Building Autonomous Learners

Woon Chia Liu • John Chee Keng Wang
Richard M. Ryan
Editors

Building Autonomous Learners

Perspectives from Research and Practice
using Self-Determination Theory

 Springer

Editors
Woon Chia Liu
National Institute of Education
Nanyang Technological University
Singapore, Singapore

John Chee Keng Wang
National Institute of Education
Nanyang Technological University
Singapore, Singapore

Richard M. Ryan
Institute for Positive Psychology
  and Education
Faculty of Health Sciences
Australian Catholic University
Strathfield, NSW, Australia

ISBN 978-981-287-629-4   ISBN 978-981-287-630-0   (eBook)
DOI 10.1007/978-981-287-630-0

Library of Congress Control Number: 2015948257

Springer Singapore Heidelberg New York Dordrecht London

Printed on acid-free paper

Springer Science+Business Media Singapore Pte Ltd. is part of Springer Science+Business Media (www.springer.com)

Foreword

The twenty-first century presents a unique, challenging and ever-changing educational landscape where the only constant appears to be change. In order to thrive and survive in such a diverse and complex environment, education systems around the globe need to rise up to the challenge of developing learners who can continue to learn on their own for life. In short, there is a need to develop *autonomous learners* who are curious, inquisitive and volitionally engaged in learning. These learners must be supported and empowered to take charge of their own learning and be driven to continuously question, make connections and seek solutions to new and unforeseen problems. This co-edited volume focuses on the important quest to build autonomous learners and presents a unique perspective bridging the nexus between research and practice.

A lot of work has been done in the field of motivation, especially with respect to student learning. However, much less emphasis has been placed on translating theories to practice. In order to address the gap, the Motivation in Educational Research Laboratory (MERL) was set up at the National Institute of Education (NIE) in 2009. True to this mission, motivational research at MERL has grown considerably in the past 5 years; this book represents the fruit of tremendous and tireless effort driven by MERL. It draws together a wide range of theoretical frameworks and practical suggestions by a group of world-renowned contributors. Many of the chapters in this book complement each other to allow the readers to have a better understanding of the nexus between theory, research and practice. In addition, a number of the chapters look at intervention studies in the Singapore classrooms, giving readers a unique insight into the psyche of Singapore students, who have drawn intense interest worldwide due to their stellar performance in internationally benchmarked tests such as Trends in Mathematics and Science Study (TIMSS), Progress International Reading Literacy Study (PRILS) and Progress for International Student Assessment (PISA) evaluations. Yet, the success of the Singapore education system goes far beyond the focus on test scores as this book will attest.

I congratulate the editors, Woon Chia Liu, John Wang and Richard Ryan, for this timely contribution to the field. As dean, Teacher Education, NIE; founders of MERL; and developer of the Self-Determination Theory, respectively, the editorial team is well-positioned to lead in this field. I also congratulate the distinguished international pool of authors from Australia, Belgium, Canada, Israel, Korea, Singapore and the USA. The rich perspectives and research of the contributing authors promise insights and research-based evidence for policymakers and teacher educators to contextualise and develop policy and programmes. The deliberate linkage of theory with practice, augmented with intervention studies in the field of education, provides multiple perspectives and strategies in which teachers, coaches and parents can use to help develop autonomous learners.

Director   Tan Oon Seng
National Institute of Education
Nanyang Technological University,
Singapore, Singapore

Acknowledgement

We are very grateful to all the contributors of this edited book. We appreciate the task was challenging, time-consuming and hard work. We hope you are pleased with the outcome as we are—a big thank you to all of you. We would also like to thank all the reviewers for their comprehensive review and insightful feedback on each chapter. Our appreciation is extended to Springer for working with us in publishing this book.

Contents

**1 Understanding Motivation in Education:
Theoretical and Practical Considerations** 1
Woon Chia Liu, John Chee Keng Wang, and Richard M. Ryan

**2 Optimizing Students' Motivation in the Era of Testing
and Pressure: A Self-Determination Theory Perspective** 9
Edward L. Deci and Richard M. Ryan

**3 The Dualistic Model of Passion: Theory, Research,
and Implications for the Field of Education** 31
Robert J. Vallerand

**4 Toward a Systematic Study of the Dark Side of Student
Motivation: Antecedents and Consequences
of Teachers' Controlling Behaviors** 59
Leen Haerens, Maarten Vansteenkiste, Nathalie Aelterman,
and Lynn Van den Berghe

**5 How Can We Create Better Learning Contexts
for Children? Promoting Students' Autonomous
Motivation as a Way to Foster Enhanced
Educational Outcomes** 83
Frédéric Guay, Valérie Lessard, and Pascale Dubois

6 Teachers' Motivation in the Classroom 107
Luc G. Pelletier and Meredith Rocchi

7 Autonomy-Supportive Teaching: What It Is, How to Do It 129
Johnmarshall Reeve

**8 An Instruction Sequence Promoting Autonomous Motivation
for Coping with Challenging Learning Subjects** 153
Avi Assor

9   **Parental Involvement and Children's Academic
     Motivation and Achievement** 169
     Wendy S. Grolnick

10   **Parental Influence and Students' Outcomes and Well-Being** 185
     Wai Cheong Eugene Chew

11   **Creating an Autonomy-Supportive
     Physical Education (PE) Learning Environment** 207
     Yew Meng How and John Chee Keng Wang

12   **Can Being Autonomy-Supportive in Teaching Improve
     Students' Self-Regulation and Performance?** 227
     John Chee Keng Wang, Betsy L.L. Ng, Woon Chia Liu,
     and Richard M. Ryan

13   **Translating Motivational Theory into Application
     of Information Technology in the Classroom** 245
     Caroline Koh

14   **Focus on Competing for Performance or Mastering New
     Knowledge? Insights from Discovering the Relations
     Between Classroom Goal Structures and Students'
     Learning in Singapore Secondary Schools** 259
     Youyan Nie

15   **Promoting Mastery-Approach Goals to Support
     the Success of the *"Teach Less, Learn More"*
     Educational Initiative** 277
     Gregory Arief D. Liem, Wee Kiat Lau, and Elaine Yu Ling Cai

Contributors

Nathalie Aelterman is affiliated at the Department of Developmental, Personality and Social Psychology of Ghent University. She recently obtained her Ph.D. in Psychology (2014) at Ghent University and is mainly interested in applying the Self-Determination Theory in educational settings and sports. In her research she particularly focuses on the stimulating and undermining effects of the social environment and the question whether social agents can successfully be trained in adopting a (more) motivating style. She has published 15 international journal papers and is a member of the editorial board of *Physical Education and Sport Pedagogy*.

Avi Assor is the head of the Educational and School Psychology programme in Ben Gurion University (BGU), Israel, where he also holds the Shane Family Chair in Education. His research focuses on socialising processes affecting children's autonomous internalisation of values and motivation for learning. Within this general domain he focuses on the harms of conditional parental regard and the benefits of teachers' and parents' support of inner directed valuing and the examination of values and goals as important components of autonomy support. In addition, he is involved in the development and assessment of school reforms aimed at enhancing students and teachers' basic psychological needs and intrinsic motivation and caring for others. He has published in *Journal of Personality and Social Psychology*, *Child Development*, *Developmental Psychology*, *Personality and Social Psychology Bulletin*, *Journal of Educational Psychology* and *Journal of Personality*. He is on the editorial board of the journal *Motivation and Emotion*.

Lynn Van den Berghe is a Ph.D. student and academic assistant in the Sport Pedagogy Research Group at the Department of Movement and Sport Sciences, Faculty of Medicine and Health Sciences, Ghent University. She received her master's degree in physical education and movement sciences in 2008 from the Catholic University of Leuven. Her dissertation is on the antecedents of burnout and (de) motivating teaching behaviour in physical education teachers and is to be finalised in 2015. She has (co-)authored ten peer-reviewed journal articles.

Elaine Yu Ling Cai has been teaching mathematics to graduating students of various learning progressions in an elementary school in Singapore for more than 10 years. She is currently a third-year doctorate in education student at the National Institute of Education, Nanyang Technological University, Singapore, and is completing her dissertation on students' learning and motivation in mathematics. Her other research interests include the solving of mathematics word problems, the model method and the Newman Error Analysis.

Wai Cheong Eugene Chew is an assistant professor at the Physical Education and Sports Science Academic Group, National Institute of Education, Nanyang Technological University. He teaches exercise psychology courses at undergraduate and graduate levels at the university. He received his bachelor of physical education from the University of Calgary (Canada) and subsequently his Ph.D. from Nanyang Technological University in 2011. His research interest and publications revolve around studies examining the motivational dynamics associated with the effects of social environmental factors, and self-regulation, on various outcomes related to people's involvement in physical activity, exercise and sports. Given his prior experience in sport management, Dr. Chew's research publications include works on sport policy, coaching development and strategy and management in sport organisations.

Edward L. Deci is the Helen F. and Fred H. Gowen Professor in the Social Sciences at the University of Rochester. He holds a Ph.D. in psychology from Carnegie-Mellon University; studied at the University of Pennsylvania, the University of London and Hamilton College; and was an interdisciplinary postdoctoral fellow at Stanford University. For more than 45 years Deci has been engaged in a programme of research on human motivation and is co-founder with Richard M. Ryan of the Self-Determination Theory. He has published ten books, including *Intrinsic Motivation* (Plenum, 1975), *Intrinsic Motivation and Self-Determination in Human Behavior* (co-authored with R. M. Ryan, Plenum, 1985) and *The Handbook of Self-Determination Research* (co-edited with R. M. Ryan, University of Rochester Press, 2002). A grantee of the National Institute of Mental Health, the National Institute of Child Health and Human Development, the National Science Foundation and the Institute of Education Sciences, Deci has lectured and consulted in 24 countries on six continents.

Pascale Dubois is a speech-language pathologist working in a school board in the Montreal area as well as in private practice. During her studies, she has worked as a research assistant in the audiology and speech-language field. She received her master's degree (speech-language pathology) in 2005 from the University of Montreal. Regularly, she has offered workshops to teachers about efficient language intervention and practices. She has worked with teenagers who have language and learning disabilities. She is particularly interested in the school to work transition of these students. She is also a Ph.D. student at the Faculty of Education at Laval University. Her areas of research interests lie in social and professional integration, self-determination and language and learning disabilities.

Wendy S. Grolnick is professor of psychology in the Frances L. Hiatt School of Psychology at Clark University in Worcester, Massachusetts, USA. She received her Ph.D. from the University of Rochester. Professor Grolnick's research, which has been supported by the National Institute of Mental Health, the William T. Grant Foundation and the Spencer Foundation, focuses on the effects of home and school environments on children's motivation as well as factors affecting the environments that parents and teachers create for their children. She has published over 60 journal articles, has written chapters in numerous books on motivation and parenting and is the author of two books: *The Psychology of Parental Control: How Well-Meant Parenting Backfires* (Lawrence Erlbaum and Associates, 2003) *and Pressured Parents, Stressed-Out Kids: Dealing with Competition While Raising a Successful Child* (Prometheus Books, 2008). Dr. Grolnick is the recipient of the William T. Grant Faculty Scholar Award and the American Psychological Association (APA) Executive Branch Science Fellowship.

Frédéric Guay is professor of counselling psychology and education at Laval University. He holds a Ph.D. in social psychology from the University of Quebec at Montreal and was a postdoctoral fellow at Laval University and a research fellow at the University of Western Sydney. His research programme has been organised by the Self-Determination Theory and Self-Concept Theory. This programme has led to publications, book chapters and scientific communications in the educational domain. He is currently the director of a professional training programme for elementary school teachers (i.e. CASIS) aiming to motivate teachers to use pedagogical practices that support students' motivational resources.

Leen Haerens is associate professor in physical education and sports pedagogy at the, Department of Movement and Sports Sciences, Faculty of Medicine and Health Sciences, Ghent University. In her Ph.D. (2003–2007) she developed and evaluated a school-based intervention aimed at promoting healthy eating and physical activity. After 1 year of postdoctoral studies, funded by the Flemish research foundation, she build up a research group in physical education and sports pedagogy. Currently she supervises eight Ph.D. students who study different aspects of motivational dynamics in physical education, starting from the Self-Determination Theory (Deci and Ryan, 2000). One of her major lines of research is built around the question "how teachers can be trained to create classroom environments in which students who lack interest in major sports can get inspired and energised towards lifelong physical activity". She has published over 50 scientific manuscripts and is associate editor of *Physical Education and Sport Pedagogy*.

Yew Meng How is currently a Ph.D. candidate at NIE, under the supervision of Prof. John Wang. His current Ph.D. research looks at creating motivating PE learning environments through autonomy support. He completed his undergraduate studies at the National University of Singapore and completed his PGDE (PE) at the National Institute of Education. His M.Ed. (human movement) degree was from the University of Western Australia. Yew Meng's prior work experience included being a PE teacher, a CCA sports officer involved in policy development and a head of Department for Student Development. He represented Singapore as a rugby player through age group and senior representation from 1996 to 2004 and coached the Singapore Schools rugby from 2001 to 2004. He was also the forwards coach for the women's National Rugby team in 2006. His research interests include the Self-Determination Theory, autonomy support in education and physical activity in youths.

Caroline Koh is assistant professor with the Psychological Studies Academic Group, National Institute of Education (NIE), Nanyang Technological University, Singapore. Prior to her current position at NIE, she taught at junior college level for a considerable number of years before a brief stint at the Ministry of Education Curriculum Planning and Development Division, Singapore. Her current teaching responsibilities include coordinating, developing curricula and conducting training for pre-service teachers, as well as professional development courses for experienced teachers. Her prime research focus is on motivation and learning, with a special interest in the use of the Self-Determination Theory in guiding research and classroom practice. In addition, she has conducted research on areas as diverse as group project work, moral development and reasoning, national education, the use of simulation-based learning and, most recently, the use of the e-portfolio as a pedagogical tool.

Wee Kiat Lau is a research assistant at the Psychological Studies Academic Group, the National Institute of Education, Nanyang Technological University, Singapore. He received his B.A. in psychology from Nanyang Technological University in 2014. He is currently involved in the research on a motivation and engagement perspective of participation in school-based co-curricular activities. His research interests include auditory processing, multisensory integration, learning and engagement and quantitative methodologies.

Valérie Lessard works as a research professional with Dr. Frederic Guay at Laval University. She completed in 2012 a Ph.D. degree in educational psychology at Laval University under the supervision of Simon Larose. From 1999 to 2012, she worked as a high school teacher and a school counsellor for four school districts in the province of Quebec (Canada). She has an extensive experience in the educational field. As a researcher and a former high school teacher, she is particularly interested in teaching practices that sustain students' motivation. Over the past few years, she also contributed to different research projects on school transition, school motivation and tracking in mathematics.

Gregory Arief D. Liem is an assistant professor at Psychological Studies Academic Group, National Institute of Education, Singapore. He has published more than 60 peer-reviewed journal articles and book chapters and co-edited 5 books. Arief currently serves as a member of the editorial board of the *Australian Journal of Guidance and Counselling, Measurement and Evaluation in Counseling and Development* and *the Asia-Pacific Education Researcher* and is also an active reviewer for numerous ISI journals. His research interests and specialisation are in the areas of motivation and engagement across various performance settings, self-related beliefs, character strengths and quantitative methodologies.

Betsy L.L. Ng is an education specialist at National University of Singapore (NUS). She graduated from the University of Melbourne with a bachelor of science degree. She obtained her master of education from the University of Sheffield and master of science and Ph.D. from Nanyang Technological University. Her Ph.D. research was on motivation and learning in education. Her other research interests include experiential learning, student-teacher relationship, science education and health psychology. She has conducted research and published papers in the areas of service learning, problem-based learning and food science. Her interest in education has led her to many years of working experience in the education industry such as an editor in a large publishing firm and a lecturer in a tertiary institution. She is a reviewer for the journal *Asia-Pacific Forum on Science Learning and Teaching*.

Youyan Nie is an assistant professor with the Psychological Studies Academic Group, National Institute of Education, Nanyang Technological University, Singapore. Her research focuses on motivation in education, especially on how to create motivational environment to promote students' learning and teachers' development.

Luc G. Pelletier holds a Ph.D. in experimental social psychology from the Université du Québec à Montreal. Following his graduate studies, he started his career at the School of Psychology, University of Ottawa, where he is now a full professor of psychology. Professor Pelletier has written more than 125 articles and book chapters mainly in the area of human and social motivation. His programme of research on motivation and self-determination focuses on how people regulate their behaviours and integrate a wide variety of behaviours into their lifestyle, the determinants of interpersonal behaviours that support basic human needs, why people sometimes fail in their attempts to regulate their actions despite being highly motivated and the influence of persuasive communication on the motivation for different activities. He is also involved in applied motivational research in the domains of education, general health and well-being, eating regulation, physical activity and sport and pro-environmental behaviours.

Johnmarshall Reeve is a professor in the Department of Education at Korea University in Seoul, South Korea. While in the USA, he received his Ph.D. from Texas Christian University and completed postdoctoral work at the University of Rochester. Professor Reeve's research interests centre on the empirical study of all aspects of human motivation and emotion with particular emphases on teachers' motivating styles, students' motivation and engagement during learning activities and the neuroscience of intrinsic motivation. He has published 50 articles on motivation in journals such as the *Journal of Educational Psychology*, 20 book chapters and 3 books, including *Understanding Motivation and Emotion*. Since 2011, Prof. Reeve has served as editor in chief of the journal *Motivation and Emotion*.

Meredith Rocchi is a Ph.D. candidate at the University of Ottawa, Canada, working under the supervision of Dr. Luc Pelletier. She is studying sport motivation from a Self-Determination Theory perspective, where her primary research focuses on coaches of all levels. Through this, she is examining environmental factors that influence coaches' motivational processes and their subsequent behaviour with their athletes. Outside of this, Meredith also examines need-supportive behaviours in sport settings with athletes and educational settings with students.

Robert J. Vallerand is currently full professor of psychology at the Université du Québec à Montréal and professorial fellow at the Australian Catholic University. His research focuses on motivational processes and most recently on the concept of passion. He has written or edited 7 books and close to 300 scientific articles and book chapters. Professor Vallerand has served as president of the *Quebec Society for Research in Psychology*, the *Canadian Psychological Association* and the *International Positive Psychology Association*. He has received numerous honours, including being elected a fellow from over a dozen learned societies such as the *American Psychological Association*, the *Association for Psychological Science*, the *Society for Personality and Social Psychology* and many others. He has also received the Adrien Pinard Career Award from the *Quebec Society for Research in Psychology*, the Donald O. Hebb Award from the *Canadian Psychological Association* (the highest research awards for a psychologist in Quebec and Canada, respectively) and the Sport Science Award from the *International Olympic Committee*.

Maarten Vansteenkiste obtained his Ph.D. at the University of Leuven (2005) under the supervision of Prof. Dr. W. Lens, Prof. Dr. E. Deci and Prof. Dr. H. De Witte. After 1 year of postdoc studies, funded by the Flemish institute for research, he accepted a position as a professor in motivation and developmental psychology at Ghent University, Belgium. Through his research, he tries to expand the Self-Determination Theory, a well-known and empirically validated motivation theory. He is especially interested in theoretically and empirically linking the Self-Determination Theory with other well-established motivation theories and has used SDT as a source of inspiration to study motivational dynamics in a variety of life domains, including education, parenting, well-being, ecology, work and sport and exercise. He has published widely about these topics in diverse high-quality journals. Currently, he is supervising several doctoral students, is an editorial board member of several journals and was awarded the Richard E. Snow Award for distinguished early career contributions to educational psychology (2009) by APA division 15.

About the Editors

Woon-Chia Liu is the Dean of Teacher Education at the National Institute of Education, Singapore. She is also an associate professor with the Psychological Studies Academic Group and a founding member of NIE's Motivation in Educational Research Laboratory. Currently, she is the President of the Educational Research Association of Singapore. She represents Singapore in the World Education Research Association (WERA) Council. Her research interests include motivation, clinical practice, mentoring, e-portfolio, as well as innovative teaching strategies such as problem-based learning.

John Chee Keng Wang is a Professor in the Physical Education and Sports Science Academic Group at the National Institute of Education, Nanyang Technological University in Singapore. He received his Ph.D. (Sport and Exercise Psychology) in 2001 from Loughborough University. Dr Wang is a Chartered Psychologist and an associate fellow of British Psychological Society. He is registered with the Health Professions Council of UK as a Sport and Exercise Psychologist. He leads the Motivation in Educational Research Lab (MERL) in NIE. His areas of research lie in the area of achievement motivation, talent development environment, self-regulation, and statistical analyses.

Richard M. Ryan is Professor at the Institute for Positive Psychology and Education at the Australian Catholic University and a Research Professor in Psychology at the University of Rochester. Ryan is a widely published researcher and theorist with over 300 papers and books in the areas of human motivation, personality, and psychological well-being. He is co-developer of *Self-Determination Theory*, a theory of human motivation that has been internationally researched and applied. He is a Fellow of the American Psychological Association, the American Educational Research Association, and an Honorary Member of the German Psychological Society (DGP).

Chapter 1
Understanding Motivation in Education: Theoretical and Practical Considerations

Woon Chia Liu, John Chee Keng Wang, and Richard M. Ryan

> *"The direction in which education starts a man will determine his future in life."*
>
> – Plato

In this era of relentless change, explosion of information, and proliferation of technological innovations, it is too simplistic to think that teachers can teach their students everything they need to know in their lifetime. In a world filled with problems that require complex solutions, and issues that are not documented in books and manuals, it is naive to attempt to "drill" and "discipline" students so that they know the "correct" answers. With this reality check, we need to take a cold hard look at what we do in classrooms and schools when we educate our students. We are doing a disservice to our students if we teach content and routines that become obsolete or impart skills that are not transferable. But more importantly, we are shortchanging our students if we champion learning processes that do not impact on life-wide learning, create learning environments that do not encourage self-determination, and develop students who do not have the drive to learn independently.

Education in the twenty-first century must strive to develop learners so that they are willing to question and find connections, create and push the boundaries, and innovate and seek out solutions. It must engage learners and empower them so that they take responsibility for their own learning and have the drive to create their own future. Inasmuch as "education is the lighting of a fire," motivation is the torch that lights and sustains the fire.

There are many definitions of motivation. Put simply, it can be defined as a force that activates, directs, and sustains goal-directed behavior. Accordingly, motivational studies attempt to examine the factors that drive and energize behavior. Across

W.C. Liu • J.C.K. Wang (✉)
National Institute of Education, Nanyang Technological University, Singapore, Singapore
e-mail: woonchia.liu@nie.edu.sg; john.wang@nie.edu.sg

R.M. Ryan
Institute for Positive Psychology and Education, Faculty of Health Sciences,
Australian Catholic University, Strathfield, NSW, Australia
e-mail: richard.ryan@acu.edu.au

© Springer Science+Business Media Singapore 2016
W.C. Liu et al. (eds.), *Building Autonomous Learners*,
DOI 10.1007/978-981-287-630-0_1

the globe, teachers are in a daily struggle to energize and direct students to engage in learning, using techniques and strategies that clearly vary in their effectiveness. Yet compared to the efforts focused on developing curricula and developing tests to assess student competencies, much less emphasis has been given to research in motivation. The title of this book, *Building Autonomous Learners: Perspectives from Research and Practice Using Self-Determination Theory*, reflects our intent to bring to the fore this critical issue.

Understanding the role of motivation in human behavior is especially important as we educate our children and prepare them to be the self-directed and lifelong learners of the twenty-first century. However, there are still gaps in our understanding of how to catalyze motivation in our schools, classrooms, and sport arenas. In particular, a lot more can be done to translate research findings into real-life applications. It is in this light that the Motivation in Educational Research Lab (MERL) was set up at the National Institute of Education (NIE), Nanyang Technological University, Singapore (http://merl.nie.edu.sg/). MERL is led by Professor John Wang and Associate Professor Woon Chia Liu and is advised by Professor Tan Oon Seng. Professors Edward Deci and Richard Ryan, the developers of the self-determination theory (SDT), are both consultants of MERL. Apart from Professors Deci and Ryan, there are 13 leading researchers in the field of motivation who are members of the international advisory panel. In addition, there are currently 14 NIE faculty members in MERL. This edited book represents the work of MERL and her associated international scholars. It consists of their work on motivation and views on issues in education, covering both the Singapore context and global perspective.

In recent years, there has been a heightened focus on international benchmarking tests such as the Trends in International Mathematics and Science Study (TIMSS), Progress in International Reading Literacy Study (PIRLS), and Program for International Student Assessment (PISA) among policy makers. Much has been made of Singapore's education system due to her students' continued and sustained high performance in international benchmarking tests. Arguably, Singapore has a sound education system, with good schools, capable school leaders and teachers, and facilities that are among the best in the world. Nonetheless, much more can and must be done in Singapore and in other education systems worldwide, if we want to prepare learners who are able to make the best of their talents and to develop a passion for learning that lasts through life.

One of the main aims of MERL is to translate theories into classroom strategies to enhance student learning. This book was conceptualized as an effort toward that end. The authors of these chapters provide unique insights into motivation from varied theoretical perspectives such as self-determination theory and achievement goal theory and others. A main feature of the book is its focus not only on theory but more importantly on practical suggestions and teaching strategies for the classroom.

This collection consists of 15 chapters presenting some of the latest theories, findings, and applications in education from renowned researchers in the field of motivation. Each chapter provides a perspective on maximizing motivation in the classroom as well as strategies for practice. It is thus more than a collection of motivation research in education. It provides teachers and parents with strategies that could enhance the development of autonomous learners and policy makers with research evidence that could impact policies. Some chapters focus on creating a self-motivating classroom climate, others on related topics such as personality traits and use of ICT in education, and still others on teachers' motivation and parental involvement.

The self-determination theory (SDT), a broad framework for the study of human motivation and personality, is the central perspective used in organizing the chapters in the book. SDT articulates a metatheory for framing motivational studies. It is a formal theory that defines intrinsic and varied extrinsic sources of motivation and gives a description of the respective roles of intrinsic and types of extrinsic motivation in cognitive and social development and in individual differences. There are six mini-theories within SDT. First, the cognitive evaluation theory (CET) looks at intrinsic motivation and factors in the classroom that can facilitate or undermine it. CET addresses the effects of extrinsic rewards, evaluations, and feedback on intrinsic motivation. The second mini-theory, organismic integration theory (OIT), focuses on the processes through which motivation for non-intrinsically motivated activities can be internalized. It thus concerns how activities that may not be "fun" can nonetheless come to be valued and embraced by students. Causality orientation theory (COT) is the third mini-theory. It focuses on individual differences in people's tendencies to orient toward environment and regulate behaviors. Fourth, the basic psychological need theory (BPNT) explains in detail the concept of the basic psychological needs and their relations to psychological health and well-being. In brief, it describes the nutriments needed by every learner to be actively and positively engaged in the school setting. A fifth framework within SDT is called the goal content theory (GCT). It distinguishes between intrinsic and extrinsic goals and their impact on motivation and well-being. GCT suggests that how students understand their overarching life goals influences their attitudes, well-being, and motivational orientations in the classroom. Finally, the relationship motivation theory (RMT) addresses the factors that lead people to maintain close relationships with others. It applies readily to the student-teacher relationship and the ways in which it can be productively enhanced. One can see from the collective breadth of these six mini-theories that SDT covers many nuances in the area of motivation, many of which are explored within the various chapters in this book.

In the context of SDT, Deci and Ryan have long argued that supporting both student and teacher autonomies has substantial advantages in terms of educational outcomes, relative to controlling strategies. In their contribution to this book, these two developers of SDT review research supporting the position. They highlight that autonomous motivation tends to flourish in situations where people experience satisfaction of their three basic psychological needs—the needs for competence, relatedness, and autonomy. In addition, they review research on goals—both mastery and performance goals and intrinsic and extrinsic goals—examining them in relation to autonomous and controlled motives. Finally, they discuss ways in which teachers can support satisfaction of their students' basic psychological needs, especially when teachers themselves are similarly supported. In conclusion, they suggest that educational policies and practices are often too narrowly focused on test outcomes and on performance in specific content areas, whereas they see higher-quality learning occurring most optimally in contexts where learners find the basic psychological need supports for active self-development.

Passion is defined as a strong inclination for a self-defining activity that we love, value, and spend a considerable amount of time on. Vallerand demonstrates that passion matters for the field of education. His chapter presents a theoretical formulation that focuses on passion with related empirical research. His dualistic model of passion posits that there are two types of passions: obsessive and harmonious. Obsessive passion represents an internally controlling pressure to engage in an activity that one loves, thereby leading to conflict with other aspects of the person's self and to maladaptive consequences. On the other hand, harmonious passion leads individuals to more autonomous engagement in an activity that they love, resulting in more adaptive outcomes. He reveals that harmonious passion for teaching is typically associated with adaptive outcomes, while obsessive passion is related to less adaptive and at times maladaptive outcomes. These findings have been obtained with respect to a number of affective, cognitive, mental, and physical health, relationship, and performance variables, across diverse populations. These findings also apply to passion for one's studies. He also addresses the role of personality and social variables in the development of passion, and he proposes directions for future research.

SDT suggests that, under the right conditions, young people are able to motivate themselves to learn. Yet, many teachers would not portray their students as naturally proactive and endowed learners, since they, more often than not, have had the experience of teaching young people who exhibit a lack of enthusiasm, are passive, refuse cooperation, and sometimes even display disruptive or aggressive behaviors. Haerens, Vansteenkiste, Aelterman, and Van den Berghe attempt to shed light on the dark side of student motivation by highlighting the antecedents and consequences of teachers' controlling behaviors in the classroom. They examine the role that experiences of need frustration play in fostering students' passivity, lack of cooperation, and/or aggressive and disruptive behaviors. They also review evidence with regard to the relationships between controlling teaching and maladaptive student outcomes. In addition, they provide insights into the wide range of antecedents that help to explain why teachers orient themselves toward a more controlling teaching style. Finally, they provide practical suggestions for teachers to avoid controlling forms of teaching.

The chapter by Guay, Lessard, and Dubois looks at the ways in which teachers can create better learning contexts for students by promoting autonomous motivation. They first describe the main instruments for measuring students' motivation according to the different motivation types proposed by SDT. Next, they discuss the potential effects of these motivation types on students' emotions, learning strategies, academic achievement, and school perseverance. Thereafter, they discuss the roles of parents, peers, and teachers in promoting certain motivation types, as well as some SDT-based school intervention programs. Finally, they derive practical implications from the reviewed studies and propose avenues for future research.

Teachers are the decisive element in the classroom. They create the learning climate and possess the power to empower or humiliate their students. As such, no book that is interested in student motivation would be complete without looking at teachers and their role in promoting a healthy learning environment. Pelletier and Rocchi review the research on teachers from the SDT perspective, while taking into consideration the role that teachers' motivation has on their behaviors with their students. More specifically, they examine how contextual factors influence teachers and how their impressions of these factors, their need satisfaction or dissatisfaction, their motivation for teaching, their general motivation, and their psychological and behavioral outcomes are related. This chapter shows that supporting teachers and providing them with a psychologically sound experience are extremely important to classroom outcomes. Since this review focuses on some of the key environmental factors that are relevant to teachers, it highlights to school administrations key areas they can work on to promote more motivated teaching and better outcomes for both the teachers and students within their own organizations.

In his chapter on autonomy-supportive teaching, Reeve notes the distinctions between autonomy-supportive teaching and controlling style of teaching. He provides evidence of the benefits students and teachers themselves gained from receiving autonomy support, and they benefit in ways that are widespread and educationally and professionally important. The goal of autonomy support is to provide students with learning activities, a classroom environment, and a student-teacher relationship that will support their daily autonomy. In addition, it allows teachers to be in sync with their students. Reeve provides multiple examples of the six acts of autonomy-supportive teaching by breaking them down to three critical moments within the instructional flow. This chapter is thus specifically targeted at teachers, focusing on how to put autonomy-supportive strategies into practice.

Assor in his chapter on instruction sequence for promoting autonomous motivation for learning especially designed for regular (often crowded) classrooms also aimed at helping teachers to provide support for student needs as part of the instruction process. There are three phases in Assor's model: (1) classroom preparation, including how classroom discussions and physical environments can create a more motivating culture and context for learning, (2) application of the sequence in individual or group work, and (3) all-classroom interim and summary discussions. The theoretical and research-based foundations for the proposed sequence are underscored as the different parts of the sequence are presented. Evidence for the effectiveness of parts of the sequence is summarized, as are the possible limitations of the sequence. Assor also points to important areas of learning and personal development in which less structured approaches might be much more beneficial.

Student learning is, of course, not only about the students and teachers. There is now ample evidence demonstrating the significant effects of parents' involvement in their children's schooling for children's school success. Yet how these effects occur and what factors facilitate parent involvement are less well understood. In her chapter on parental involvement and children's academic achievement, Grolnick focuses on how parent involvement exerts its effects. She examines multiple forms of involvement (e.g., at school, at home), parents' motivations for being involved (whether more controlled or autonomous), and whether involvement is provided in a more controlling versus autonomy-supportive manner. In addition, the chapter provides evidence for a model in which parent involvement affects children's achievement largely by facilitating children's inner motivational resources of perceived competence, perceived control, and autonomous self-regulation. Some guidelines for autonomous parenting are presented.

In Chew's chapter on parental influences on students' outcome and well-being, he traces the development and trends in the study of parental influence, focusing on its relations to child outcomes pertaining to school-related concerns and pursuits, and indicators of well-being. The emergence of SDT as the theoretical framework for such investigations is discussed. In the process, key parenting dimensions or styles important to the development of the child are identified. In line with the emphasis on the holistic development of students, a scoping review of the current research on parental influence on adolescent outcomes in the sports domain was conducted. Results showed that the research on parental influence in the sports domain pay little attention to the identified parenting styles or dimensions. Relevant to the discussion, highlights of findings from recent studies by this author on the effects of parenting dimensions on student-athletes' motivational factors and well-being are presented.

Similar to Reeve's chapter, How and Wang focus on how to create an autonomy-supportive environment in physical education (PE). Research has found that PE teachers' motivational styles have a substantial impact on students' engagement in learning and can influence children to adopt physically active lifestyles. This chapter presents a strong case for an autonomy-supportive PE classroom through research-based evidence. Additionally, this chapter also provides practical suggestions to enable PE teachers to implement an autonomy-supportive style in their teaching of PE.

Wang, Ng, Liu, and Ryan present a research study on the effectiveness of autonomy-supportive intervention in students' perceived autonomy support, psychological needs, learning strategies, and achievement in Singapore schools. Results revealed that from pre- to post-intervention, students taught by autonomy-supportive teachers had significant positive changes in perceived autonomy support, needs, self-efficacy, self-regulated learning, and grades. Students in the autonomy-supportive condition were also more self-efficacious and autonomous in learning than those in the control condition, as shown by increased achievement. Implications and limitations are discussed.

The twenty-first century is one characterized by technological revolution, so it is important that Koh looks at student motivation and the use of information and communication technology (ICT) in the classroom. The current impetus is for the main stakeholders in education, ranging from high-ranking policy makers and school leaders to teachers and students at ground level, to get on the bandwagon of mining the so-called "golden" opportunities that ICT has to offer. However, formal research into the effectiveness of ICT-powered tools in facilitating teaching and learning has just started to emerge, and there is a pressing need to review the extent to which conventional theories are applicable to ICT-infused learning contexts.

Koh's chapter focuses particularly on three commonly used ICT tools, namely, the e-portfolio, blogs, and YouTube videos to promote learner motivation, and the extent to which conventional theories of motivation are able to explain what is currently observed. She specifically discusses the extent to which students' self-determination, self-efficacy, and self-regulation are promoted through the infusion of ICT in their learning.

Nie uses achievement goal theory to examine the relations between classroom goal structures and students' learning in Singapore's secondary schools. Data were collected from more than 8000 Secondary 3 students in 247 classes across 39 schools. The results from both English and mathematics classrooms show consistent findings. In essence, classroom mastery goal structure is found to be positively related to students' academic self-efficacy, interest and enjoyment, personal mastery goal orientation, and engagement, whereas classroom performance goal structure is found to be positively related to personal performance avoidance goal orientation and negatively related to academic achievement. Specifically, in English classrooms, classroom performance goal structure is positively related to avoidance coping and negatively related to engagement. In general, the results from this large-scale study suggest that adopting classroom mastery goals, rather than focusing on performance goals, is a more effective motivational strategy.

Liem and colleagues continue this focus on achievement goals, providing a synthesis of the empirical work on the adoption of achievement goals and its impacts on academic, social, and well-being outcomes and discussing the relevance of the TARGET framework to the *teach less, learn more* (TLLM) initiative. The TLLM is an educational approach initiated in 2004 by Mr. Lee Hsien Loong, Prime Minister of Singapore, in fostering students' motivation and engagement in both academic and nonacademic arenas so that they are better prepared to face future life challenges. Given the benefits and also potential detriments of emphasizing the pursuit of performance goals, Liem et al. propose that Singaporean students would benefit from educational practices focusing on the pursuit of mastery goals or task-based goals. The practical implications of achievement goal theory for the implementation of the TLLM policy are highlighted.

In summary, the chapters in this book consist of the latest findings and theory advancements and applications in education from the SDT and achievement theory framework. The ultimate goal of this collection is to convey to educators and policy makers the latest information on the importance of building autonomous learners, along with policy implications and practical strategies for practice in school, classroom, and home. We hope that you will find these chapters useful and enlightening.

Chapter 2
Optimizing Students' Motivation in the Era of Testing and Pressure: A Self-Determination Theory Perspective

Edward L. Deci and Richard M. Ryan

For the past quarter century, there has been substantial discussion in many countries about the quality of educational systems. To a significant degree, these discussions have been prompted by concerns about economic competition among nations. The focus has been primarily on how well a country's students are achieving relative to the students of other countries, the idea being that the results of achievement test scores represent a good indicator of how well the countries are likely to fare in the international marketplace during future decades. However debatable that premise may be, policymakers have paid close attention to students' test scores, such as those derived from the Programme for International Student Assessments (PISA; National Center for Education Statistics, Institute of Education Sciences, 2009) and the Trends in International Mathematics and Science Study (TIMSS; National Center for Education Statistics, Institute of Education Sciences, 2011).

In some nations (e.g., Germany, Singapore), the test results are primarily used as information concerning where resources might be most needed and/or to support research and experiments in curricular impact and change. In others, however, the use and interpretation of tests has been more controlling than informational in nature. For example, in the USA, evidence of not being at the top of international rankings has been used to place external pressures on school systems from both state and federal legislation to hold the systems "accountable" for test score outcomes, especially in areas of mathematics and English. These pressures are especially heavy for schools serving high concentrations of poverty, which tend to be low performing. In turn, this *test-based accountability* pressure has spawned an

E.L. Deci (✉)
University of Rochester, Rochester, NY, USA
e-mail: deci@psych.rochester.edu

R.M. Ryan
Institute for Positive Psychology and Education, Faculty of Health Sciences,
Australian Catholic University, Strathfield, NSW, Australia
e-mail: richard.ryan@acu.edu.au

© Springer Science+Business Media Singapore 2016
W.C. Liu et al. (eds.), *Building Autonomous Learners*,
DOI 10.1007/978-981-287-630-0_2

industry of metrics and "aligned" curricula, some of which have become mandatory state-administered achievement tests, with "high stakes" attached to outcomes. Most noteworthy have been the *No Child Left Behind* legislation endorsed by President Bush and the *Race to the Top* legislation endorsed by President Obama, both of which focus on a narrow range of human motivation and learning in the service of promoting school achievement in the prescribed areas.

Such high-stakes policies represent, among other things, an explicit *motivational* strategy. By applying rewards and sanctions to districts, schools, and teachers based on a narrow set of student performances, the idea is to incentivize students, teachers, and schools to improve on these indicators. This approach to educational improvement is intended to drive higher achievement with more rewards and more fear of punishment. In fact, both the operant behavioral perspective (e.g., Skinner, 1953), which postulates that reinforcements strengthen behaviors, and the expectancy theories (e.g., Vroom, 1964; Wigfield & Eccles, 2000), which maintain that people engage in behaviors they expect will lead to desired outcomes (i.e., rewards), are frequently cited to support the logic of this control-oriented school improvement approach (e.g., see Kellaghan, Madaus, & Raczek, 1996).

Yet, as pointed out by Ryan and Brown (2005), these high-stakes testing approaches neither represent classical behaviorist strategies, nor do they fully reflect modern expectancy theories. The reason, as they highlighted, is that this controlling approach actually involves incentivizing, reinforcing, or rewarding *outcomes* rather than *behaviors*. Doing so means that any behaviors that might lead to those outcomes could be strengthened. Of course, teachers improving their teaching and students exerting more effort and being more engaged in learning are among the behaviors that could be strengthened. But so too could behaviors such as "teaching to the test," narrowing curricula, or even cheating by the students, teachers, or administrators. Past research has shown that in controlling contexts there is a tendency for people to take a short path to desired outcomes (Shapira, 1976), and indeed there is evidence that some school systems subjected to the pressures of high-stakes testing have often taken paths that involve "gaming the system," including straightforward cheating, at both school and district levels (e.g., Aviv, 2014; McNeil & Valenzuela, 2000; Moon, Callahan, & Tomlinson, 2003). Moreover, at least in the USA, such pressuring reforms based on incentives, sanctions, and accountability have not led to meaningful improvements in learning and achievement (e.g., Amrein & Berliner, 2002; Hout & Elliott, 2011).

An Autonomy-Supportive Approach

An alternative approach to improving schools involves supporting rather than externally controlling the motivation of teachers and students. Based on a quite different metatheory, *self-determination theory* (SDT; Deci & Ryan, 2000) begins with the assumption that people are by nature active and engaged. When in supportive or nurturing social conditions, they are naturally inclined to take in knowledge and values and to more fully integrate the regulation of behaviors. People have, that is, an evolved tendency to grow and learn (Ryan & Hawley, in press). Indeed, this process of taking in and assimilating knowledge and behaviors is the essence of development (Piaget, 1971; Werner, 1948).

The naturalness of the human propensity to grow and learn is obvious in children prior to school. Children spend much of their time actively playing; they manipulate and experiment on their environments, and they take delight in making things happen and discovering new knowledge. Children can turn almost anything into a toy, at times finding the box that a doll or a fire truck came in as interesting as the toy itself. They marvel at all kinds of things, such as what happens when they push light switches or hit particular keys on their parents' cell phones. This is all part of exploring their world and is an extremely powerful engine of learning.

In motivational terms, such activity is said to be *intrinsically motivated* (Deci, 1975; Harlow, 1950; White, 1959). When intrinsically motivated, people engage in behaviors because they spontaneously experience interest and enjoyment when they do, and these behaviors do not require separable consequences such as tangible rewards or the avoidance of punishments. Spontaneous satisfaction and enjoyment, which are integrally intertwined with the behaviors themselves, are all the consequences that are necessary. Within *self-determination theory* (SDT; Deci & Ryan, 1985; Ryan & Deci, 2000b), intrinsic motivation is considered a natural propensity of human life, and it is a great source of energy for people's engagement with the world and their learning from it. Yet because these intrinsic assimilative propensities are expected to flourish in supportive contexts, when they are not manifest, SDT would look first and foremost to the interpersonal context to understand what may be forestalling or disrupting their expression.

Closely related to intrinsic motivation is another category of autonomous motivation, namely, *fully internalized extrinsic motivation*. Students can be autonomously motivated even when the focal activities are not interesting if they appreciate and accept the value or importance of the activities for themselves (Ryan, Connell, & Deci, 1985). As we elaborate later in the chapter, a substantial body of research has now shown that even in formal school settings—elementary, secondary, college, and professional schools—students who have higher levels of intrinsic motivation (interest) and autonomous internalized motivation (value) learn and perform better and display greater classroom adjustment and better psychological well-being than those whose levels of autonomous motivation are low (e.g., Ryan & Deci, 2000a, 2013).

It is thus extremely interesting that so much of the thinking about school reform and about the motivation of teachers and students that might facilitate greater achievement in schools gives little or no attention to fostering intrinsic motivation or supporting autonomy more generally within school settings. Stated differently, policymakers as well as some educators have focused on how to control outcomes rather than on how to create the social-contextual conditions that yield autonomous motivation and the enhanced outcomes of learning and wellness consistently associated with it (Ryan & Deci, 2015).

Intrinsic Motivation

The concept of intrinsic motivation, which was introduced into the psychological literature in the 1950s (Harlow, 1950; White, 1959), emerged primarily from research with rats and primates. Researchers repeatedly found that animals readily engaged in learning and exploratory and manipulative behaviors and moreover that those behaviors could not be satisfactorily explained by the drive or reinforcement theories of motivation that were prominent at that time (e.g., Hull, 1943). A new approach to motivation was necessary to provide a meaningful account of both exploratory behaviors in animals and normal development in humans (see White, 1959), and the concept of intrinsic motivation provided a useful starting point for such an approach.

Intrinsic motivation is considered a prototype of autonomous behaviors, which means that such behaviors are performed with a full sense of willingness, volition, and choice (e.g., Deci & Ryan, 2000; Ryan & Deci, 2000b). When intrinsically motivated, people experience an internal perceived locus of causality for their behavior (de Charms, 1968)—that is, they feel initiative and ownership in acting (Deci & Ryan, 1991). As already noted, the play of children is a characteristic example of intrinsically motivated behavior, and many leisure-time pursuits of adults also fall into that category. So too are many aspects of learning and work, especially if the tasks have been designed to be interesting. Because aspects of learning and work can be intrinsically motivated, researchers began many years ago to examine contextual factors that support and enhance intrinsic motivation as well as those that thwart and diminish it.

Classroom Climates

Early classroom studies by Deci, Schwartz, Sheinman, and Ryan (1981) were based on the hypothesis that teachers' orientations toward supporting students' autonomy versus controlling their behavior would create different climates or ambiences within their classrooms, which would in turn impact the students' intrinsic motivation and well-being. These researchers developed a self-report assessment for teachers that indexed their degree of autonomy support versus control. Just before the beginning of a school year, the researchers had teachers from fourth through sixth grades in several schools complete the scale. Two months later, there were assessments done in those classrooms of the students' intrinsic motivation, perceived competence, and self-esteem. Analyses indicated that the students of teachers who were more autonomy supportive were more intrinsically motivated, perceived themselves to be more competent at schoolwork, and had higher self-esteem than the students of teachers whose self-reported motivational strategies were more controlling. It appeared that within just 2 months, the teachers of late-elementary students had affected the students' motivation and feelings of competence as a function of the degree to which the teachers were autonomy supportive versus controlling.

Subsequent research continued to replicate and extend such findings, showing that the autonomy support versus control of both teachers and parents was related to the students' autonomous motivation, well-being, and school performance (Ryan & Grolnick, 1986). In one study, for example, Roth, Assor, Niemiec, Ryan, and Deci (2009) found that when parents of high school students were autonomy supportive, their children experienced more choice and displayed an interest-focused school engagement, whereas when the parents were controlling their children experienced inner compulsion and showed a grade-focused school engagement. In short, having teachers and parents who were autonomy supportive was associated not only with the students' autonomous motivation but also with their wellness and learning outcomes (e.g., Chirkov & Ryan, 2001; Grolnick & Ryan, 1989; Grolnick, Ryan, & Deci, 1991).

Teachers who are controlling are prone to use rewards, punishments, demands, and evaluative pressures to control behavior and to foster desired achievement outcomes, all of which have been experimentally found to undermine autonomous motivation (Deci, Koestner & Ryan, 1999; Deci, Spiegel, Ryan, Koestner, & Kauffman, 1982; Ryan & Deci, 2015). In contrast, autonomy-supportive approaches entail taking students' perspectives, acknowledging their needs and feelings, providing support when they face obstacles, and providing choice and supporting initiative where possible. In addition, positive, nonevaluative feedback that is informational rather than pressuring supports autonomy (Henderlong & Lepper, 2002). These elements of autonomy support have also been examined widely in experiments and field studies (Patall, Cooper, & Robinson, 2008; Reeve & Jang, 2006). It is interesting to note in this regard that although there has been some controversy about whether choice and autonomy are also important in eastern cultures, research has provided strong evidence that they have positive effects on Asian as well as Western children (e.g., Bao & Lam, 2008; Jang, Reeve, Ryan, & Kim, 2009). These factors likely to be used by autonomy-supportive teachers—for example, positive feedback and choice—are important because they provide people with satisfaction of what we refer to as basic psychological needs. That is, we have postulated that all people need to feel both competent and autonomous in order to be healthy, effective, and intrinsically motivated (Deci & Ryan, 2000). Thus, when teachers and parents behave in ways that allow students to satisfy those needs, there will be more positive educational outcomes.

In sum, research has suggested that autonomy-supportive classrooms tend to facilitate greater intrinsic motivation among students and that offering choice and providing positive feedback are among the factors that autonomy-supportive teachers are likely to implement in their classrooms. Such teachers would be capitalizing on the fact that students are inherently active, intrinsically motivated to engage their environments, and inclined to learn from their natural interactions. Yet, as already mentioned, recent ideas about school reform tend to ignore these inherent tendencies toward learning and to, instead, focus on controlling use of rewards, competition, evaluations, threats, and surveillance, all of which have been found to be detrimental to intrinsic motivation, autonomy, well-being, and learning.

Autonomous Extrinsic Motivation

As previously noted, central to people's nature is the process of integration, which involves the internalization and reciprocal assimilation of knowledge and experience, thus making the people more unified within their sense of self (Ryan & Deci, 2012). In terms of motivation, this process is particularly pertinent to people's motivation for activities that are not interesting but are believed by teachers and parents to be important for students to do in order for them to effectively negotiate their world. Because these behaviors are not interesting, people are not intrinsically motivated to do them, so extrinsic motivation must come into play. However, as we have seen, use of extrinsic motivators can be quite detrimental for autonomy and intrinsic motivation. Fortunately, research has shown that extrinsic motivators are less likely to be detrimental if the motivators are implemented in an autonomy-supportive social context, such as autonomy-supportive classrooms or homes. For example, Ryan, Mims, and Koestner (1983) found that when monetary rewards were given in an autonomy-supportive way, participants were much more intrinsically motivated than when they were given in a controlling way. Further, such rewards that were performance contingent and given in an autonomy-supportive context were not detrimental relative to a neutral condition with neither rewards nor feedback.

In considering the extrinsic motivation of uninteresting activities, Ryan and Deci (2000a) argued that extrinsic motivators and structures can be internalized and integrated to varying degrees, and the degree to which a motivator or structure is internalized and assimilated will affect the degree to which the ensuing behavioral regulation will be autonomous. More specifically, these researchers argued that there are four types of regulation for extrinsically motivated behaviors that vary in their degree of autonomy. The least autonomous is referred to as *external regulation*, and the regulators in such cases are the classic rewards and punishments widely given to control people's behaviors. In general, as reviewed above, when behaviors are externally regulated using contingent rewards and sanctions, they tend to be very low in autonomy—that is, these controllers of behavior foster an external perceived locus of causality and thus can have various negative consequences.

A second type of extrinsic motivation involves a partial internalization in which a regulation or contingency is taken in by a person but not accepted as his or her own. This type of internalization, referred to as introjection, involves internalizing an external control but maintaining its controlling nature in a form very much like it had been when the regulation was external. However, now, because the regulation is within the person, it is as if one part of the person were controlling the rest. Examples of *introjected regulation* are contingent self-esteem and ego-involvement (Deci & Ryan, 1995; Ryan, 1982). In each case, a person's sense of worth is dependent on meeting some standard, and to the degree that the person does not, the regulatory process essentially criticizes and derogates the person, so he or she ends up feeling low self-esteem. Introjected regulation, although internal to the person, is controlling and is experienced as being external to the person's sense of self—indeed, it is experienced as pressure *on* the self.

Internalization can, however, function more effectively with people coming to understand the value of uninteresting behaviors for themselves and thus being willing to accept responsibility for those behaviors. In SDT this is referred to as *identified regulation* and is indicative of people being volitional in carrying out the behaviors because they act from a sense of the behaviors' value. Thus, whereas external and introjected regulations are relatively controlling, identified regulation is relatively autonomous. Finally, when people are able to integrate identifications with other aspects of themselves, the internalization is complete. *Integrated regulation* represents the most mature form of extrinsic motivation, because with it the person wholeheartedly accepts the importance and value of the behaviors. This type of regulation is highly autonomous and shares many consequences with intrinsic motivation, which is the prototype of autonomous motivation.

The integration process, through which people internalize and assimilate values and motivation, is the means for becoming autonomous when acting in accord with norms and mores of the social world. As such, it represents optimal socialization, and it is fueled by people's needs for autonomy and relatedness. Like competence and autonomy, SDT considers relatedness to be a basic psychological need that must be satisfied for healthy effective engagement with the world. Thus, to the extent that people are able to satisfy their basic psychological needs for relatedness, competence, and autonomy by internalizing the regulation of uninteresting behaviors, the more likely they will be to do so. These psychological needs are all ones that can be supported or ignored in classroom contexts.

Basic Needs, Integration, and Autonomy

In fact, one of the most important aspects of SDT is its specification of the three basic psychological needs whose support is essential to integrative functioning and wellness. Most theories that use the concept of psychological needs (e.g., McClelland, 1965) view them as learned and study them as individual differences in need strength. However, SDT views the three basic psychological needs as evolved and universal (e.g., see Ryan & Hawley, in press), and thus the theory specifies that the needs must be satisfied in order for people to perform effectively and coherently, as well as to be psychologically well. As such, rather than focusing on individual differences in the strength of needs for making predictions about outcomes, SDT gives empirical attention to the degree to which the needs have been or are being satisfied versus frustrated, hypothesizing that greater satisfaction of the basic needs will be related to more positive outcomes. As well, the theory examines social-contextual factors that either support or thwart satisfaction of the basic needs as a basis for making predictions and prescriptions.

As already noted, research has indicated that social-contextual conditions (e.g., the provision of choice, perspective taking) that support satisfaction of the need for autonomy lead to enhanced autonomous motivation (e.g., Patall et al. 2008), whereas autonomy frustration (e.g., with controlling language) leads to undermining (e.g.,

Koestner, Ryan, Bernieri, & Holt, 1984). Contexts that support satisfaction of the competence need (e.g., with positive feedback) also facilitate autonomous motivation (e.g., Ryan et al., 1983), whereas those that thwart it (e.g., with loss of a competition) diminish the motivation (e.g., Reeve & Deci, 1996). Contexts that support relatedness (e.g., with responsiveness) enhance autonomous motivation (La Guardia, Ryan, Couchman, & Deci, 2000), whereas those that thwart it (e.g., though rejection) decrease autonomy (Legate, DeHaan, Weinstein & Ryan, 2013). Further, many studies have shown that satisfaction of all three needs promotes autonomous motivation, whereas thwarting any of the needs is detrimental to the motivation (e.g., Chen et al., in press). Accordingly, one of the important functions of the concept of basic psychological needs is that it provides accounts of social-contextual influences on intrinsic motivation and integration, and it provides a basis for making a priori predictions about the effects on motivation of factors in the social situation. If some factor seems logically like it would enhance satisfaction of people's psychological needs, it is appropriate to hypothesize positive consequences, whereas if it seems likely that a factor would thwart one or more of the needs, it would be hypothesized to have negative consequences.

Need Satisfaction, Autonomous Motivation, Learning, and Wellness

Many studies have examined the relations of both social-contextual need supports and autonomous motivation to learning and well-being outcomes, covering the range from elementary schools to universities. We provide only a few examples. Grolnick and Ryan (1987) found that, in a study of fifth-grade students who read passages appropriate to their grade level, those who were in noncontrolling learning contexts, where they experienced greater need satisfaction, displayed better conceptual learning and more positive affect than did students in the more controlling classrooms. A study of college students' learning showed comparable results (Benware & Deci, 1984).

Research in high school classes by Jang, Reeve, and Deci (2010) involved trained observers rating the behavior of both teachers and students. The researchers found that ratings of teachers' autonomy support positively predicted ratings of student engagement and further that ratings of teachers' provisions of structure accounted for additional variance in engagement. Structure concerns making clear to students how to attain desired classroom outcomes, and the research indicates that when this structure is provided by teachers in an autonomy-supportive way, the structure complements autonomy support in facilitating student engagement (Griffith & Grolnick, 2014).

In high school physical education classes, autonomy-supportive teaching was found to predict student autonomous motivation for physical activity (Hagger, Chatzisarantis, Barkoukis, Wang, & Baranowski, 2005), and the relation between teacher autonomy support and student autonomous motivation was mediated by the students' basic psychological need satisfaction (Standage, Duda, & Ntoumanis, 2006).

Research in university-level organic chemistry classes involved students attending weekly workshops led by instructors who varied in the degree to which they were autonomy supportive versus controlling (Black & Deci, 2000). Results revealed that students who experienced their instructors as more autonomy supportive showed increases in their level of autonomous motivation during the semester and that they got better grades in the course after controlling for the variance explained by their general achievement. In other words, after controlling for indicators of ability and skill, students' autonomous motivation for this particular course predicted their performance in the course, thus paralleling results from younger students (e.g., Miserandino, 1996).

In medical schools, students who experienced their instructors as more autonomy supportive learned the course material more fully and put it into more effective use 6 months later relative to students who experienced their instructors as more controlling (Williams & Deci, 1996). Further medical students who, in their fourth year in the program, chose specialties for their residencies were likely to pick the specialty that had had the most autonomy-supportive preceptor during the students' third year in the program (Williams, Saizow, Ross, & Deci, 1997). Also, researchers found that, in law schools, having more autonomy-supportive instructors had a positive effect on students' autonomous motivation, their course grades, and the scores on their bar exams (Sheldon & Krieger, 2007).

To summarize, research in schools with elementary, secondary, university, and professional schools have all similarly found that classroom climates that support satisfaction of students' basic psychological needs for competence, autonomy, and relatedness tend to enhance the students' autonomous motivation. This results in better learning and performance, along with more positive affective experiences, than is the case with pressured climates, which lead to controlled motivation. With the large body of research showing the substantial advantages of autonomous rather than controlled motivation for the desired educational outcomes of conceptual learning, effective performance, and psychological well-being, it seems ever more clear that approaches to education reform that are based primarily on incentives, pressures, and controls for motivating effective education are misguided and lack an evidence base.

Goals and Motives

The concept of goals has been a central one in the study of motivation for half a century. Goals presumably represent the ends toward which people are motivated. Some are explicit, others less so. We briefly address two approaches to studying goals that have been used in the field of education. Our primary foci will be on whether goals are differentially effective in predicting positive educational outcomes and how goals and motives might relate to each other in predicting those outcomes. The first approach to studying goals in education that we discuss was developed within the achievement motivation tradition and the second within the self-determination tradition. We discuss each in turn as they relate to pressuring contexts and autonomous motivation.

Achievement Goals and Autonomous Motives

The approach to studying goals that has received the greatest attention in the education literature is the achievement goal approach. The approach began by distinguishing between *mastery goals*, which involve learning in order to enhance one's own competence, and *performance goals*, which involve learning in order to appear better than others. Subsequently, the performance goals were further differentiated into *performance-approach* goals and *performance-avoidance* goals (Elliot, 1999). The former involves pursuing positive performance goal outcomes (e.g., doing better than someone else), whereas the latter involves avoiding negative performance goal outcomes (e.g., not doing worse than someone else). In this and other approach-avoidance literatures, there is ample evidence that avoidance orientations are associated with appreciable negative consequences. Indeed, performance-avoidance goals, relative to performance-approach goals, have been found to result in poorer learning, performance, and well-being outcomes. In contrast, mastery goals are generally associated with strong well-being and sometimes with high performance on achievement tasks (Elliot, 2005).

In contrast to mastery goals, performance goals are very much focused on performance in a normative way, which is quite consistent with the strong national attempt to improve achievement in order to surpass the achievement of students from other nations. To more fully understand how performance-approach goals might relate to educational outcomes, researchers have used autonomy-related concepts from SDT to examine whether the achievement goal effects that have been found in previous research might be explained in part or in full by autonomous versus controlled motives. That is, if people pursue performance-approach goals for autonomous motives, will the consequences be more positive than if pursued for controlled motives, and if the goals and motives compete for variance, will they explain independent variance?

Vansteenkiste et al. (2010) simultaneously examined the strength of performance-approach goals and the autonomous versus controlled motives for pursuing those goals to predict self-regulated learning, test anxiety, and persistence among high school students, all outcomes that have been effectively predicted by performance-approach goals (e.g., Elliot, 2005). Vansteenkiste and colleagues found first that both the autonomous and controlled motives were significant predictors of outcomes, with autonomy positively predicting the self-regulated learning strategies and persistence and controlled motives being negative predictors of such variables and a positive predictor of test anxiety. However, when the strength of the performance-approach goals was entered into the analyses with these motives, performance-approach goals did not predict significant variance in any of the seven outcome variables. In other words, people's motives for predicting performance-approach goals were more important than the strength of the goals themselves in predicting various educational outcomes.

Benita, Roth, and Deci (2014) conducted two studies to examine the importance of people's autonomous and controlled motives when pursuing mastery goals. As already noted, mastery goals have typically been effective in predicting affective outcomes and some performance outcomes. Further, it is noteworthy that, with their focus on improving oneself rather than outperforming others, the mastery goals are less consistent with the national obsession toward achievement and therefore with the national pressure to perform. Benita and colleagues examined mastery goals in relation to autonomous versus controlled motives for pursuing those goals and also to autonomy-supportive versus controlling educational climates within which the goals were being pursued. In the first study, autonomous motives for pursuing mastery goals led to more interest and engagement than goals for which the motives were controlled. In another study, the researchers found that mastery goals that were adopted within an autonomy-supportive context led to more positive emotional experiences than the goals adopted in controlling contexts. In sum, this research on mastery goals, like the previously reviewed research on performance-approach goals, indicates that understanding the relations of achievement goals to educational outcomes is facilitated by an examination of the motives people have for pursuing the goals or the motivational contexts within which the goals were adopted (see also Vansteenkiste, Lens, Elliot, Soenens, & Mouratidise, 2014). In all of these studies of achievement goals, controlling or pressuring contexts and controlled motives for pursuing goals were found to have negative correlates.

Intrinsic and Extrinsic Goals

The second approach to studying goals in educational contexts concerns intrinsic goals versus extrinsic goals, the former being focused on learning in order to contribute to society, to be physically fit, or to grow as a person and the latter being focused more on obtaining wealth, becoming socially recognized, or having greater power or influence. In this research, either intrinsic or extrinsic goals were emphasized in learning settings as the aims of learning, and both learning and performance outcomes were examined (e.g., Vansteenkiste, Simons, Lens, Sheldon, & Deci, 2004).

This research on intrinsic and extrinsic goals in education evolved out of earlier research by Kasser and Ryan (1993, 1996), which had examined whether, if people's aspirations or life goals were intrinsic versus extrinsic, they would be psychologically healthier. In short, the researchers found that the stronger people's extrinsic goals were, relative to their intrinsic goals, the less psychologically healthy they tended to be, and this goal effect was independent of whether people's motives for pursuing the goals were autonomous or controlled (Sheldon, Ryan, Deci, & Kasser,

2004). Further, attainment of extrinsic goals predicted ill-being rather than well-being (Niemiec, Ryan, & Deci, 2009).

In the experiments done in schools, researchers manipulated people's goals with respect to specific learning opportunities. For example, when junior college students were learning about sustainability, some were told that their learning about recycling and reusing could help them save money (an extrinsic goal), while others were told that the learning would help them contribute to the community (an intrinsic goal). Results indicated that those who learned with the intrinsic goal learned more and performed better when taking a test or explaining the material to others than did those who learned with the extrinsic goal (Vansteenkiste et al., 2004). This intrinsic goal effect was especially strong if the goals were communicated in an autonomy-supportive way. In other words, both the goals and the motives predicted independent variance and the two interacted positively.

In short, studies of the intrinsic and extrinsic goals showed that learning in order to attain intrinsic goals such as community contribution tended to satisfy basic psychological needs and promote well-being, whereas pursuit and attainment of extrinsic goals such as financial accumulation tended to thwart basic psychological needs and promoted ill-being. This research also opens up the question of what goals and motives we are orienting students toward or implicitly promoting in schools, as we prepare them for confidently entering a world of varied opportunities. With the pressures associated with competition to achieve more than others, it seems that we may be fostering extrinsic and performance goals as well as controlled motives.

SDT in the Classroom: Supporting Basic Psychological Needs

Perhaps the most important message from the research reviewed thus far is that when students' motivation is autonomous, they display more positive educational outcomes than when their motivation is controlled and that the students are more autonomously motivated when the teachers create classroom climates that support the students' basic psychological needs for competence, autonomy, and relatedness.

Support for students' basic needs begins with *teachers taking the students' perspectives* when they are interacting in school (e.g., Deci, Eghrari, Patrick, & Leone, 1994; Koestner et al., 1984). It is quite easy for teachers to slip into a mode of viewing classroom activities from their own perspective, in terms of how they think things should be, as if all students were highly motivated for all courses and would be ready to do whatever the teachers think they should. However, it is likely that the situation will often not be like that in classrooms. So it becomes essential for teachers to try to understand how the students tend to see things and to relate in terms of the students' perspectives.

Many teachers have a lot of experience working with students, and they may well have accumulated a lot of information about how students see both school-related and personal matters. They may know, for example, that some students find some courses quite boring and that some students feel a very low sense of competence for at least some of their courses, which can be very draining of the students' motivation. Knowing such things could be useful for teachers in new situations, so they could be open to the students being bored or feeling incompetent. Still, students and their circumstances vary greatly, so even highly experienced teachers will not necessarily know what is going on for a student at a given time. That makes it especially important, when teachers sense that something is wrong for a student, to take interest in what is happening for that student, appreciating both inner and outer obstacles to motivation. When the time is right, the teachers can ask the students what is happening to them, doing it in an accepting and supportive way, so the students will not become defensive. If the teachers listen carefully, they can really understand what the students might be going through and will be able to work with them more effectively.

If teachers are able to take students' perspectives, it is likely to come naturally that they will refrain from pressuring the students to do what they, the teachers, want them to do. For example, the use of controlling language, with directives and words that convey control—words such as should, must, and have to—has been shown to diminish intrinsic motivation and impair internalization (Deci et al., 1994; Ryan, 1982), so when teachers are mindful of this and convey a sense of invitation rather than coercion, they will be more effective in promoting autonomy, engagement, learning, and wellness. Reeve (this volume) describes that in detail.

Research has found various other things to be important in the classroom as well. For example, providing students the opportunity to make choices either independently or as a group can help them feel more autonomous and competent and thus more engaged in the activities they played a role in selecting (e.g., Patall et al., 2008). Of course, there are certain things students need to do or learn, but there is often room for the students to make choices about what, when, and how to engage in learning activities. For example, it is important for students to read, but in some settings with very low achievement levels in language arts, letting them read almost anything they choose is better than having them not read what they have been told they have to read but do not find interesting or understandable. Providing opportunities for choice is likely to enhance students' autonomous motivation and engagement. Along with making choices, having opportunities to explore and try new things without pressure is also useful for students. Of course, teachers want students to succeed, but at times letting them make mistakes as they try something for themselves can be a more important learning opportunity than pressuring them to succeed. Indeed, natural learning is often a series of trials and experiments rather than continuous success, and teachers can be more accepting of this sometimes bumpy trajectory of discovery and learning.

Providing autonomy support does not mean that teachers are "permissive" and allow students to do whatever they want. As we said when reviewing Jang et al.'s (2010) study, optimally, teachers also provide structure, including clear guidelines, goals, and limits, but this does not require a controlling attitude or approach. Structure can be provided in autonomy-supportive ways, and when that is the case, it is likely to facilitate internalization of the structures and the goals underlying them. For example, Deci et al.'s (1994) experiment showed that providing a meaningful rationale when asking students to do something facilitated their internalization of the request (see also Jang, 2008). This also suggests that we should not be surprised when the internalization of structures, rules, or limits may be poor if the structures are arbitrary or have no rationale.

Feedback is also important in the classroom. Many studies have shown that specific and clear positive feedback about what was done well tends to enhance autonomous motivation (see Deci et al., 1999). But evaluative feedback can have a negative effect because, even when the feedback is "positive," it can be experienced as controlling, and when it is, it can catalyze an extrinsic orientation in the learner (e.g., Ryan, 1982). Similarly, although negative feedback has been shown to undermine intrinsic motivation because it is often done in a way that conveys incompetence (Deci & Cascio, 1972), negative feedback is sometimes important and does not necessarily have negative consequences. That requires treating the interaction as a problem-solving session in which, after being clear about what is being addressed, the student is asked how he or she sees the situation—that is, what was going on with him or her. Then, the interaction continues with the "recipient of the feedback" playing an active role in considering how he or she might handle the situation more effectively next time. In sum, the functional impact of feedback will depend on whether it is experienced as effectance relevant and informational or as controlling.

Classroom facilitation does not end with autonomy and competence. Relatedness to teachers is a substantial predictor of motivation in the classroom. Relatedness is fostered when it is clear the child feels welcomed and cared for in a given context. Teachers foster relatedness from the initial smile at the door to the concern when there are failures or difficulties in academic tasks. What is compelling to us is that relatedness is also highly correlated with perceived autonomy support. That is, caring for and connecting with a student is typically associated with more support for autonomy.

Most teachers, when free to teach, try to find ways to support interest and value in learning, thus promoting autonomy. They work to build a structured classroom that guides behavior and scaffolds the learning tasks so that each can see growth. Yet teachers themselves are also under pressure in many schools around the globe, and they do not feel the freedom they need to nurture student learning and development. The less autonomy, competence, and relatedness teachers themselves experience in their jobs, the less able they are to facilitate the students' autonomy and learning.

What Teachers Need

Teachers can become more autonomous, competent, and relationally supportive through many pathways. One path of course is specific training. For example, Kaplan and Assor (2012) described an intervention program in which Israeli teachers received training to be more autonomy supportive. Those who received the intervention subsequently had students who displayed less aggression and negative affect than did the students of teachers who were in the control group. Cheon, Reeve, and Moon (2012) designed and implemented an intervention for physical education teachers to enhance their support for autonomy. Observer and student ratings confirmed the success of the intervention, including showing enhancement of students' psychological needs in trained teachers. In fact, a meta-analysis of studies examining the effects of training for teacher autonomy support found that interventions can enhance autonomy support as assessed with student perceptions and observer ratings (Su & Reeve, 2011).

Although training can sharpen skills, we also find that many teachers are daily ongoingly trying to support the psychological needs of children. Yet varied demands of the workplace can make that mission more difficult. Teachers often feel a lack of control over either the process or content of their teaching. Many find themselves subjected to prescribed curricula, controlling standards, or top-down evaluations and supervision.

To practice their craft well, SDT suggests that, just like their students, teachers need support for autonomy. For example, Nie, Chua, Yeung, Ryan, and Chan (2014) recently studied teachers' motivation in Chinese public schools. They found that teachers who experienced more autonomy support from their supervisors also evidenced more intrinsic motivation and identified regulation in their role as teachers. They also had more job satisfaction and fewer physical symptoms. In contrast, teachers who perceived their supervisors to be controlling reported more amotivation and external motivation to teach, as well as lower job satisfaction and greater workplace stress. Fernet, Guay, Senécal, and Austin (2012) showed that, when teachers experienced increases in overload and in student disruptive behaviors, the teachers experienced less autonomous motivation for teaching and less perceived competence. Those experiences in turn lead to greater emotional exhaustion and less sense of personal accomplishment. Bartholomew, Ntoumanis, Cuevas, and Lonsdale (2014) found that more teacher job pressure predicted greater burnout and that frustration of the basic psychological needs mediated this relation.

In sum, there is considerable evidence that when teacher needs are frustrated by thwarting environmental pressures, the teachers tend to be less autonomously motivated to teach and more prone to burnout. Furthermore, as Pelletier, Séguin-Lévesque, and Legault (2002) found, both pressures from above (e.g., test pressures, controlling principals) and pressures from below (unmotivated or resistant students) can negatively affect teachers' autonomous motivation for teaching. In turn, Pelletier et al. found that the less autonomous teachers' motivations were for teaching, the less autonomy supportive they were with their students. Similarly, Roth, Assor, Kanat-Maymon, and Kaplan (2007) found that teachers who were more autonomously motivated for teaching had students who perceived them to be more autonomy supportive. In contrast, teachers who felt controlled in their classrooms were seen as more controlling by students. Finally, Holzberger, Philipp, and Kunter (2014) recently showed that even high teacher self-efficacy does not enhance instructional quality if teachers' intrinsic need satisfaction is low. This shows how there are systemic positive effects of attending to the needs of teachers, as support for their needs allows them to provide a more facilitating and supportive motivational environment for their students.

Conclusion

In this chapter, we pointed out that many countries have become concerned about the education of their students whom they believe are not performing adequately as reflected in the countries' rankings on international achievement tests. In some instances, test information has usefully informed educational improvement efforts, whereas in others it has led to policies and practices that represent controlling approaches to school reform. We have questioned the effectiveness of these controlling approaches, particularly high-stakes testing, citing relevant evidence (e.g., Hout & Elliott, 2011).

We focused on an alternative to the pressure-and-test approach. In this view, we see schools as an important locus for nurturing students' learning and holistic personal development through supporting their basic psychological needs. Need-supportive conditions have been found consistently to be effective in promoting greater engagement, learning, and well-being among students. We discussed the importance of fostering intrinsic motivation as a prototype of autonomous learning and further explained how extrinsic motivation can become internalized and integrated so students can engage in less interesting tasks with more autonomy. We also reviewed evidence that social-contextual factors that thwart the basic psychological needs for autonomy, competence, or relatedness have negative effects on autonomous motivation, learning, and well-being, whereas those that support basic psychological needs have correspondingly positive effects.

We also discussed two approaches to the study of goals in education and found that, although research has shown that goals can predict educational outcomes, whether people's motives for pursuing the goals are autonomous versus controlled predicts significant variance in those outcomes, sometimes overshadowing the goal effects. Thus, although mastery or performance goals can differentially affect outcomes, what may be more critical is the relative autonomy of the individual's pursuit of such goals.

Given that research indicates that the more autonomous approaches have clear advantages over the controlling approaches for educational outcomes, we argued that teachers can effectively put the principles of a self-determination theory approach into practice in the classroom. Training can facilitate such practice, as can providing the professional need supports teachers require. Specifically, teachers need to have their own autonomy supported to be able to effectively and flexibly meet the needs of their students.

We believe it is right for educators and policymakers both to assess educational outcomes and to devote energy and resources toward enhancing students' learning. Yet our overall point is that, rather than fetishizing specific outcomes in math or language, reformers, educational administrators, and policymakers should begin to care more about the quality of students' and teachers' engagement, volition, and wellness within the school setting. It is our strong belief, supported by substantial empirical evidence, that, when teachers have the resources and permission to attend to the basic psychological needs of students, the students will indeed become more actively engaged in learning and will more readily internalize a value for achieving. Ultimately this process-oriented approach will result in improved achievement outcomes. Ironically, when officials instead attempt to force or control teachers and students to attain specific metrics, it crowds out good classroom practices, does harm to student development, and in the end fails to produce the desired outcomes. In sum, we would like to see nations trying just as hard to race to the top in student need satisfaction and wellness, which would result in more productive, well-educated, and fulfilled citizens across the globe.

References

Amrein, A. L., & Berliner, D. C. (2002). High-stakes testing, uncertainty, and student learning. *Education Policy Analysis Archives, 10*(18), 110–123. Retrieved 3 Sep 2006, from http://epaa.asu.edu/epaa/v10n18/.

Aviv, R. (2014, July 21). Wrong answer. *The New Yorker*, pp. 54–65.

Bao, X.-H., & Lam, S.-F. (2008). Who makes the choice? Rethinking the role of autonomy and relatedness in Chinese children's motivation. *Child Development, 79*, 269–283. doi:10.1111/j.1467-8624.2007.01125.x.

Bartholomew, K. J., Ntoumanis, N., Cuevas, R., & Lonsdale, C. (2014). Job pressure and ill-health in physical education teachers: The mediating role of psychological need thwarting. *Teaching and Teacher Education, 37*, 101–107. doi:10.1016/j.tate.2013.10.006.

Benita, M., Roth, G., & Deci, E. L. (2014). When are mastery goals more adaptive? It depends on experiences of autonomy support and autonomy. *Journal of Educational Psychology, 106*, 258–267. doi:10.1037/a0034007.

Benware, C., & Deci, E. L. (1984). Quality of learning with an active versus passive motivational set. *American Educational Research Journal, 21*, 755–765. doi:10.3102/00028312021004755.

Black, A. E., & Deci, E. L. (2000). The effects of student self-regulation and instructor autonomy support on learning in a college-level natural science course: A self-determination theory perspective. *Science Education, 84*, 740–756.

Chen, B., Vansteenkiste, M., Beyers, W., Boone, L., Deci, E. L., Duriez, B., et al. (in press). Basic psychological need satisfaction, need frustration, and need strength across four cultures. *Motivation and Emotion, 39*(2), 216–236.

Cheon, S. H., Reeve, J., & Moon, I. S. (2012). Experimentally based, longitudinally designed, teacher-focused intervention to help physical education teachers be more autonomy supportive toward their students. *Journal of Sport and Exercise Psychology, 34*, 365–396.

Chirkov, V. I., & Ryan, R. M. (2001). Parent and teacher autonomy-support in Russian and U.S. adolescents: Common effects on well-being and academic motivation. *Journal of Cross Cultural Psychology, 32*, 618–635. doi:10.1177/0022022101032005006.

de Charms, R. (1968). *Personal causation: The internal affective determinants of behavior*. New York: Academic.

Deci, E. L. (1975). *Intrinsic motivation*. New York: Plenum. doi:10.1007/978-1-4613-4446-9.

Deci, E. L., & Cascio, W. F. (1972, April). *Changes in intrinsic motivation as a function of negative feedback and threats*. Presented at the Eastern Psychological Association, Boston.

Deci, E. L., Eghrari, H., Patrick, B. C., & Leone, D. R. (1994). Facilitating internalization: The self-determination theory perspective. *Journal of Personality, 62*, 119–142. doi:10.1111/j.1467-6494.1994.tb00797.x.

Deci, E. L., Koestner, R., & Ryan, R. M. (1999). A meta-analytic review of experiments examining the effects of extrinsic rewards on intrinsic motivation. *Psychological Bulletin, 125*, 627–668. doi:10.1037/0033-2909.125.6.627.

Deci, E. L., & Ryan, R. M. (1985). *Intrinsic motivation and self-determination in human behavior.* New York: Plenum.

Deci, E. L., & Ryan, R. M. (1991). A motivational approach to self: Integration in personality. In R. Dienstbier (Ed.), *Nebraska symposium on motivation* (Perspectives on motivation, Vol. 38, pp. 237–288). Lincoln, NE: University of Nebraska Press.

Deci, E. L., & Ryan, R. M. (1995). Human autonomy: The basis for true self-esteem. In M. Kernis (Ed.), *Efficacy, agency, and self-esteem* (pp. 31–49). New York: Plenum.

Deci, E. L., & Ryan, R. M. (2000). The "what" and "why" of goal pursuits: Human needs and the self-determination of behavior. *Psychological Inquiry, 11*, 227–268. doi:10.1207/S15327965PLI1104_01.

Deci, E. L., Schwartz, A. J., Sheinman, L., & Ryan, R. M. (1981). An instrument to assess adults' orientations toward control versus autonomy with children: Reflections on intrinsic motivation and perceived competence. *Journal of Educational Psychology, 73*, 642–650. doi:10.1037/0022-0663.73.5.642.

Deci, E. L., Spiegel, N. H., Ryan, R. M., Koestner, R., & Kauffman, M. (1982). Effects of performance standards on teaching styles: Behavior of controlling teachers. *Journal of Educational Psychology, 74*, 852–859. doi:10.1037/0022-0663.74.6.852.

Elliot, A. J. (1999). Approach and avoidance motivation and achievement goals. *Educational Psychologist, 34*, 169–189. doi:10.1207/s15326985ep3403_3.

Elliot, A. J. (2005). A conceptual history of the achievement goal construct. In A. Elliot & C. Dweck (Eds.), *Handbook of competence and motivation* (pp. 52–72). New York: Guilford Press.

Fernet, C., Guay, F., Senécal, C., & Austin, S. (2012). Predicting intraindividual changes in teacher burnout: The role of perceived school environment and motivational factors. *Teaching and Teacher Education, 28*, 514–525. doi:10.1016/j.tate.2011.11.013.

Griffith, S. F., & Grolnick, W. S. (2014). Parenting in Caribbean families: A look at parental control, structure, and autonomy support. *Journal of Black Psychology, 40*(2), 166–190. doi:10.1177/0095798412475085.

Grolnick, W. S., & Ryan, R. M. (1987). Autonomy in children's learning: An experimental and individual difference investigation. *Journal of Personality and Social Psychology, 52*, 890–898. doi:10.1037/0022-3514.52.5.890.

Grolnick, W. S., & Ryan, R. M. (1989). Parent styles associated with children's self-regulation and competence in school. *Journal of Educational Psychology, 81*, 143–154. doi:10.1037/0022-0663.81.2.143.

Grolnick, W. S., Ryan, R. M., & Deci, E. L. (1991). The inner resources for school achievement: Motivational mediators of children's perceptions of their parents. *Journal of Educational Psychology, 83*, 508–517. doi:10.1037/0022-0663.83.4.508.

Hagger, M. S., Chatzisarantis, N. L. D., Barkoukis, V., Wang, C. K. J., & Baranowski, J. (2005). Perceived autonomy support in physical education and leisure-time physical activity: A cross-cultural evaluation of the trans-contextual model. *Journal of Educational Psychology, 97*, 287–301. doi:10.1037/0022-0663.97.3.376.

Harlow, H. F. (1950). Learning and satiation of response in intrinsically motivated complex puzzle performance by monkeys. *Journal of Comparative and Physiological Psychology, 43*, 289–294. doi:10.1037/h0058114.

Henderlong, J., & Lepper, M. R. (2002). The effects of praise on children's intrinsic motivation: A review and synthesis. *Psychological Bulletin, 128*, 774–795. doi:10.1037/0033-2909.128.5.774.

Holzberger, D., Philipp, A., & Kunter, M. (2014). Predicting teachers' instructional behaviors: The interplay between self-efficacy and intrinsic needs. *Contemporary Educational Psychology, 39*, 100–111. doi:10.1016/j.cedpsych.2014.02.001.

Hout, M., & Elliott, S. W. (Eds.). (2011). For the Committee on Incentives and Test-Based Accountability in Public Education, Board on Testing and Assessment, Division of Behavioral and Social Sciences and Education, National Research Council of The National Academies. *Incentives and test-based accountability in education*. Washington, DC: National Academy Press.

Hull, C. L. (1943). *Principles of behavior: An introduction to behavior theory*. New York: Appleton-Century-Crofts.

Jang, H. (2008). Supporting students' motivation, engagement, and learning during an uninteresting activity. *Journal of Educational Psychology, 100*, 798–811. doi:10.1037/a0012841.

Jang, H., Reeve, J., Ryan, R. M., & Kim, A. (2009). Can self-determination theory explain what underlies the productive, satisfying learning experiences of collectivistically oriented Korean students? *Journal of Educational Psychology, 101*, 644–661. doi:10.1037/a0014241.

Jang, H., Reeve, J., & Deci, E. L. (2010). Engaging students in learning activities: It's not autonomy support or structure, but autonomy support and structure. *Journal of Educational Psychology, 102*, 588–600. doi:10.1037/a0019682.

Kaplan, H., & Assor, A. (2012). Enhancing autonomy-supportive I-Thou dialogue in schools: Conceptualization and socio-emotional effects of an intervention program. *Social Psychology of Education*. doi:10.1007/s11218-012-9178-2.

Kasser, T., & Ryan, R. M. (1993). A dark side of the American dream: Correlates of financial success as a central life aspiration. *Journal of Personality and Social Psychology, 65*, 410–422. doi:10.1037/0022-3514.65.2.410.

Kasser, T., & Ryan, R. M. (1996). Further examining the American dream: Differential correlates of intrinsic and extrinsic goals. *Personality and Social Psychology Bulletin, 22*(3), 280–287. doi:10.1177/0146167296223006.

Kellaghan, T., Madaus, G. F., & Raczek, A. (1996). *The use of external examinations to improve student motivation*. Washington, DC: American Educational Research Association.

Koestner, R., Ryan, R. M., Bernieri, F., & Holt, K. (1984). Setting limits on children's behavior: The differential effects of controlling versus informational styles on intrinsic motivation and creativity. *Journal of Personality, 52*, 233–248. doi:10.1111/j.1467-6494.1984.tb00879.x.

La Guardia, J. G., Ryan, R. M., Couchman, C. E., & Deci, E. L. (2000). Within-person variation in security of attachment: A self-determination theory perspective on attachment, need fulfillment, and well-being. *Journal of Personality and Social Psychology, 79*, 367–384. doi:10.1037/0022-3514.79.3.367.

Legate, N., De Haan, C. R., Weinstein, N., & Ryan, R. M. (2013). Hurting you hurts me too: The psychological costs of complying with ostracism. *Psychological Science*. doi:10.1177/0956797612457951.

McClelland, D. C. (1965). Toward a theory of motive acquisition. *American Psychologist, 20*, 321–333. doi:10.1037/h0022225.

McNeil, L., & Valenzuela, A. (2000). *The harmful effects of the TAAS system of testing in Texas: Beneath the accountability rhetoric*. Cambridge, MA: Harvard Civil Rights Project.

Miserandino, M. (1996). Children who do well in school: Individual differences in perceived competence and autonomy in above average children. *Journal of Educational Psychology, 88*, 203–214. doi:10.1037/0022-0663.88.2.203.

Moon, T. R., Callahan, C. M., & Tomlinson, C. A. (2003, April 28). Effects of state testing programs on elementary schools with high concentrations of student poverty: Good news or bad news? *Current Issues in Education, 6*(8). Retrieved 14 May 2003, from http://cie.ed.asu.edu/volume6/number8/.

National Center for Education Statistics, Institute of Education Sciences. (2009). Highlights from PISA 2009: Performance of U.S. 15-year-old students in reading, mathematics, and science literacy in an international context. Retrieved from: http://nces.ed.gov/pubsearch/pubsinfo.asp?pubid=2011004.

National Center for Education Statistics, Institute of Education Sciences. (2011). Highlights from TIMSS 2011: Mathematics and science achievement of U.S. fourth- and eighth-grade students in an international context. Retrieved from: http://nces.ed.gov/pubsearch/pubsinfo. asp?pubid=2013009.

Nie, Y., Chua, B. L., Yeung, A. S., Ryan, R. M., & Chan, W. Y. (2014). The importance of autonomy support and the mediating role of work motivation for well-being. Testing self-determination theory in a Chinese work organisation. *International Journal of Psychology*. doi:10.1002/ijop.12110.

Niemiec, C. P., Ryan, R. M., & Deci, E. L. (2009). The path taken: Consequences of attaining intrinsic and extrinsic aspirations in post-college life. *Journal of Research in Personality, 73*(3), 291–306. doi:10.1016/j.jrp.2008.09.001.

Patall, E. A., Cooper, H., & Robinson, J. C. (2008). The effects of choice on intrinsic motivation and related outcomes: A meta-analysis of research findings. *Psychological Bulletin, 134*, 270–300. doi:10.1037/0033-2909.134.2.270.

Pelletier, L. G., Seguin-Levesque, C., & Legault, L. (2002). Pressure from above and pressure from below as determinants of teachers' motivation and teaching behaviors. *Journal of Educational Psychology, 94*, 186–196. doi:10.1037/0022-0663.94.1.186.

Piaget, J. (1971). *Biology and knowledge*. Chicago: University of Chicago Press.

Reeve, J., & Deci, E. L. (1996). Elements within the competitive situation that affect intrinsic motivation. *Personality and Social Psychology Bulletin, 22*, 24–33. doi:10.1177/0146167296221003.

Reeve, J., & Jang, H. (2006). What teachers say and do to support students' autonomy during a learning activity. *Journal of Educational Psychology, 98*, 209–218.

Roth, G., Assor, A., Kanat-Maymon, Y., & Kaplan, H. (2007). Autonomous motivation for teaching: How self-determined teaching may lead to self-determined learning. *Journal of Educational Psychology, 99*, 761–774. doi:10.1037/0022-0663.99.4.761.

Roth, G., Assor, A., Niemiec, C. P., Ryan, R. M., & Deci, E. L. (2009). The emotional and academic consequences of parental conditional regard: Comparing conditional positive regard, conditional negative regard, and autonomy support as parenting practices. *Developmental Psychology, 45*, 1119–1142. doi:10.1037/a0015272.

Ryan, R. M. (1982). Control and information in the intrapersonal sphere: An extension of cognitive evaluation theory. *Journal of Personality and Social Psychology, 43*, 450–461. doi:10.1037/0022-3514.43.3.450.

Ryan, R. M., & Brown, K. W. (2005). Legislating competence: The motivational impact of high stakes testing as an educational reform. In A. J. Elliot & C. S. Dweck (Eds.), *Handbook of competence* (pp. 354–374). New York: Guilford Press.

Ryan, R. M., Connell, J. P., & Deci, E. L. (1985). A motivational analysis of self-determination and self-regulation in education. In C. Ames & R. E. Ames (Eds.), *Research on motivation in education: The classroom in milieu* (pp. 13–51). New York: Academic.

Ryan, R. M., & Deci, E. L. (2000a). Intrinsic and extrinsic motivations: Classic definitions and new directions. *Contemporary Educational Psychology, 25*, 54–67. doi:10.1006/ceps.1999.1020.

Ryan, R. M., & Deci, E. L. (2000b). Self-determination theory and the facilitation of intrinsic motivation, social development, and well-being. *American Psychologist, 55*, 68–78. doi:10.1037/0003-066X.55.1.68.

Ryan, R. M., & Deci, E. L. (2012). Multiple identities within a single self: A self-determination theory perspective on internalization within contexts and cultures. In M. R. Leary & J. P. Tangney (Eds.), *Handbook of self and identity* (2nd ed., pp. 225–246). New York: Guilford.

Ryan, R. M., & Deci, E. L. (2013). Toward a social psychology of assimilation: Self-determination theory in cognitive development and education. In B. Sokol, F. M. E. Grouzet, & U. Muller (Eds.), *Self-regulation and autonomy: Social, developmental, educational, and neurological dimensions of human contact* (pp. 191–207). New York: Cambridge University Press.

Ryan, R. M., & Deci, E. L. (2015). Promoting self-determined school engagement: Motivation, learning, and well-being. In K. R. Wentzel & D. Miele (Eds.), *Handbook on motivation at school* (2nd ed.). New York: Routledge. in press.

Ryan, R. M., & Grolnick, W. S. (1986). Origins and pawns in the classroom: Self-report and projective assessments of children's perceptions. *Journal of Personality and Social Psychology, 50*, 550–558.

Ryan, R. M., & Hawley, P. (in press). Naturally good? Basic psychological needs and the proximal and evolutionary bases of human benevolence. In M. Leary & K. W. Brown (Eds.). *The psychology of hypoegoic behavior*. New York: Guilford.

Ryan, R. M., Mims, V., & Koestner, R. (1983). Relation of reward contingency and interpersonal context to intrinsic motivation: A review and test using cognitive evaluation theory. *Journal of Personality and Social Psychology, 45*, 736–750. doi:10.1037/0022-3514.45.4.736.

Shapira, Z. (1976). Expectancy determinants of intrinsically motivated behavior. *Journal of Personality and Social Psychology, 34*, 1235–1244. doi:10.1037/0022-3514.34.6.1235.

Sheldon, K. M., & Krieger, L. S. (2007). Understanding the negative effects of legal education on law students: A longitudinal test of self-determination theory. *Personality and Social Psychology Bulletin, 33*, 883–897. doi:10.1177/0146167207301014.

Sheldon, K. M., Ryan, R. M., Deci, E. L., & Kasser, T. (2004). The independent effects of goal contents and motives on well-being: It's both what you pursue and why you pursue it. *Personality and Social Psychology Bulletin, 30*, 475–486. doi:10.1177/0146167203261883.

Skinner, B. F. (1953). *Science and human behavior*. New York: Macmillan.

Standage, M., Duda, J. L., & Ntoumanis, N. (2006). Students' motivational processes and their relationships to teacher ratings in school physical education: A self-determination theory approach. *Research Quarterly for Exercise and Sport, 77*, 100–110. doi:10.1080/02701367.2006.10599336.

Su, Y.-L., & Reeve, J. (2011). A meta-analysis of the effectiveness of intervention programs designed to support autonomy. *Educational Psychology Review, 23*, 159–188. doi:10.1007/s10648-010-9142-7.

Vansteenkiste, M., Lens, W., Elliot, A. J., Soenens, B., & Mouratidise, A. (2014). Moving the achievement goal approach one step forward: Toward a systematic examination of the autonomous and controlled reasons underlying achievement goals. *Educational Psychologist, 49*(3), 153–174. doi:10.1080/00461520.2014.928598.

Vansteenkiste, M., Simons, J., Lens, W., Sheldon, K. M., & Deci, E. L. (2004). Motivating learning, performance, and persistence: The synergistic effects of intrinsic goal contents and autonomy-supportive contexts. *Journal of Personality and Social Psychology, 87*, 246–260. doi:10.1037/0022-3514.87.2.246.

Vansteenkiste, M., Smeets, S., Soenens, B., Lens, W., Matos, L., & Deci, E. L. (2010). Autonomous and controlled regulation of performance-approach goals: Their relations to perfectionism and educational outcomes. *Motivation and Emotion, 34*, 333–353. doi:10.1007/s11031-010-9188-3.

Vroom, V. H. (1964). *Work and motivation*. New York: Wiley.

Werner, H. (1948). *Comparative psychology of mental development*. New York: International Universities Press.

White, R. W. (1959). Motivation reconsidered: The concept of competence. *Psychological Review, 66*, 297–333. doi:10.1037/h0040934.

Wigfield, A., & Eccles, J. S. (2000). Expectancy-value theory of achievement motivation. *Contemporary Educational Psychology, 25*, 68–81. doi:10.1006/ceps.1999.1015.

Williams, G. C., & Deci, E. L. (1996). Internalization of biopsychosocial values by medical students: A test of self-determination theory. *Journal of Personality and Social Psychology, 70*, 767–779. doi:10.1037/0022-3514.70.4.767.

Williams, G. C., Saizow, R., Ross, L., & Deci, E. L. (1997). Motivation underlying career choice for internal medicine and surgery. *Social Science and Medicine, 45*, 1705–1713.

Chapter 3
The Dualistic Model of Passion: Theory, Research, and Implications for the Field of Education

Robert J. Vallerand

"To every young person listening tonight who's contemplating their career choice: If you want to make a difference in the life of our nation; if you want to make a difference in the life of a child—become a teacher. Your country needs you."

(Barak Obama, President of the United States, State of the Union Address, 2011)

It is very telling that out of all the professions that President Obama could have chosen to "make a difference in the life of a child (and a country)," teaching is the one he chose. Teaching is indeed a very important profession for a number of reasons. One of these deals with the opportunity that teachers have to leading children unto a lifelong path of self-growth and discovery. There is nothing more rewarding for a teacher than to see some of his or her students being passionate for a given subject. This is because he or she knows that in all likelihood, those who have found a passion for something in school will do well in society and contribute to it. Passionate teachers connect with their students, instill persistence and the joy of learning, and go a long way in helping students becoming passionate themselves and succeed in school and to eventually find a satisfying career and lead a meaningful life. We now see the link with Obama's statement. Accordingly, the role of passion in teaching has started to generate much interest in recent years (e.g., Day, 2004; Greenberger, 2012; Phelps & Benson, 2012).

But let us not get ahead of ourselves. What is passion? What are some of its effects? How does it develop? Are all passions equal or are some more positive than

R.J. Vallerand (✉)
Laboratoire de Recherche sur le Comportement Social Département de Psychologie, Université du Québec à Montréal, Station "Ctr-ville", Montreal, QC, P. O. Box. 8888, H3C 3P8, Canada

Australian Catholic University, Strathfield, NSW, Australia
e-mail: Vallerand.bob@gmail.com

© Springer Science+Business Media Singapore 2016
W.C. Liu et al. (eds.), *Building Autonomous Learners,*
DOI 10.1007/978-981-287-630-0_3

others? The purpose of this chapter is to look at these various issues and document some of the ways through which passion matters for the field of education. Using the Dualistic Model of Passion (Vallerand, 2010, 2015), research is presented that shows that passion matters greatly for both students and teachers on a number of dimensions. In the first section, I present a brief history on the concept of passion. Then, second, the Dualistic Model of Passion (Vallerand, 2008, 2010, 2015; Vallerand et al., 2003) is presented. The third section reviews research dealing with the role of passion in the different outcomes that matter for both teachers and students. Then, in the fourth section, I discuss the development of passion. Finally, the last section offers some conclusions and applications that passion may offer to the field of education.

On the Concept of Passion

Interestingly, very little research has focused on passion in the psychological literature until recently. And yet, passion has generated a lot of attention from philosophers. Indeed, centuries of scholarship has been devoted to passion, especially from an emotional perspective. Three positions have emerged (see Vallerand, 2015). The first posits that passion entails a loss of reason and control (see Plato, 429–347 BC and Spinoza, 1632–1677). In line with the etymology of the word passion (from the Latin "passio" for suffering), people who have a passion are seen as experiencing some suffering. They are slaves to their passion as it comes to control them. The second perspective portrays passion in a more positive light. One example is René Descartes (1596–1650) who defines passions as strong emotions with inherent behavioral tendencies that can be positive as long as reason underlies the behavior. The Romantics, especially Jean-Jacques Rouseau (1712–1778), Helvetius (1715–1771), and Diderot (1713–1784), all presented passion as essential to a healthy, fulfilled living. Hegel (1770–1831) argues that passions are necessary to reach the highest levels of achievement and Kierkegaard (1813–1855) even writes, "To exist, if we do not mean by that only a pseudo existence, cannot take place without passion." Thus, this second view of passion portrays passion in a more positive light as some positive outcomes may be experienced when individuals are in control of their passion. Taken together, these two positions highlight the duality of passion.

Little is known, however, about a third perspective of passion that emerged at the turn of the twentieth century, at the junction of philosophy and psychology. This third position suggests that some passions are "good" and others are "bad." For instance, basing himself on the work of Descartes, Kant (1724–1804), and Ribot (1907), Joussain (1928) proposed that there were two broad types of passion: the "noble" passions oriented toward the well-being or benefit of others or society and the "selfish" passions that seek personal satisfaction. Of additional interest, Joussain further suggested that passions could interact among themselves in at least two ways. First, some passions can conflict with other passions and in fact crowd out other passions and try to extinguish them. Second, other passions can peacefully coexist with others. In fact, Joussain proposed that "virtue is to be obtained through the *equilibrium* that we establish among our passions and the multiple consequences that they create for us and others, keeping in mind the knowledge that we have of the world and ourselves" (p. 103; translation from French and italics are mine). Inherent in such a statement is that all passions are not equivalent and that they may play different roles in the outcomes that we experience. As we shall see, this is clearly one of the themes of this chapter.

Unfortunately, Joussain did not conduct research on passion and very little scholarship or research has followed his work until recently. The few psychologists who have looked at the concept have underscored its motivational aspect. For instance, some authors have proposed that people will spend large amounts of time and effort in order to reach their passionate goals (see Frijda, Mesquita, Sonemans, & Van Goozen, 1991) or working on the activity that they love (Baum & Locke, 2004). Nearly all empirical work on passion has been conducted in the area of passionate love (e.g., Hatfield & Walster, 1978). Although such research is important, it does not deal with the main topic at hand, namely, passion for activities. Finally, although other related constructs such as positive addiction (Glasser, 1976), grit (Duckworth, Peterson, Matthews, & Kelly, 2007), and intrinsic motivation (Deci & Ryan, 2000) have been proposed, they are conceptually different (the reader is referred to Vallerand, 2015, Chap. 2, for conceptual comparisons between passion and these and other concepts). Of great importance is the fact that none of these constructs reflects the duality inherent in passion underscored by philosophers and early psychologists. Furthermore, none of these concepts or theories can explain why something that you love can be "bad" for you.

The Dualistic Model of Passion

The Dualistic Model of Passion (DMP; Vallerand, 2010, 2015) proposes that people engage in various activities throughout life in order to grow as individuals. After a period of trial and error that would appear to start in early adolescence (Erikson, 1968), most people will eventually start to show preference for some activities, especially those that are perceived as particularly enjoyable and important and that have some resonance with how they see themselves. These activities become passionate activities. In line with the above, Vallerand et al. (2003) define passion as a strong inclination toward a self-defining activity that one loves, finds important and meaningful, and invests time and energy in. These activities come to be so self-defining that they represent central features of one's identity. For instance, the teacher who has a passion for teaching is not simply teaching, he or she sees him- or herself as a "teacher," and the student who has developed a passion for playing the guitar perceives him- or herself as a "guitarist."

The DMP further posits that there are two types of passion. The DMP postulates that activities that people like (or love) will also be internalized in the person's identity and self to the extent that these are highly valued and meaningful for the person

(Aron, Aron, & Smolan, 1992; Csikszentmihalyi, Rathunde, & Whalen, 1993). Furthermore, it is proposed that there are two types of passion, obsessive and harmonious, that can be distinguished in terms of how the passionate activity has been internalized. Obsessive passion results from a controlled internalization of the activity into one's identity. In line with self-determination theory (Deci & Ryan, 2000; Ryan & Deci, 2000), such an internalization process leads to values and regulations associated with the activity to be at best partially internalized in the self and at worse to be internalized in the person's identity but completely outside the integrating self (Deci & Ryan, 2000), in line with the ego-invested self (Hodgins & Knee, 2002). A controlled internalization originates from intra- and/or interpersonal pressure typically because certain contingencies are attached to the activity such as feelings of social acceptance or self-esteem (Lafrenière, Bélanger, Vallerand, & Sedikides, 2011; Mageau, Carpentier, & Vallerand, 2011), or because the sense of excitement derived from activity engagement is uncontrollable. People with an obsessive passion can thus find themselves in the position of experiencing an uncontrollable urge to partake in the activity they view as important and enjoyable. They cannot help but to engage in the passionate activity. Consequently, they risk experiencing conflicts and other negative affective, cognitive, and behavioral consequences during and after activity engagement. For example, when confronted with the possibility of playing some music with his friends or prepare his class lecture for the next day, a teacher with an obsessive passion for music may not be able to resist the invitation and will go and jam with his friends instead of preparing the lecture. During the musical session, he might feel upset with himself for playing instead of working on the lecture. He might therefore have difficulties focusing on the task at hand (playing the guitar) and may not experience as much positive affect and flow as he could while playing.

It is thus proposed that with obsessive passion, individuals come to display a rigid persistence toward the activity, as oftentimes they can't help but to engage in the passionate activity. This is so because ego-invested rather than integrative self-processes (Hodgins & Knee, 2002) are at play with obsessive passion leading the person to eventually become dependent on the activity. While such persistence may lead to some benefits in the long term (e.g., improved performance at the activity), it may also come at a cost for the individual, potentially leading to less than optimal functioning within the confines of the passionate activity because of the lack of flexibility that it entails. Furthermore, such a rigid persistence may lead the person to experience conflict with other aspects of his or her life when engaging in the passionate activity (when one should be doing something else, for instance), as well as to frustration and rumination about the activity when prevented from engaging in it. Thus, if the teacher has an obsessive passion for music but nevertheless manages to say no to his friends and to music, he still may end up suffering because of the difficulties of concentrating on the lecture preparation due to ruminations about the lost opportunity to play music.

Conversely, harmonious passion results from an autonomous internalization of the activity into the person's identity and self. In line with self-determination theory (Deci & Ryan, 2000; Ryan & Deci, 2000), such internalization occurs when individuals have freely accepted the activity as important for them without any contingencies attached to it (e.g., Mageau et al., 2011). This type of internalization emanates from the intrinsic and integrative tendencies of the self (Deci & Ryan, 2000; Ryan & Deci, 2003) and produces a motivational force to engage in the activity willingly and engenders a sense of volition and personal endorsement about pursuing the activity.

When harmonious passion is at play, individuals freely choose to engage in the beloved activity. With this type of passion, the activity occupies a significant but not overpowering space in the person's identity and is in harmony with other aspects of the person's life. In other words, with harmonious passion the authentic integrating self (Deci & Ryan, 2000) is at play allowing the person to fully partake in the passionate activity with mindfulness (Brown & Ryan, 2003) and an openness that is conducive to positive experiences (Hodgins & Knee, 2002). Consequently, people with a harmonious passion should be able to fully focus on the task at hand and experience positive outcomes both during task engagement (e.g., positive affect, concentration, flow, etc.) and after task engagement (general positive affect, satisfaction, etc.). Thus, there should be little or no conflict between the person's passionate activity and his or her other life activities. Furthermore, when prevented from engaging in their passionate activity, people with a harmonious passion should be able to adapt well to the situation and focus their attention and energy on other tasks that need to be done. Finally, with harmonious passion, the person is in control of the activity and can decide when to and when not to engage in the activity. Thus, when confronted with the possibility of playing music with his friends or preparing the class lecture to be delivered the next day, the teacher with a harmonious passion for playing the guitar can readily tell his friends that he'll take a rain check and proceed to be fully immersed in the preparation of the lecture without thinking about the missed opportunity to play the guitar. People with a harmonious passion are able to decide to forego activity engagement on a given day if needed or even to eventually terminate the relationship with the activity if they decide it has become a permanent negative factor in their life. Thus, behavioral engagement in the passionate activity can be seen as flexible.

Research on Passion

Initial Research on the Concept of Passion and the DMP

Initial contemporary research on the construct of passion for activities (Vallerand et al., 2003) focused on three different goals: (1) to determine the prevalence of passion for an activity in people's lives, (2) to develop the Passion Scale, and (3) to test the validity of some of the elements of the passion constructs. In the initial study, Vallerand and colleagues (2003, Study 1) had over 500 college students complete the Passion Scale with respect to an activity that they loved, that they valued, and in which they invested time and energy (i.e., the main passion definition criteria), as well as other scales allowing them to test predictions derived from the DMP. A large variety of passionate activities were reported ranging from physical activity and sports to watching movies, playing a musical instrument, and reading. Participants reported engaging in one specific passionate activity for an average of 8.5 h per week and had been engaging in that activity for almost 6 years. Thus, clearly passionate activities are meaningful to people and are long-lasting in nature. Of importance regarding the first purpose of this research, 84 % of participants indicated that they had at least a moderate level of passion for a given activity in their lives (they scored at least four out of seven on a question asking them if their favorite activity was a "passion" for them). In a similar vein, a subsequent study (Philippe, Vallerand, & Lavigne, 2009) with over 750 participants ranging in age from 18 to 90 years using a more stringent criterion of having a mean of 5 out of 7 on four criteria of passion (loving the activity, activity valuation, activity engagement, and perceiving the activity as a passion) revealed that 75 % of participants had a high level of passion for an activity in their life. These findings have been obtained in other countries as well (see Lecoq & Rimé, 2009; Liu, Chen, & Yao, 2011; Stenseng, 2008). Overall, these results reveal that the prevalence of passion is rather high and is not limited to simply a few individuals. Passion pervades people's lives!

Of additional interest for the present topic is the fact that at least three studies have assessed the level of passion of teachers using the criteria discussed above. In a first study, Carbonneau, Vallerand, Fernet, and Guay (2008) asked a large number of experienced elementary and secondary school teachers to complete the Passion Scale as well as the passion criteria. Using a cutoff score of 4 on the mean of the criteria, it was found that 93 % of the teachers were found to be at least moderately passionate for teaching. Using similar procedures, Fernet and colleagues (Fernet, Lavigne, & Vallerand, 2014) replicated these findings with novice teachers in two studies (Study 1 = 94 %; Study 2 = 93 %). These findings reveal that most teachers are passionate for their teaching.

A second goal of the initial passion research dealt with the development of the Passion Scale. Vallerand et al. (2003, Study 1) conducted exploratory and confirmatory factor analyses supporting the presence of two factors corresponding to the two types of passion. These findings on the factor validity of the Passion Scale have been replicated in at least 20 studies in a variety of settings and activities (see Vallerand, 2015, Chap. 4 for a complete review). Further, more recently, Marsh et al. (2013) have provided support not only for the bifactorial nature of the Passion Scale but also for its invariance as a function of gender, language (French and English), and several types of activities. The Passion Scale consists of two subscales of six items each reflecting obsessive (e.g., "I almost have an obsessive feeling toward this activity") and harmonious passion (e.g., "This activity is in harmony with other activities in my life"). Furthermore, internal consistency analyses have shown that both subscales are reliable (typically 0.75 and above). Finally, test-retest correlations over periods ranging from 4 to 6 weeks revealed moderately high stability values (in the 1980s, Rousseau, Vallerand, Ratelle, Mageau, & Provencher, 2002), thereby supporting the factorial validity and reliability of the scale.

With respect to the third purpose of the initial passion research of Vallerand et al. (2003, Study 1), a series of critical findings with partial correlations (controlling for the correlation between the two types of passion) revealed that both harmonious and obsessive passions were positively associated with the passion criteria, thereby providing support for the definition of passion. In addition, both types of passion were found to relate to one's identity, and obsessive passion was found to more strongly relate to a measure of conflict with other life activities than harmonious passion. These findings support the view that both harmonious and obsessive passions are indeed a "passion" as each one reflects the definition of the passion construct (see also Marsh et al., 2013, for additional support on the construct validity of the passion concept). Furthermore, research provided support for the hypotheses dealing with affect, wherein harmonious passion positively predicted positive affect both during and after engagement in the passionate activity, while obsessive passion was unrelated to positive affect but positively related to negative affect, especially after task engagement and while prevented from engaging in the activity. Finally, other studies in this initial research (Vallerand et al., 2003) have also shown that obsessive (but not harmonious) passion correlated to rigid persistence in ill-advised activities (Vallerand et al., Studies 3 and 4). Of interest is the fact that the above findings obtained with the Passion Scale have been replicated in several studies using experimental inductions of the two types of passion (see Bélanger, Lafrenière, Vallerand, & Kruglanski, 2013; Lafrenière, Vallerand, & Sedikides, 2013). Overall, these results provide important support for the conceptual validity of the two types of passion and their divergent effects on various outcomes.

Since the 2003 Vallerand et al. initial publication, approximately 200 studies have been conducted on the role of passion in a host of cognitive, affective, behavioral, relational, and performance outcomes experienced within the realms of hundred of passionate activities conducted in both our own and other laboratories. Most of these studies have used the DMP as a theoretical framework. In the present paper, we do not address research on all of these various outcomes (see Vallerand, 2010, 2015 for a review) but rather focus on research on the role of passion in some key outcomes such as psychological well-being, physical health, expert performance, and interpersonal relationships.

Passion and Psychological Well-Being

Initial research sought to determine if there was a link between passion for an activity and psychological well-being. The main premise was that if you can engage in an activity that you love and that you care about (in education or elsewhere), this should have a positive influence on your psychological well-being. The first study was conducted by Rousseau and Vallerand (2003) and it involved senior citizens. Measures of psychological well-being (e.g., life satisfaction, meaning in life, and vitality) and ill-being (anxiety and depression) were included in this study. Having a harmonious passion for an activity was expected to promote psychological well-being, while being obsessively passionate or non-passionate should not. Furthermore, because experiencing positive psychological states is the antithesis of psychological ill-being, it was also hypothesized that harmonious passion should protect against ill-being. Research supported these hypotheses. For instance, in this particular study, harmonious passion toward one's favorite activity (e.g., playing cards, playing music, etc.) positively predicted positive indices of psychological well-being but negatively predicted indices of ill-being. Conversely, obsessive passion positively predicted anxiety and depression, was negatively related to life satisfaction, and was unrelated to vitality and meaning in life. Thus, harmonious passion was found to serve promoting and protective functions with respect to well-being, while the less than optimal role of obsessive passion was demonstrated.

Subsequent research conducted with teachers replicated and extended these findings. For instance, using a prospective design, Carbonneau et al. (2008) showed that having a harmonious passion for teaching predicted an *increase* in life satisfaction over a 3-month period. Teachers who had a predominant harmonious passion for their teaching were happier in their life 3 months later than they were at the start of the study! No such benefits were found with obsessive passion. Similar findings were obtained with undergraduate students. Thus, having a harmonious passion for one's studies (in this case psychology majors) predicted being happier in one's life in general than having an obsessive passion (Vallerand et al., 2007, Study 2). No relationships were found for obsessive passion. Similar findings were obtained with student athletes who were harmoniously passionate for their sport (e.g., Vallerand, Rousseau, Grouzet, Dumais, & Grenier, 2006, Studies 2 and 3; Vallerand et al., 2008, Study 2). It should be noted that teachers and students are not the only ones to experience these differential effects of harmonious and obsessive passion on psychological well-being as such findings have been replicated with a different population across the life span using a variety of psychological well-being measures (for reviews see Vallerand, 2010, 2015, Chap. 8).

It should be noted that the above research only included passionate people. So, we don't know if passion provides an advantage relative to the absence of passion. Philippe et al. (2009) conducted two studies with close to 1,000 participants across the life span to address this issue. Using the passion criteria described previously, the authors (Philippe et al., Study 1) distinguished those individuals who were highly passionate for an activity in their life (a mean of 5 and more on a 7-pt scale on the four passion criteria) from those who were not (below a mean of 5 on the passion criteria). Furthermore, in line with Vallerand and Houlfort (2003), among the passionate individuals, they distinguished those who were "harmoniously passionate" (those with a higher z-score on the harmonious passion than on the obsessive passion subscale) from those who were "obsessively passionate" (those with a higher z-score on the obsessive than on the harmonious passion subscale) and then compared the three groups on various psychological well-being indices. The results showed that being harmoniously passionate for a given activity leads to higher levels of psychological well-being relative to being obsessively passionate and non-passionate. These findings thus replicate the findings of the research reviewed above on the positive role of harmonious passion in psychological well-being. In addition, it was found that non-passionate and obsessively passionate individuals did not differ. A subsequent study (Philippe et al., 2009, Study 2) replicated these findings and, in addition, using a 1-year prospective design, revealed that both obsessively passionate and non-passionate individuals experienced a slight, but significant, *decrease* in psychological well-being over time, while harmoniously passionate individuals experienced a significant *increase* in psychological well-being over the 1-year period. Thus, overall, it would appear that harmonious passion promotes psychological well-being, while obsessive passion and being non-passionate undermine it.

Other research has looked at the processes mediating the positive effects of passion on psychological well-being. One such mediator is the repeated experience of situational (or state) positive affect during the course of engagement of the passionate activity. Research has supported the adaptive role of positive affect in a variety of outcomes, including psychological well-being (e.g., Lyubomorsky, King, & Diener, 2005; Sedikides, Wildschut, Arndt, & Routledge, 2008). For instance, in one important line of research, Fredrickson (2001) has proposed and found support for her Broaden-and-Build Theory that posits that positive emotions are adaptive because they broaden people's thought-action repertoires and self and allow people to build resources over time leading to better decisions and higher levels of psychological well-being. Thus, such cumulative experience of positive affect may facilitate psychological well-being. Of major importance is the fact that research has shown that harmonious passion positively contributes to the experience of positive affect during activity engagement, while obsessive passion does not and may even facilitate the experience of negative affect (e.g., Vallerand et al., 2003, Studies 1 and 2; Vallerand et al., 2006, Studies 2 and 3). Since passionate individuals engage on average 8 h per week in their passionate activity, this means that harmonious passion can lead people to experience somewhere around 8 h of cumulative positive affect per week on top of what may be experienced in other life domains. Furthermore, harmonious passion has been found to protect against negative affect, while OP leads to negative affect and is either unrelated or weakly related to positive affect *following* task engagement (e.g., Mageau & Vallerand, 2007; Philippe, Vallerand, Houlfort, Lavigne, & Donahue, 2010; Vallerand et al., 2003, Studies 1 and 2; Vallerand et al., 2006, Studies 2 and 3). Thus, this analysis suggests that having a harmonious passion can lead people to experience cumulative (and repeated) experiences of positive affect that should facilitate and sustain psychological well-being as well as protect against psychological ill-being. However, such should not be the case for obsessive passion as it should mainly promote negative affect and psychological ill-being.

A research by Rousseau and Vallerand (2008) tested the above hypothesis with respect to the role of the promotion function of positive affect in the passion-psychological well-being relation. At Time 1, participants who were passionate toward exercise completed the Passion Scale with respect to physical activity, as well as measures of psychological well-being. A few weeks later, at Time 2, immediately following an exercise bout, participants completed situational measures of positive and negative affect. Finally, 3 weeks later at Time 3, they completed measures of psychological well-being again. Results from a structural equation modeling analysis revealed that harmonious passion positively predicted positive affect that, in turn, led to increases in psychological well-being from Time 1 to Time 3. On the other hand, obsessive passion was unrelated to positive affect but positively predicted negative affect. The latter did not predict psychological well-being. Finally, obsessive passion directly and negatively predicted psychological well-being. These basic findings have been replicated in the work domain, especially with teachers and administrators in several commission school boards (Houlfort, Philippe, Vallerand, & Ménard, 2014, Study 3).

The role of flow as a mediator in the harmonious passion-psychological well-being relationship has also been ascertained. For instance, in a study with undergraduate students, Carpentier, Mageau, and Vallerand (2012) showed that harmonious passion for one's favorite activity positively predicted the experience of flow in both the passionate activity and their studies. Flow, in both activities, in turn, positively predicted psychological well-being. These findings are important because they suggest that having a harmonious passion for a leisure activity (such as gaming or sports) can actually allow one to fully immerse in one's studies and even experience flow in them, leading to high levels of psychological well-being. It is when the passion for such outside activities is obsessive that negative effects take place in one's studies.

In other research, the role of flow as a mediator of the *protective* effects of harmonious passion on burnout was assessed with both teachers and students. Previous research has shown that obsessive passion (for either teaching or studying) is conducive to burnout, while harmonious passion seems to protect against it in both teachers (Carbonneau et al., 2008; Trépanier, Fernet, Austin, Forest, & Vallerand, 2014) and students (e.g., Stoeber, Childs, Kayward, & Feast, 2011). Lavigne, Forest, & Crevier-Braud (2012) conducted two studies, one with a cross-sectional design (Study 1) and one with a longitudinal design (Study 2) in order to assess the mediating role of flow in these effects of passion. Because both studies yielded highly similar findings, only the longitudinal study is presented here. In this study, administrators completed the Passion Scale for their work as well as measures of flow at work and burnout at two different time points, 6 months apart. Structural equation modeling analyses were conducted on the data and showed that harmonious passion for work positively predicted *increases* in flow over time that, in turn, predicted *decreases* in burnout over time. Obsessive passion was unrelated to flow but directly and positively predicted increases in burnout. It would thus appear that positive work experiences (such as flow) do mediate the protective effects of harmonious passion on psychological ill-being.

In sum, it would appear that harmonious passion promotes psychological well-being and prevents ill-being, largely because it leads the person to experience some positive experiences (i.e., positive affect and flow) during task engagement and allows the person to cognitively disengage from the passionate activity when not physically engaging in it (Carpentier et al., 2012). Conversely, it would appear that obsessive passion may not promote psychological well-being because it is unrelated to positive emotions and flow during task engagement. However, obsessive passion may facilitate negative states of ill-being such as burnout because of the rigid persistence it entails and the conflict it creates with other aspects of one's life.

In sum, the passion that teachers bring to the classroom matters not only for their students and what can be transmitted to them but also for the teachers themselves and their psychological well-being. To the extent that their passion is harmonious, teachers should be able to avoid burnout so prevalent in the teaching profession and experience a life that includes both satisfying work and a rich life outside of it. This conclusion also applies to students.

Passion and Physical Health

Passion can also affect one's physical health in a number of ways. One obvious way is that passion for exercise will facilitate one's physical health through the sustained engagement that it will induce over time. Although some students may be passionate for sedentary forms of activities such as gaming (e.g., Lafrenière, Vallerand, Donahue, & Lavigne, 2009), a substantial percentage of students are passionate for physical activity and sports. In fact, in the initial study on passion (Vallerand et al., 2003, Study 1), fully 60 % of college students indicated that they had a passion for some form of individual or a team sport or physical activity! Clearly, physical activity brings about a host of physiological and cardiovascular benefits (Wells, 2012). And we know that people who are passionate for a given activity engage in this activity on average 8.5 h per week. Thus, having a passion for physical activity and sports should lead people to engage in such activities for several hours each week on a recurrent basis, thereby experiencing important physiological benefits. What does the research say on this issue?

Research on this issue leads to a number of conclusions. First, based on the passion criteria discussed previously (love of the activity, activity valuation, time and energy commitment, and the activity being part of identity), participants are highly passionate for physical activities as diverse as aerobic classes, yoga, weight training, running, or competitive sports (Carbonneau, Vallerand, & Massicotte, 2010, Studies 1 and 2; Halvari, Ulstad, Bagoien, and Skjesol, 2009; Parastatidou, Doganis, Theodorakis, & Vlachopoulos, 2012; Stephan, Deroche, Brewer, Caudriot, & Le Scanff, 2009). Furthermore, another research with sport samples that has not assessed the passion criteria has nevertheless shown participants to display high levels of harmonious and/or obsessive passion in sport activities such as basketball (Vallerand et al., 2006, Studies 1, 2, and 3; Vallerand et al., 2008, Study 1), water polo and synchronized swimming (Vallerand et al., Study 2), ice hockey (Amiot, Valleran, & Blanchard, 2006), and soccer refereeing (Philippe et al., 2009, Studies 1 and 2). Thus, passion seems implicated in physical activity engagement and students were participants in several of those studies.

A second finding of importance is that both the harmonious and obsessive passions predict *heavy* engagement in physical activity. Thus, being passionate about physical activity leads people to engage in highly demanding physical regimens (e.g., Parastatidou et al., 2012). And the more demanding the training, the more physiological benefits one derives from training. Furthermore, of interest is the fact that obsessive passion appears to lead to higher levels of activity engagement than harmonious passion. This last finding may reflect the rigid persistence that obsessive passion induces in people where they may train no matter what, irrespective of conditions. The net result may be that overall having an obsessive passion leads one to exercise slightly more. A third and related conclusion is that the above studies show that the two types of passion also predict sustained engagement over time. It thus appears that the two types of passion for a specific type of physical activity leads one to remain engaged in this activity for years. Finally, it should be noted that several of the studies on this issue were conducted with students. Thus, it would appear that several students should be able to reap the physical benefits of regular engagement in physical activity. What we don't know, however, is the extent to which such sustained engagement has some positive effects on school outcome such as concentration in the classroom and better grades. Research on this issue would appear important.

Another benefit derived from regular engagement in physical activity is that people will develop the appropriate muscular endurance that will allow them to engage successfully in exercise while protecting themselves from experiencing injuries. Thus, passion should indirectly lead people to be resistant to acute (or little nagging) injuries that less frequent exercisers will experience. Because their body is not ready to sustain the physical demands of the activity, non-passionate, less assiduous, exercisers get injured. Further, because both types of passion lead to sustained regular engagement in physical activity, they should both protect against acute injuries (such as muscle pulls and twisted ankles).

In one study, Rip, Fortin, and Vallerand (2006) asked modern-jazz dance students and professional dancers with an average of 11 years of dance experience to complete a questionnaire that contained the Passion Scale for dancing and various questions pertaining to injuries. One of the questions focused on the number of days over the past 12 months when they could not dance because of acute injuries, defined as injuries such as muscle pulls, twisted ankles, and the like that were not recurring or chronic injuries. Results from partial correlations revealed that both the harmonious and obsessive passions were *negatively* correlated with the number of days missed because of acute injuries. In other words, the more one is passionate (either harmonious or obsessive), the less one is severely injured. Thus, being passionate for some form of physical activity such as dance serves to protect the person from acute injuries while engaging in the activity.

Another issue with physical activity deals with one's behavior when one gets injured. As is the case with dancers (Turner & Wainwright, 2003) and most exercisers, people sometimes get injured when engaging in physical activity. Obsessive passion, as we have seen in this chapter, induces rigid persistence. Therefore, when injured, obsessive passion should lead people to refuse to stop and to wish to continue dancing, thereby aggravating the injury and leading to chronic injuries. On the other hand, with harmonious passion, the person is mindful and in control of the activity. Therefore, persistence is expected to be flexible, allowing the harmoniously passionate dancers to let go and to stop dancing when injured and especially if there is a risk of developing a chronic injury. In Rip et al. (2006) study, dancers completed the Passion Scale for dancing as well as questions pertaining to chronic injuries incurred over the past year. Results from partial correlations revealed that obsessive passion was positively related to the number of weeks missed due to chronic injuries, whereas harmonious passion was unrelated to chronic injuries. Stephan et al. (2009) have also found obsessive passion to be a risk factor for injuries.

Research has started to look at how passion for a nonphysical form of activity may lead to over-engagement in the passionate activity that may have some implications for one's health. One such type of activity is gaming. Gaming is of interest because people, and especially students and young adults, may engage in these activities for excessively long periods of time, leading them to disregard biological needs such as hunger, thirst, and sleep. Over time, such neglect may take its toll on physical health and people may come to experience illnesses, sometimes serious ones. Stories abound of people who engaged in gaming for days without stopping and who ended up experiencing serious health problems as a result (e.g., Chuang, 2006). In fact, in some cases, prolonged engagement in gaming has led to death. Because of the rigid persistence it entails, obsessive passion may positively predict such extreme health problems. Indeed, people with an obsessive passion cannot let go of the activity, become oblivious to their biological needs, and may experience severe health problems. Conversely, because harmonious passion allows one to remain mindful during activity engagement and entails a flexible persistence in the activity, the person should then be able to stop activity engagement when the time comes to attend to one's biological needs. Thus, harmonious passion should prevent the occurrence of negative health consequences due to excessive gaming.

In a first study on gaming (Lafrenière et al., 2009), participants were male and female massively multiplayer online gaming players. These games are interactive and always ongoing, 24 h a day. Thus, the nature of the game encourages players to engage almost continuously in it. On average, participants in this study engaged in their favorite gaming activity (e.g., World of Warcraft) for 22 h per week. Lafrenière et al. asked participants to complete a number of scales online, including the Passion Scale for gaming and a scale assessing negative physical symptoms (with respect to various minor acute physical problems such as appetite loss, sleep disorders, dry eyes, etc.). Results revealed that, controlling for age, gender, and the number of hours spent on gaming, obsessive passion for gaming was found to positively predict negative physical symptoms. In contrast, harmonious passion was unrelated to physical symptoms. These findings were replicated in a second study on passion for gaming (Przybylski, Weinstein, Ryan, & Rigby, 2009) using a large number of male and female video game players from a variety of types of video games and a broad *positive* measure of physical health instead of a measure of negative symptoms. Only obsessive passion was found to negatively affect health. Harmonious passion had no relationship with the positive health measure.

These two studies on passion for gaming activities converge: obsessive passion seems to negatively affect one's health, while harmonious passion is unrelated to it. However, it should be noted that these two studies simply measured passion and health at the same point in time. It is then difficult to make the case that passion has *causal* influences on health. One study (Carbonneau et al., 2010, Study 2) went further and looked at *changes* in health outcomes that took place over a 3-month period as a function of passion for exercise. Carbonneau et al. (Study 2) had Canadian men and women passionate for yoga complete the Passion Scale and a negative physical symptoms measure similar to that used by Lafrenière et al. at Time 1 and again at Time 2, 3 months later. The results from structural equation modeling analyses (controlling for the number of weekly hours and years of involvement in yoga) revealed that only harmonious passion predicted *decreases* in (negative) physical symptoms over the 3-month period. Obsessive passion did not predict changes in negative physical symptoms.

Overall, these findings are important because they underscore the fact that we need to go beyond mere activity engagement to determine the type of outcomes that will be experienced by the person. The *quality* of activity engagement matters. If the type of passion matters even with an activity like yoga, it should matter with most activities. In light of the obesity crisis that we are experiencing worldwide, future research on how best to promote passion for physical activity in our students would appear to represent an important future research direction. Similarly, we need some research to determine how such passion for exercise can be funneled more positively to foster adaptive outcomes in the classroom for students. As the Romans were saying centuries ago, "mens sanae in coporae sano."

Passion and Performance

Research in the area of expert performance reveals that to reach international levels in most domains (sport, music, arts, etc.), one must put in roughly 10,000 h of practice over a 10-year period (Ericsson & Charness, 1994; Starkes & Ericsson, 2003). One important type of practice is called deliberate practice. Deliberate practice entails engaging in the activity with clear goals of improving on certain task components (Ericsson & Charness, 1994). For instance, a student in a music class may work hard on mastering a new strumming technique for hours until it is successfully mastered. I believe that passion represents the major reason why the guitarist will persist engaging in deliberate practice although it is not easy or even fun to do so. Indeed, if one is to engage in the activity for long hours over several years and sometimes a lifetime, one must love the activity dearly and have the desire to persist in the activity especially when times are rough. Thus, the two types of passion (harmonious and obsessive) should lead to engagement in deliberate practice that, in turn, should lead to improved performance.

The above model was tested in a study with student athlete basketball players (Vallerand et al., 2008, Study 1). Male and female student athletes (basketball players) completed scales assessing their passion for basketball as well as deliberate practice (based on Ericsson & Charness, 1994). Coaches independently rated the athletes' performance. Results from a path analysis revealed that both types of passion led to engagement in deliberate practice in basketball which, in turn, led to objective performance. These findings were replicated in a prospective design with dramatic arts students (Vallerand et al., 2007, Study 1). Of additional interest, harmonious passion toward dramatic arts was positively and significantly related to life satisfaction, while obsessive passion was unrelated to it. This is in line with research reported previously on passion and psychological well-being. It thus appears that both types of passion positively contribute to deliberate practice and thus, indirectly, to performance. However, with harmonious passion, there is a bonus effect as one may reach high levels of performance while being happy at the same time. One need not choose between the performance and happiness if harmonious passion is involved.

One of the main features of performance's progress over time deals with the achievement goals that one pursues in the activity. Such goals should contribute to keeping one deeply involved in the mastery pursuit of the activity through continuous engagement in deliberate practice. One important goal theory is that of Elliot (1997). This author proposed that achievement goals should represent important mediators between passion and deliberate practice. Elliot and colleagues (Elliot & Church, 1997; Elliot & Harackiewicz, 1996) have distinguished between three types of achievement goals: mastery goals (which focus on the development of competence and task mastery), performance-approach goals (which focus on the attainment of personal competence relative to others), and performance-avoidance goals (which focus on avoiding incompetence relative to others). Harmonious passion, being a rather pure autonomous form of regulation, should be positively related to mastery goals but not to performance goals of either type. On the other hand, obsessive passion, being a more pressured, internally controlling, form of regulation, should lead the individual to feel compelled to seek any and all forms of success at the activity and may even evoke concerns about doing poorly. As such, obsessive passion should be positively related to mastery and performance-approach goals, as well as performance-avoidance goals.

A study with student athletes involved in water polo and synchronized swimming (including some who were part of the junior national teams) was conducted over an entire season to test the above model (Vallerand et al., 2008, Study 2). Early in the season, at Time 1, individuals completed the Passion Scale, the Achievement Goals Scale, and scales assessing psychological well-being. At Time 2, in February, they completed the Deliberate Practice Scale. Finally, at the end of the season, at Time 3, coaches assessed individuals' performance over the entire season. Results of a path analysis yielded support for the proposed model. Harmonious passion was found to lead to mastery goals that, in turn, led to deliberate practice that positively predicted objective performance. On the other hand, obsessive passion was positively related to all three goals. While performance-approach goals did not predict any variables in the model, performance-avoidance goals *negatively* predicted performance over the 5-month period. In other words, performance-avoidance goals can lead to performance decrements over time! Finally, harmonious passion was positively associated with psychological well-being, while obsessive passion was unrelated to it. This basic model was replicated in other research involving both student and professional musicians of international stature (Bonneville-Roussy, Lavigne, & Vallerand, 2011) and students who had a passion toward studying psychology as their future profession with objective exam scores in a psychology course serving as a measure of performance (Vallerand et al., 2007, Study 2).

The above findings lead to the conclusion that there are two roads to excellence, the harmonious and the obsessive roads. The harmonious road is characterized by the sole goal of wanting to improve (i.e., mastery goal), which leads to deliberate practice and high levels of performance. Furthermore, one experiences a happy life in the process. On the other hand, the obsessive path to excellence is paved with both adaptive (i.e., mastery) and maladaptive (i.e., performance-avoidance) goals and there is no link to psychological well-being. While both types of passion may lead to high levels of performance, obsessive passion may achieve this at a psychological cost relative to harmonious passion. These findings are important for the field of education and lead to some interesting questions such as "Which road to success is presented to students by teachers?" and "How does such a road to performance contribute to students' harmonious and obsessive passion and performance?"

Passion and Interpersonal Relationships

So far, we have seen in this chapter that how one engages in a given activity has a profound impact on psychological and physical health and performance. These are important intrapersonal consequences. Because roughly 80 % of the passionate activities are engaged in with other people (Lecoq & Rimé, 2009, Study 2), it would also appear reasonable to suggest that being passionate for an activity should influence the quality of relationships that one develops in this area. Is it the case?

In a study on massively multiplayer online role-playing games such as *World of Warcraft*, Utz, Jonas, and Tonkens (2012) asked a large number of gamers to complete the Passion Scale for gaming and scales assessing the number of friends that they have online, the quality of such friendships, and the number of hours they engage in gaming each week. Controlling for the number of weekly hours played, results from regression analyses revealed that both the harmonious and obsessive passions positively predicted the number of friends online. However, only harmonious passion positively predicted the *quality* of such friendships. These findings, on the quality of *existing* friendships, were replicated by Philippe et al. (2010) with respect to *new* friendships in a number of settings, including in sports with student athletes (Philippe et al., Study 3) and education with students involved in work-study groups (Philippe et al., Study 4). It would thus appear that harmonious passion positively contributes to both the development of new friendships and the maintenance of existing friendships of high quality within the purview of the passionate activity. On the other hand, obsessive passion may actually hinder the quality of such relationships.

If harmonious passion facilitates the development and maintenance of high-quality relationships, then what are the mediating processes involved? Conversely, what is it that obsessive passion does to prevent the person from connecting positively with others? We have seen previously that when harmonious passion is at play, people experience positive affective states, while with obsessive passion, people mainly experience negative affect or, at best, a mixture of positive and negative affect (for reviews, see Vallerand, 2008, 2010, 2015, Chap. 7). Of great importance is the fact that emotions serve some functions, including some that are social in nature (Frijda & Mesquita, 1994). In particular, emotions serve to communicate our emotional state to others. Thus, if we experience positive emotions while engaging in a team activity such as soccer, it may bring other people closer to us, as people typically want to connect with happy people. In addition, the Broaden-and-Build Theory posits that positive emotions allow people to open up not only to themselves (having full access to the self) but also to their surroundings and to others (see Fredrickson, 2001; Waugh & Fredrickson, 2006). The opposite effects should take place with negative emotions because they constrict the self, instead of opening it up. The person is then defensive and stays to him- or herself, and consequently instead of connecting with others, he or she is then likely to remain aloof, to shy away from others while showing an unhappy face. And if we look unhappy, we may keep others at a distance, as people typically do not want to interact with unhappy people (Fowler & Christakis, 2008). Overall, these are *not* the best conditions for inviting others to connect with us and to develop friendships.

In sum, because of the different types of emotions that they promote, the harmonious and obsessive passions should differentially affect the quality of relationships that people will develop within the purview of the passionate activity. Philippe et al. (2010) tested the proposed processes in a series of studies. In one study conducted within educational settings with work-study groups (Philippe et al., Study 4), students who did not know each other at the beginning of the term completed the Passion Scale toward their studies in management. Then, at the end of the term, 15 weeks later, they indicated the positive and negative emotions experienced within their study groups over the semester and reported on the positive (connectedness) and negative (seclusion) interpersonal aspects that they had experienced during the term. Furthermore, participants were asked to rate their perceptions of each of their teammates' quality of interpersonal relationships developed with the other people in the study group over the semester on the positive and negative interpersonal dimensions. It was hypothesized that harmonious passion would positively predict positive affect, but negatively predict negative affect, experienced over the semester. Conversely, obsessive passion was expected to be unrelated to positive affect and to positively predict negative affect. In turn, positive and negative affects experienced in the study group over the semester were hypothesized to respectively predict the positive and negative relationship assessments performed by both the participants and their fellow students. Results from the structural equation modeling analyses provided support for the hypotheses. These findings were replicated in work and sport settings (see Philippe et al., Studies 1–3).

Research reviewed above involved the quality of relationships with teammates and workmates. What characterizes such relationships is that people are at the same level, with no one having a higher status than the other. However, we do not know if these principles uncovered in same status relationships also apply in "one-up" relationships where different status takes place. For example, does passion matter in teacher–student, work supervisor–subordinate, and coach–athlete relationships? Scientists have looked at this issue with student athletes and their coaches (Jowett, Lafrenière, & Vallerand, 2013; Lafrenière, Jowett, Vallerand, Donahue, & Lorimer, 2008, Studies 1 and 2). Such research has looked at both sides of the issue—that is, at both the passion of the coach and that of the athlete in assessing its role in the quality of the relationship. For instance, research in the Lafrenière et al. (2008) article looked at the role of passion in the quality of the relationship between athletes and their coaches. Study 1 involved British student athletes who completed the Passion Scale for their sport and a scale assessing their perceptions of the quality of their relationship with their coach on a number of indices. Results revealed that athletes' harmonious passion toward their sport was positively related to most indices of relationship satisfaction with their coach, whereas obsessive passion was negatively related to some and unrelated to the other indices.

In their second study, Lafrenière and colleagues (2008, Study 2) attempted to reproduce the sequence obtained in the Philippe et al. (2010) study, this time with coaches. The authors had over 100 French–Canadian coaches from different sports complete the Passion Scale for coaching and a scale assessing the quality of their relationships with their athletes (the Quality of Interpersonal Relationship Scale; Senécal, Vallerand, & Vallières, 1992). In addition, coaches also completed a scale assessing the emotions they experience while coaching. Results from a path analysis showed that harmonious passion for coaching predicted positive emotions while coaching that, in turn, predicted the quality of relationships with the athletes. Obsessive passion was unrelated to positive affect or relationship quality.

In sum, the findings from the Lafrenière and colleagues' (2008) research underscore the fact that passion matters with respect to the quality of relationships involving "supervisor–supervisee" types of relationship and that the same mediating processes are at play as in same-level relationships. These findings have important implications for the field of education where teachers' passion for their teaching may affect the quality of relationships that they both develop and maintain with their students. This conclusion may also apply to other "one-up" relationships such as those involving school principals and teachers. Future research on these issues would appear important.

There is a second way through which passion can affect our relationships. Specifically, according to the DMP, passion toward an activity can also influence our relationships in other areas of our lives through the conflict it might create. Thus, obsessive passion should lead to conflict and problems in other life activities, while this should not be the case for harmonious passion. Vallerand et al. (2003, Study 1) had shown that obsessive (but not harmonious) passion for an activity was positively associated with experiencing conflict between activity engagement and other aspects of one's life. Another study (Séguin-Lévesque, Laliberté, Pelletier,

Blanchard, & Vallerand, 2003) showed that in controlling for the number of hours that people engaged in the Internet, obsessive passion for the Internet was positively related to conflict with one's spouse, while harmonious passion was unrelated to it. Finally, a subsequent study tested more directly the mediating role of conflict between obsessive passion and the quality of the romantic relationship with one's partner. In this study (Vallerand et al., 2008, Study 3), 150 English soccer fans from the United Kingdom were asked to complete a questionnaire assessing passion toward soccer as a fan, perceptions of conflict between soccer and the loved one, and the satisfaction with one's intimate relationship. Structural equation modeling analyses were conducted and revealed that having an obsessive passion for one's soccer team predicted conflict between soccer and the loved one. Conflict, in turn, negatively predicted satisfaction with the relationship. While harmonious passion was negatively related to conflict, the effects only approached statistical significance.

Based on the findings reported in this section, one can conclude that there is support for the perspective that a passion for an enjoyable and meaningful activity can have a profound impact on the quality of relationships that one develops and maintains both within the purview of the passionate activity and outside of it. Research would appear warranted to determine how teachers' and principals' passion for their work conflicts with their own romantic relationships and family life.

As a closing note to this section on the role of passion in outcomes, it should be underscored that the research conducted on passion and outcomes has been largely correlational in nature. Thus, a caveat is in order as pertains to causality issues. Two points are in order on this issue. First, it should be reiterated that studies that have used a cross-lagged panel design (Carbonneau et al., 2008; Lavigne et al., 2012, Study 2) have found that passion predicted changes in outcomes over time, whereas outcomes did not predict changes in passion. These findings thereby suggest that the direction of causality is indeed from passion to outcomes. Of greater interest is the study of Lafrenière et al. (2013, Study 2) who have used an experimental design where participants were randomly assigned to conditions of harmonious, obsessive, or no passion and then completed a scale assessing life satisfaction. The results revealed that harmonious passion led to higher levels of psychological well-being relative to the other two conditions that did not differ. Another research by Bélanger et al. (2013) has used experimental inductions of passion to replicate findings obtained with the Passion Scale as pertains to goal conflict. Thus, it can safely be concluded that passion can produce some important outcomes that matter for both teachers and students.

On the Development of Passion

According to the DMP (Vallerand, 2008, 2010, 2015; Vallerand et al., 2003; Vallerand & Houlfort, 2003), there are at least three processes involved in the transformation of an interesting activity into a passion: activity valuation, identification with the activity, and internalization of the activity in one's identity. These three issues are discussed in turn. Activity valuation refers to the importance one gives to an activity. In line with past research (Aron et al., 1992; Deci, Eghrari, Patrick, & Leone, 1994), an activity is likely to be internalized when it is highly valued and meaningful. Consequently, activity valuation should facilitate the internalization of the activity into one's identity and by the same token should facilitate the development of passion. Parents, teachers, and coaches all play an important role in children's or students' valuation of a given activity (e.g., Eccles & Wigfield, 2002). For instance, adults can underscore the value of an activity either by being themselves passionate about it, by spending time with children in the context of the activity, or by encouraging specialization in the activity at the expense of other activities.

Identification with the activity is a second important process in the development of passion (Schlenker, 1985). When an interesting activity becomes so important that it contributes to one's identity or has the potential to do so in the future, individuals are more likely to become passionate about this particular activity. Indeed, enjoying science and having the perception that one may become a scientist later on (a possible self, Markus & Nurius, 1986) should make this potential identity element salient, thereby facilitating its internalization in identity (Houser-Marko & Sheldon, 2006) and the development of passion for this field.

Finally, the type of passion that will develop depends on the type of internalization that takes place. As mentioned previously, in line with self-determination theory (Ryan & Deci, 2000), two types of internalization can take place: autonomous and controlled. Two important variables can determine the type of internalization process that will occur: the social environment and one's personality. To the extent that one's social environment (e.g., parents, teachers, coaches, principals) is autonomy supportive, an autonomous internalization is likely to take place (e.g., Vallerand, 1997; Vallerand, Fortier, & Guay, 1997), leading to harmonious passion. Conversely, to the extent that one's social environment is controlling, a controlled internalization will take place, leading to obsessive passion. Similarly, if an individual has an autonomous personality orientation (as indexed by the Global Motivation Scale; Guay, Mageau, & Vallerand, 2003), then, the autonomous internalization process should kick in, leading to harmonious passion. On the other hand, when one's personality orientation is more of the controlled type, the controlled internalization process should be in operation, leading to obsessive passion.

These hypotheses were tested in two series of studies (Mageau et al., 2009, Studies 1–3; Vallerand et al., 2006; Studies 1 and 3). In Study 3 of a first series of studies (Mageau et al., 2009, Study 3), first year high school students who had never played a musical instrument before and who were taking their first music class completed a series of questionnaires early in the term, assessing activity selection and valuation (perceived parental activity valuation and perceived parental and child activity specialization), autonomy support from parents and music teachers, as well as identity processes. The authors sought to see who would develop a passion for music by the end of the semester and which type they would display (i.e., harmonious or obsessive passion). Results from discriminant analyses revealed that the students who ended up being passionate for music (only 36 % of the sample) at the end of the term had, earlier in the term, reported higher levels of activity valuation and specialization, identity processes, and parental and teacher autonomy support than those students who did not develop a passion. Furthermore, among those who ended up being passionate, it was found that high perceived autonomy support from close adults (parents and music teachers) and children's valuation for music were conducive to the development of harmonious passion. High levels of parental perceived valuation for music and *lack of* autonomy support (i.e., controlling behavior) were found to predict the development of obsessive passion. Results of two other studies involving students interacting in sports and music settings revealed that both perceived parental autonomy support (Mageau et al., Study 1) and actual autonomy support (as reported by the parents themselves; Mageau et al., Study 2) were conducive to harmonious passion and the lack of such support to obsessive passion. In sum, the results of the Mageau et al. studies demonstrate the role of activity valuation, identity processes, and autonomy support from significant adults in the development of a passion in general and harmonious and obsessive passion in particular.

In the second series of studies, Vallerand et al. (2006, Studies 1 and 3) tested the role of activity valuation and personality variables in the occurrence of the two types of passion among student athletes. In the first study (Vallerand et al., Study 1), results from a path analysis revealed that activity valuation coupled with an autonomous internalization style (as assessed by the Global Motivation Scale; Guay et al., 2003) predicted harmonious passion. Obsessive passion was predicted by activity valuation coupled with a controlled internalization style. These findings were replicated in a second study (Vallerand et al., 2006, Study 3) using a short longitudinal design. Thus, personality factors also play a role in the development of both types of passion.

The studies discussed so far pertained to activities where participants had been engaging in the activity for just a few months or years. Thus, these studies pertained more to the *initial* development of passion. However, once developed, passion can also undergo an ongoing development as it is affected by a variety of social and personal variables (Vallerand, 2010, 2015). For instance, in a study with students enrolled in a college music program and with an average of over 7 years of musical experience (Bonneville-Roussy, Vallerand, & Bouffard, 2013), results from a path analysis revealed that a musical identity coupled with autonomy support from one's music teachers predicted harmonious passion toward music, while obsessive passion was predicted by a musical identity coupled with controlling behavior from one's music teachers. Thus, autonomy support (or its lack of support) also plays a role in the *ongoing* development of passion.

Other research have looked at social factors pertaining to the task as determinants of passion. In studies with novice teachers, Fernet et al. (2014, Study 1) found that experiencing some levels of autonomy as to how to perform one's teaching positively predicted harmonious passion but negatively predicted obsessive passion for teaching. These findings were replicated and extended in a second study (Fernet et al., Study 2) again with teachers using a cross-lagged panel design over a 12-month period. Of major importance, results from structural equation modeling showed that task autonomy predicted an *increase* in harmonious passion for teaching and a decrease in obsessive passion over time. Of importance, the two types of passion did not predict changes in task autonomy, suggesting that the direction of causality is from task autonomy to passion and not the other way around.

Other task elements may also affect the type of passion that will be activated when engaging in the activity. Two of these are the task demands and task resources (Bakker & Demerouti, 2007). Task demands refer to task that impose pressure or restrictions that one has to cope with while engaging in the activity. Because task demands should be experienced as controlling in nature, they should connect with elements that have been internalized in a controlled fashion and therefore facilitate obsessive passion. Thus, the more one experiences pressure to perform a demanding activity, the more one is to mobilize and use obsessive passion to get the job done. In addition, experiencing pressure to get the job done could even undermine harmonious passion as such pressure may disrupt harmony among one's various life domains. Conversely, task resources can be seen as support that one has access to in order to better perform one's task. Task resources can be seen as affordances to efficiently perform the task as one chooses to do so. Thus, they should trigger elements that have been internalized in an autonomous fashion, including harmonious passion. Indeed, knowing that one has access to resources and support to autonomously perform a task that one loves should lead one to experience harmonious passion for the task and the adaptive outcomes that follow. In sum, task resources should facilitate harmonious passion, while task demands should facilitate obsessive passion.

Trépanier et al. (2014) conducted a large-scale study with over 1,000 nurses to test the above hypotheses. Participants completed the Passion Scale for their work, a scale to assess job demands (e.g., "I have to display high levels of concentration and precision at work") and job resources (e.g., "I have access to useful information that helps me carry out complex tasks"). Results from structural equation modeling provided support for the hypotheses. Specifically, task resources were found to positively predict harmonious passion, while task demands positively predicted obsessive passion. In addition, task demands were found to undermine harmonious passion. In other words, having an inordinate amount of work that one has to do fosters obsessive, and may even diminish harmonious, passion.

The results reviewed in this section show that one's social environment and personality are important factors in the initial development of passion. It should be kept in mind that task characteristics such as task autonomy, demands, and resources play an important role in ongoing development of passion and in making operative the harmonious and obsessive passions that are already present in ourselves. Thus, in addition to the social environment, task properties need to be taken into account when attempting to explain and predict the passion displayed toward a given activity. Research is needed in order to determine how teachers' behavior influences students' development of passion for various school subjects and, in the long term, the career they choose. Similarly, the role of principals in influencing the working life of teachers and their passion for teaching needs to be empirically assessed. Such research should lead to important applications at various levels of the education system.

Conclusions

The purpose of the present chapter was to introduce the concept of passion and show its relevance to the field of education. In so doing, we have presented the Dualistic Model of Passion (e.g., Vallerand, 2010, 2015; Vallerand et al., 2003). The research reviewed in this chapter leads to two major conclusions. First, there is an overwhelming support for the Dualistic Model of Passion. The model defines passion as a strong inclination toward a self-defining activity that one loves, finds important, and devotes significant amount of time and energy. Furthermore, two types of passion are proposed depending on how the activity representation has been internalized in one's identity. Whereas harmonious passion entails control of the activity and a harmonious coexistence of the passionate activity with other activities of the person's life, obsessive passion entails the relative lack of control over the passionate activity, rigid persistence, and conflict with other life activities. Research reviewed provided strong support for the existence of the two types of passion as well as for the processes that the DMP posits that they entail (see Vallerand, 2015 for additional information on the DMP and related research).

The second major conclusion is that passion would appear quite relevant for the field of education. Indeed, passion is directly relevant to the world of education for teachers and students and also principals. We have seen that passion leads to important effects for both teachers and students on a variety of outcomes that include psychological well-being, physical health, meaningful relationships, and high levels of performance. Beyond such effects, however, I suggest that the research discussed in this chapter leads to a number of applications for the field of education. I will only mention a few here. First, teachers should keep in mind the important role that they play in helping their students navigate through this period of self-growth and learning that they go through while in school. Teachers can influence greatly whether their students find certain school subjects passionate. Helping students find some connection with their identity and to experience the joy of mastering a challenging subject in the classroom is essential to a lifelong pursuit of knowledge and self-discovery conducive to developing a passion for a future career. Such connection can be done through the transfer of the teachers' own passion for a given subject, but it need not be. Helping students find their own passion is also important and perhaps even more so as it focuses on the students' own choices and sense of identity. Second, school life does not place only in the classroom. Therefore, helping students discover passionate school activities that take place *outside* the classroom such as sports, arts, music, and the like should help students connect with their school and rekindle or maintain their interest for classroom activities (Fredricks, Alfeld, & Eccles, 2010). Indeed, once children run to school to engage in extracurriculum activities that they love, it becomes much easier to fully engage in more demanding curriculum activities. And entering the classroom with a smile on one's face makes things much easier in the classroom, especially if the teachers are engaging and passionate about their subjects. Such a school setting where passion is encouraged both inside and outside the classroom may go a long way in preventing high school dropout and fostering success at school that may generalize later on to life in general.

Finally, school principals should keep in mind that they also play an important role in the ongoing development of their school teachers' passion. Because well over 90 % of novice teachers come in the profession with a passion for teaching (Fernet et al., 2014), it is the responsibility of the school principals to maintain their teachers' flame for teaching alive. Such may not be an easy task, however, as 50 % of novice teachers leave the profession in the first 5 years! The research reviewed in this chapter reveals that providing some levels of job autonomy and autonomy support and facilitating the presence of additional resources while keeping demands to a minimum should help keeping passion alive and make sure that it is harmonious. Too often, new teachers end up having what appear to them as an overbearing weight on their shoulders while more seasoned teachers watch them flounder. By keeping demands at a minimum and providing appropriate support and resources such as a mentor, principals may help novice teachers maintain their harmonious passion for teaching, experience more adaptive outcomes both at school and outside of it, and eventually remain in the profession.

For centuries philosophers have asked the question "How can people's lives be most worth living?" Theory and research reveal that one answer to this question is by having in one's life a harmonious passion toward an enjoyable and meaningful activity. In light of the various outcomes that follow from one's passion both for teachers and students, future research in education would therefore appear to be not only promising but also of extreme importance.

References

Amiot, C., Vallerand, R. J., & Blanchard, C. M. (2006). Passion and psychological adjustment: A test of the person-environment fit hypothesis. *Personality and Social Psychology Bulletin, 32*, 220–229.

Aron, A., Aron, E. N., & Smollan, D. (1992). Inclusion of other in the self scale and the structure of interpersonal closeness. *Journal of Personality and Social Psychology, 63*, 596–612.

Bakker, A. B., & Demerouti, E. (2007). The job demands-resources model: State of the art. *Journal of Managerial Psychology, 22*, 309–328.

Baum, J. R., & Locke, E. A. (2004). The relationship of entrepreneurial traits, skill, and motivation to subsequent venture growth. *Journal of Applied Psychology, 89*, 587–598.

Bélanger, J. J., Lafrenière, M.-A. K., Vallerand, R. J., & Kruglanski, A. W. (2013). When passion makes the heart grow colder: The role of passion in alternative goal suppression. *Journal of Personality and Social Psychology, 104*, 126–147.

Bonneville-Roussy, A., Lavigne, G. L., & Vallerand, R. J. (2011). When passion leads to excellence: The case of musicians. *Psychology of Music, 39*, 123–138.

Bonneville-Roussy, A., Vallerand, R. J., & Bouffard, T. (2013). The roles of autonomy support and harmonious and obsessive passions in educational persistence. *Learning and Individual Differences, 24*, 22–31.

Brown, K. W., & Ryan, R. M. (2003). The benefits of being present: Mindfulness and its role in psychological well-being. *Journal of Personality and Social Psychology, 84*, 822–848.

Carbonneau, N., Vallerand, R. J., Fernet, C., & Guay, F. (2008). The role of passion for teaching in intra and interpersonal outcomes. *Journal of Educational Psychology, 100*, 977–988.

Carbonneau, N., Vallerand, R. J., & Massicotte, S. (2010). Is the practice of Yoga associated with positive outcomes? The role of passion. *The Journal of Positive Psychology, 5*, 452–465.

Carpentier, J., Mageau, G. A., & Vallerand, R. J. (2012). Ruminations and flow: Why do people with a more harmonious passion experience higher well-being? *Journal of Happiness Studies, 13*(3), 501–518.

Chuang, Y. C. (2006). Massively multiplayer online role-playing game-induced seizures: A neglected health problem in Internet addiction. *Cyberpsychology and Behavior, 9*, 451–456.

Csikszentmihalyi, M., Rathunde, K., & Whalen, S. (1993). *Talented teenagers: The roots of success and failure*. New York: Cambridge University Press.

Day, C. (2004). *A passion for teaching*. New York: Routledge Falmer.

Deci, E. L., Eghrari, H., Patrick, B. C., & Leone, D. R. (1994). Facilitating internalization: The self-determination perspective. *Journal of Personality, 62*, 119–142.

Deci, E. L., & Ryan, R. M. (2000). The "what" and "why" of goal pursuits: Human needs and the self-determination of behavior. *Psychological Inquiry, 11*, 227–268.

Duckworth, A. L., Peterson, C., Matthews, M. D., & Kelly, D. R. (2007). Grit: Perseverance and passion for long-term goals. *Journal of Personality and Social Psychology, 92*, 1087–1101.

Eccles, J. S., & Wigfield, A. (2002). Motivational beliefs, values, and goals. *Annual Review of Psychology, 53*, 109–132.

Elliot, A. J. (1997). Integrating "classic" and "contemporary" approaches to achievement motivation: A hierarchical model of approach and avoidance achievement motivation. In P. Pintrinch & M. Maehr (Eds.), *Advances in motivation and achievement* (Vol. 10, pp. 143–179). Greenwich, CT: JAI Press.

Elliot, A. J., & Church, M. A. (1997). A hierarchical model of approach and avoidance achievement motivation. *Journal of Personality and Social Psychology, 72*, 218–232.

Elliot, A. J., & Harackiewicz, J. M. (1996). Approach and avoidance achievement goals and intrinsic motivation: A mediational analysis. *Journal of Personality and Social Psychology, 70*, 968–980.

Ericsson, K. A., & Charness, N. (1994). Expert performance. *American Psychologist, 49*, 725–747.

Erikson, E. H. (1968). *Identity: Youth and crisis*. New York: W.W. Norton.

Fernet, C., Lavigne, G., & Vallerand, R. J. (2014). Fired up with passion: The role of harmonious and obsessive passion in burnout in novice teachers. *Work and Stress, 28*, 270–288.

Fowler, J. H., & Christakis, N. A. (2008). Dynamic spread of happiness in a large social network: Longitudinal analysis over 20 years in the Framingham Heart Study. *BMJ [British Medical Journal], 337*, 1–9.

Fredricks, J. A., Alfeld, C., & Eccles, J. (2010). Developing and fostering passion in academic and nonacademic domains. *Gifted Child Quarterly, 54*, 18–30.

Fredrickson, B. L. (2001). The role of positive emotions in positive psychology: The Broaden-and build theory of positive emotions. *American Psychologist, 56*, 218–226.

Frijda, N. H., & Mesquita, B. (1994). The social roles and functions of emotions. In S. Kitayama & H. R. Markus (Eds.), *Emotion and culture: Empirical studies of mutual influence* (pp. 51–87). New York: Cambridge University Press.

Frijda, N. H., Mesquita, B., Sonnemans, J., & Van Goozen, S. (1991). The duration of affective phenomena or emotions, sentiments and passions. In K. T. Strongman (Ed.), *International review of studies on emotion* (Vol. 1, pp. 187–225). New York: Wiley.

Glasser, W. (1976). *Positive addiction*. New York: Harper & Row.

Greenberger, S. W. (2012). Teacher passion and distance education theory. *Journal of Instructional Research, 1*, 34–41.

Guay, F., Mageau, G. A., & Vallerand, R. J. (2003). On the hierarchical structure of self-determined motivation: A test of top-down, bottom-up, reciprocal, and horizontal effects. *Personality and Social Psychology Bulletin, 29*, 992–1004.

Halvari, H., Ulstad, S. O., Bagøien, T. E., & Skjesol, K. (2009). Autonomy support and its links to physical activity and competitive performance: Mediations through motivation, competence, action orientation and harmonious passion, and the moderator role of autonomy support by perceived competence. *Scandinavian Journal of Educational Research, 53*(6), 533–555.

Hatfield, E., & Walster, G. W. (1978). *A new look at love*. Reading, MA: Addison-Wesley.

Hodgins, H. S., & Knee, R. (2002). The integrating self and conscious experience. In E. L. Deci & R. M. Ryan (Eds.), *Handbook on self-determination research: Theoretical and applied issues* (pp. 87–100). Rochester, NY: University of Rochester Press.

Houlfort, N., Philippe, F., Vallerand, R. J., & Ménard, J. (2014). On passion as heavy work investment and its consequences. *Journal of Managerial Psychology, 29*, 25–45.

Houser-Marko, L., & Sheldon, K. M. (2006). Motivating behavioral persistence: The self-as-doer construct. *Personality and Social Psychology Bulletin, 32*, 1037–1049.

Joussain, A. (1928). *Les passions humaines* [The human passions]. Paris: Ernest Flammarion.

Jowett, S., Lafrenière, M.-A. K., & Vallerand, R. J. (2013). Passion for activities and relationship quality: A dyadic approach. *Journal of Social and Personal Relationship, 30*, 734–749.

Lafrenière, M.-A. K., Bélanger, J. J., Sedikides, C., & Vallerand, R. J. (2011). Self-esteem and passion for activities. *Personality and Individual Differences, 51*, 541–544.

Lafrenière, M.-A., Jowett, S., Vallerand, R. J., Donahue, E. G., & Lorimer, R. (2008). Passion in sport: On the quality of the coach-player relationship. *Journal of Sport and Exercise Psychology, 30*, 541–560.

Lafrenière, M.-A. K., Vallerand, R. J., Donahue, E. G., & Lavigne, G. L. (2009). On the costs and benefits of gaming: The role of passion. *Cyberpsychology & Behavior, 12*, 285–290.

Lafrenière, M.-A. K., Vallerand, R. J., & Sedikides, C. (2013). On the relation between self-enhancement and life satisfaction: The moderating role of passion. *Self and Identity, 12*, 516–530.

Lavigne, G. L., Forest, J., & Crevier-Braud, L. (2012). Passion at work and burnout: A two-study test of the mediating role of flow experiences. *European Journal of Work and Organizational Psychology, 21*(4), 518–546.

Lecoq, J., & Rimé, B. (2009). Les passions: Aspects émotionnels et sociaux. *Revue Européenne de Psychologie Appliquée/European Review of Applied Psychology, 59*, 197–209.

Liu, D., Chen, X.-P., & Yao, X. (2011). From autonomy to creativity: A multilevel investigation of the mediating role of harmonious passion. *Journal of Applied Psychology, 96*, 295–309.

Lyubomirsky, S., King, L., & Diener, E. (2005). The benefits of frequent positive affect: Does happiness lead to success? *Psychological Bulletin, 131*, 803–855.

Mageau, G., Carpentier, J., & Vallerand, R. J. (2011). The role of self-esteem contingencies in the distinction between obsessive and harmonious passion. *European Journal of Social Psychology, 6*, 720–729.

Mageau, G., & Vallerand, R. J. (2007). The moderating effect of passion on the relation between activity engagement and positive affect. *Motivation and Emotion, 31*, 312–321.

Mageau, G. A., Vallerand, R. J., Charest, J., Salvy, S.-J., Lacaille, N., Bouffard, T., et al. (2009). On the development of harmonious and obsessive passion: The role of autonomy support, activity valuation, and identity processes. *Journal of Personality, 77*, 601–645.

Markus, H., & Nurius, P. (1986). Possible selves. *American Psychologist, 41*(9), 954–969.

Marsh, H. W., Vallerand, R. J., Lafreniere, M. A. K., Parker, P., Morin, A. J. S., Carbonneau, N., et al. (2013). Passion: Does one scale fit all? Construct validity of two-factor Passion Scale and psychometric invariance over different activities and languages. *Psychological Assessment, 25*, 796–809.

Parastatidou, I. S., Doganis, G., Theodorakis, Y., & Vlachopoulos, S. P. (2012). Exercising with passion: Initial validation of the Passion Scale in exercise. *Measurement in Physical Education and Exercise Science, 16*, 119–134.

Phelps, P. H., & Benson, T. R. (2012). Teachers with a passion for the profession. *Action in Teacher Education, 34*, 65–76.

Philippe, F. L., Vallerand, R. J., Houlfort, N., Lavigne, G., & Donahue, E. G. (2010). Passion for an activity and quality of interpersonal relationships: The mediating role of positive and negative emotions. *Journal of Personality and Social Psychology, 98*, 917–932.

Philippe, F., Vallerand, R. J., & Lavigne, G. (2009). Passion does make a difference in people's lives: A look at well-being in passionate and non-passionate individuals. *Applied Psychology Health and Well-Being, 1*, 3–22.

Przybylski, A. K., Weinstein, N., Ryan, R. M., & Rigby, C. S. (2009). Having to versus wanting to play: Background and consequences of harmonious versus obsessive engagement in video games. *Cyberpsychology & Behavior, 12*, 485–492.

Ribot, T. (1907). *Essai sur les passions*. Paris: Alcan.

Rip, B., Fortin, S., & Vallerand, R. J. (2006). The relationship between passion and injury in dance students. *Journal of Dance Medicine & Science, 10*, 14–20.

Rousseau, F. L., & Vallerand, R. J. (2003). Le rôle de la passion dans le bien-être subjectif des aînés [The role of passion in the subjective well-being of the elderly]. *Revue Québécoise de Psychologie, 24*, 197–211.

Rousseau, F. L., & Vallerand, R. J. (2008). An examination of the relationship between passion and subjective well-being in older adults. *International Journal of Aging and Human Development, 66*, 195–211.

Rousseau, F. L., Vallerand, R. J., Ratelle, C. F., Mageau, G. A., & Provencher, P. (2002). Passion and gambling: On the validation of the Gambling Passion Scale (GPS). *Journal of Gambling Studies, 18*, 45–66.

Ryan, R. M., & Deci, E. L. (2000). Self-determination and the facilitation of intrinsic motivation, social development, and well-being. *American Psychologist, 55*, 68–78.

Ryan, R. M., & Deci, E. L. (2003). On assimilating identities of the self: A self-determination theory perspective on internalization and integrity within cultures. In M. R. Leary & J. P. Tangney (Eds.), *Handbook of self and identity* (pp. 253–272). New York: Guilford.

Schlenker, B. R. (1985). Identity and self-identification. In B. R. Schlenker (Ed.), *The self and social life* (pp. 65–99). New York: McGraw-Hill.

Sedikides, C., Wildschut, T., Arndt, J., & Routledge, C. (2008). Nostalgia: Past, present, and future. *Current Directions in Psychological Science, 17*, 304–307.

Séguin-Lévesque, C., Laliberté, M.-L., Pelletier, L. G., Blanchard, C., & Vallerand, R. J. (2003). Harmonious and obsessive passion for the internet: Their associations with the couple's relationships. *Journal of Applied Social Psychology, 33*, 197–221.

Senécal, C. B., Vallerand, R. J., & Vallières, E. F. (1992). Construction et validation de l'Échelle de la Qualité des Relations Interpersonnelles (EQRI). *Revue Européenne de Psychologie Appliquée, 42*, 315–322.

Starkes, J. L., & Ericsson, K. A. (Eds.). (2003). *Expert performance in sports: Advances in research on sport expertise*. Champaign, IL: Human Kinetics.

Stenseng, F. (2008). The two faces of leisure activity engagement: Harmonious and obsessive passion in relation to intrapersonal conflict and life domain outcomes. *Leisure Sciences, 30*, 465–481.

Stephan, Y., Deroche, T., Brewer, B. W., Caudroit, J., & Le Scanff, C. (2009). Predictors of perceived susceptibility to sport-related injury among competitive runners: The role of previous experience, neuroticism, and passion for running. *Applied Psychology An International Review, 58*, 672–687.

Stoeber, J., Childs, J. H., Hayward, J. A., & Feast, A. R. (2011). Passion and motivation for studying: Predicting academic engagement and burnout in university students. *Educational Psychology, 31*, 513–528.

Trépanier, S.-G., Fernet, C., Austin, S., Forest, J., & Vallerand, R. J. (2014). Linking job demands and resources to burnout and work engagement: Does passion underlie these differential relationships? *Motivation and Emotion, 38*, 353–366.

Turner, B. S., & Wainwright, S. P. (2003). Corps de ballet: The case of the injured ballet dancer. *Sociology of Health & Illness, 25*, 269–288.

Utz, S., Jonas, K. J., & Tonkens, E. (2012). Effects of passion for massively multiplayer online role-playing games on interpersonal relationships. *Journal of Media Psychology Theories Methods and Applications, 24*, 77.

Vallerand, R. J. (1997). Toward a hierarchical model of intrinsic and extrinsic motivation. *Advances in Experimental and Social Psychology, 29*, 271–360.

Vallerand, R. J. (2008). On the psychology of passion: In search of what makes people's lives most worth living. *Canadian Psychology, 49*, 1–13.

Vallerand, R. J. (2010). On passion for life activities: The dualistic model of passion. In M. P. Zanna (Ed.), *Advances in experimental social psychology* (Vol. 42, pp. 97–193). New York: Academic.

Vallerand, R. J. (2015). *The psychology of passion*. New York: Oxford University Press.

Vallerand, R. J., Blanchard, C. M., Mageau, G. A., Koestner, R., Ratelle, C. F., Léonard, M., et al. (2003). Les passions de l'âme: On obsessive and harmonious passion. *Journal of Personality and Social Psychology, 85*, 756–767.

Vallerand, R. J., Fortier, M. S., & Guay, F. (1997). Self-determination and persistence in a real-life setting: Toward a motivational model of high school dropout. *Journal of Personality and Social Psychology, 72*, 1161–1176.

Vallerand, R. J., & Houlfort, N. (2003). Passion at work: Toward a new conceptualization. In S. W. Gilliland, D. D. Steiner, & D. P. Skarlicki (Eds.), *Emerging perspectives on values in organizations* (pp. 175–204). Greenwich, CT: Information Age Publishing.

Vallerand, R. J., Mageau, G. A., Elliot, A., Dumais, A., Demers, M.-A., & Rousseau, F. L. (2008). Passion and performance attainment in sport. *Psychology of Sport & Exercise, 9*, 373–392.

Vallerand, R. J., Ntoumanis, N., Philippe, F., Lavigne, G. L., Carbonneau, C., Bonneville, A., et al. (2008). On passion and sports fans: A look at football. *Journal of Sports Sciences, 26*, 1279–1293.

Vallerand, R. J., Rousseau, F. L., Grouzet, F. M. E., Dumais, A., & Grenier, S. (2006). Passion in sport: A look at determinants and affective experiences. *Journal of Sport & Exercise Psychology, 28*, 454–478.

Vallerand, R. J., Salvy, S. J., Mageau, G. A., Elliot, A. J., Denis, P., Grouzet, F. M. E., et al. (2007). On the role of passion in performance. *Journal of Personality, 75*, 505–534.

Waugh, C. E., & Fredrickson, B. L. (2006). Nice to know you: Positive emotions, self-other overlap, and complex understanding in the formation of new relationships. *Journal of Positive Psychology, 1*, 93–106.

Wells, G. (2012). *Superbodies: Peak performance secrets from the world's best athletes*. New York: Harper Collins.

Chapter 4
Toward a Systematic Study of the Dark Side of Student Motivation: Antecedents and Consequences of Teachers' Controlling Behaviors

Leen Haerens, Maarten Vansteenkiste, Nathalie Aelterman, and Lynn Van den Berghe

Self-determination theory (SDT; Deci & Ryan, 2000; Ryan, Deci, & Vansteenkiste, 2015) holds the assumption that individuals are inherently proactive and endowed with a natural tendency to learn and develop. A rectilinear consequence following this assumption is that in educational settings, where learning is at the heart of almost every activity, students are naturally engaged, enthusiastic, and dedicated to learn. Yet, SDT also maintains that for learners' curiosity and interests to unfold, contextual supports are required. That is, under the right conditions, young people are able to motivate themselves to learn (Deci, 1995).

However, many teachers do not portray their students as naturally proactive and endowed learners, since they encounter difficulties to motivate young people who in their opinion lack enthusiasm or are even passive, defiant, and disruptive (Way, 2011). Consistent with such observations, SDT maintains, much as individuals have the potential for growth, they equally have the vulnerability to be passive, self-centered, or even aggressive and hostile toward others (Vansteenkiste & Ryan, 2013). The present chapter then particularly focuses on those conditions that can awake these

L. Haerens (✉) • L. Van den Berghe
Department of Movement and Sports Sciences,
Ghent University, Ghent, Belgium
e-mail: Leen.Haerens@UGent.be; L.VandenBerghe@UGent.be

M. Vansteenkiste
Department of Developmental, Personality and Social Psychology,
Ghent University, Ghent, Belgium
e-mail: Maarten.Vansteenkiste@UGent.be

N. Aelterman
Department of Movement and Sports Sciences,
Ghent University, Ghent, Belgium

Department of Developmental, Personality and Social Psychology,
Ghent University, Ghent, Belgium
e-mail: nathalie.aelterman@ugent.be

© Springer Science+Business Media Singapore 2016   59
W.C. Liu et al. (eds.), *Building Autonomous Learners*,
DOI 10.1007/978-981-287-630-0_4

vulnerabilities and elicit negative student behaviors and feelings (e.g., passivity and boredom, defiant and disruptive behaviors). Consistent with SDT, recent work revealed that such negative behaviors are more likely to arise in educational situations where teachers adopt a more controlling teaching style.

Understanding the Processes Underlying Students' Maladaptive Motivational Functioning

Distinguishing Between Need Satisfaction and Need Frustration

A central tenet of SDT is that students will thrive more when their basic psychological needs for autonomy (i.e., experiencing a sense of volition and psychological freedom), competence (i.e., experiencing a sense of effectiveness), and relatedness (i.e., experiencing closeness and mutuality in interpersonal relationships) are fulfilled as the satisfactions of these needs serve as the essential vitamins that energize personal growth and integrity (Ryan & Deci, 2002; Vansteenkiste, Niemiec, & Soenens, 2010). These psychological needs are considered to be inherent and, hence, universally critical. That is, regardless of gender, social class, and cultural background, individuals are said to be benefit from experiencing a sense of volition, mastery, and mutual care (Deci & Ryan, 2000; Vansteenkiste et al., 2010).

SDT posits that stimulating learning environments will nurture these basic needs, thereby catalyzing a "bright" pathway toward more optimal functioning and well-being. In contrast, learning environments that actively block or forestall these needs will elicit experiences of need frustration, which manifests as feelings of pressure and internal conflict (i.e., autonomy frustration), feelings of inferiority or failure (i.e., competence frustration), and feelings of loneliness and alienation (i.e., relatedness frustration). In turn, the frustration of these psychological needs activates a "dark" pathway involving a shift toward suboptimal or even maladaptive motivational functioning (Ryan & Deci, 2000; Vansteenkiste & Ryan, 2013). In other words, when students experience their class activities as a daunting duty, when they feel inadequate or isolated, they will pay an emotional price. The immediate consequence of the experience of need frustration involves ill-being and the depletion of students' energetic resources, which, in turn, engenders malfunctioning (e.g., reduced self-control; Ryan & Deci, 2000, 2008; Vansteenkiste & Ryan, 2013).

At first sight need frustration seems the exact opposite of need satisfaction such that they represent the opposite poles of a single continuum. Yet, it is increasingly recognized that experiences of need frustration cannot be equated with experiences of low need satisfaction. The frustration of the psychological needs requires a more active blocking and undermining of them rather than a mere deprivation. To illustrate, although students may experience little room for initiative taking (low autonomy satisfaction), may not feel very confident to complete a task effectively (low competence satisfaction), or might not feel well connected with the teacher or their classmates (low relatedness satisfaction), it is especially when they feel controlled and pressured (autonomy frustration), when they feel like a failure (competence frustration), or when they feel isolated (high relatedness frustration) that their psychological needs get frustrated.

According to more recent developments within SDT, both experiences of need satisfaction and need frustration have separate roots (e.g., classroom climate, teacher's style) and differential implications for students' motivational functioning at school. To understand and predict students' passivity and indifference, their feelings of resentment, and their aggressive and disruptive behaviors, it would especially be crucial to investigate the distinct role of experiences of need frustration (Bartholomew, Ntoumanis, Ryan, Bosch, & Thogersen-Ntoumani, 2011a, Bartholomew, Ntoumanis, Ryan, & Thøgersen-Ntoumani, 2011b; Vansteenkiste & Ryan, 2013). A number of recent studies have begun to shed light on this issue, which are discussed in the next section.

The Distinct Role of Experiences of Need Frustration

Bartholomew and colleagues (2011b) were pioneers to initiate a set of studies on the specific role of need frustration in the sport domain. After having developed a scale to measure psychological need frustration separately from need satisfaction (see also Chen et al., 2015; Sheldon & Hilpert, 2012), they showed in a follow-up study (Bartholomew et al., 2011a) that need satisfaction related predominantly to positive outcomes (i.e., vitality and positive affect), while need frustration related particularly to negative outcomes, which were either self-reported (i.e., depressive symptoms, burnout, and disordered eating) or objectively recorded (i.e., acute stress as indexed by S-IGA). The critical role of need frustration for predicting maladaptive outcomes was subsequently confirmed in samples as diverse as soccer players (Balaguer et al., 2012), sport coaches (Stebbings, Taylor, Spray, & Ntoumanis, 2012), physical education teachers (Bartholomew et al., 2011a, Bartholomew, Ntoumanis, Cuevas, & Lonsdale, 2014), and employees (Gillet, Fouquereau, Forst, Brunault, & Colombat, 2012).

While these studies assessed need satisfaction and need frustration at the domain level, Sheldon and Hilpert (2012) and Chen et al. (2015) developed and formally validated a new global measure of need satisfaction and need frustration. While Sheldon and Hilpert included American University students only, Chen et al. validated their new measure in a cross-culturally diverse sample, including participants from four different nations (i.e., Belgium, China, Peru, the US). In their study Chen et al. (2015) reported evidence that a six-factor model, involving the satisfaction and frustration of the three separate needs, yielded a superior fit compared to a three-factor model involving the three needs. Further, whereas need satisfaction related primarily to well-being, need frustration related primarily to ill-being. Consistent with SDT's universality claim, these associations were found to hold regardless of individuals' cultural background. Using an adaptation of the Chen et al. measure at the situational level, Haerens, Aelterman, Vansteenkiste, Soenens, & Van Petegem (2015) reported that need satisfaction as experienced during a single physical education class related primarily to autonomous motivation, while need frustration related more closely to controlled motivation and amotivation.

Two additional issues deserve being mentioned. First, across this rapidly growing body of work that focuses on the distinct roles of need frustration and need satisfaction, the strength of the association between need satisfaction and need frustration has varied. While items tapping into both sets of experiences have been found to load onto different factors, studies have reported need satisfaction and need frustration to be only moderately negatively correlated (e.g., Bartholomew et al., 2011b; Haerens et al., 2015), while other studies found a more substantial negative correlation between both (i.e., Bartholomew et al., 2011a; Gillet et al., 2012). Multiple factors could account for these differences including the fact that studies were conducted at different levels of generality (i.e., global, domain, situational; Vallerand, 1997), focused on different domains, sampled different age groups, and made use of different sets of items. Future research could examine whether any of these factors contribute to systematic variation in the association between need satisfaction and need frustration.

Second, the exact term that has been used to refer to the frustration of individuals' needs by different authors has varied. Whereas Bartholomew and colleagues (2011a, 2011b) used the term *need thwarting*, and Sheldon and Hilpert (2012) introduced the term *dissatisfaction*, following Vansteenkiste and Ryan (2013), Chen et al. (2015) and Haerens et al., (2015) used the term *need frustration*. Throughout this chapter, we prefer using the term need frustration above the other two terms for the following reasons. The term need frustration aims to tap into individuals' personal experiences, whereas the term need thwarting yields a stronger reference to contextual features that undermine or forestall individuals' psychological needs. Indeed, as explained in greater detail below, the thwarting of individuals' psychological needs is assumed to elicit feelings of need frustration. As for the term dissatisfaction, this term refers in our view primarily to the deprivation of individuals' psychological needs and thus insufficiently captures the more active frustration of them.

Need-Thwarting Teaching

Conceptualization

Much like the experience of need frustration cannot be simply equated with an absence of need-satisfying experiences, it is increasingly recognized that need thwarting involves more than absence of need support (Bartholomew et al., 2011b; Vansteenkiste & Ryan 2013). That is, teachers' lack of nurturance of students' psychological needs does not necessarily imply that they actively block or forestall their needs. For need thwarting to occur, a more active contextual interference and undermining role is required. Yet, the very thwarting of students' psychological needs does by definition imply the absence of need support, suggesting that the relation between contextual need thwarting and contextual need support is asymmetrical (Vansteenkiste & Ryan, 2013).

Consistent with such theorizing, autonomy-supportive and controlling teaching have been found to be modestly negatively interrelated (e.g., Assor, Kaplan, & Roth, 2002; De Meyer et al., 2014; Haerens et al., 2015). To illustrate, when teachers do not explicitly provide choices and do not actively encourage students' initiative (i.e., are low in autonomy support), this does not automatically imply that they actively thwart students' need for autonomy (e.g., using pressuring language and punishments). Moreover, teachers can also have a more neutral style that is neither supporting nor thwarting students' need for autonomy.

Controlling teaching then involves the ignorance of the students' perspective at the advantage of the teachers' agenda and the use of pressures to make them act, think, or feel in a particular way (Grolnick, 2003; Reeve, 2009). According to SDT, a controlling style can be expressed in at least two different ways, that is, as externally or internally controlling teaching (Ryan, 1982; Soenens & Vansteenkiste, 2010; Vansteenkiste, Simons, Lens, Soenens, & Matos, 2005). Externally controlling teaching refers to the activation of a sense of external obligation in students by using rather overt and observable controlling strategies, such as (threats of) punishments, deadlines (e.g., Amabile, Dejong, & Lepper, 1976), pressuring rewards (e.g., Deci, Koestner, & Ryan, 1999), and explicitly controlling language, like "you must" (e.g., Reeve, 2009; Ryan & Niemiec, 2009). Internally controlling teaching involves the use of tactics that trigger internally pressuring (i.e., introjected) forces in learners by appealing to students' feelings of guilt (e.g., Vansteenkiste et al., 2005), by eliciting shame and anxiety (e.g., Soenens, Sierens, Vansteenkiste, Dochy, & Goossens, 2012), or by triggering ego involvement and contingent self-worth (Ryan, 1982). An exemplary statement of a physical education teacher provoking internal pressure would be: "Everyone should be able to do the following exercise. Even a toddler can do this!" The activation of such internal pressures may also happen in a more covert and subtle way, for instance, through the facial expression of disappointment or the withdrawal of attention when students fail to meet certain standards (i.e., conditional regard) (Soenens & Vansteenkiste, 2010).

In addition to being controlling, teachers can also thwart students' needs, in particular their need for competence, by creating a chaotic environment (Reeve, 2009). Chaotic teachers create confusion among students by exerting an illogical and incoherent structure when introducing tasks and expressing ambiguous feedback or even destructive criticism (Reeve & Jang, 2006). In a chaotic environment, students get ambiguous, unclear, or even incorrect information, which elicits a sense of competence frustration. In addition, chaotic teachers provide unclear and confusing rules for adequate behavior, which creates an atmosphere of permissiveness. Finally, the need for relatedness can be thwarted when teachers create an emotionally cold learning environment for students. Uninvolved teachers are unfriendly and even reject or exclude (some) students (Skinner & Belmont, 1993).

The few studies that addressed the unique role of need-thwarting behaviors mainly focused on the dimension of controlling teaching (e.g., De Meyer et al., 2014; Haerens et al., 2015; Soenens et al., 2012), whereas the dimensions of chaotic and cold teaching have only scarcely been investigated (but see Van den Berghe et al., 2013).

Yet, this might be a worthwhile issue for future research. That is because teachers who do not provide clear guidelines on how to attain the learning goals and, hence, are low in structure do not necessarily actively thwart students' need for competence, for instance, by severely criticizing the students' functioning. Similarly, teachers may be less involved or caring and, hence, be low in relatedness support, yet, this does not mean they exclude or reject students, thereby eliciting feelings of relatedness frustration. These findings and assumptions imply that, just as need satisfaction and need frustration are preferably assessed as separate constructs, the so-called "dark" side of a teachers' interpersonal style deserves to be studied in its own right (De Meyer et al., 2014; Haerens et al., 2015; Vansteenkiste & Ryan, 2013).

Notwithstanding the need to examine the role of student perceptions of chaotic and cold teaching behaviors in future studies, given the dearth of the studies regarding these teaching dimensions, the remainder of the chapter particularly deals with controlling teaching behaviors. Specifically, we review evidence with regard to the effects and antecedents of controlling teaching.

Effects of Controlling Teaching

Controlling Teaching and Student Outcomes From the initial development of SDT, teachers' degree of controlling teaching has been examined (e.g., Deci, Schwartz, Sheinman, & Ryan, 1981). Yet, because controlling teaching was assessed along a unidimensional continuum, with autonomy-supportive teaching representing the positive pole and controlling teaching the negative pole, the distinct effects of controlling teaching could not be examined. More recent studies did address the detrimental role of controlling teaching per se by devising a separate measure for controlling teaching and revealed that controlling teaching hampers secondary school students' positive functioning in the classroom (e.g., De Meyer et al., 2014).

To illustrate, student-perceived external controlling teaching, including teachers' interference with students' pace of working and suppression of students' criticisms, was negatively associated with students' effort and persistence to learn among elementary school children (Assor, Kaplan, Kanat-Maymon, & Roth, 2005). Among secondary school students, a conditionally approving attitude, involving the use of intrusive and manipulative practices such as shaming students and using guilt induction, negatively related to students' academic performance, a relation that could be explained by students' reduced autonomous motivation to learn and less frequent engagement in self-regulatory learning strategies (Soenens et al., 2012). Further, observational (e.g., Reeve & Jang, 2006) and experimental studies (e.g., Flink, Boggiano, & Barrett, 1990) have shown that the use of controlling strategies undermines students' interest, creativity, and performance. For instance, Koestner, Ryan, Bernieri, & Holt (1984) showed that 6–7-year-old children were more creative in their painting when guidelines on how to paint were introduced in an informational manner (e.g., providing a rationale for staying within the paper borders) rather than in a controlling way (e.g., using controlling language and referring to being a "good boy/girl"). More recently, Vansteenkiste et al. (2005) showed among late elementary school children that the use of guilt-inducing and "should" language undermined deep-level learning compared to an autonomy-supportive style of introducing the same learning activity, while no differences were found for superficial learning. Presumably, the induced pressure had led the children to engage in some learning, yet, at the cost of a full absorption in the learning activity, which is required for deep-level learning to take place.

Apart from hampering growth, SDT suggests that the exposure to a controlling environment, especially when enduring, will engender a host of negative learning outcomes, such as passivity, and even school dropout (Deci & Ryan, 2000; Vansteenkiste & Ryan, 2013). Consistent with this, perceived controlling teaching has been associated with feelings of anger and anxiety and restricted engagement among elementary school students (Assor et al., 2005) as well as poor quality motivation (Soenens et al., 2012). Complementing the work on student-perceived controlling teaching, the observation of controlling teaching during a single physical education class, although low in incidence, was found to relate to more pressured motivation (i.e., controlled motivation) and feelings of discouragement (i.e., amotivation; De Meyer et al., 2014).

Controlling Teaching and Defiance In response to a controlling environment, students might not only rigidly or slavishly comply with the teacher's requests (i.e., controlled motivation) or become passive, discouraged, and indifferent (i.e., amotivation), they can also display more active forms of defensive functioning including oppositional defiance (Haerens et al., 2015). Oppositional defiance involves a blunt rejection of the requests made by an authority figure and the tendency to engage in the opposite behavior (Vansteenkiste, Soenens, Van Petegem, & Duriez, 2014). Because the behavior originates in direct reaction to the encountered external forces, it represents a rather pressured form of functioning; it reflects the tendency to seek distance from authority figures, yet in a non-volitional way (Van Petegem, Soenens, Vansteenkiste, & Beyers, 2015).

A few studies have begun to investigate relationships between controlling agents and oppositional defiance. For instance, in the parenting domain, Van Petegem, Soenens, Vansteenkiste, & Beyers (2015) showed in a series of four studies that children are more likely to be oppositional defiant when they perceive their parents as being controlling, an effect that could be accounted for by elicited experiences of need frustration in the parent-child relationship. Haerens et al. (2015) found a more direct relationship between controlling teaching and oppositional defiance that was not accounted for by feelings of need frustration among secondary school students reporting on their experiences during physical education. De Meyer et al. (2015) went beyond these cross-sectional studies by making use of an experimental design, in which participants were shown a videotape of a teacher acting in a controlling way. Participants who imagined taking a class with a controlling teacher indicated to be more likely to defy the teacher, an effect that could be accounted for by experiences of need frustration.

Apart from engaging in oppositional defiance, students may also not participate or disengage from an activity for more autonomous reasons. That is, students can display reflective defiance, a possibility that was suggested in the context of (health) behavior change (Vansteenkiste & Van de Broeck, 2014; Vansteenkiste, Williams, & Resnicow, 2012). Whereas oppositional defiance reflects a straightforward opposition against the teacher's requests pushed by emerging impulses to rebel and, hence, involves little reflection and consideration of the socializing agents' request as such, students engaging in reflective defiance oppose against these requests after having seriously thought about them. Thus, reflectively defiant students are more considerate of their reasons for not doing what is requested, such that they more volitionally disengage from the activity. Students could refuse to participate in or disengage from the activity because in their opinion the offered activities truthfully do not make sense to them or because they are highly competent in the subject at hand and see little challenge in the offered activities. We thus suggest that it is entirely possible that some students, after reflection and negotiation with their teacher, willingly decide to oppose against the teacher's requests (Vansteenkiste et al., 2014). From an educational perspective, more reflective forms of defiance do not necessarily represent a negative outcome. On the contrary, since reflective defiance is hypothesized to be more autonomous in nature, it is possible that it may not yield the counterproductive outcomes that oppositional defiance yields. Yet, as far as we know, studies examining whether and how controlling teaching relates to these distinct forms of defiance are virtually nonexistent.

Do Some Students Benefit from a Controlling Teaching Style? Teachers and teacher educators are not always convinced of the detrimental effects of controlling teaching (e.g., De Meyer et al., 2015). Their argument is that in real-life contexts a controlling and stricter teaching style is needed for at least certain types of students. Before providing a brief overview of the available research addressing this question, two issues need clarification.

First, teachers' reliance on controlling strategies should not be confused with their provision of structure and guidance (Reeve, 2009). The suggestion within SDT to limit the use of a controlling teaching style does not imply that teachers need to refrain from setting expectations or from providing scaffolds while monitoring children's learning process. Indeed, students in general (Jang, Reeve, & Deci, 2010), and especially those who are anxious and uncertain (Mouratidis, Vansteenkiste, Michou, & Lens, 2013), benefit from structure.

Second, SDT does recognize the fact that controlling teaching may yield some, especially behavioral, benefits, such as compliance and superficial learning. Yet, the problematic outcomes associated with controlling teaching especially begin to emerge when the pressures are fading and students are no longer supervised. Moreover, the behavioral benefits associated with controlling socialization often come with an emotional cost, as indexed by reduced well-being and heightened anxiety and depressive symptoms (Grolnick & Pomerantz, 2009; Soenens & Vansteenkiste, 2010; Reeve, 2009).

A lot of research within the SDT tradition has addressed the question to what extent the hypothesized effects of controlling teaching are universal, that is, generalize across students' age, educational level, cultural background (e.g., Jang, Reeve, Ryan, & Kim, 2009), and motivational orientation. Recent research particularly has begun to address the question whether individuals displaying a particular profile react differently to autonomy-supportive and controlling socialization practices (e.g., Rietzschel, Slijkhuis, & Van Yperen, 2014). With respect to the educational domain, De Meyer et al. (2015) examined whether teachers' matching beliefs, that is, their belief that they need to match their teaching style to the motivational orientation of the child, would hold. Making use of a video-based experimental approach as described above, they reported that students who watched a controlling teacher, relative to those who watched an autonomy-supportive teacher, reported less optimal outcomes (e.g., higher need frustration and more oppositional defiance). Importantly, in direct contradiction to the teachers' laymen beliefs, this desirable effect of an autonomy-supportive, relative to a controlling, teaching style emerged independent of students' personal controlled motivation as assessed prior to watching the videos. These findings support the idea that a controlling approach is detrimental, even to students who function in a controlled way themselves, despite of the match between the teachers' approach and the students' motivational profile.

Observing Controlling Teaching

Advantages of Observations Consistent with SDT's claim that especially behavior that is subjectively perceived as controlling by the students will be most predictive of maladaptive motivational outcomes (Black & Deci, 2000; Jang, Reeve, Ryan, & Kim, 2009), most previous studies typically relied on student reports of teaching behaviors. Indeed, for students to feel hampered in their functioning, they probably need to hold the perception that their teacher is pressuring them to act, think, or feel in a teacher-prescribed way. Yet, to gain deeper insight in what controlling teaching behaviors exactly look like and to move this line of research forward, observational measures are needed (Reeve et al., 2014).

In fact, we believe the use of observational measures yields several advantages. First, observations allow one to gain a richer understanding in the specific ways how controlling teaching manifests during particular periods of the lesson (e.g., the beginning of a lesson). Insight in this situation-specific manifestation is crucially important to understand the real nature of teacher-student interactions. In fact, observations provide the opportunity to measure and identify what really happens during specific acts of instructions (e.g., yells, losing patience). Insight in these more concrete controlling behaviors is richer and more informative when compared to more generic assessments of teacher's overall controlling style, as is the case in most available student reports.

Second, the exclusive reliance on student reports causes problems of shared method variance, such that associations obtained between perceived controlling teaching and student outcomes get artificially inflated. The use of observations can overcome this methodological limitation.

Third, the simultaneous observation of controlling behaviors and its student-perceived assessment allow addressing a number of under-investigated issues. For instance, given that the association between observed and student-perceived controlling behaviors is far from perfect, the question can be raised whether discrepancies can be predicted by particular psychological characteristics. Further, the simultaneous use of both observations and self-reports allows one to examine whether both yield an independent contribution in the prediction of outcomes. Although the perception of teacher control should come with a cost, it is also possible that, at least in some situations, students do not consciously need to notice the teachers' controlling behaviors to suffer from it in terms of experienced need frustration and related negative outcomes. There is at least one experimental study (Reeve & Tseng, 2011) that revealed that the effects of experimentally induced controlling instructions on objective indicators of stress (i.e., salivary cortisol) were not mediated by participants' subjective perceived control.

Fourth, as previous research has shown that teachers do not always report accurately about the way they teach (Mosston & Ashworth, 2002), videotapes of teachers' lessons could be used as a tool to foster teachers' reflection on and evaluation of their own engagement in controlling teaching behavior. By detecting specific critical moments that occur during the course of a lesson during which teachers are engaging in controlling behaviors, teachers may come to a deeper understanding of what it means for them personally to be controlling. Moreover, identifying the factors that elicited these controlling behaviors may form the starting point to begin avoiding such practices and to identify occasions during the lesson where there is room to be less controlling.

What Observation Studies Tell Us Given the present chapter's focus on the distinct role of controlling teaching behaviors in the prediction of need frustration and maladaptive outcomes (i.e., dark pathway), we limit ourselves to the discussion of those studies that included separate observations of controlling teaching, such that a unique score for observed controlling teaching could be derived (e.g., Van den Berghe et al., 2013).

A first set of experimental studies was conducted in the laboratory where pairs of individuals either took up the role of a teacher or a student. For instance, Deci, Spiegel, Ryan, Koestner, and Kauffman (1982) conducted an experimental laboratory-based study in which psychology students instructed their peers on a puzzle task. A list of controlling behaviors, such as "asking controlling questions," "uttering directives and criticisms," and "imposing deadlines," was observed. Consistent with SDT, students adopting the teacher role turned out to be more controlling when they were held accountable for their students' performing up to certain standards compared to those that received no standards for students' learning. Reeve and Jang (2006) built on this work by showing that these observed controlling teaching behaviors, elicited by a pressuring context, also had detrimental effects on the students, such as decreased levels of perceived autonomy.

Although highly informative, a potential pitfall of these studies is that they were conducted in a rather artificial laboratory setting (but see Flink et al., 1990), with students working on rather intrinsically motivating activities. Moreover, the teaching situation was limited to teacher-student pairs that were formed right before the experiment, and controlling behaviors were coded for only a short period of time. The daily class reality is however more complex, as students build up a relation with a teacher that lasts for at least a certain period of time and they often work on non-interesting activities. Most teachers teach a larger group of students for lessons of approximately 50 min at secondary school and sometimes entire days in elementary school. Consequently, it is possible that some of the controlling practices that were identified and studied in the laboratory (Deci et al., 1982; Reeve & Jang, 2006) are only rarely observed in real life.

To test whether the findings of previous studies would hold in a real teaching context, De Meyer and colleagues (2015) videotaped and observed controlling teaching behaviors in the context of a naturalistic and authentic physical education lesson and investigated how these related to students' quality of motivation. The coded controlling behaviors mainly referred to pressuring students, such as when a teacher commands students (e.g., "No one stops until I say so"), yells at the students (e.g., "Mary and Thomas, are you deaf?"), exercises power over the students by interfering and demanding respect (e.g., "You have to be silent when I speak"), uses destructive criticism (e.g., "Unbelievable, it is really not difficult to simply copy my demonstration and still you do something else"), is irritated or loses patience (e.g., "Nicky, its time you start doing what I asked"), does not allow input from the students (e.g., "No, that won't work. I am the one who puts together the teams"), or pressures students by making an appeal to their self-confidence by inducing feelings of guilt and shame ("I am really disappointed in the performance of some students of this class" – when looking at Sophie and her friend). When teachers engaged more frequently in these visibly controlling behaviors, students reported that they experienced their teachers as more controlling and, in turn, that they felt more pressured to engage in the lesson (i.e., controlled motivation) and were more amotivated (De Meyer et al., 2014). Interestingly, these associations were obtained even though the occurrence of controlling teaching behavior was low, which might suggest that even a sporadic exposure to controlling teaching behaviors may increase students' perception of exerted control by the teacher and prompt a less adaptive form of motivation. Research in the area of controlling parenting similarly revealed that, even though levels of control are typically low, controlling parenting does represent a strong and robust predictor of maladaptive developmental outcomes (e.g., Soenens, Vansteenkiste, & Luyten, 2010).

Given that a controlling teaching approach seems to results in detrimental effects, it is important to understand why teachers are inclined to engage in such an approach. In the following, we review the current literature on antecedents of a controlling teaching style.

Antecedents of Controlling Teaching

A Taxonomy of Distal Antecedents Antecedents of teaching behaviors are usually divided into three categories, that is, (a) factors from above, (b) factors from below, and (c) factors from within (Grolnick, 2003). These factors can be facilitating such that they subsequently elicit a more need-supportive teaching style, but they can also be more pressuring with the implication of eliciting a more controlling style. In light of the focus of the present chapter on controlling teaching, we will particularly focus on identified pressuring antecedents from above, below, and within.

Pressuring factors from above refer to the demands teacher encounter within the wider school environment, such as pressures from school boards and principals (Pelletier, Seguin-Levesque, & Legault, 2002) or following from school administration (Pelletier & Sharp, 2009; Taylor, Ntoumanis, & Smith, 2009). Pressures from within refer to personal characteristics of the teacher, including their own personality functioning (Van den Berghe et al., 2013). Finally, also students' characteristics (Pelletier et al., 2002) or so-called pressures from below (e.g., defiance) can elicit a controlling style. These three groups of pressuring factors can then be considered as more distal variables that may feed into more proximal antecedents, including teachers' motivation for teaching as well as the beliefs they hold with respect to the effectiveness and feasibility of adopting a controlling style. We first discuss the three mentioned groups of distal pressuring factors (above, within, and below) to end with the proximal antecedents of controlling teaching including teachers' motivation and beliefs.

Pressuring Factors from Above The school climate can put multiple demands on teachers. In many countries, the government provides predefined curricula with obligatory standards for teachers (and students) to obtain. A school climate highly emphasizing these performance-based standards through competition and high-stakes testing can lead teachers to exert pressure on their students (Reeve et al., 2014). In fact, within such a climate teachers are more strongly held accountable for their students' performances, such that they become more inclined to transmit this performance-based agenda onto their students (Deci et al., 1982; Pelletier et al., 2002; Reeve, 2009; Soenens et al., 2012). Consistent with this reasoning, Deci et al. (1982) revealed that "teachers" were more controlling when they were held accountable for their students' performance. Also, a more recent correlational study of Soenens and colleagues (2012) confirmed that a pressuring school environment indirectly relates to more controlling teaching behavior. As such, many of the ideas developed and findings obtained within the SDT literature do not align with the current emphasis on teachers' accountability for students' performance and the related pressures teachers experience when they are teaching toward tests. Indeed, to the extent that teachers teach to the test, students' deep engagement in meaningful and interesting learning activities likely gets forestalled (Vansteenkiste, Simons, Lens, Sheldon, & Deci, 2004).

Pressures from Within Individuals' general causality orientations represent relatively enduring motivational orientations reflecting people's understanding of how they initiate and regulate their behavior in specific life domains and situations (Deci & Ryan, 1985; 2002). Three causality orientations have been distinguished. First, teachers with an autonomy orientation typically regulate their behavior based on their own interests and personally valued standards and they experience a sense of volition and freedom when engaging in activities. Second, an impersonal orientation refers to the feeling of ineffectiveness and to the experience that one's behavior is beyond one's intentional control. Third, teachers with a controlled orientation experience their behavior as controlled and pressured by other people, social norms, and cultural values. A controlled orientation is hypothesized to constitute a more pressuring personal orientation that tends to translate into more controlling interactions with relevant others. This is because control-oriented teachers that are more likely to be preoccupied by their own concerns and agenda, are more likely to directly transmit their own pressuring experiences (e.g., external evaluations, pressuring school leaders, or their own teaching agenda) onto their students, thereby engaging in more controlling practices. Based on self-reports in preservice teachers, Reeve (1998) indeed found that control-oriented preservice teachers engage more frequently in controlling teaching strategies. These findings were strengthened in a recent study of Van den Berghe et al. (2013) who showed that a controlled orientation (as reported by in-service teachers) related to more controlling teaching as observed by an external observer.

Such findings call for an individualized approach when trying to reach control-oriented teachers. When school leaders or CPD providers want to support control-oriented teachers' psychological needs for autonomy, competence, and relatedness during training, it is critical to examine whether control-oriented teachers are not only more controlling but possibly also less receptive for change than autonomy-oriented teachers (Su & Reeve, 2011). In that respect, CPD trainers might consider to include reflective activities for teachers on their own engagement in controlling practices and the effects these practices can have on students' motivational experiences and learning in the classroom.

Pressures from Below Students' lack of motivation, as manifested through amotivation or discouragement as well as oppositional defiance, can not only follow from a controlling teaching style but may also yield an influence on subsequent teaching behaviors. Skinner, Kindermann, Connell, and Wellborn (2009), for instance, argued that student disengagement in terms of passivity, giving up, or refraining from putting effort into the lessons can act as a de-energizing resource that negatively affects teachers because they receive negative feedback on their functioning when they observe their students. When teachers expected that their students would be less motivated, they were not only interacting less frequently with them; they were also more controlling toward them (Sarrazin, Tessier, Pelletier, Trouilloud, & Chanal, 2006). Similar positive relationships between students' disengagement and teachers' need-thwarting behaviors were found by Van den Berghe, Cardon, Tallir,

Kirk, & Haerens (2015) who observed and coded the first 3-min intervals of 100 physical education lessons.

There is certainly a need to further explore this fallow land of how and under which conditions students' behaviors trigger teachers to enact in a more controlling way. Observation studies would allow to conduct critical incident analyses (Flanagan, 1954), which involves observing, identifying, and qualitatively analyzing specific critical moments that occur during the course of a lesson in order to understand what happens before and after a teacher enacts in a controlling way.

Proximal Antecedents: Teaching Motivation and Beliefs These different distal antecedents may feed onto teachers' teaching style by playing onto more proximal antecedents, such as the teachers' motivation for the profession. The role teacher motivation plays in relation to teachers' way of interacting with the students in the classroom has become a topic of interest over the past decade (Richardson, Karabenick, & Watt, 2014). Studies in the educational context revealed that more controlled as opposed to autonomous motivation related to more controlling interactions with students (Pelletier et al., 2002). These findings suggest that teachers, who predominantly teach for controlled reasons such as the pressure to comply with curriculum standards or the pressure to being acknowledged and recognized by principals or colleagues, are probably at higher risk for engaging in controlling teaching behaviors.

In reality, many teachers combine autonomous and controlled reasons to teach to a different degree. While some teachers might feel pressured to prepare their classes very well to prove themselves to colleagues and their students (i.e., controlled motivation), they might also value the importance of their subject and enjoy the interactions with students at the same time (i.e., autonomous motivation). The question then arises which type of motivational profile, involving a particular combination of autonomous and controlled reasons, relates to a controlling teaching style. In one informative study, Van den Berghe et al. (2014) showed that especially teachers, who typically enjoy and personally value interacting with their students, that is, those who display a more autonomously motivated profile, reported being more need supportive, but this study did not include dimensions of need-thwarting teaching (i.e., controlling teaching) (Van den Berghe et al., 2014). Thus, more research is needed to explore how naturally occurring combinations of motives to engage in the teaching profession relate to a controlling teaching style.

Next to teachers' motivation, also the beliefs that teachers hold can serve as a second proximal factor that helps explain why teachers orient themselves toward or hold onto a controlling teaching style (Korthagen, 2004; Pajares, 1992; Reeve et al., 2014; Roth & Weinstock, 2013). A first belief that may explain teachers' tendency to adopt a controlling style concerns the perceived effectiveness of a controlling teaching style. For example, some teachers may believe it is sometimes necessary or even beneficial to rely on controlling practices, such as threats of punishment or criticism, to prompt students' cooperation. Reeve et al. (2014) and De Meyer et al. (2015) indeed showed that teachers who believed that a controlling style is more effective also tended to engage in a controlling style more frequently. A second belief that explains why teachers orient themselves to one style or another is the belief it is too difficult or too challenging to avoid engaging in a controlling style during everyday instruction (Reeve et al., 2014).

Although no prior research addressed this issue, these proximal antecedents (i.e., teaching motivation and beliefs) may develop differently depending on the interplay with the pressuring distal factors from above, within, or below. To illustrate, teachers who are exposed to pressures from the school board, who endorse a more controlled orientation, or who are frequently confronted with disengaged students may come to belief that a controlling approach is more effective. How these distal and proximal factors interact with each other and translate into a teachers' behavior in the classroom is an interesting avenue for future research.

Controlling Teaching: Future Directions

In this chapter, it became clear that the body of educationally oriented research on controlling teaching is still in its infancy. Most of the work that has been done so far was cross-sectional (Haerens et al., 2015; Soenens et al., 2012) or experimental (Flink et al., 1990; Koestner et al., 1984; Niemiec & Ryan, 2009) in nature. However, an evolving number of studies across different life domains such as parenting (Van Petegem et al., 2015), health counseling (Ng, Ntoumanis, Thogersen-Ntoumani, Stott, & Hindle, 2013; Verstuyf, Vansteenkiste, Soenens, Boone, & Mouratidis, 2013), coaching (Balaguer et al., 2012; Bartholomew et al., 2011a; Stebbings et al., 2012), and education (De Meyer et al., 2014; Deci et al., 1982; Reeve & Jang, 2006) all point in the same direction, that is, toward the detrimental effects of a controlling approach. Hence, the study of controlling teaching deserves greater attention in future research, thereby making use of more sophisticated designs. We sketch three research themes that can be addressed in future work, that is, the necessity for (a) longitudinal work, (b) research relying on person-centered analytical strategies, and (c) intervention work addressing the role of controlling teaching.

First, one topic that could be examined is whether controlling teaching and need frustration form an escalating negative cycle, such that both get interwoven with each other over time (see Jang, Kim, & Reeve, 2012; examples on autonomy support). Indeed, children may not only defy controlling teachers, but the teachers themselves may increase their use of controlling strategies when noticing expression of need frustration such as oppositional defiance and associated misbehavior. In this respect, when adolescents perceived their parents to rely on a controlling style to introduce and monitor parental prohibitions, they were more likely to defy the prohibitions over a 1-year period, with oppositional defiance equally eliciting increases in controlling prohibitions over time (Vansteenkiste, et al., 2014).

Second, given that most past work was limited to one dimension of need-thwarting teaching behavior (i.e., controlling teaching), future research could try to do a better job at conceptualizing and measuring chaotic and cold teaching.

This may provide more detailed insights in the associations and interactions between different dimensions of need-thwarting teaching behavior and students' motivation. Relatedly, an important aim for future research is to further address the interplay of need-thwarting and need-supportive teaching behaviors. Recent work suggests that observed (e.g., Van den Berghe et al., 2013) and self-reported (e.g., Haerens et al., 2015) autonomy-supportive and controlling behaviors are only modestly negatively related. This implies that at least some teachers may score simultaneously high on autonomy-supportive and controlling behaviors. Because autonomy-supportive and controlling behaviors can co-occur in different doses, it becomes interesting to explore their effects and their co-variation as a function of the timing and taught content of the lesson. As an example of this person-centered approach, Matosic and Cox (2014) recently showed that athletes of coaches who were perceived to be predominantly autonomy-supportive displayed higher levels of need satisfaction and more adaptive motivational outcomes, when compared to athletes of coaches who were perceived to be mainly controlling. Interestingly, the results also revealed that moderate levels of perceived coach control were not necessary bad, at least when combined with high perceived autonomy support. The authors primarily included positive student outcomes in their study. Yet, given the discussed dark pathway associated with a controlling approach, it would make sense to also include maladaptive motivational outcomes (e.g., need frustration, resentment, oppositional defiance) to investigate whether such outcomes would especially become more salient if social agents such as teachers or coaches are perceived to be controlling.

Third, in light of the emerging evidence on the detrimental effects of controlling teaching, we suggest that it is timely to start thinking about the development of effective continuous professional development (CPD) programs for teachers that allow them to gain insight into their way of interacting with the students and its effects on students' motivation and learning. There are already a few examples of effective programs focusing on the enhancement of need-supportive teaching available in the literature (e.g., Aelterman et al., 2013, Aelterman, Vansteenkiste, Van den Berghe, De Meyer, & Haerens, 2014; Cheon, Reeve, Yu, & Jang, 2014; Tessier, Sarrazin, & Ntoumanis, 2010), but evidence-based CPD programs focusing on the reduction of controlling teaching are lacking. As Cheon and Reeve (2013) suggest, asking teachers to replace their use of controlling teaching strategies by autonomy-supportive ones is probably a more difficult transition for them to make, because it requires giving up a certain approach (i.e., letting controlling teaching go) rather than expanding their existing style (i.e., become more autonomy supportive). Overall, if we want to design effective CPD programs to reduce controlling teaching, we need insights into the wide range of antecedents that help to explain why teachers adopt a controlling teaching style. The identification of these antecedents would be helpful to identify these teachers who are most vulnerable for the adoption of a controlling style and are perhaps most resistant to change.

Conclusion: A Helicopter View

Historically, SDT scholars have been primarily concerned with identifying the critical motivational processes and contexts that foster positive outcomes, including intrinsic motivation, creativity, and well-being. Over the past couple of years, however, perhaps under influence of a growing body of studies conducted within the area of psychopathology (Ryan, et al., 2015), an increasing number of studies have focused on the factors that elicit maladaptive functioning in non-clinical individuals (Ryan & Deci, 2000; Vansteenkiste & Ryan, 2013). Such work is illuminating at the theoretical level because it allows moving beyond the consideration of need-supportive contexts and need-satisfying experiences by also taking into account the fairly distinct role of contextual need thwarting and associated need frustration. Practically speaking, this work seems equally timely because, at least within the Belgian educational context, it is our impression that schools increasingly face students who are indifferent, defiant, or even aggressive and that school directories and teachers call for help in dealing with these students. The identification of critical teaching variables that relate to these maladaptive outcomes is then a first step to develop intervention programs that allow teachers to more effectively handle such students. We end by providing a set of practical suggestions that follow from the presented studies and insights.

Practical Recommendations

Controlling teaching involves the minimization, ignorance, or even denial of the students' perspective at the advantage of the teachers' agenda and the use of pressures to make students act, think, or feel in a particular way (Grolnick, 2003; Reeve, 2009). Examples of more overt observable controlling strategies that teachers can best avoid are:

- (Threats of) deadlines and punishments (e.g., "You really must do this otherwise you will lose two points")
- Pressuring awards (e.g., "Only if you read 10 min every day, you get a reward")
- Yelling (e.g., "Mary and Thomas, are you deaf?") and commanding (e.g., "No one stops until I say so")
- Using destructive criticism (e.g., "Unbelievable, it is really not difficult to simply do what is asked")
- Losing patience or becoming irritated (e.g., "Nicky, I am getting sick of your behavior")
- Denying input from the students (e.g., "No, I do not want to hear it, just get started with what you have to do")
- Using explicitly controlling language, like "you must" or "you have to"

More covered forms of controlling teaching refer to tactics to appeal to students' feelings of guilt, to elicit shame and anxiety, or to trigger ego involvement and contingent self-worth. An exemplary statement of a teacher provoking such internal pressure would be: "Everyone should be able to do the following exercise. Even a toddler can do this!" Or "I am really disappointed in the performance of some students of this class." Teachers can also display facial expressions of disappointment or withdraw attention when students fail to meet certain standards.

If teachers would want to become less controlling, there are a number of considerations they can take into account. First, the suggestion within SDT to limit the use of a controlling teaching style does not imply that teachers need to refrain from structuring the learning process by setting expectations or providing scaffolds while monitoring children's learning. Indeed, students in general (Jang, Reeve, & Deci, 2010), and especially those who are anxious and uncertain (Mouratidis, Vansteenkiste, Michou, & Lens, 2013), benefit from structure. Rules and expectations can thus be consequently monitored, but preferably in an autonomy-supportive way. This means that students understand why a rule is introduced and are preferably involved in the process of establishing rules and determining consequences in case of rule violation.

Second, as teachers' view on their teaching style is often discrepant from how their student perceives them (Mosston & Ashworth, 2002), teachers may have the mistaken impression that they are not controlling, while in the eyes of the students, they are. Obtaining self-reports of the students themselves, possibly in conjunction with videotaping the lesson, is then a useful tool to get an insight in their own engagement in controlling teaching behaviors. Further, by detecting specific critical moments during which a teacher is more likely to engage in controlling behaviors, teachers may come to a deeper understanding of what it means to be controlling and when they are most likely to be so. Moreover, identifying the factors (e.g., Do they experience pressures from school board? Are they discouraged because some students are displaying disruptive behavior?) that elicited these controlling behaviors may form the starting point to begin avoiding such practices. Yet, to move away from controlling practices, teachers will also need to be given an alternative and to be trained in adopting an autonomy-supportive style. Given the strong focus high-performance standards and frequent testing in contemporary classrooms, it is also worthwhile to reconsider certain didactical and pedagogical approaches (e.g., marking every lesson, the way marks are communicated). Some of these approaches may be generally accepted and expected, yet have fairly great likelihood of engendering controlling strategies.

Finally, it is important to know that some of the abovementioned controlling strategies may yield behavioral benefits, such as compliance and superficial learning. These initial positive effects may reinforce the use of control and help to explain why at least some teachers believe that a controlling style is necessary or even beneficial to prompt students' cooperation. Yet, the problematic outcomes associated with controlling teaching especially begin to emerge when the pressures are fading and students are no longer supervised. Moreover, the behavioral benefits associated with controlling socialization often come with an emotional cost, as indexed by reduced well-being and heightened anxiety and depressive symptoms.

References

Aelterman, N., Vansteenkiste, M., Van den Berghe, L., De Meyer, J., & Haerens, L. (2014). Fostering a need-supportive teaching style: Intervention effects on physical education teachers' beliefs and teaching behaviors. *Journal of Sport and Exercise Psychology, 36*(3), 595–609. doi:10.1123/jsep.2013-0229.

Aelterman, N., Vansteenkiste, M., Van Keer, H., De Meyer, J., Van den Berghe, L., & Haerens, L. (2013). Development and evaluation of a training on need-supportive teaching in physical education: Qualitative and quantitative findings. *Teaching and Teacher Education, 29*, 64–75. doi:10.1016/j.tate.2012.09.001.

Amabile, T. M., Dejong, W., & Lepper, M. R. (1976). Effects of externally imposed deadlines on subsequent intrinsic motivation. *Journal of Personality and Social Psychology, 34*, 92–98. doi:10.1037//0022-3514.34.1.92.

Assor, A., Kaplan, H., Kanat-Maymon, Y., & Roth, G. (2005). Directly controlling teacher behaviors as predictors of poor motivation and engagement in girls and boys: The role of anger and anxiety. *Learning and Instruction, 15*, 397–413. doi:10.1016/j.learninstruc.2005.07.008.

Assor, A., Kaplan, H., & Roth, G. (2002). Choice is good, but relevance is excellent: Autonomy-enhancing and suppressing teacher behaviours predicting students' engagement in schoolwork. *British Journal of Educational Psychology, 72*, 261–278. doi:10.1348/000709902158883.

Balaguer, I., González, L., Fabra, P., Castillo, I., Mercé, J., & Duda, J. L. (2012). Coaches' interpersonal style, basic psychological needs and the well- and ill-being of young soccer players: A longitudinal analysis. *Journal of Sports Sciences, 30*(15), 1619–1629. doi:10.1080/02640414.2012.731517.

Bartholomew, K. J., Ntoumanis, N., Cuevas, R., & Lonsdale, C. (2014). Job pressure and ill-health in physical education teachers: The mediating role of psychological need thwarting. *Teaching and Teacher Education, 37*, 101–107. doi:10.1016/j.tate.2013.10.006.

Bartholomew, K. J., Ntoumanis, N., Ryan, R. M., Bosch, J. A., & Thogersen-Ntoumani, C. (2011a). Self-determination theory and diminished functioning: The role of interpersonal control and psychological need thwarting. *Personality and Social Psychology Bulletin, 37*(11), 1459–1473. doi:10.1177/0146167211413125.

Bartholomew, K. J., Ntoumanis, N., Ryan, R. M., & Thøgersen-Ntoumani, C. (2011b). Psychological need thwarting in the sport context: Assessing the darker side of athletic experience. *Journal of Sport & Exercise Psychology, 33*(1), 75–102.

Black, A. E., & Deci, E. L. (2000). The effects of instructors' autonomy support and students' autonomous motivation on learning organic chemistry: A self-determination theory perspective. *Science Education, 84*(6), 740–756. doi:10.1002/1098-237x(200011)84:6<740::aid-sce4>3.0.co;2-3.

Chen, A., Vansteenkiste, M., Beyers, W., Boone, L., Deci, E. L., & Deeder, J. (2015). Psychological need satisfaction and desire for need satisfaction across four cultures. *Motivation and Emotion, 39*(2), 216–236.

Cheon, S. H., & Reeve, J. (2013). Do the benefits from autonomy-supportive PE teacher training programs endure? A one-year follow-up investigation. *Psychology of Sport and Exercise, 14*(4), 508–518. doi:10.1016/j.psychsport.2013.02.002.

Cheon, S. H., Reeve, J., Yu, T. H., & Jang, H. R. (2014). The teacher benefits from giving autonomy support during physical education instruction. *Journal of Sport & Exercise Psychology, 36*, 331–346. doi:10.1123/jsep.2013-0231.

De Meyer, J., Soenens, B., Vansteenkiste, M., Aelterman, N., Van Peteghem, S., & Haerens, L. (2015). Do students with different motivational orientations benefit from autonomy supportive teaching and suffer from controlling teaching? Manuscript submitted for publication, in press.

De Meyer, J., Tallir, I. B., Soenens, B., Vansteenkiste, M., Aelterman, N., Van den Berghe, L., et al. (2014). Does observed controlling teaching behavior relate to students' motivation in physical education? *Journal of Educational Psychology, 106*, 541–554. doi:10.1037/a0034399.

Deci, E. L. (1995). *Why we do what we do: Understanding self-motivation.* New York: Penguin Books.

Deci, E. L., Koestner, R., & Ryan, R. M. (1999). A meta-analytic review of experiments examining the effects of extrinsic rewards on intrinsic motivation. *Psychological Bulletin, 125*(6), 627–668. doi:10.1037/0033-2909.125.6.627.

Deci, E. L., & Ryan, R. M. (1985). The general causality orientations scale: Self-determination in personality. *Journal of Research in Personality, 19*(2), 109–134. doi:10.1016/0092-6566(85)90023-6.

Deci, E. L., & Ryan, R. M. (2000). The "what" and "why" of goal pursuits: Human needs and the self-determination of behavior. *Psychological Inquiry, 11*(4), 227–268. doi:10.1207/s15327965pli1104_01.

Deci, E. L., & Ryan, R. M. (2002). *Handbook of self-determination research*. Rochester, NY: The University of Rochester Press.

Deci, E. L., Schwartz, A. J., Sheinman, L., & Ryan, R. M. (1981). An instrument to assess adults' orientations toward control versus autonomy with children: Reflections on intrinsic motivation and perceived competence. *Journal of Educational Psychology, 73*, 642–650.

Deci, E. L., Spiegel, N. H., Ryan, R. M., Koestner, R., & Kauffman, M. (1982). Effects of performance standards on teaching styles: Behavior of controlling teachers. *Journal of Educational Psychology, 74*(6), 852–859. doi:10.1037//0022-0663.74.6.852.

Flanagan, J. C. (1954). The critical incident technique. *Psychological Bulletin, 51*(4), 327–358. doi:10.1037/h0061470.

Flink, C., Boggiano, A. K., & Barrett, M. (1990). Controlling teaching strategies: Undermining children's self-determination and performance. *Journal of Personality and Social Psychology, 59*(5), 916–924. doi:10.1037//0022-3514.59.5.916.

Gillet, N., Fouquereau, E., Forst, J., Brunaults, P., & Colombat, P. (2012). The impact of organizational factors on psychological needs and their relations with well-being. *Journal of Business and Psychology, 27*, 437–450. doi:10.1007/s10869-011-9253-2.

Grolnick, W. S. (2003). *The psychology of parental control: How well-meant parenting backfires*. Mahwah, NJ: L. Erlbaum Associates.

Grolnick, W. S., & Pomerantz, E. M. (2009). Issues and challenges in studying parental control: Toward a new conceptualization. *Child Development Perspectives, 3*, 165–170.

Haerens, L., Aelterman, N., Vansteenkiste, M., Soenens, B., & Van Petegem, S. (2015). Do perceived autonomy-supportive and controlling teaching relate to physical education students' motivational experiences through unique pathways? Distinguishing between the bright and dark side of motivation. *Psychology of Sport and Exercise, 16*, 26–36. http://dx.doi.org/10.1016/j.psychsport.2014.08.013.

Jang, H., Kim, E. J., & Reeve, J. (2012). Longitudinal test of self-determination theory's motivation mediation model in a naturally occurring classroom context. *Journal of Educational Psychology, 104*(4), 1175–1188. doi:10.1037/a0028089.

Jang, H., Reeve, J., Ryan, R. M., & Kim, A. (2009). Can self-determination theory explain what underlies the productive, satisfying learning experiences of collectivistically oriented Korean students? *Journal of Educational Psychology, 101*(3), 644–661. doi:10.1037/a0014241.

Jang, H., Reeve, J., & Deci, E. L. (2010). Engaging students in learning activities: It is not autonomy support or structure but autonomy support and structure. *Journal of Educational Psychology, 102*, 588–600. doi:10.1037/a0019682.

Koestner, R., Ryan, R. M., Bernieri, F., & Holt, K. (1984). Setting limits on children's behavior: The differential effects of controlling vs informational styles on intrinsic motivation and creativity. *Journal of Personality, 52*(3), 233–248. doi:10.1111/j.1467-6494.1984.tb00879.x.

Korthagen, F. A. J. (2004). In search of the essence of a good teacher: Towards a more holistic approach in teacher education. *Teaching and Teacher Education, 20*(1), 77–97. doi: http://dx.doi.org/10.1016/j.tate.2003.10.002.

Matosic, D., & Cox, A. E. (2014). Athletes' motivation regulations and need satisfaction across combinations of perceived coaching behaviors. *Journal of Applied Sport Psychology, 26*(3), 302–317. doi:10.1080/10413200.2013.879963.

Mosston, M., & Ashworth, S. (2002). *Teaching physical education* (5th ed.). San Fransisco: Benjamin Cummings.

Mouratidis, A., Vansteenkiste, M., Michou, A., & Lens, W. (2013). Perceived structure and achievement goals as predictors of students' self-regulated learning and affect and the mediating role of competence need satisfaction. *Learning and Individual Differences, 23*, 179–186. doi:10.1016/j.lindif.2012.09.001.

Ng, J. Y., Ntoumanis, N., Thogersen-Ntoumani, C., Stott, K., & Hindle, L. (2013). Predicting psychological needs and well-being of individuals engaging in weight management: The role of important others. *Applied Psychology: Health and Well-Being, 5*(3), 291–310. doi:10.1111/aphw.12011.

Niemiec, C. P., & Ryan, R. M. (2009). Autonomy, competence, and relatedness in the classroom applying self-determination theory to educational practice. *Theory and Research in Education, 7*(2), 133–144.

Pajares, M. F. (1992). Teachers' beliefs and educational research: Cleaning up a messy construct. *Review of Educational Research, 62*(3), 307–332. doi:10.3102/00346543062003307.

Pelletier, L. G., Seguin-Levesque, C., & Legault, L. (2002). Pressure from above and pressure from below as determinants of teachers' motivation and teaching behaviors. *Journal of Educational Psychology, 94*(1), 186–196. doi:10.1037//0022-0663.94.1.186.

Pelletier, L. G., & Sharp, E. C. (2009). Administrative pressures and teachers' interpersonal behaviour in the classroom. *Theory and Research in Education, 7*(2), 174–183. doi:10.1177/1477878509104322.

Reeve, J. (1998). Autonomy support as an interpersonal motivating style: Is it teachable? *Contemporary Educational Psychology, 23*(3), 312–330. doi:10.1006/ceps.1997.0975.

Reeve, J. (2009). Why teachers adopt a controlling motivating style toward students and how they can become more autonomy supportive. *Educational Psychologist, 44*(3), 159–175. doi:10.1080/00461520903028990.

Reeve, J., & Jang, H. S. (2006). What teachers say and do to support students' autonomy during a learning activity. *Journal of Educational Psychology, 98*(1), 209–218. doi:10.1037/0022-0663.98.1.209.

Reeve, J., & Tseng, C. M. (2011). Cortisol reactivity to a teacher's motivating style: The biology of being controlled versus supporting autonomy. *Motivation and Emotion, 35*(1), 63–74. doi:10.1007/s11031-011-9204-2.

Reeve, J., Vansteenkiste, M., Assor, A., Ahmad, I., Cheon, S. H., Jang, H., et al. (2014). The beliefs that underlie autonomy-supportive and controlling teaching: A multinational investigation. *Motivation and Emotion, 38*(1), 93–110. doi:10.1007/s11031-013-9367-0.

Rietzschel, E. F., Slijkhuis, M., & Van Yperen, N. W. (2014). Close monitoring as a contextual stimulator: How need for structure affects the relation between close monitoring and work outcomes. *European Journal of Work and Organizational Psychology, 23*(3), 394–404.

Richardson, P. W., Karabenick, S. A., & Watt, H. M. G. (2014). *Teacher motivation: Theory and practice*. Hoboken: Taylor and Francis.

Roth, G., & Weinstock, M. (2013). Teachers' epistemological beliefs as an antecedent of autonomy-supportive teaching. *Motivation and Emotion, 37*(3), 402–412. doi:10.1007/s11031-012-9338-x.

Ryan, R. M. (1982). Control and information in the intrapersonal sphere: An extension of cognitive evaluation theory. *Journal of Personality and Social Psychology, 43*(3), 450–461. doi:10.1037//0022-3514.43.3.450.

Ryan, R. M., & Deci, E. L. (2000). The darker and brighter sides of human existence: Basic psychological needs as a unifying concept. *Psychological Inquiry, 11*, 319–338.

Ryan, R. M., & Deci, E. L. (2002). An overview of self-determination theory. In E. L. Deci & R. M. Ryan (Eds.), *Handbook of self-determination research* (pp. 3–33). Rochester, NY: University of Rochester Press.

Ryan, R. M., & Deci, E. L. (2008). From ego depletion to vitality: Theory and findings concerning the facilitation of energy available to the self. *Social and Personality Psychology Compass, 2*(2), 702–717. doi:10.1111/j.1751-9004.2008.00098.x.

Ryan, R. M., Deci, E. L., Vansteenkiste, M. (2015). Autonomy and autonomy disturbances in self-development and psychopa-thology: Research on motivation, attachment, and clinical process. To appear In D. Cicchetti (Ed.), *Developmental psychopathology* (3rd Edn). New York: Wiley.

Ryan, R. M., & Niemiec, C. P. (2009). Self-determination theory in schools of education: Can an empirically supported framework also be critical and liberating? *Theory and Research in Education, 7*(2), 263–272. doi:10.1177/1477878509104331.

Sarrazin, P. G., Tessier, D. P., Pelletier, L. G., Trouilloud, D. O., & Chanal, J. P. (2006). The effects of teachers' expectations about students' motivation on teachers' autonomy-supportive and controlling behaviors. *International Journal of Sport and Exercise Psychology, 4*(3), 283–301.

Sheldon, K. M., & Hilpert, J. C. (2012). The balanced measure of psychological needs (BMPN) scale: An alternative domain general measure of need satisfaction. *Motivation and Emotion, 36*(4), 439–451. doi:10.1007/s11031-012-9279-4.

Skinner, E. A., & Belmont, M. J. (1993). Motivation in the classroom: Reciprocal effects of teacher behavior and student engagement across the school year. *Journal of Educational Psychology, 85*(4), 571–581. doi:10.1037/0022-0663.85.4.571.

Skinner, E. A., Kindermann, T. A., Connell, J. P., & Wellborn, J. G. (2009). Engagement and disaffection as organizational constructs in the dynamics of motivational development. In K. R. Wentzel & A. Wigfield (Eds.), *Handbook of motivation at school* (pp. 223–246). New York/London: Routledge.

Soenens, B., Sierens, E., Vansteenkiste, M., Dochy, F., & Goossens, L. (2012). Psychologically controlling teaching: Examining outcomes, antecedents, and mediators. *Journal of Educational Psychology, 104*(1), 108–120. doi:10.1037/a0025742.

Soenens, B., & Vansteenkiste, M. (2010). A theoretical upgrade of the concept of parental psycho-logical control: Proposing new insights on the basis of self-determination theory. *Developmental Review, 30*(1), 74–99. doi:10.1016/j.dr.2009.11.001.

Soenens, B., Vansteenkiste, M., & Luyten, P. (2010). Toward a domain-specific approach to the study of parental psychological control: Distinguishing between dependency-oriented and achievement-oriented psychological control. *Journal of Personality, 78*(1), 217–256. doi:10.1111/j.1467-6494.2009.00614.x.

Stebbings, J., Taylor, I. M., Spray, C. M., & Ntoumanis, N. (2012). Antecedents of perceived coach interpersonal behaviors: The coaching environment and coach psychological well- and ill-being. *Journal of Sport & Exercise Psychology, 34*(4), 481–502.

Su, Y.-L., & Reeve, J. (2011). A meta-analysis of the effectiveness of intervention programs designed to support autonomy. *Educational Psychology Review, 23*(1), 159–188. doi:10.1007/s10648-010-9142-7.

Taylor, I. M., Ntoumanis, N., & Smith, B. (2009). The social context as a determinant of teacher motivational strategies in physical education. *Psychology of Sport and Exercise, 10*(2), 235–243. doi:10.1016/j.psychsport.2008.09.002.

Tessier, D., Sarrazin, P., & Ntoumanis, N. (2010). The effect of an intervention to improve newly qualified teachers' interpersonal style, students motivation and psychological need satisfaction in sport-based physical education. *Contemporary Educational Psychology, 35*(4), 242–253. doi:10.1016/j.cedpsych.2010.05.005.

Vallerand, R. J. (1997). Toward a hierarchical model of intrinsic and extrinsic motivation. In M. P. Zanna (Ed.), *Advances in experimental social psychology* (Vol. 29, pp. 271–360). New York: Academic.

Van den Berghe, L., Soenens, B., Aelterman, N., Cardon, G., Tallir, I. B., & Haerens, L. (2014). Within-person profiles of teachers' motivation to teach: Associations with need satisfaction at work, need-supportive teaching, and burnout. *Psychology of Sport and Exercise, 15*(4), 407–417. doi:10.1016/j.psychsport.2014.04.001.

Van den Berghe, L., Cardon, G., Tallir, I., Kirk, D., & Haerens, L. (2015). Dynamics of needsupportive and need-thwarting teaching behavior: The bidirectional relationship with student engagement and disengagement in five-minute intervals. *Physical Education and Sport Pedagogy*. In revision.

Van den Berghe, L., Soenens, B., Vansteenkiste, M., Aelterman, N., Cardon, G., Tallir, I. B., et al. (2013). Observed need-supportive and need-thwarting teaching behavior in physical education: Do teachers' motivational orientations matter? *Psychology of Sport and Exercise, 14*, 650–661. doi:10.1016/j.psychsport.2013.04.006.

Van Petegem, S., Soenens, B., Vansteenkiste, M., & Beyers, W. (2015). Rebels with a cause? Adolescent defiance from the perspective of reactance theory and self-determination theory. *Child Development, 86*(3), 903–918. doi:10.1111/cdev.12355.

Vansteenkiste, M., Niemiec, C., & Soenens, B. (2010). The development of the five mini-theories of self-determination theory: An historical overview, emerging trends, and future directions. In T. C. Urdan & S. A. Karabenick (Eds.), *Advances in motivation and achievement* (The decade ahead, Vol. 16, pp. 105–166). Bingley, UK: Emerald Publishing.

Vansteenkiste, M., & Ryan, R. M. (2013). On psychological growth and vulnerability: Basic psychological need satisfaction and need frustration as a unifying principle. *Journal of Psychotherapy Integration, 23*, 263–280. doi:10.1037/a0032359.

Vansteenkiste, M., Simons, J., Lens, W., Sheldon, K. A., & Deci, E. L. (2004). Motivating learning, performance, and persistence: The synergistic effects of intrinsic goal contents and autonomy-supportive contexts. *Journal of Personality and Social Psychology, 87*, 246–260.

Vansteenkiste, M., Simons, J., Lens, W., Soenens, B., & Matos, L. (2005). Examining the motivational impact of intrinsic versus extrinsic goal framing and autonomy-supportive versus internally controlling communication style on early adolescents' academic achievement. *Child Development, 76*, 483–501. doi:10.1111/j.1467-8624.2005.00858.x.

Vansteenkiste, M., Soenens, B., Van Petegem, S., & Duriez, B. (2014). Longitudinal associations between adolescent perceived degree and style of parental prohibition and internalization and defiance. *Developmental Psychology, 50*, 229–236. doi:10.1037/a0032972.

Vansteenkiste, M., & Van den Broeck, A. (2014). Understanding motivational dynamics among unemployed individuals: Insights from the self-determination theory perspective. In U. C. Klehe, & E. A. J. Van Hooft (Eds.). *Handbook of job loss and job search*. Oxford: Oxford University Press.

Vansteenkiste, M., Williams, G. C., & Resnicow, K. (2012). Toward systematic integration between self-determination theory and motivational interviewing as examples of top-down and bottom-up intervention development: Autonomy or volition as a fundamental theoretical principle. *International Journal of Behavioral Nutrition and Physical Activity, 9*, 11. doi:10.1186/1479-5868-9-23.

Verstuyf, J., Vansteenkiste, M., Soenens, B., Boone, L., & Mouratidis, A. (2013). Daily ups and downs in women's binge eating symptoms: The role of basic psychological needs, general self-control, and emotional eating. *Journal of Social and Clinical Psychology, 32*, 335–361.

Way, S. M. (2011). School discipline and disruptive classroom behavior: The moderating effects of student perceptions. *Sociological Quarterly, 52*, 346–375. doi:10.1111/j.1533-8525.2011.01210.x.

Chapter 5
How Can We Create Better Learning Contexts for Children? Promoting Students' Autonomous Motivation as a Way to Foster Enhanced Educational Outcomes

Frédéric Guay, Valérie Lessard, and Pascale Dubois

The consequences of school dropout are far reaching, for both individuals and the overall population. School dropout has generated about 1.9 billion dollars a year in costs (in lost taxes, additional social services, and return-to-school costs) in the province of Quebec, Canada (*Groupe d'action sur la persévérance et la réussite scolaires au Québec*; Ménard, 2009). At the individual level, less education translates into less social engagement compared to higher-educated individuals, particularly in terms of voting, volunteer work, and blood donation. Moreover, non-high-school graduates earn much lower annual incomes than graduates, and their unemployment rate is 2.1 times higher. They also have shorter life expectancy (Ménard, 2009).

Given the extent of this problem and the consequences for both individuals and society, we need to gain a better understanding of the factors that enable certain students to persevere in school and graduate while others do not. Can this problem be explained solely by students' learning difficulties and family characteristics? According to self-determination theory (SDT, Ryan & Deci, 2009), this is a reductionist view. Instead, SDT suggests that the learning environment in which students develop their academic competences must also be taken into account. For example, instead of nurturing curiosity and a desire to learn, some schools place the accent on control, reward, assessment, and competition, which impede the development of high-quality motivation. It was found that students who were sensitive to strict control simply abandoned their studies (Vallerand, Fortier, & Guay, 1997), probably in order to maintain their psychological integrity. Few adults in the job market would be happy to work in a highly controlled climate that quashed all initiative. Such working environments would drive many adults to quit. According to SDT (Ryan & Deci, 2009), students, even very young ones, would be no exception.

F. Guay (✉) • V. Lessard • P. Dubois
Université Laval, Québec, QC, Canada
e-mail: Frederic.Guay@fse.ulaval.ca; Valerie.Lessard@fse.ulaval.ca

© Springer Science+Business Media Singapore 2016
W.C. Liu et al. (eds.), *Building Autonomous Learners*,
DOI 10.1007/978-981-287-630-0_5

In recent decades, many empirical studies have used SDT as a conceptual framework to examine education environments. Most of these studies have considered the contribution of personal and environmental factors to the understanding of students' academic achievement, engagement, creativity, and well-being. The popularity of SDT among education researchers is due in part to the practical applications that have been generated (Pintrinch, 2003). For example, studies have demonstrated that the negative effect of controlling teaching practices on students' motivation has led to the development of teacher training programs designed to reduce teachers' use of such practices and increase their use of autonomy-supportive practices (e.g., Connell & Klem, 2000; Guay, Falardeau, & Valois, 2012; Reeve, Jang, Carrell, Jeon, & Barch, 2004). In this chapter, we describe the main instruments used to measure the types of motivation proposed by SDT. We then address the potential effects of these motivation types on students' emotions, learning strategies, academic achievement, and school perseverance. In addition, we look at the roles of parents, teachers, and peers in fostering certain motivation types. Some SDT-based intervention programs are then presented. Finally, we offer some practical implications of the reviewed studies and we propose several avenues for future research. We refer the reader to Deci and Ryan (2002) and Ryan and Deci (2009) for definitions of the main concepts and a complete presentation of the postulates of SDT.

Measuring School Motivation

Parents and teachers generally feel that motivation, or lack thereof, is associated with academic achievement. It is believed that students who work hard have a better chance of passing their exams. However, according to SDT, motivation is not a one-dimensional notion that is equivalent to effort. On the contrary, motivation is a multidimensional concept that varies in terms of quality. Students are said to have high-quality motivation when it is driven by intrinsic, integrated, or identified regulation and lower-quality motivation when it is driven by external or introjected regulation.

Various approaches have been adopted to measure students' motivation toward learning, including projective techniques and behavioral observations. However, these two approaches can be difficult to apply in the classroom. Consequently, in this review, we decided to cover questionnaires, which are easier to use to measure students' motivation. However, whereas motivation is easier to assess with questionnaires, the procedure must be rigorous. Therefore, questionnaire development and evaluation are key issues in the school motivation research. For instance, unless the metrological quality of the questionnaire has been well demonstrated, it is difficult to compile valid research results that advance the knowledge and lead to effective interventions and new education policies. In this chapter, we present the two currently most widely used instruments to assess student motivation: the Academic Motivation Scale (AMS, Vallerand et al., 1989) and the Self-Regulation Questionnaires developed by Ryan and Connell (1989). In addition, we present a new instrument designed to assess motivation in young elementary school students toward different school subjects.

The Academic Motivation Scale (AMS)   Vallerand and colleagues (1989) developed the Academic Motivation Scale (AMS) to measure three types of intrinsic motivation (knowledge, accomplishment, and stimulation), three types of extrinsic motivation (identified, introjected, and external), and amotivation. The scale contains 28 evenly distributed statements designed to assess the seven regulation types. Students are first asked why they are attending their high school, college, or university. They then rate the 28 responses to the question on a 5-point Likert scale ranging from (1) *does not correspond at all* to (5) *corresponds exactly*. The scale is available free online at the following site: http://www.er.uqam.ca/nobel/r26710/ LRCS/echelles_en.htm. It is noteworthy that the AMS has been used and validated in many countries, including Canada (Vallerand et al., 1992, 1993), Mexico (Lucas, Izquierdo, & Alonso, 2005), the United States (Fairchild, Horst, Finney, & Barron, 2005), France (Blanchard, Vrignaud, Lallemand, Dosnon, & Wach, 1997), and Greece (Barkoukis, Tsorbatzoudis, Grouios, & Sideridis, 2008).

In the first study to investigate the metrological quality of the French version of the scale, Vallerand et al. (1989) confirmed the seven-factor structure of the instrument and its convergent and divergent validity (see also Vallerand et al., 1992, 1993). More recently, Guay, Morin, Litalien, Valois, and Vallerand (2015) reviewed all the studies that evaluated the metrological quality of the original version of the AMS. They made the following observations: (1) score reliability was supported for all subscales, with most Cronbach's alphas above the critical value of 0.70; (2) the majority of studies supported the scale's factor validity, and confirmatory factor analyses supported the seven-factor structure, although some studies obtained low fit indices to the theoretical model; and (3) although the instrument validity was demonstrated in several aspects, certain shortcomings were observed: notably, some studies did not reproduce the simplex correlation pattern among the motivation types (Grouzet, Otis, & Pelletier, 2006; Otis, Grouzet, Frederick, & Pelletier, 2005; Ryan & Connell, 1989; Vallerand et al., 1989). In other words, stronger and more positive correlations were found between more distal motivations on the self-determination continuum (e.g., intrinsic motivation and introjected regulation) than between more proximal motivations (e.g., intrinsic motivation and identified regulation). The fact that the simplex correlation pattern was not supported in some studies brings into question one of the central postulates of SDT that the driving force for a given behavior varies in terms of quality. More precisely, because introjected motivation is positively associated with intrinsic motivation, we may conclude that this form of motivation is important for individual adaptation to the school environment. Hence, motivation would not be a question of quality, but rather intensity. Accordingly, given these somewhat inconclusive findings, Fairchild et al. (2005) proposed that the AMS items be revised to improve the construct validity.

Our research team (Guay et al., 2015) felt that Fairchild et al.'s suggestion was premature. Before undertaking a revision of the AMS items, we first wanted to understand why introjected and intrinsic motivation were so strongly correlated when measured by the AMS and why the fit indices for the theoretical model were so weak in some studies. It was suggested that the statistical methods used to date may have been responsible for these results. Accordingly, our team used a new method that takes into account the interrelationships between all the AMS items (i.e., exploratory structural equation modeling, ESEM). Results of two studies conducted in secondary school and college students appeared to support this hypothesis. Using this new statistical method, the correlations between intrinsic and introjected motivation were substantially lower and the fit indices for the measurement models were improved, supporting the validity of the AMS.

The Self-Regulation Questionnaire Ryan and Connell (1989) also developed an academic motivation scale called the Academic Self-Regulation Questionnaire (SRQ-A). It assesses three types of extrinsic motivation (external, introjected, and identified) as well as intrinsic motivation. The questionnaire items address the reasons that children do their schoolwork. It was developed for students in late elementary school and the beginning of middle school. It contains 32 evenly distributed statements assessing the four abovementioned motivation types. Students respond on a 4-point scale ranging from (1) *not at all true* to (4) *very true*. The questionnaire is available online at the following site: http://www.selfdeterminationtheory.org/ questionnaires.

Ryan and Connell's (1989) results underscore the questionnaire's validity and reliability. More specifically, the simplex correlation pattern between the four motivation types is supported (i.e., adjacent motivations on the continuum are more strongly and positively correlated than more distally placed motivations). Their studies also confirm that each motivation type has its own indicators (factorial validity), and each motivation type predicts different variables associated with academic achievement (see Ryan & Deci, 2009). Furthermore, the SRQ-A has been used with students and learners in different cultures, including Germany (Levesque, Zuehlke, Stanek, & Ryan, 2004; Wild & Krapp, 1995), Japan (Hayamizu, 1997; Yamauchi & Tanaka, 1998), Belgium (Vansteenkiste, Zhou, Lens, & Soenen, 2005), and throughout North America (Grolnick, Ryan, & Deci, 1991).

To our knowledge, the AMS and the SRQ-A are currently the primary instruments used to measure the motivation types proposed by SDT in education settings. Although highly useful, these two scales assess different types of motivation in relation to schoolwork in general, without considering the fact that motivations could differ across school subjects. Nevertheless, a growing number of researchers are examining motivation more specifically in relation to individual school subjects (see Elliot, 2005; Gottfried, 1985, 1990; Green, Martin, & Marsh, 2007; Pintrich, 2003), which raises the compelling question of whether the motivation types proposed by SDT are school subject-specific.

Elementary School Motivation Scale (ESMS) Our team recently developed an adapted version of the AMS to assess three types of motivation (intrinsic, identified regulation, and controlled regulation – combining introjection and external regulation) toward three school subjects (reading, writing, and mathematics; Guay et al., 2010). The items were adapted for elementary school children. Three items each assessed the three motivation types toward the three school subjects. Children were asked to indicate how often they performed school tasks on a 4-point scale ranging from (1) *no, never* to (4) *yes, all the time*. The full scale is provided in French and English in the appendix to Guay et al.'s (2010) article. Results provide reasonable support for the scale's factorial structure and good support for its convergent and divergent validity and the internal consistency of the item scores.

Moreover, results revealed that certain motivations were school subject-specific and others were not. For example, intrinsic motivation appeared to differ across mathematics, writing, and reading. Thus, students who enjoyed doing mathematics did not necessarily enjoy reading as much. This differentiation effect was also obtained for identified regulation, but not for controlled regulation. Consequently, it would be useful to assess intrinsic and identified regulation separately for different school subjects. Other authors have developed instruments to assess subject-specific motivation types (e.g., De Naeghel, Van Keer, & Vansteenkiste, 2010). We hope that researchers will pursue this avenue in order to better identify how different motivation types contribute to academic achievement.

In summary, education researchers apparently have valid and reliable instruments for assessing students' regulations. At this stage, we cannot claim that any one instrument is superior to another. The choice of instrument depends primarily on the research objectives and the target population.

Fostering Learning and Academic Achievement

The fundamental hypothesis of SDT is that students whose behaviors are regulated by self-determined motivations (i.e., intrinsic and identified regulation) will have more positive cognitive, behavioral, and emotional outcomes at school. Below, we present some studies that address these three outcomes.

Behavioral Outcomes

Perseverance In a survey study of over 4,000 high school students, Vallerand et al. (1997) demonstrated that students who dropped out of high school had lower intrinsic motivation, lower identified regulation, and higher amotivation compared to students who stayed in school (see also Vallerand & Bissonnette, 1992 for similar findings). No difference was found in external regulation. Surprisingly, students who persevered also showed higher introjected regulation than dropouts. In a similar study conducted in a sample of rural high school students, Hardre and Reeve (2003) showed that self-determined forms of motivation were associated with lower intentions to drop out, even when students' prior academic achievement was considered (see also Blanchard, Pelletier, Otis, & Sharp, 2004; Otis et al., 2005; Ratelle, Larose, Guay & Senécal, 2005). Vansteenkiste, Simons, Lens, Sheldon, and Deci

(2004, Study 2) demonstrated that self-determined motivation and perseverance in college students (measured using students' choice to do supplementary readings and problems) could be improved more by activating intrinsic academic goals (students were motivated by the intrinsic pleasure associated with the task or because the task reflected their integrated values) rather than extrinsic goals (students were motivated by external pressures or internal pressures such as guilt or intention to protect their self-esteem). Furthermore, a positive association was found between self-determined motivation and intentions to persevere in university graduate students (see Litalien & Guay, 2015). This relationship was indirect, mediated through students' perceived competence. In other words, doctoral students who pursue their studies because they enjoy them or because they find the program important for their personal development would feel more competent academically, which would encourage them to persevere in the program.

Thus, many studies on perseverance indicate that when students are motivated to do their schoolwork in a self-determined manner, they tend to persevere. That said, introjected regulation has also been positively linked to perseverance (Otis et al., 2005; Vallerand et al., 1997; Vansteenkiste et al., 2004), which goes against the postulates of SDT. Thus, introjection could improve perseverance, particularly at school, because students are often required to perform boring academic tasks. However, this type of motivation might come with psychological costs, including the development of less-than-optimal cognitive strategies as well as lower well-being and creativity.

Studies have also focused on the relationships between self-determined motivation and perseverance in specific school subjects. Generally, results are in line with the abovementioned studies: self-determined motivation is positively associated with perseverance (e.g., Black & Deci, 2000, for chemistry; Noels, Clément, & Pelletier, 2001, for language). For example, Lavigne, Vallerand, and Miquelon (2007) tested a model of intentions to persevere in science studies in a sample of 728 fourth-year high school students (aged 15 and 16 years) attending public schools in the Greater Montreal Area. Their results showed that students with strong intentions to persevere in science reported significantly higher intrinsic motivation and identified regulation and lower introjected regulation and amotivation than students with weak intentions to persevere. Thus, the more that motivation toward the sciences was self-determined, the greater the intentions to persevere in the field. Because external regulation was not assessed in this study, no conclusions could be drawn as to its effects.

Academic Achievement Numerous studies have established that self-determined motivation is positively associated with academic achievement (Fortier, Vallerand, & Guay, 1995; Grolnick et al., 1991; Guay & Vallerand, 1997; Miserandino, 1996; Ratelle, Guay, Vallerand, Larose, & Senécal, 2007, studies 2 and 3). Even more importantly, Guay and Vallerand (1997) demonstrated that self-determined motivation predicted higher achievement over one school year. Moreover, Guay, Ratelle, Roy, and Litalien (2010) in a study in over 900 high school students found that students with higher self-determined academic motivation raised their grades over a 1-year period. Therefore, if we compare two students with similar performance at a given time, the student whose motivation is more self-determined has a greater chance of performing better the following year than the student whose motivation is less self-determined.

The above studies assessed self-determined motivation with an index that combines the different regulation types proposed by SDT. However, this does not allow a detailed analysis of the relationships between the motivation types proposed by SDT and academic achievement. In a field and experimental study, Burton, Lydon, D'Alessandor, and Koestner (2006) showed that, of the two most commonly investigated types of self-determined motivation in education (i.e., intrinsic and identified), only identified motivation predicted academic performance. On the other hand, intrinsic motivation predicted students' psychological well-being. The authors concluded that the two motivation types act in tandem: intrinsic motivation enables students to preserve their psychological well-being at school when coping with academic problems, whereas identified regulation enables students to invest more effort into their studies and therefore perform better academically. In light of these findings, future research could attempt to gain a more in-depth understanding of the different types of motivation, including the controlled types (introjected and external), in relation to students' academic achievement.

Although it did not directly assess motivation types, a study in 2,520 students addressed the psychological needs proposed by SDT and found that attending college or university with the motivation to satisfy the needs for autonomy and competence was associated with higher academic achievement and greater intentions to persevere (Guiffrida, Lynch, Wall, & Abel, 2013). However, motivation to satisfy the need for relatedness showed a different relationship with academic achievement: results underscored that this motivation was associated with lower academic achievement. This result is surprising, as positive peer relationships have been associated with higher academic achievement in elementary school children (Guay, Boivin, & Hodges, 1999). According to Guiffrida et al. (2013), it is probable that students who are motivated to develop positive relationships with peers have put less effort in their academic work. Nevertheless, results indicated that attending college or university to satisfy the need for relatedness to professors and school staff was linked to higher academic achievement. Therefore, motivation to satisfy the need for relatedness could at times be beneficial and at other time not, especially if this need conflicts with other goals, such as developing disciplinary competences. Taken together, these studies indicate that when students invest in their studies for self-determined motives or to fulfill certain basic psychological needs, they tend to perform better (see Ryan & Deci, 2009).

At a time when schools are increasingly using rigorous admissions criteria (grades, admission tests) to select students, we must not be persuaded by the philosophy that we have to create a competitive environment if we want students to do well at school. In fact, the research has demonstrated exactly the opposite: the heavier the external pressure placed on students, the worse their performance. Nevertheless, as in all research domains, these results have not been entirely corroborated. Some studies have found weak correlations between self-determined motivations and academic performance (Cokley, Bernard, Cunningham, & Motoike, 2001; Fairchild et al., 2005). Further research is therefore needed in order to gain a deeper understanding of these contradictory results.

Cognitive Outcomes

Learning and Seeking Challenges Students with self-determined motivation retain information more easily, consolidate material better (e.g., Benware & Deci, 1984; Grolnick & Ryan, 1987; Vansteenkiste et al., 2004), and are more inclined to attempt to accomplish difficult tasks in order to develop their competences (e.g., Boggiano, Main, & Katz, 1988).

In an experimental study of fifth-grade elementary students, Grolnick and Ryan (1987) noted that students learned and retained knowledge differently according to their degree of autonomy. Students who expected to be assessed (i.e., low autonomy condition) showed weaker conceptual learning than students who did not expect to be assessed (i.e., high autonomy condition). Similar results were obtained by Vansteenkiste and colleagues (2004), who observed that self-determined motivation acted as an explanatory variable in the relationship between goals, classroom climate (controlling or autonomy-supportive), and superficial versus deep-level processing of learning material. They demonstrated that the pursuit of intrinsic goals combined with an autonomy-supportive classroom climate produced a positive effect on the use of "less superficial" learning strategies and test performance. For example, students who read a text and relate it to information that they have already learned are using a deeper-level learning strategy that is associated with better performance. Inversely, students who skip the parts of the text that they do not understand very well are using a superficial learning strategy that is associated with weaker performance.

Oxford and Ehrman (1995) examined the relationship between adults' language learning strategies and various factors such as competence, sex, aptitude, learning style, personality type, motivation, and anxiety. They found a significant positive association between intrinsic motivation and the use of metacognitive strategies (paying attention, consciously seeking opportunities to practice, planning language tasks, self-evaluating one's progress, and error monitoring). Vandergrift (2005) examined the relationships between motivation, metacognition, and competence in oral comprehension in 57 students aged 13 and 14 years and learning French as a second language. Students were administered a questionnaire to assess their degree of amotivation, intrinsic motivation, and extrinsic motivation types in relation to second language learning. A metacognitive awareness questionnaire was used to assess the strategies that the students used when listening to French texts. As expected, significant correlations were obtained between the motivation types and strategy uses. The more self-determined the motivation (intrinsic or identified over introjected or external), the stronger the association with the use of metacognitive strategies for language learning (see Baleghizadeh & Rahimi, 2011, for similar results in university students). Results also indicated that most of the strategies were negatively correlated with amotivation. In summary, the above studies converge toward the conclusion that self-determined motivations play an influential role in fostering the use of various metacognitive strategies.

Affective Outcomes

In line with the postulates of SDT, Vallerand and colleagues (1989) showed that students with higher self-determined motivation reported more positive emotions in class, greater enjoyment of schoolwork, and greater satisfaction at school (see also Black & Deci, 2000; Ryan & Connell, 1989). Moreover, Black and Deci (2000) demonstrated that students who took college chemistry courses for self-determined reasons (versus controlled reasons) perceived themselves as less anxious about passing the courses (Black & Deci, 2000). In a study of German and American students, Levesque et al. (2004) investigated the associations between motivation types and subjective well-being. They showed that, despite differences in mean self-determined motivation between the two groups (German students felt significantly higher self-determined motivation than American students), self-determined motivation was positively associated with subjective well-being in both groups. With respect to introjected regulation, as mentioned above, studies (e.g., Vallerand et al., 1997) have correlated it positively to school perseverance. However, Ryan and Connell (1989) found a positive correlation between introjected regulation and cognitive anxiety in children, supporting the hypothesis that introjection may come with affective costs for students.

Academic Motivation: A Student-Centered Approach

Studies addressing relationships between the motivation types and student outcomes have demonstrated the importance of promoting self-determined forms of motivation. Most of these studies adopted an approach that centers on this variable by determining relationships between the motivation types and various adaptation indices. However, they did not compare students' motivation profiles using a person-centered approach. In one study (Ratelle et al., 2007), we used a person-centered approach to examine motivation in high school students. More specifically, we determined whether students would present different motivation profiles and whether certain profiles would be more beneficial than others for students' adjustment to school. The analyses revealed three distinct profiles, including one that combined high self-determined (intrinsic and identified regulation) and controlled (external and introjected regulation) motivations. Students with this profile had more positive school adjustment indices (i.e., higher performance, better concentration and satisfaction, and less absenteeism and anxiety). Surprisingly, we did not find a profile characterized by low controlled motivation and high self-determined motivation. In other words, we were unable to identify a group of students who attended high school solely for self-determined reasons. This anomalous result may be attributed to the high school climate, which was probably too controlling to foster this particular profile. We consequently examined a college setting, which offers students more choice (e.g., program selection, flexible schedules, ability to drop certain courses without penalty). In this study, we discovered a profile characterized by high self-determined motivation and low controlled motivation. This group of students was more perseverant than the group with high self-determined and controlled motivation. Taken together, Ratelle et al.'s (2007) results suggest that students' motivation profiles are sensitive to the educational setting and that students would be more likely to develop a self-determined profile in college than in high school. Furthermore, these results support the hypothesis that self-determined forms of motivation are the most beneficial for school adjustment.

Hayenga and Corpus (2010) also used a person-centered approach to determine associations between different motivation profiles and academic achievement in high school. Of the 343 students studied, those with "high-quantity" (high intrinsic and extrinsic motivation) and "good-quality" (high intrinsic and low extrinsic motivation) profiles tended to earn better grades than students with "low-quantity" (low motivation) and "poor-quality" (low intrinsic and high extrinsic motivation) profiles. However, students with a "good-quality" profile obtained better grades than students with all other profiles.

Boiché, Sarrazin, Grouzet, Pelletier, and Chanal (2008) also used a person-centered approach to investigate high school students' motivation in physical education, a subject that is characterized by fewer constraints. They found a self-determined motivation profile associated with higher grades in physical education compared to other motivation profiles (see also Gillet, Vallerand, & Rosnet, 2009). Taken together, these studies evidence the importance of comparing motivation profiles. Moreover, they suggest that the classroom or school climate can be an influential factor in fostering a motivation profile in which self-determined motivation predominates over controlled motivation.

Determinants of Academic Motivation: The Role of Parents, Teachers, and Peers

Assuming that self-determined motivation is optimal for students, it is important to identify the environmental conditions that can contribute to develop it. The SDT-based research has demonstrated that autonomy support is instrumental for mobilizing students' motivational resources. Below, we review the research on autonomy support with respect to three significant individuals in students' lives: parents, teachers, and peers.

Autonomy Support Provided by Parents

Because parents are the primary agents of socialization in their child's life, we would expect them to have a significant influence on students' self-determined motivation (Pomerantz, Grolnick, & Price, 2005). Parents who are autonomy-supportive consider their children's perspectives, provide them with opportunities to act within certain guidelines, and offer meaningful rationales to explain why they must do less interesting activities. This enables the child to develop a more self-determined motivation toward school. These findings have emerged from studies that employed a variety of objective methods to assess parents' autonomy support, including external judges (Grolnick & Ryan, 1989), parents' logbooks (Aunola, Viljaranta, Lehtinen, & Nurmi, 2013), and children's evaluations (Grolnick et al., 1991; Niemiec et al., 2006; Ratelle et al., 2005; Vallerand et al., 1997).

Researchers have frequently used students' perceptions to assess the degree of autonomy support provided by parents. In general, mothers tend to be perceived as more autonomy-supportive than fathers (Grolnick et al., 1991), even though perceptions of mother's and father's autonomy support also tend to be positively associated (Niemiec et al., 2006). However, when assessed by external judges, mother's and father's degree of autonomy support appear to be rather similar (Grolnick & Ryan, 1989).

In attempts to predict self-determined academic motivation, contradictory results have been obtained on the relative influence of the two parents. Some studies (e.g., Grolnick et al., 1991; Guay & Chanal, 2008) provided evidence that autonomy support by both parents significantly predicted greater self-determined motivation in children. Others (e.g., d'Ailly, 2003; Grolnick & Ryan, 1989) have noted that only autonomy-supportive mothers produced greater self-determined academic motivation in their children. The study by Gillet, Vallerand, and Lafrenière (2012) concurs with this conclusion by demonstrating that students' perceptions of mother's autonomy support alone were associated with self-determined academic motivation, with no association with perceptions of father's autonomy support. Because most of the researches on parental autonomy support have considered either the mother's parenting style or the combined styles of both parents, further studies are needed to untangle the separate roles of mother and father in supporting their child's autonomy. For example, it would be instructive to examine whether having two autonomy-supportive parents is associated with more self-determined regulation. In the absence of this optimal parental condition, would at least one autonomy-supportive parent help protect the child from the negative outcomes associated with a controlling style by the other parent (see Simons & Conger, 2007)?

Certain factors could moderate the positive relationship between parents' autonomy support and the child's development of self-determined motivation. First, it is arguable that the influence of autonomy support would diminish as children grow up. It is known that as children mature they become more independent from their parents when performing academic tasks. However, studies in children in elementary school (Grolnick & Ryan, 1989; Grolnick et al., 1991), high school (Vallerand et al., 1997), college, and university (Ratelle, Guay, Larose, & Senécal, 2004, Ratelle et al., 2005; Vansteenkiste et al., 2005) have shown that autonomy support by parents is instrumental for the development of self-determined motivation. Thus, even young adults continue to benefit from having autonomy-supportive parents. The effect could be even stronger during times of stress, such as the transition to high school or college (Grolnick, Kurowski, Dunlap, & Hevey, 2000; Ratelle et al., 2004, 2005). For example, our results revealed that students' perceptions of autonomy support by parents were associated with more self-determined regulation trajectories during the transition to college (Ratelle et al., 2004).

We might also contend that parental autonomy support benefits only "normal" students or those living in Western cultures. More specifically, we would expect students with emotional handicaps and/or learning problems to function more effectively in settings where their behaviors are regulated by reinforcements (Maag, 2001; see Deci, Hodges, Pierson, & Tomassone, 1992, for a discussion). In addition, we would expect students from cultures that emphasize interdependence among their members to benefit less from an autonomy-supportive parenting style compared to students from more individualistic cultures. Nevertheless, studies have demonstrated many advantages associated with autonomy support, for both students with learning problems (Deci et al., 1992) and students in collectivist cultures such as China (d'Ailly, 2003; Vansteenkiste et al., 2005) and Russia (Chirkov & Ryan, 2001).

Autonomy Support Provided by Teachers

Because teachers are the primary adults who interact with children at school, they are expected to exert a significant influence on children's self-determined motivation. Like parents, autonomy-supportive teachers foster self-determined motivation in their students (Reeve, 2002, 2006). It is noteworthy that this conclusion has been drawn for students in elementary school (e.g., Ryan & Grolnick, 1986), high school (e.g., Trouilloud, Sarrazin, Bressoux, & Bois, 2006), and college and university (e.g., Williams & Deci, 1996). In addition, the same conclusion was drawn for students with severe behavioral problems (e.g., Savard, Joussemet, Pelletier, & Mageau, 2013). Again like parents, and irrespective of education level or children's problems, teachers who adopt an autonomy-supportive teaching style contribute to more self-determined motivation in their students. Although most studies have assessed students' perceptions of teaching styles, similar results have been obtained using teachers' perceptions (e.g., Deci, Schwartz, Sheinman, & Ryan, 1981). Moreover, the advantages of teachers' autonomy support for students' motivation do not appear to be culture dependent, as similar results have been found in non-Western cultures such as Russia (Chirkov & Ryan, 2001) and China (Hardré, Chen, Huang, Chiang, Jen, & Warden, 2006).

Some studies have attempted to determine how autonomy support benefits students enrolled in demanding (and often rigid) university programs. For example, in a study conducted in medical students, having an autonomy-supportive professor predicted higher self-determined motivation in students. In addition, this effect was sustained over a 2-year period (Williams & Deci, 1996). Another study by Sheldon and Krieger (2007) found that law students who perceived higher autonomy support by their professors reported higher self-determined motivation. These results suggest that teachers' autonomy support can offset the negative effects associated with certain characteristics of these academic programs (e.g., heavy demands, competition, and rigidity).

Combined Assessment of Autonomy Support Provided by Parents and Teachers

So far, we have presented the separate contributions of parents and teachers to students' self-determined motivation. In fact, very few studies have assessed the combined contribution of parents and teachers to explain this motivation type. In a sample of Chinese elementary school students, d'Ailly (2003) determined the contribution of autonomy support by significant adults to students' motivational resources and academic achievement. Results suggest that parents (and particularly mothers) played a similar role to that of teachers in explaining self-determined motivation (see also Gillet et al., 2012). In another study in a sample of high school students in Quebec (Canada), autonomy support by parents was a better predictor of students' feeling of autonomy compared to autonomy support by teachers and school administrators (Vallerand et al., 1997). It was noteworthy that autonomy support by teachers and by administrators contributed similarly to students' feeling of autonomy. Students' feeling of autonomy was in turn positively associated with self-determined academic motivation. This suggests that in education settings, adults other than teachers can contribute to students' development of motivational resources. Vallerand et al.'s (1997) study is the only one to assess the role of perceived autonomy support by administrators in academic motivation.

Few studies have verified whether students' motivation is more self-determined when several significant persons provide them with autonomy support versus only a few significant persons. To respond to this question, Guay, Ratelle, Vitaro, and Vallerand (2013) examined a sample of 1,407 high school students. First, correlation analyses revealed that perceptions of autonomy support by three significant persons (mother, father, and teacher) were relatively independent, indicating that high school students are capable of differentiating between social relationships and can assess their separate roles. Using a student-centered statistical approach, the authors then identified autonomy support profiles. Among other things, results showed that students who perceived receiving autonomy support from their mother, father, and teacher had higher grades, were more self-determinedly motivated (intrinsic and identified regulation), and perceived themselves as more academically competent than students who perceived these three significant persons as less autonomy-supportive. Moreover, it appeared that autonomy support by mother and teacher was sufficient to maintain students' self-determined motivation and perceived competence, although for best outcomes, all sources (including father) should support student autonomy (additive effect). Thus, it is possible that the father–child relationship would focus more on the performance, mastery, and development of competence than for the interactions characterizing the other relationships (Collins & Russell, 1991). Consequently, autonomy support by father could be more influential than autonomy support by other sources in fostering academic achievement.

Autonomy Support Provided by Peers

In the SDT research, very few studies have examined the role of autonomy support by peers. Nevertheless, studies in other research fields have demonstrated that peers play an instrumental role, sometimes surpassing that of parents, in fostering certain behaviors in youths, such as greater autonomy and self-regulation of action (Villacorta, Koestner, & Lekes, 2003). Guay, Senécal, Gauthier, and Fernet (2003) proposed a model whereby autonomy support by peers and parents predicts career indecision in students through perceived competence and autonomy. This model was tested in a sample of 834 Quebec students attending college. Results showed that the higher the perceived autonomy support by parents and peers, the higher the perceived competence in career decision activities. These perceptions were in turn associated with less career indecision (Guay et al., 2003). Accordingly, peers appear to have considerable influence on the development of student motivation (see also Villacorta et al., 2003).

Other studies conducted in non-education settings have demonstrated that autonomy support by peers is influential for the development of more self-determined motivation (intrinsic and identified) in youths (e.g., Pihu & Hein, 2007; Beiswenger & Grolnick, 2010, in physical activity settings). However, further studies are needed to gain a deeper understanding of how autonomy support by peers fosters motivation in students of all ages and across a variety of education settings.

School Intervention Programs

Self-determination theory (SDT) has guided the development of intervention programs designed to develop more self-determined school motivation and hence to improve students' perseverance and academic achievement. We present below several examples of such programs.

First, some intervention programs have targeted autonomy support by teachers in order to foster more self-determined motivation in students (Su & Reeve, 2011). In general, studies have shown that interventions designed to teach teachers how to support autonomy in their students result in higher student perceptions of autonomy support (e.g., Amrita, 2011; Cheon, Reeve, & Moon, 2012; Reeve et al., 2004). Furthermore, the impact of these interventions is not limited to students' perceptions. For example, Reeve and colleagues (2004) developed a program to enhance engagement in high school students by teaching teachers how to support students' autonomy. Teachers in the experimental group received autonomy support training. In a series of classroom observations, the judges assessed the autonomy support provided by each teacher and their students' engagement in academic tasks. Trained teachers showed significantly more autonomy-supportive behaviors compared to control teachers. In addition, the more that teachers used autonomy-supportive practices in class, the more engaged their students were in their tasks. Similarly, Kaplan and Assor (2012) developed a teacher training program focusing on the importance of having autonomy-supportive talks and discussions with high school students. The program was implemented in 18 classes of Grade 7 students (420 students). Results showed that having autonomy-supportive talks and discussions with students was associated with higher positive emotions in students, more positive perceptions of the teacher, and fewer negative emotions and violence in class. In summary, these studies provide evidence of the importance of providing teachers with better training in autonomy-supportive practices and suggest that these practices could help students feel more supported, experience more positive emotions, and develop more self-determined school motivation.

In their meta-analysis, Su and Reeve (2011) shed light on the conditions liable to foster more effective intervention programs to develop autonomy support. Such programs would be most effective when they: (a) cover several elements of autonomy support (e.g., providing meaningful rationales for tasks, acknowledging students' perspectives and feelings, offering choices, nurturing motivational resources, and using non-controlling language); (b) are given over a period of about 1–3 h in a laboratory setting, where nuisance effects can be controlled; and (c) engage teachers in knowledge- and skill-based activities using a variety of media (e.g., paper and electronic). In addition, these programs appear to be more effective when they are offered to teachers rather than principals and other school administrators or when they are offered to novice teachers just beginning their career.

Other multiple-element intervention programs have been developed to promote more self-determined motivation in students and to enhance their competence in various school subjects. To illustrate this type of program and the outcomes for students, we present two programs that were developed for elementary school reading and writing. First, the Reading Within Family and School program (LiFuS; for German-speaking children in Switzerland) was developed by Villiger and colleagues to promote reading in fourth-year elementary school children (Villiger, Niggli, Wandeler, & Kutzelmann, 2012). The study examined the effects of a family–school intervention program designed to create family and school environments that support motivation to read and hence improve students' reading motivation and text comprehension. In order to determine the specific contribution of the family environment, the program was administered to a group without ($n=244$) and with ($N=225$) parents' participation. Results showed that the family–school intervention had significant effects on students' reading enjoyment and curiosity. In addition, the effect on reading enjoyment remained at the 5-month follow-up. However, no effect was observed on self-concept in reading or on text comprehension. These results underscore the importance of promoting self-determined reading, not only at school but in the family as well.

The CASIS-Écriture training program (cooperation, authentic activities, support for autonomy, involvement, and structure) was designed to help elementary school teachers increase their students' motivation in writing (Guay et al., 2012). The program aims to develop five pedagogical practices: cooperation, meaningful activities, autonomy support, engagement, and structuring. An evaluation study (Guay et al., 2012) conducted in 18 teachers and 273 students in second-year elementary school revealed that students of teachers who received the CASIS training (experimental group) improved significantly over the school year in self-determined writing motivation compared to control students (whose teachers did not receive CASIS training), who showed decreased self-determined writing motivation. Moreover, students in the experimental group performed better than controls on a dictation at the end of the school year while controlling for ability at the beginning of the school year. In light of these results (and despite the small sample), it appears that enriching teaching practices through professional training would be an effective way to motivate students to write and therefore to improve their writing skills.

Various SDT-related intervention programs have been created and evaluated in an effort to intervene more effectively with at-risk clients. Konrad and colleagues (2007) reviewed studies that evaluated SDT-based intervention programs for students with learning problems (LP) and/or attention deficit hyperactivity disorder (ADHD). Results showed that autonomy-supportive interventions have been the most frequently studied, followed by interventions combining autonomy support and one or several other SDT-related components. In their meta-analysis, Shogren and colleagues (2004) investigated the efficacy of using choice making as an intervention to reduce problem behavior. Results showed that, overall, providing choice opportunities to students resulted in clinically significant reductions in problem behavior.

In sum, an impressive number of STD-based intervention programs have emerged in recent years, and the research has demonstrated their overall effectiveness in helping students (from elementary to high school and college and with a variety of learning and behavioral problems) to develop more self-determined school motivation. In addition, many training programs for parents and educators have emphasized autonomy-supportive practices. However, other elements (e.g., structured learning activities and adults' engagement with students) have been examined as well and could be explored further to gain a deeper understanding of how they contribute to students' motivation.

Conclusion: Practical Implications for Teachers and Future Perspectives

We have presented an overview of education studies based on self-determination theory (SDT), revealing a number of relevant observations. First, the different types of intrinsic and extrinsic motivation can be assessed with a variety of reliable and valid scales. In addition, studies have demonstrated that certain motivation types are school subject-specific. It would be useful in future research to explore why self-determined regulations differ across school subjects, compared to controlled motivations, which differ less. Could self-determined regulations be governed more by the school environment, with controlled regulations governed more by other factors, such as the student's personality and family environment? In addition, the more that students' motivation is self-determined, the better their academic performance, the longer they persist, the better they learn, the greater their satisfaction, and the more positive their emotions at school. Studies using a person-centered approach also suggest that a profile characterized by high self-determined and controlled motivation is generally associated with positive outcomes but that more benefits result from a purely self-determined motivation profile (high self-determined and low controlled motivation). Future research could seek to understand why a large proportion of students have a high self-determined and controlled motivation profile. How was this profile developed? What environmental factors at school and at home led to this particular development?

We have also discovered that parents, peers, and teachers who support students' autonomy can foster self-determined motivation. However, the unique contribution of father's autonomy support to the development of students' self-determined school motivation has received little attention, along with the role of peers. Could fathers play a distinct role in nurturing students' motivational resources? Furthermore, could the parents exert a mutual influence on their ability to support their child's autonomy? More specifically, would an autonomy-supportive parent influence the partner to become more autonomy-supportive? Finally, we must emphasize that certain intervention programs appear to be effective in fostering students' self-determined motivation. However, further intervention studies are needed to more definitively determine whether the benefits of these programs are felt across diverse student populations (e.g., students with learning problems, with disadvantaged parents, from different ethnic groups). Taken together, the findings of the studies reviewed here provide support for the various postulates of STD.

In light of these various findings, what are the practical implications for teachers? Several suggestions could be proposed, but we focus herein only on four of them. First and foremost, learning activities proposed by teachers should be intrinsically motivating. This might sound obvious, but frequently we notice that teachers use pedagogical activities that are tedious thereby having the unfortunate consequence of not nurturing children's intrinsic curiosity (e.g., overuse of rote learning instead of focusing on rich educational tasks). Teachers are thus invited to create educational tasks that are authentic or meaningful for children. This could be achieved by knowing more about students' interests and preferences. Second, in order to support children's autonomy, it is important to: (1) acknowledge their negative feelings, (2) provide meaningful rationales for performing an activity, (3) use a language that it is non-controlling (avoiding threat, punishments or rewards to motivate behaviors), (4) offer choices in various learning activities, and (5) nurture motivational resources (Su & Reeve, 2011). Third, teachers should provide feedback that foster students' perceived competence and autonomous learning. According to Hattie and Timperley (2007), the main purpose of feedback is to diminish the gap between students' current performance and their expected performance. This gap can be reduced when the teacher provides feedback clarifying the objective and success criteria, informing students about their current performance in direct and concrete terms, and guiding them toward goal achievement. Fourth, it is important to establish positive relationships with students. For example, it may be useful to schedule a time to meet individually with students. Cooperative work is a pedagogical practice that allows individual meetings because teachers have not to focus their attention on other students since they are busy. The teacher, during these meetings, may take the time to discuss with students about their values, needs, and interests. In such a context, students would feel connected to their teachers because they are interested in their preferences and emotional states rather than on their grades.

We hope that this brief overview will inspire new research directions and innovative intervention programs. Also, we encourage educators to draw on the available research in an effort to improve their pedagogical and educational practices in order to help students realize their full potential.

References

Amrita, K. (2011). *Effects of teacher autonomy support intervention on Thai students' motivation: A self-determination theory perspective.* Doctoral dissertation, Universiti Utara Malaysia. Retrieved from http://etd.uum.edu.my/2966/

Aunola, K., Viljaranta, J., Lehtinen, E., & Nurmi, J. E. (2013). The role of maternal support of competence, autonomy and relatedness in children's interests and mastery orientation. *Learning and Individual Differences, 25*, 171–177. doi:10.1016/j.lindif.2013.02.002.

Baleghizadeh, S., & Rahimi, A. H. (2011). The relationship among listening performance, metacognitive strategy use and motivation from a self-determination theory perspective. *Theory and Practice in Language Studies, 1*, 61–67. doi:10.4304/tpls.1.1.61-67.

Barkoukis, V., Tsorbatzoudis, H., Grouios, G., & Sideridis, G. (2008). The assessment of intrinsic and extrinsic motivation and amotivation: Validity and reliability of the Greek version of the academic motivation scale. *Assessment in Education: Principles, Policy & Practice, 15*, 39–55. doi:10.1080/09695940701876128.

Beiswenger, K. L., & Grolnick, W. S. (2010). Interpersonal and intrapersonal factors associated with autonomous motivation in adolescents' after-school activities. *Journal of Early Adolescence, 30*(3), 369–394. doi:10.1177/0272431609333298.

Benware, C., & Deci, E. L. (1984). Quality of learning with an active versus passive motivational set. *American Educational Research Journal, 21*, 755–765. doi:10.3102/00028312021004755.

Black, A. E., & Deci, E. L. (2000). The effects of instructors' autonomy support and students' autonomous motivation on learning organic chemistry: A self-determination theory perspective. *Science Education, 84*(6), 740–756. doi:10.1002/1098-237X(200011)84:6<740::AID-SCE4>3.0.CO;2-3.

Blanchard, C., Pelletier, L., Otis, N., & Sharp, E. (2004). Rôle de l'autodétermination et des aptitudes scolaires dans la prédiction des absences scolaires et l'intention de décrocher. *Revue des Sciences de l'éducation, 30*(1), 105–123. doi:10.7202/011772ar.

Blanchard, S., Vrignaud, P., Lallemand, N., Dosnon, O., & Wach, M. (1997). Validation de l'échelle de motivation en éducation auprès de lycéens français. *L'Orientation Scolaire et Professionnelle, 26*, 33–56.

Boggiano, A. K., Main, D. S., & Katz, P. A. (1988). Children's preference for challenge: The role of perceived competence and control. *Journal of Personality and Social Psychology, 54*, 134–141. doi:10.1037/0022-3514.54.1.134.

Boiché, J. C. S., Sarrazin, P. G., Grouzet, F. M. E., Pelletier, L. G., & Chanal, J. (2008). Students' motivation profiles and achievement outcomes in physical education: A self-determination perspective. *Journal of Educational Psychology, 100*, 688–701. doi:10.1037/0022-0663.100.3.688.

Burton, K. D., Lydon, J. E., D'Alessandro, D. U., & Koestner, R. (2006). The differential effects of intrinsic and identified motivation on well-being and performance: Prospective, experimental, and implicit approaches to self-determination theory. *Journal of Personality and Social Psychology, 91*, 750–762. doi:10.1037/0022-3514.91.4.750.

Cheon, S. H., Reeve, J., & Moon, I. S. (2012). Experimentally based, longitudinally designed, teacher-focused intervention to help physical education teachers be more autonomy supportive toward their students. *Journal of Sport & Exercise Psychology, 34*, 365–396. Retrieved from https://bmri.korea.ac.kr/file/board_data/publications/1349685409_1.pdf.

Chirkov, V. I., & Ryan, R. M. (2001). Parent and teacher autonomy-support in Russian and U.S. adolescents: Common effects on well-being and academic motivation. *Journal of Cross Cultural Psychology, 32*, 618–635. doi:10.1177/0022022101032005006.

Cokley, K. O., Bernard, N., Cunningham, D., & Motoike, J. (2001). A psychometric investigation of the academic motivation scale using a United States sample. *Measurement and Evaluation in Counseling and Development, 34*, 109–119. doi:10.1037/0033-2909.107.2.238.

Collins, W. A., & Russell, G. (1991). Mother-child and father-child relationships in middle childhood and adolescence: A developmental analysis. *Developmental Review, 11*(2), 99–136. doi:10.1016/0273-2297(91)90004-8.

Connell, J. P., & Klem, A. M. (2000). You can get there from here: Using a theory of change approach to plan urban education reform. *Journal of Educational and Psychological Consulting, 11*, 93–120. doi:10.1207/s1532768Xjepc1101_06.

D'Ailly, H. (2003). Children's autonomy and perceived control in learning: A model of motivation and achievement in Taiwan. *Journal of Educational Psychology, 95*, 84–96. doi:10.1037/0022-0663.95.1.84.

De Naeghel, J., Van Keer, H., & Vansteenkiste, M. (2010). *Measuring reading motivation in elementary school.* Paper presented at the Fourth International Conference on Self-Determination Theory. Abstract retrieved from http://hdl.handle.net/1854/LU-3130850

Deci, E. L., Hodges, R., Pierson, L., & Tomassone, J. (1992). Autonomy and competence as motivational factors in students with learning disabilities and emotional handicaps. *Journal of Learning Disabilities, 25*, 457–471. doi:10.1177/002221949202500706.

Deci, E. L., & Ryan, R. M. (2002). *Handbook of self-determination research.* Rochester, NY: The university of Rochester Press.

Deci, E. L., Schwartz, A. J., Sheinman, L., & Ryan, R. M. (1981). An instrument to assess adults' orientations toward control versus autonomy with children: Reflections on intrinsic motivation and perceived competence. *Journal of Educational Psychology, 73*, 642–650. doi:10.1037/0022-0663.73.5.642.

Elliot, A. J. (2005). A conceptual history of the achievement goal construct. In A. J. Elliot & C. S. Dweck (Eds.), *Handbook of competence and motivation* (pp. 52–72). New York: Guilford Press.

Fairchild, A. J., Horst, S. J., Finney, S. J., & Barron, K. E. (2005). Evaluating existing and new validity evidence for the academic motivation scale. *Contemporary Educational Psychology, 30*, 331–358. doi:10.1016/j.cedpsych.2004.11.001.

Fortier, M. S., Vallerand, R. J., & Guay, F. (1995). Academic motivation and school performance: Toward a structural model. *Contemporary Educational Psychology, 20*, 257–274. doi:10.1006/ceps.1995.1017.

Gillet, N., Vallerand, R., & Lafrenière, M. A. (2012). Intrinsic and extrinsic school motivation as a function of age: The mediating role of autonomy support. *Social Psychology of Education: An International Journal, 15*, 77–95. doi:10.1007/s11218-011-9170-2.

Gillet, N., Vallerand, R. J., & Rosnet, E. (2009). Motivational clusters and performance in a real-life setting. *Motivation and Emotion, 33*, 49–62. doi:10.1007/s11031-008-9115-z.

Gottfried, A. E. (1985). Academic intrinsic motivation in elementary and junior high school students. *Journal of Educational Psychology, 77*, 631–645. doi:10.1037/0022-0663.77.6.631.

Gottfried, A. E. (1990). Academic intrinsic motivation in young elementary school children. *Journal of Educational Psychology, 82*, 525–538. doi:10.1037/0022-0663.82.3.525.

Green, J., Martin, A., & Marsh, H. W. (2007). Motivation and engagement in English, mathematics and science high school subjects: Towards an understanding of multidimensional domain specificity. *Learning and Individual Differences, 17*, 269–279. doi:10.1016/j.lindif.2006.12.003.

Grolnick, W. S., Kurowski, C. O., Dunlap, K. G., & Hevey, C. (2000). Parental resources and the transition to junior high. *Journal of Research on Adolescence, 10*, 465–488. doi:10.1207/SJRA1004_05.

Grolnick, W. S., & Ryan, R. M. (1987). Autonomy in children's learning: An experimental and individual difference investigation. *Journal of Personality and Social Psychology, 52*, 890–898. doi:10.1037/0022-3514.52.5.890.

Grolnick, W. S., & Ryan, R. M. (1989). Parent styles associated with children's self-regulation and competence in school. *Journal of Educational Psychology, 81*, 143–154. doi:10.1037/0022-0663.81.2.143.

Grolnick, W. S., Ryan, R. M., & Deci, E. L. (1991). Inner resources for school performance: Motivational mediators of children's perceptions of their parents. *Journal of Educational Psychology, 83*, 508–517. doi:10.1037/0022-0663.83.4.508.

Grouzet, F. M. E., Otis, N., & Pelletier, L. G. (2006). Longitudinal cross-gender factorial invariance of the academic motivation scale. *Structural Equation Modeling: A Multidisciplinary Journal, 13*, 73–98. doi:10.1207/s15328007sem1301_4.

Guay, F., Boivin, M., & Hodges, E. V. (1999). Predicting change in academic achievement: A model of peer experiences and self-system processes. *Journal of Educational Psychology, 91*, 105–115. doi:10.1037/0022-0663.91.1.105.

Guay, F., & Chanal, J. (2008). Meet the parents: Mothers and fathers' contextual and psychological resources associated to adolescents' perceptions of parental autonomy support. In H. W. Marsh, R. G. Craven, & D. M. McInerney (Eds.), *Self-processes, learning, and enabling human potential: Dynamic new approaches* (Advances in self research, Vol. 3, pp. 145–169). Charlotte, NC: Information Age Publishing.

Guay, F., Chanal, J., Ratelle, C. F., Marsh, H. W., Larose, S., & Boivin, M. (2010). Intrinsic identified and controlled types of motivation for school subjects in young elementary school children. *British Journal of Educational Psychology, 80*, 711–735. doi:10.1348/0007099 10X499084.

Guay, F., Falardeau, E., & Valois, P. (2012). Évaluer l'efficacité et l'impact du programme d'intervention "CASIS-écriture" pour augmenter la motivation des élèves du primaire envers l'écriture. Rapport de recherche inédit.

Guay, F., Morin, A. J., Litalien, D., Valois, P., & Vallerand, R. J. (2015). Application of exploratory structural equation modeling to evaluate the Academic Motivation Scale. *Journal of Experimental Education, 83(1):*51–82. doi:10.1080/00220973.2013.876231.

Guay, F., Ratelle, C. F., Roy, A., & Litalien, D. (2010). Academic self-concept, autonomous academic motivation, and academic achievement: Mediating and additive effects. *Learning and Individual Differences, 20*, 644–653. doi:10.1006/ceps.1995.1017.

Guay, F., Ratelle, C. F., Vitaro, F., & Vallerand, R. J. (2013). The number of autonomy supportive relationships: Is having more better for motivation, perceived competence, and grades? *Contemporary Educational Psychology, 38*, 375–382. doi:10.1016/j.cedpsych.2013.07.005.

Guay, F., Senécal, C., Gauthier, L., & Fernet, C. (2003). Predicting career indecision: A self-determination theory perspective. *Journal of Counseling Psychology, 50*(2), 165–177. doi:10.1037/0022-0167.50.2.165.

Guay, F., & Vallerand, R. J. (1997). Social context, students' motivation, and academic achievement: Toward a process model. *Social Psychology of Education, 1*, 211–233. doi:10.1007/BF02339891.

Guiffrida, D. A., Lynch, M. F., Wall, A. F., & Abel, D. S. (2013). Do reasons for attending college affect academic outcomes?: A test of a motivational model from a self-determination theory perspective. *Journal of College Student Development, 54*, 121–139. doi:10.1353/csd.2013.0019.

Hardré, P. L., Chen, C. H., Huang, S. H., Chiang, C. T., Jen, F. L., & Warden, L. (2006). Factors affecting high school students' academic motivation in Taiwan. *Asia Pacific Journal of Education, 26*, 189–207.

Hardre, P. L., & Reeve, J. (2003). A motivational model of rural students' intentions to persist in, versus drop out of high school. *Journal of Educational Psychology, 95*, 347–356. doi:10.1037/0022-0663.95.2.347.

Hattie, J., & Timperley, H. (2007). The power of feedback. *Review of Educational Research, 77*, 81–112.

Hayamizu, T. (1997). Between intrinsic and extrinsic motivation: Examination of reasons for academic study based on the theory of internalization. *Japanese Psychological Research, 39*, 98–108. doi:10.1111/1468-5884.00043.

Hayenga, A., & Corpus, J. (2010). Profiles of intrinsic and extrinsic motivations: A person-centered approach to motivation and achievement in middle school. *Motivation and Emotion, 34*(4), 371–383. doi:10.1007/s11031-010-9181-x.

Kaplan, H., & Assor, A. (2012). Enhancing autonomy-supportive I–Thou dialogue in schools: Conceptualization and socio-emotional effects of an intervention program. *Social Psychology of Education, 15*(2), 251–269. doi:10.1007/s11218-012-9178-2.

Konrad, M., Fowler, C. H., Allison, R. W., Test, D. W., & Wood, W. M. (2007). Effects of self-determination interventions on the academic skills of students with learning disabilities. *Learning Disability Quarterly, 30*(2), 89–113. Retrieved from http://www.jstor.org/stable/30035545.

Lavigne, G. L., Vallerand, R. J., & Miquelon, P. (2007). A motivational model of persistence in science education: A self-determination theory approach. *European Journal of Psychology of Education, 22*(3), 351–369. doi:10.1007/BF03173432.

Levesque, C., Zuehlke, A. N., Stanek, L. R., & Ryan, R. M. (2004). Autonomy and competence in German and American university students: A comparative study based on self-determination theory. *Journal of Educational Psychology, 96*, 68–84. doi:10.1037/0022-0663.96.1.68.

Litalien, D., & Guay, F. (2015). Dropout Intentions in PhD Studies: A Comprehensive Model Based on Interpersonal Relationships and Motivational Resources. *Contemporary Educational Psychology, 41*, 218–231.

Lucas, J. M., Izquierdo, J. G. N., & Alonso, J. L. N. (2005). Validación de la versión española de la Echelle de Motivation en Education. *Psicothema, 17*, 344–34. Téléchargé à partir de http://www.psicothema.com/psicothema.asp?id=3110.

Maag, J. W. (2001). Rewarded by punishment: Reflections on the disuse of positive reinforcement in schools. *Exceptional Children, 67*, 173–186. Retrieved from http://www.opi.mt.gov/pdf/MBI/14SessionIV/AR/PositiveReinforcement.pdf.

Ménard. (2009). *Décrochage scolaire au Québec: Coûts et conséquences*. Québec, Canada: Groupe d'action sur la persévérance et la réussite scolaires au Québec.

Miserandino, M. (1996). Children who do well in school: Individual differences in perceived competence and autonomy in above-average children. *Journal of Educational Psychology, 88*, 203–214. doi:10.1037/0022-0663.88.2.203.

Niemiec, C. P., Lynch, M. F., Vansteenkiste, M., Bernstein, J., Deci, E. L., & Ryan, R. M. (2006). The antecedents and consequences of autonomous self-regulation for college: A self-determination theory perspective on socialization. *Journal of Adolescence, 29*, 761–775. doi:10.1016/j.adolescence.2005.11.009.

Noels, K. A., Clément, R., & Pelletier, L. G. (2001). Intrinsic, extrinsic, and integrative orientations of French Canadian learners of English. *Canadian Modern Language Review/La Revue canadienne des langues vivantes, 57*(3), 424–442. doi:10.3138/cmlr.57.3.424.

Otis, N., Grouzet, F. M. E., & Pelletier, L. G. (2005). Latent motivational change in an academic setting: A 3-year longitudinal study. *Journal of Educational Psychology, 97*, 170–183. doi:10.1037/0022-0663.97.2.170.

Oxford, R. L., & Ehrman, M. E. (1995). Adults' language learning strategies in an intensive foreign language program in the United States. *System, 23*, 359–386. doi:10.1016/0346-251X(95)00023-D.

Pihu, M., & Hein, V. (2007). Autonomy support from physical education teachers, peers and parents among school students: Trans-contextual motivation model. *Acta Kinesiologiae Universitatis Tartuensis, 12*, 116–128.

Pintrich, P. R. (2003). A motivational science perspective on the role of student motivation in learning and teaching contexts. *Journal of Educational Psychology, 95*, 667–686. doi:10.1037/0022-0663.95.4.667.

Pomerantz, E. M., Grolnick, W. S., & Price, C. E. (2005). The role of parents in how children approach achievement: A dynamic process perspective. In A. J. Elliot & C. S. Dweck (Eds.), *Handbook of competence and motivation* (pp. 229–278). New York: Guilford Publications.

Ratelle, C. F., Guay, F., Larose, S., & Senécal, C. (2004). Family correlates of trajectories of academic motivation during a school transition: A semiparametric group-based approach. *Journal of Educational Psychology, 96*, 743–754. doi:10.1037/0022-0663.96.4.743.

Ratelle, C. F., Guay, F., Vallerand, R. J., Larose, S., & Senécal, C. (2007). Autonomous, controlled, and amotivated types of academic motivation: A person-oriented analysis. *Journal of Educational Psychology, 4*, 734–746.

Ratelle, C. F., Larose, S., Guay, F., & Senécal, C. (2005). Perceptions of parental involvement and support as predictors of college students' persistence in a science curriculum. *Journal of Family Psychology, 19*, 286–293. doi:10.1037/0022-0663.99.4.734.

Reeve, J. (2002). Self-determination theory applied to educational settings. In E. L. Deci & R. M. Ryan (Eds.), *Handbook of self-determination research* (pp. 183–203). Rochester, NY: University of Rochester Press.

Reeve, J. (2006). Teachers as facilitators: What autonomy-supportive teachers do and why their students benefit. *Elementary School Journal, 106*, 225–236. doi:10.1086/501484.

Reeve, J., Jang, H., Carrell, D., Jeon, S., & Barch, J. (2004). Enhancing students' engagement by increasing teachers' autonomy support. *Motivation and Emotion, 28*, 147–169. doi:10.1023/B:MOEM.0000032312.95499.6f.

Ryan, R. M., & Connell, J. P. (1989). Perceived locus of causality and internalization: Examining reasons for acting in two domains. *Journal of Personality and Social Psychology, 57*, 746–761. doi:10.1037/0022-3514.57.5.749.

Ryan, R. M., & Deci, E. L. (2009). Promoting self-determined school engagement: Motivation, learning, and well-being. In K. R. Wentzel & A. Wigfield (Eds.), *Handbook on motivation at school* (pp. 171–196). New York: Routledge.

Ryan, R. M., & Grolnick, W. S. (1986). Origins and pawns in the classroom: Self-report and projective assessments of individual differences in children's perceptions. *Journal of Personality and Social Psychology, 50*, 550–558. doi:10.1037/0022-3514.50.3.550.

Savard, A., Joussemet, M., Pelletier, J. E., & Mageau, G. A. (2013). The benefits of autonomy support for adolescents with severe emotional and behavioral problems. *Motivation and Emotion, 37*(4), 688–700. doi:10.1007/s11031-013-9351-8.

Sheldon, K. M., & Krieger, L. S. (2007). Understanding the negative effects of legal education on law students: A longitudinal test of self-determination theory. *Personality and Social Psychology Bulletin, 33*, 883–897. doi:10.1177/0146167207301014.

Shogren, K. A., Faggella-Luby, M. N., Bae, S. J., & Wehmeyer, M. L. (2004). The effect of choice-making as an intervention for problem behavior: A meta-analysis. *Journal of Positive Behavior Interventions, 6*(4), 228–237. doi:10.1177/10983007040060040401.

Simons, L. G., & Conger, R. D. (2007). Linking mother–father differences in parenting to a typology of family parenting styles and adolescent outcomes. *Journal of Family Issues, 28*, 212–241. doi:10.1177/0192513X06294593.

Su, Y. L., & Reeve, J. (2011). A meta-analysis of the effectiveness of intervention programs designed to support autonomy. *Educational Psychology Review, 23*(1), 159–188. doi:10.1007/s10648-010-9142-7.

Trouilloud, D., Sarrazin, P., Bressoux, P., & Bois, J. (2006). Relation between teachers' early expectations and students' later perceived competence in physical education classes: Autonomy-supportive climate as a moderator. *Journal of Educational Psychology, 98*, 75–86. doi:10.1037/0022-0663.98.1.75.

Vallerand, R. J., & Bissonnette, R. (1992). Intrinsic, extrinsic, and amotivational styles as predictors of behavior: A prospective study. *Journal of Personality, 3*, 599–620. doi:10.1111/j.1467-6494.1992.tb00922.x.

Vallerand, R. J., Blais, M. R., Brière, N. M., & Pelletier, L. G. (1989). Construction et validation de l'Echelle de Motivation en Education. *Canadian Journal of Behavioural Sciences, 21*, 323–349. doi:10.1037/h0079855.

Vallerand, R. J., Fortier, M. S., & Guay, F. (1997). Self-determination and persistence in a real-life setting: Toward a motivational model of high school dropout. *Journal of Personality and Social Psychology, 72*, 1161–1176. doi:10.1037/0022-3514.72.5.1161.

Vallerand, R. J., Pelletier, L. G., Blais, M. R., Brière, N. M., Senécal, C., & Vallières, E. F. (1992). The academic motivation scale: A measure of intrinsic, extrinsic, and amotivation in education. *Educational and Psychological Measurement, 52*, 1003–1019. doi:10.1177/0013164492052004025.

Vallerand, R. J., Pelletier, L. G., Blais, M. R., Brière, N. M., Senécal, C., & Vallières, E. F. (1993). On the assessment of intrinsic, extrinsic, and amotivation in education: Evidence on the concurrent and construct validity of the academic motivation scale. *Educational and Psychological Measurement, 53*, 159–172. doi:10.1177/0013164493053001018.

Vandergrift, L. (2005). Relationships among motivation orientations, metacognitive awareness and proficiency in L2 Listening. *Applied Linguistics, 26*, 70–89. doi:10.1093/applin/amh039.

Vansteenkiste, M., Simons, J., Lens, W., Sheldon, K. M., & Deci, E. L. (2004). Motivating learning, performance, and persistence: The synergistic role of intrinsic goals and autonomy-support. *Journal of Personality and Social Psychology, 87*, 246–260. doi:10.1037/0022-3514.87.2.246.

Vansteenkiste, M., Zhou, M., Lens, W., & Soenens, B. (2005). Experiences of autonomy and control among Chinese learners: Vitalizing or immobilizing? *Journal of Educational Psychology, 96*, 755–764. doi:10.1037/0022-0663.97.3.468.

Villacorta, M., Koestner, R., & Lekes, N. (2003). Further validation of the motivation toward the environment scale. *Environment and Behavior, 35*(4), 486–505. doi:10.1177/0013916503035004003.

Villiger, C., Niggli, A., Wandeler, C., & Kutzelmann, S. (2012). Does family make a difference? Mid-term effects of a school/home-based intervention program to enhance reading motivation. *Learning and Instruction, 22*(2), 79–91. doi:10.1016/j.learninstruc.2011.07.001.

Wild, K. P., & Krapp, A. (1995). Elternhaus und intrinsische lernmotivation [Parents' home and intrinsic motivation to learn]. *Zeitschrift fu¨r Pa¨dagogik, 41*, 579–595.

Williams, G. C., & Deci, E. L. (1996). Internalization of biopsychosocial values by medical students: A test of self-determination theory. *Journal of Personality and Social Psychology, 70*, 767–779. doi:10.1037/0022-3514.70.4.767.

Yamauchi, H., & Tanaka, K. (1998). Relations of autonomy, self-referenced beliefs and self-regulated learning among Japanese children. *Psychological Reports, 82*, 803–816. doi:10.2466/pr0.1998.82.3.803.

Chapter 6
Teachers' Motivation in the Classroom

Luc G. Pelletier and Meredith Rocchi

Introduction

Over the last 50 years, researchers in educational psychology have directed most of their attention to the study of students' motivation for the purpose of understanding the ways in which teachers can enhance or undermine students' motivation, well-being, and functioning (Meece, Anderman, & Anderman, 2006; Ryan & Deci, 2009; Wang & Holcombe, 2010; Zimmerman, 2008). Traditionally, teachers have not been the central focus of this research and there has been little systematic and theory-driven attention dedicated to teachers' motivation The focus on students' motivation and their experience in the classroom has tended to overlook the centrality of teachers' motivation as a critical determinant of teachers' own experience and the interpersonal behaviors directed at students and thereby to students' motivation and the quality of their learning.

As society increasingly holds teachers accountable for students' performances, and given the role that teachers play in students' motivation, there has been a recent surge of interest in applying well-developed theories of motivation, to the domain of teaching. The purpose has been to determine if the educational context has a positive or negative effect on teachers' motivation to teach, their well-being, and the climate being created in the classroom. Since a teacher's ultimate purpose is to work with the students, a large majority of this research has continued to examine teachers within the context of their behavior and interactions with their students. More specifically, motivation researchers have turned their attention to several aspects of the complex educational environment to determine if some of the factors associated

L.G. Pelletier (✉) • M. Rocchi
University of Ottawa, Ottawa, ON, Canada
e-mail: Luc.Pelletier@uOttawa.ca; Meredith.rocchi@gmail.com

© Springer Science+Business Media Singapore 2016   107
W.C. Liu et al. (eds.), *Building Autonomous Learners*,
DOI 10.1007/978-981-287-630-0_6

with that environment could have a positive or a negative impact on teachers' interpersonal behaviors with their students and ultimately on student's motivation (Pelletier & Patry, 2006; Pelletier & Sharp, 2009).

More recently, motivation researchers who have developed robust theories in relation to student learning in educational contexts have turned their attention to teachers' motivation, to see whether the same principles that have guided the research on students' motivation might have the same explanatory power with regard to teachers. Motivational psychology has provided a comprehensive framework for examining the factors acting on teachers, while taking into consideration their teaching behaviors, and speaks to the conditions that lead to a successful or unsuccessful experience (Hagger & Chatzisarantis, 2007).

Putting the Educational Context in Context

Teaching is a very complex vocation that requires many talents and skills. Teachers not only translate educational philosophy and objective into knowledge and skills and transfer them to students in the classroom; they are also responsible for the climate in which these activities take place. Depending on the context, teachers are not only required to teach their students, but they are also expected to be motivators, leaders, administrators, life coaches, planners, performers, and negotiators.

Teachers' motivation is influenced by several factors affecting the global school climate, such as teachers' attitude to work, their desire to participate in the pedagogical processes within the school environment, their participation in extracurricular activities, and, more specifically, their interest in students' motivation inside and outside of the classroom. Therefore, teachers are responsible for the improvement of knowledge; the physical conditions of the classroom through orderliness, discipline, and control; and the diagnosis of student's feelings, attitudes, and motivation inferred by their behavior and response in the classroom environment.

Research has shown that teachers have the capacity to create environments that help foster their students' motivation toward learning, which also helps them achieve their potential (Ryan & Deci, 2009). Research examining the specific mechanics of the teacher-student relationship has found that this relationship influences engagement (Assor, Kaplan, & Roth, 2002), well-being (Van Petegem, Aelterman, Van Keer, & Rosseel, 2008), and motivation (Noels, Clement, & Pelletier, 1999).

In recent years, research has examined the factors that influence teachers directly. Self-determination theory (SDT; Deci & Ryan, 1985, 2000; Ryan & Deci, 2009), a leading theory of motivation, can provide important insight into the understanding of teachers' motivation, including the reasons they choose to become teachers, continue to teach, experience success, and enjoy what they do, and it can guide future research in this area.

Self-Determination Theory: A Brief Overview

SDT is a theory of motivation, built on the assumption that all humans, including both students and teachers, have innate tendencies to grow and to integrate ongoing life experiences (Deci & Ryan, 2000; Ryan & Deci, 2009). As we have seen throughout this book, according to SDT, there are three distinct types of motivation (amotivation, extrinsic motivation, and intrinsic motivation) that lead to different affective, cognitive, and behavioral outcomes based on the degree to which the behavior has been internalized and integrated into the self. Internalization refers to the assimilation of values or external demands, while integration refers to the final step of this process when the values or external demands become an integral part of the personality of the person. This process can be viewed in terms of a continuum where types of motivation are divided into behavioral regulations that are placed from the least internalized (or self-determined) to the most (Ryan, 1995).

When considering the continuum, Deci and Ryan (2000) propose that the least internalized (or self-determined) form of motivation is amotivation, which consists of nonregulation. It is marked by a lack of intention to act (Deci & Ryan, 2002). Moving along the continuum toward more self-determined forms of motivation is extrinsic motivation, in which Deci and Ryan (1985, 2000) suggest it can be divided into four types of regulation, from the least internalized to the most: external, intro- jected, identified, and integrated. Finally, the most self-determined motivation orientation is intrinsic regulation, where pleasure derived from the behavior is found in the behavior itself. It is characterized by a spontaneous engagement in the activity that is fuelled by interest, curiosity, and the difficulty of the task (Deci & Ryan, 2002).

It is important to note that although the process of internalization is a natural human tendency, SDT posits that the extent it will occur depends on the satisfaction of the three basic needs (autonomy, competence, and relatedness). Autonomy is seen when an individual acts in line with his or her own interests and values. In this case, behavior is an expression of the self, and the origin of behaviors comes from within. Competence is seen in an individual's interactions with the environment, when they have the opportunity to seek challenges, express their capacities, and develop their confidence. Finally, relatedness is seen as a sense of belonging with others and the community as a whole. It is achieved through interpersonal connec- tions and reciprocal care between others. These three needs are said to be innate, universal across cultures, and evident in all development periods (Deci & Ryan, 2002).

Contextual Motivation for Teaching

Extensive research using the SDT framework has examined individuals' motivation in specific life domains and contexts, and teaching is no exception. SDT posits, through the hierarchical model of intrinsic and extrinsic motivation, that there is a sequence to explain the interactions between social environments, motivation, and behaviors. Specifically, factors within the social context of an activity will impact someone's motivation quality for that activity. Then, depending on the quality, this motivation will lead to different behavioral or psychological outcomes for that person (Deci & Ryan, 2002; Vallerand, 1997). The contextual factors do not necessarily impact motivation directly; instead their influence can be indirect through the extent to which they satisfy or thwart the basic psychological needs (Deci & Ryan, 2000; Deci, Schwartz, Sheinman, & Ryan, 1981; Vallerand, 1997). Contextual factors include the structure of a specific environment, like the educational environment (i.e., educational policies), as well as the people within it (i.e., the colleagues, the principal, the administrators). When considering other people, the extent to which they will support teachers' basic psychological needs is dependent on the extent they engage in need-supportive interpersonal behaviors (Deci & Ryan, 1985), that is, how their interpersonal behaviors support others' need for autonomy, competence, and relatedness. An environment that supports the three basic psychological needs will promote improved motivation quality, while an environment that thwarts psychological needs leads to decreased motivation quality.

Next, looking at the quality of motivation, SDT has examined the outcomes associated with different motivation qualities. In general, the higher-quality or more self-determined types of motivation (identified, integrated, and intrinsic regulation) are considered optimal when compared with the lower-quality or least self-determined types of motivation (amotivation, external, and introjected regulation). Specifically, the more self-determined motivation styles are found to lead to improved psychological outcomes like self-esteem, life satisfaction, well-being, and health and improved behavioral outcomes such as increased learning, interest, performance, and persistence (Mageau & Vallerand, 2003). Alternatively, less self-determined motivation styles are associated with negative psychological outcomes like decreased health and vitality and decreased behavioral outcomes like persistence, effort, and success (Deci & Ryan, 2000).

Since humans are interdependent and social beings and interpersonal interactions are a key part of the human experience, SDT takes into account how motivation relates to people's behavior with others, where the focus has been on need-supportive interpersonal behaviors. When considering need-supportive and need-thwarting interpersonal behaviors, autonomy-supportive behaviors have received by far the most empirical attention (e.g., Pelletier, Fortier, Vallerand, & Brière, 2001; Standage, Duda, & Ntoumanis, 2005). These behaviors are described as providing choice, providing a rationale for tasks, acknowledging others' perspectives, giving opportunities for initiative, and promoting task involvement (Mageau & Vallerand, 2003). The opposite of an autonomy-supportive interpersonal style would be a controlling style (or autonomy-thwarting style). When someone engages in controlling interpersonal behaviors, they use rewards, incorporate intimidating feedback, make demands without providing a rationale, use conditional regard, and use excessive personal control (Bartholomew, Ntoumanis, & Thøgersen-Ntoumani, 2009). Next, competence-supportive behaviors include using positive expectancies, encouraging learning, providing positive feedback, acknowledging improvements, believing others can meet their goals, and encouraging their others to improve (Sheldon & Filak, 2008; Taylor, Ntoumanis, & Standage, 2008). The opposite would involve using a competence-thwarting style and would include emphasizing others' faults, discouraging others from trying difficult tasks, focusing on what they do wrong, sending them the messages that are inadequate, and doubting their capacity to improve (Sheldon & Filak, 2008). Finally, relatedness-supportive interpersonal behaviors occur when someone understands, supports, and cares for others. They would do this by being warm, showing they are interested in what others do, relating to them, and showing that they genuinely like them (Jones, Armour, & Potrac, 2004). Alternatively, someone would not be supporting others' need for relatedness if they were distant, did not connect with them, did not include them in activities, did not listen, and were not available when they needed them (Sheldon & Filak, 2008).

Research in SDT has suggested that increased motivation quality is associated with increased use of need-supportive interpersonal behaviors, while decreased motivation quality is associated with increased need-thwarting interpersonal behaviors (Sheldon & Filak, 2008). In the educational context, this suggests that when someone like a teacher experiences high-quality motivation for an activity or life domain, they are more likely to engage in need-supportive interpersonal behaviors (autonomy, competence, and relatedness support) that will create an environment that promotes an increase in motivation quality for students (Deci & Ryan, 2000). Alternatively, a teacher who experiences lower-quality motivation for teaching is more likely to engage in need-thwarting interpersonal behaviors and create an environment that undermines motivation quality in students (Bartholomew, Ntoumanis, Ryan, Bosch, & Thogersen-Ntoumani, 2011). Findings suggest that this sequence is especially relevant in supervisor-subordinate relationships (i.e., teacher-student, parent-child, coach-athlete) as the supervisor plays a major role in setting the interpersonal climate for the subordinate (Mageau & Vallerand, 2003).

As discussed previously, the primary role of a teacher is to instruct and influence students. Therefore, a large majority of research examining the teaching context in SDT has focused on the extent teachers' behaviors help improve the motivation quality of their students. More recently, researchers have begun to examine teachers' motivation separately (Eyal & Roth, 2011; Fernet, Senécal, Guay, March, & Dowson, 2008; Roth, Assor, Kanat-Maymon, & Kaplan, 2007; Sørebø, Halvari, Gulli, & Kristiansen, 2009; Spittle, Jackson, & Casey, 2009; Wang & Liu, 2008; Wilkesmann & Schmid, 2014). This research provides support for assessing teachers' motivation toward teaching as a whole (Pelletier, Séguin-Lévesque, & Legault, 2002; Taylor et al., 2008) or as specific job tasks (Fernet et al., 2008; i.e., class preparation, teaching, evaluation of students, classroom management, administrative tasks, and complementary tasks) as defined by SDT. Also, this research has shown that a teacher who is intrinsically motivated may undertake a task like teaching for its own sake, for the satisfaction it provides, or for the feeling of accomplishment and self-actualization, while an extrinsically motivated teacher may perform the activity of teaching as a duty in order to obtain some reward such as salary, avoid sanction, or comply with request from administrators.

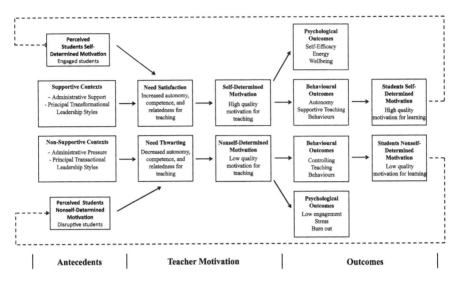

Fig. 6.1 A process model of the effects of the educational context on teachers' motivation, teachers' outcomes, teachers' interpersonal behaviors, and students' motivation

Through this research, the antecedents (i.e., contextual factors) of teachers' motivation, as well as the behavioral and psychological outcomes of their motivation, have begun to be identified. This growing body of literature focuses on the teachers' themselves and how the social context affects their need satisfaction and their motivation for teaching, their well-being, and their teaching behaviors. More specifically, as illustrated in Fig. 6.1, the school administration (i.e., the structure of the school system, the administrators, the principal), as part of teachers' social context, can satisfy or thwart teachers' basic psychological needs (i.e., being autonomy supportive or controlling with them). This in turn leads to teachers being more or less self-determined in their motivation for teaching, which results in corresponding positive or negative outcomes related to teachers' psychological experiences and behaviors with their students. At this point, an element of reciprocity is introduced because teachers and students are part of a common social context (i.e., the classroom context) and they are each part of each other's social context. Thus, as autonomy-supportive teachers positively affect students' self-determined motivation, the teachers' motivation and the quality of their experience are also positively affected by the students' motivation and behavior. Inversely, as controlling teachers negatively affect students' self-determined motivation, the teachers' motivation and the quality of their experience are also affected by the students' motivation and behavior. Almost all the components of this hypothesized sequence have been tested and will be described below.

Antecedents of Teachers' Motivation

According to SDT, contextual factors will influence teachers' motivation quality either directly or through the extent to which they help teachers meet their psychological needs while teaching. Previous research has identified a number of contextual factors related to either the structure of the teaching environment or the people within it that have an impact on teachers' motivation. These factors are discussed in details below.

Administrative Pressure

One area of the teaching context that has received a lot of attention is the impact of administrative pressure on teachers. This pressure can take many forms including imposing demands such as time constraints or deadlines, performance evaluations, pressures to conform to certain teaching methods, or making teachers accountable for their students' level of performance (Pelletier et al., 2002; Reeve, 2002). These pressures can originate directly from the school administration or indirectly from school boards and parents that demand results.

The first studies on administrative pressures within the SDT framework examined how they affected teachers' interpersonal behaviors directly. Deci, Speigel, Ryan, Koestner, and Kauffman (1982) provided the first test of the relations between the pressure that came from above, interpersonal behaviors, and intrinsic motivation. Participants in this study were instructed to help students learn to become better problem solvers, and some were further instructed that it was their job to ensure that their students performed "up to high standards." The results showed that teachers who had been pressured to have their students achieve high standards were more critical of the students, used more hints and more directive language, and were more controlling than teachers who did not have to face such performance standards. In a field experiment of this question, Flink, Boggiano, and Barrett (1990) looked at a school-based curriculum for elementary students. The results were similar to those of the laboratory study: teachers who faced external pressure toward higher standards were shown to be more likely to engage in controlling and instructing behaviors in their classrooms. The pressured teachers were also less effective: their students showed poorer performance on objective test-score outcomes.

Once the initial studies found an important link between administrative pressures and teachers' interpersonal behaviors, a subsequent series of studies examined whether these effects occurred through the processes proposed by SDT. In a study of 254 teachers, Pelletier and colleagues (2002) showed that the relationship between administrative pressures in the workplace and teachers' autonomy-supportive behaviors was mediated by the effect of these pressures on their motivation. More specifically, the more teachers felt pressured by colleagues, the administration, and constraints of the curriculum, the less self-determined was their motivation and, in turn, the less autonomy support they showed their students.

Fernet, Guay, and Senecal, (2004) identified additional sources of administrative pressure for teachers. They examined the relationship between job demands (work stressors like overload, role ambiguity, role conflict, and stress), job control (a measure of perceived autonomy at work), and teacher's motivation and its subsequent impact on burnout. The results found that job control (perceived autonomy) moderates the relationship between job demands and burnout for teachers who have a self-determined motivation for teaching.

Recent studies included one more step to this link, finding that administrative pressures led teachers to feel less need satisfaction. In a study, Taylor and colleagues (2008) reported that the more teachers perceived job pressure (defined as time constraints, pressure from school authorities, and evaluation based on students' performance), the less they felt that their basic needs for competence, autonomy, and relatedness were satisfied. The level of need satisfaction was directly linked to teachers' self-determined motivation, which in turn impacted the extent to which they provided meaningful rationales, instrumental help, and support and gained an understanding of the students. In a separate study, through a series of interviews, teachers confirm that pressures from above affect their choice of motivational strategies and behaviors in class (Taylor, Ntoumanis, & Smith, 2009). They said that factors such as time constraints, performance evaluations, and pressure from the school administration to conform to certain teaching methods impacted their use of motivational teaching strategies. Teachers reported being more controlling when they felt pressured to conform to certain teaching methods. They also felt that they were less autonomy supportive when they felt pressured by time constraints in lessons.

In more recent studies that focused on teacher burnout and well-being, Fernet, Guay, Senécal, and Austin (2012) examined the impacts of a number of factors, including perceptions of classroom overload, on teachers' motivation and burnout during the course of a school year. The results suggest that perceptions of classroom overload had a negative impact on teachers' motivation for teaching. Alternatively, Bartholomew and colleagues (Bartholomew, Ntoumanis, Cuevas, & Lonsdale, 2014) found that perceptions of time constraints, school authorities, and colleagues had a negative impact on psychological need satisfaction and well-being. In a study that examined perceptions of administrative support, instead of pressure, Carson and Chase (2009) found that administrative support had a significant positive impact on teachers' need for relatedness, which was significantly related to an increase in motivation for teaching.

The association between pressure at work and teachers' self-determined motivation is consistent with several studies inspired by SDT (Ryan & Deci, 2000). According to SDT, the effect of external events on intrinsic motivation and self-determination depends on whether an individual perceives contexts as supportive of autonomy or controlling. Thus, these studies show that teachers do indeed perceive administrative pressures as controlling, which lead to lower need satisfaction and higher levels of controlled motivation (or non-self-determined) toward teaching.

Principals

School principals play a key role in determining the overall culture and environment of a school; they can be perceived as being part of the administration or, because of their leadership position, they can play a critical role in teachers' motivation. For instance, despite "the pressure that could come from above," principals can help teachers in a number of different ways including providing pedagogical resources, reducing administrative tasks, and providing emotional support (Fernet et al., 2012). Previous research in SDT has shown that leadership styles have an impact on an individual's need for autonomy and, subsequently, their motivation quality (e.g., Sheldon, Turban, Brown, Barrick, & Judge, 2003). Research using the full-range model of leadership (Bass & Avolio, 1994) has examined transformational and transactional leadership styles. Results have shown that transformational leadership styles are associated with increased motivation quality, while transactional styles are associated with a decrease in motivation quality (Gagné & Deci, 2005). Transformational leadership occurs when an individual in a position of power provides subordinates with a clear vision and opportunities for intellectual stimulation and demonstrates concern for each individual. Alternatively, transactional leadership styles are characterized by controlling behavior, offering contingent rewards, and complying with rules and policies. Eyal and Roth (2011) examined principals' leadership styles and the subsequent impact on teachers' motivation for teaching and teacher burnout. This study examined 122 elementary school teachers and asked them to report on their principal's leadership behaviors, their motivation for teaching, and their emotional exhaustion (burnout). The results suggested principals' transformational leadership styles (focus on empowerment and an organizational vision) were negatively associated with burnout and that this relationship was partially mediated by self-determined motivation for teaching. Alternatively, transactional leadership styles (controlling practices, monitoring, and enforcing compliance) were positively associated with burnout and non-self-determined motivation for teaching.

Students' Motivation

Significant amounts of research have focused on how teachers' behaviors impact students; however, since the teaching and learning social environments are intertwined, the motivational sequences for teachers and students become reciprocal.

When someone in a position of authority believes that the subordinate is intrinsically motivated, or highly self-determined, they are more likely to experience an increase in their own quality of motivation and they may become more autonomy supportive (Pelletier et al., 2002; Pelletier & Vallerand, 1996). For example, several studies have shown that teachers or individuals in a supervising role behave differently depending on the subordinate's performance or productivity. Barrow (1976) and Lowin and Craig (1968) examined supervisors' reactions following an increase or decrease in the subordinate's performance and productivity. They observed that supervisors were more supportive, kind, and considerate when subordinates were perceived as productive. When subordinates were perceived as unproductive, supervisors became more controlling and relied on punishment to motivate them.

Regarding self-determination more specifically, studies in the laboratory and in the classroom have shown that when teachers believed that students were autonomously motivated, they were more autonomy supportive and less controlling (Pelletier & Vallerand, 1996; Skinner & Belmont, 1993) and that the impact of students' motivation on teachers' interpersonal behaviors was actually mediated by teachers' motivation (Pelletier et al., 2002; Taylor & Ntoumanis, 2007; Taylor et al., 2008). In sum, these results support the idea that when teachers interact with students, they often rely on their perceptions on the students' motivation as guides to their interpersonal behaviors. In turn, their interpersonal behaviors may influence their students' motivation in such a way that it may create the motivation that was perceived and then confirmed the teachers' initial perceptions whether it was accurate or inaccurate because it was based on false beliefs (Pelletier & Vallerand, 1996).

In a more recent study, Fernet and colleagues (Fernet et al., 2012) examined a different dimension of students' motivation and its relationship with teachers' motivation. They examined the extent to which teachers reported that their students were disruptive (i.e., how much noise they made) and its relationship with teachers' motivation. Results suggest that perceptions of disruptive behavior had a significant negative relationship with motivation for teaching.

It is important to note that students may impact teachers indirectly through the school administration. In some contexts, teachers feel that they are responsible for students who may not be motivated or able to meet the administration's standards. In these instances teachers should experience a pressure from students because their lack of motivation or their low performance reinforces the administration's perception that something needs to be done. Then teachers may perceive a pressure to behave in a controlling manner to be sure that the administration's standards are achieved.

Outcomes of Teachers' Motivation

Several studies have examined the outcomes of teachers' motivation for the purposes of understanding their behavior in the classroom or their psychological experiences related to teaching. In line with previous research in SDT, research in the teaching context has demonstrated that high-quality motivation leads to positive behavioral and psychological outcomes, while lower-quality motivation leads to negative psychological and behavioral outcomes.

Behavioral Outcomes

One area of teacher behavioral outcomes that has received a lot of attention is teachers' use of need-supportive interpersonal behaviors. The majority of studies have focused on autonomy support and thwarting (control) and have examined the relationship between motivation quality and the use of these behaviors. Autonomy-supportive teachers are responsive (spend time listening, acknowledge the student's feelings and perspective) and supportive (praise the quality of performance), explicative (provide a rationale for tasks and limits); they provide opportunities for choice, initiative taking, and independent work; and they offer student discussion time. In opposition, controlling teachers take charge (hold the instructional materials, use directives/commands), shape students toward a right answer (give solutions), motivate through pressure (threats, criticisms, and deadlines), and do not allow students to work at their own pace or voice opinions contrary to their own (Assor, Kaplan, Kanat-Maymom, & Roth, 2005; Reeve, 2002; Reeve & Jang, 2006; Sarrazin, Tessier, Pelletier, Trouilloud, & Chanal, 2006). Results have shown that teachers who have an autonomy-supporting style (as opposed to a controlling style) facilitate intrinsic motivation and self-determination in their students. This is associated with many positive consequences for students, such as increased positive emotions, decreased feelings of distraction and anxiety in class, increased prolonged effort, learning centered on comprehension, improved grades, and less likelihood of dropout (Reeve, Deci, & Ryan, 2004; Ryan & Brown, 2005; Ryan & Deci, 2009).

In order to understand why some teachers engage in need-supportive behaviors and others do not, research began to examine the relationship between teachers' motivation quality and their use of autonomy-supportive interpersonal behaviors (e.g., Pelletier et al., 2002; Taylor et al., 2008). In line with SDT, they found that self-determined motivation for teaching predicted an increase in reported use of autonomy-supportive interpersonal behaviors with students.

Roth, Assor, Kanat-Maymon, and Kaplan (2007) believe the relationship between teachers' motivation, autonomy-supportive interpersonal behaviors with students, and students' motivation occurs for at least two reasons. First, high-quality motivation for teaching should increase the teachers' interest in the subjects they teach, which should lead to a better mastery of the subjects and to the provision of better rationale or examples in their teaching, more creativity in teaching, and more involvement in their teaching activities. Second, teachers with higher-quality motivation for teaching should have a better understanding of the benefits associated with an autonomous orientation and recognize its potential to foster quality learning. For this reason, they should prefer that their students learn in a context that is conducive to that type of motivation and the type of values associated with it. In a similar study, Taylor and Ntoumanis (2007) suggested that the link between teachers' motivation and their students' motivation may occur because teachers' motivation translates into different behaviors as viewed by their students. Students rated self-determined teachers as supporting their autonomy more and providing more structured teaching and more involvement, which in turn was associated with higher-quality motivation for learning. They found that non-self-determined motivation for teaching leads to controlling teaching, which in turn contributes to lower-quality motivation among students.

Other behavioral outcomes of teachers' motivation have also begun to be examined. For example, Gorozidis and Papaioannou (2014) tested a model looking at whether teachers' motivation quality predicted their intentions to participate in training activities. They found that autonomous motivation had a positive relationship with intentions to participate, while controlled motivation had a significant negative relationship.

Social Contagion of Motivation

It is also possible that the association between the teacher's motivation and students' motivation may be explained by a social phenomenon called *Social Contagion of Motivation*. As shown by Wild, Enzle, Nix, and Deci (1997) and Radel, Sarrazin, Legrain, and Wild (2010), participants who were taught a skill by a non-self-determined teacher reported lower interest in learning and lower task enjoyment than those taught by a self-determined teacher, despite receiving the same standardized lesson. A study by Garbarino (1975) suggests that this may be related to changes in subtle change in teacher's behavior that are related to their motivation. This study found that rewarded teachers were more critical and demanding of their students than volunteer teachers. Consequently, students who were taught by rewarded teachers made more errors while learning a specific skill. Recent studies by Roth and colleagues (2007) and Taylor and Ntoumanis (2007) suggest that the link between teachers' motivation and their students' motivation may occur because teachers' motivation translates into different levels of autonomy-supportive behaviors, as viewed by their students (e.g., "The teacher encourages me to work in my own way," "The teacher explains why it is important to study certain subjects in school"), higher perceived involvement, and time spent with their students. As discussed in the previous section, this leads to more autonomous motivation for learning, while controlled motivation for teaching leads to controlling teaching, which, in turn, contributes to lower levels of self-determined motivation among students.

Psychological

A number of studies have investigated the relationship between teachers' motivation quality and their likelihood of experiencing a burnout from teaching. When teachers experience burnout, they typically suffer from emotional exhaustion, depersonalization, and decreased feelings of personal accomplishments (Maslach & Jackson, 1981). Teachers will often describe not having the capacity to provide meaningful contributions and feeling like they cannot make a positive impact on their students or in their work (Schaufeli, Leiter, & Maslach, 2009).

In a study examining the relationship between the six different types of behavioral regulation according to SDT and burnout, Fernet and colleagues (Fernet et al., 2008) found that the there was a significant relationship between the different subtypes of teachers' motivation and burnout, as described by depersonalization and emotional exhaustion. They found a simplex-like pattern where the autonomous types of regulation (internal, integrated, and identified) had a negative relationship with burnout, while the controlled types of regulation (introjected, external, and nonregulation) had a positive relationship with reported burnout. In line with these findings, Eyal and Roth (2011) found a significant relationship between controlled motivation for teaching and emotional exhaustion, and Fernet and colleagues (Fernet et al., 2012) found a negative relationship between autonomous motivation and emotional exhaustion.

In two studies examining motivational clusters for teachers, Van den Berghe and colleagues (den Berghe et al., 2013; Van den Berghe et al., 2014) found that both the high-quality (high autonomous motivation) and high-quantity (high autonomous and high controlled motivation) motivation profiles experienced less burnout than the other groups. Since the high-quantity group also experienced less likelihood of burnout, this suggests that autonomous motivation may have an energizing effect on the teachers and helps them circumvent burnout. On a more positive note, Fernet and colleagues (Fernet et al., 2008) also found a positive relationship between autonomous motivation for teaching and teachers' reported self-efficacy for teaching.

Discussion and Future Directions

SDT (Deci & Ryan, 2000; Ryan & Deci, 2009) can provide important insight into the understanding of teachers' motivation including the reasons they do different tasks related to their work, continue to teach, experience success, and impact their students' motivation. The study of teachers' motivation represents not only another sector where research in SDT can be applied, but this sector also represents a domain with its own challenging characteristics that could improve our knowledge on the causes, consequences, and mechanisms of students' motivation. More specifically, in agreement with research in other life domains, research has examined how environmental and contextual factors influence teachers and how their impressions of the teaching environment, their need satisfaction or dissatisfaction, their motivation for teaching, and their use of need-supportive or need-thwarting behaviors with students and psychological outcomes are related. Research has shown that when the administration imposes restrictions, makes teachers responsible for their students' performance, and pressures or rewards teachers to produce good student performance and teachers believe that their students are extrinsically motivated or not motivated, it is likely that these factors may undermine teachers' own psychological needs for teaching. This undermines their motivation quality toward their own work which, in turn, may lead them to be more controlling with their students. As such, teachers' motivation plays an important role in promoting a healthy teaching environment, and this review can inform school administrations by demonstrating why they should take care to ensure that their teachers are supported and having a psychologically sound experience. This review focused on some of the key environmental factors that are relevant to teachers, and it provides school administrations some key areas they can work on specifically to promote, within their own organizations, more motivated teaching and better outcomes for students.

Although the studies described in this chapter are consistent with SDT, more studies on the entire sequence illustrated in Fig. 6.1 are required to demonstrate how the factors relate to each other and how these relationships unfold over time. It would also be important to consider how some factors may be more important than others, that they may explain more variance in teachers' motivation, and that they may represent a more strategic battle to fight. For example, even if teachers learn to use autonomy-supportive strategies, these efforts could be in vain if no efforts are made to reduce the pressure that comes from the school administration or the educational system.

Although the proposed model could be useful for understanding how factors like educational policies or administrative decisions may make their ways through the school system and impact teachers' and eventually students' motivation, it may be important to consider that all teachers are not necessarily affected by the *pressure that could come from above* and the *pressure that could come from below* in the same way. More specifically, although some teachers may be exposed to administrative pressure and students that are less motivated, they may not become less self-determined toward teaching and turn toward controlling strategies when interacting with their students. Therefore, it is important for future research to examine how individual factors like dispositions, experience, personal characteristics, social factors like support from colleagues, and cultural factors (e.g., countries with different philosophy of education) may help teachers become more or less resilient toward factors that could otherwise undermine their motivation quality.

We also need more research that assesses the outcomes of teachers' motivation and the implications that a perception of decline in teachers' motivation may have for the educational system and the school administrators. Like the research on the relationship between teachers' perception of their students' motivation and the self-fulfilling consequences that these perceptions have on teachers' interpersonal behaviors toward their students, research should also examine this relationship with administrative pressure. Specifically, it would be important to examine whether teachers' low motivation for teaching that results from administrative pressure leads administrators to rely more and more on controlling strategies (e.g., making teachers accountable) to motivate teachers and if that leads administrators of the school system to make decisions that undermine their attempts to improve the situation.

Practical Suggestions

Motivating teachers to be fully engaged in teaching represents a challenging task. Below are some practical implications and key lessons learned from the present research on teachers' motivation and self-determination theory regarding the optimal ways to deal with the factors that could affect teachers' motivation.

How can administrations help? Research has shown that when the administration imposes restrictions about a curriculum, makes teachers responsible for their students' performance, and pressures or rewards teachers to produce good student performance, it is likely that teachers will become controlling with students. It is possible that these conditions may directly affect teachers' behaviors or that they may undermine teachers' psychological needs (mainly autonomy) and motivation toward their own work that leads them to be more controlling with their students. How might administrations be more need supportive? Evidently, they cannot eliminate all time constraints or performance evaluations, nor would they necessarily want to; however, administrations should carefully consider the objectives of any constraints or evaluations they have in place and ensure that they achieve the desired results. A first practical implication of the research discussed in the present chapter is that school administrators (and teachers as well) should be mindful of the factors that can undermine teachers' motivation, and when possible, administrators should consider whether or not the factors they have in place contribute unintentionally to the low levels of motivation in teachers.

A second implication has to do with the factors that have been shown to affect directly teachers' motivation. School administrators and school principals play a key role in determining the overall culture and environment of a school; because of their leadership position, they can play a critical role in teachers' motivation. For instance, principals can help teachers in a number of different ways including providing pedagogical resources, reducing administrative tasks, and providing emotional support. If administrators, and more specifically principals, realize that they do contribute to teachers' low motivation, they should consider directly minimizing the impact of some factors by (a) considering ways to reduce teachers' workload or giving them options about how they want to structure it, (b) providing them with options about the ways they want to organize and communicate the educational curriculum, (c) providing constructive feedback to teachers about the ways they teach and the ways they could be autonomy supportive with their students, (d) providing step-by-step procedures (i.e., implementation goals and implementation intentions), and (e) means of tracking progress and providing constructive feedback about their teaching.

A third practical implication is related to the way that administrators could implement the administrative structure in a school environment. SDT suggests that having structure is important, but the way in which limits are set and communicated within a given structure can make it controlling. Research suggests that the provision of a rationale is a particularly important element of communicating justifications for an activity in an autonomy-supportive way (Deci, Eghrari, Patrick, & Leone, 1994).

Research also suggests communicating this rationale in the form of a clear mission and vision framed in terms of intrinsic goals (Vansteenkiste, Lens, & Deci, 2006), as opposed to high-stakes standards (Ryan & Brown, 2005), may serve this role in an organizational context and then may promote a supportive climate for teaching. One study of Australian teachers provides an initial hint that this may prove a fruitful avenue: the more teachers understood and agreed with the school mission and its associated goals, the more personal accomplishment they felt, and the less they suffered from emotional exhaustion and depersonalization (Dorman, 2003). This suggests that in the long run, less administrative pressure may not only be beneficial for the students' motivation, it may also be beneficial for the teachers' well-being as well.

The last implication deals with students' motivation. A critical factor that could affect teachers' motivation is their perceptions of their students' motivation. One way to overcome this is to train teachers to ensure that they are need supportive with their students. A few recent studies have shown that teachers can learn how to increase their use of autonomy-supportive behaviors with their students through teaching (Tessier, Sarrazin, & Ntoumanis, 2008), by being shown how to be autonomy supportive (Tessier, Sarrazin, & Ntoumanis, 2010), and by being educated about SDT (Reeve, Jang, Carrell, Jeon, & Barch, 2004). Although this strategy is covered in more details in other chapters of this book, it may be important to consider three different reasons for doing this. That is, by being autonomy supportive with their students, teachers may not only increase the motivation of their students, they may also impact their own motivation in three different ways. First, teachers should feel more motivated because they are more competent and effective in promoting more motivation and engagement in their students. Next, the increase motivation in their students should lead teachers to have a positive perception that students are motivated, and this, in turn, should create more motivation in teachers. Finally, the increase motivation in students should reduce the need from the administration to put pressure on the teachers to produce motivated and engaged students, and this in turn should foster more motivation in teachers.

Summary of Practical Implications

- School administrations and teachers should be mindful of the factors that can undermine teachers' motivation, and when possible, administrators should consider whether or not the factors they have in place contribute unintentionally to the low levels of motivation in teachers.
- Administrators should review the objectives of any constraints or evaluations they have in place to motivate teachers and ensure that they are not perceived as being controlling by teachers and that they are achieving the desired results.
- Because of their leadership position, school administrators and school principals can have an impact on teachers' motivation by determining the overall culture and environment of a school and by determining the resources that could be

available for teachers. When it is possible, principals can help teachers in a number of different ways by (a) providing pedagogical resources, (b) reducing administrative tasks, and (c) providing emotional support.

- Administrators and principals can minimize the impact of several factors that affect teachers' motivation. They can (a) reduce teachers' workload or give them options about how they want to structure it, (b) provide teachers with options about the ways they want to organize and communicate the educational curriculum, (c) provide constructive feedback to teachers about the ways they teach and the ways they could be autonomy supportive with their students, (d) provide step-by-step procedures and means of tracking their progress as teachers, and (e) provide constructive feedback about their teaching.
- Administrators can facilitate the implementation of the administrative structure in a school environment (a) by communicating justifications and providing a rationale for an activity and (b) by communicating this rationale in the form of a clear mission and vision framed in terms of intrinsic goals as opposed to high-stakes standards.
- A critical factor that could affect teachers' motivation is their perceptions of their students' motivation. As indicated in other chapters of this book, one way to increase students' motivation is to train teachers to be need supportive with their students. Teachers can learn to increase their use of autonomy-supportive behaviors by learning how to be autonomy supportive and by being educated about SDT.
- By being autonomy supportive with their students, teachers may not only increase the motivation of their students, they may also impact their own motivation in three different ways: (a) teachers may feel more motivated because they are more competent and effective in promoting more motivation and engagement in their students; (b) the increase motivation in their students should lead teachers to have a positive perception that their students are motivated, and this, in turn, should create more motivation in teachers; (c) the increase motivation in students should reduce the need from the administration to put pressure on the teachers to produce motivated and engaged students, and this in turn should foster more motivation in teachers.

References

Assor, A., Kaplan, H., Kanat-Maymom, Y., & Roth, G. (2005). Directly controlling teacher behaviors as predictors of poor motivation and engagement in girls and boys: The role of anger and anxiety. *Learning and Instruction, 15,* 397–413.

Assor, A., Kaplan, H., & Roth, G. (2002). Choice is good, but relevance is excellent: Autonomy-enhancing and suppressing teacher behaviours in predicting student's engagement in school work. *British Journal of Educational Psychology, 72,* 261–278.

Barrow, J. C. (1976). Worker performance and task complexity as causal determinants of leader behavior, style, and flexibility. *Journal of Applied Psychology, 61,* 433–440.

Bartholomew, K. J., Ntoumanis, N., Cuevas, R., & Lonsdale, C. (2014). Job pressure and ill-health in physical education teachers: The mediating role of psychological need thwarting. *Teaching and Teacher Education, 37,* 101–107.

Bartholomew, K. J., Ntoumanis, N., Ryan, R. M., Bosch, J. A., & Thogersen-Ntoumani, C. (2011). Self-determination theory and diminished functioning: The role of interpersonal control and psychological need thwarting. *Personality and Social Psychology Bulletin, 37,* 1459–1473.

Bartholomew, K. J., Ntoumanis, N., & Thøgersen-Ntoumani, C. (2009). A review of controlling motivational strategies from a self-determination theory perspective: Implications for sports coaches. *International Review of Sport and Exercise Psychology, 2,* 215–233.

Bass, B. M., & Avolio, B. J. (1994). *Improving organizational effectiveness through transformational leadership.* Thousand Oaks, CA: Sage.

Carson, R. L., & Chase, M. A. (2009). An examination of physical education teacher motivation from a self-determination theoretical framework. *Physical Education and Sport Pedagogy, 14,* 335–353.

Deci, E., & Ryan, R. (1985). *Intrinsic motivation and self-determination in human behavior.* New York: Plenum.

Deci, E., & Ryan, R. (2002). *Handbook of self-determination.* Rochester, NY: University of Rochester Press.

Deci, E. L., Eghrari, H., Patrick, B. C., & Leone, D. (1994). Facilitating internalization: The self determination theory perspective. *Journal of Personality, 62,* 119–142.

Deci, E. L., & Ryan, R. M. (2000). The "what" and "why" of goal pursuits: Human needs and the self-determination of behavior. *Psychological Inquiry, 11,* 227–268.

Deci, E. L., Schwartz, A. J., Sheinman, L., & Ryan, R. M. (1981). An instrument to assess adults' orientations toward control versus autonomy with children: Reflections on intrinsic motivation and perceived competence. *Journal of Educational Psychology, 73,* 642–650.

Deci, E. L., Spiegel, N. H., Ryan, R. M., Koestner, R., & Kauffman, M. (1982). Effects of performance standards on teaching behavior of controlling teachers. *Journal of Educational Psychology, 74,* 852–859.

den Berghe, V., Cardon, G., Aelterman, N., Tallir, I., Vansteenkiste, M., & Haerens, L. (2013). Emotional exhaustion and motivation in physical education teachers: A variable-centered and person-centered approach. *Journal of Teaching in Physical Education, 32,* 305–320.

Dorman, J. P. (2003). Relationship between school and classroom environment and teacher burnout: A LISREL analysis. *Social Psychology of Education, 6,* 107–127.

Eyal, O., & Roth, G. (2011). Principals' leadership and teachers' motivation: Self-determination theory analysis. *Journal of Educational Administration, 49,* 256–275.

Fernet, C., Guay, F., Senécal, C., & Austin, S. (2012). Predicting intraindividual changes in teacher burnout: The role of perceived school environment and motivational factors. *Teaching and Teacher Education, 28,* 514–525.

Fernet, C., Guay, F., & Senecal, C. (2004). Adjusting to job demands: The role of work, self-determination and job control in predicting burnout. *Journal of Vocational Behavior, 65,* 39–56.

Fernet, C., Senécal, C., Guay, F., March, H., & Dowson, M. (2008). The Work Tasks Motivation Scale for Teachers (WTMST). *Journal of Career Assessment, 16,* 256–279.

Flink, C., Boggiano, A. K., & Barrett, M. (1990). Controlling teaching strategies: Undermining children's self-determination and performance. *Journal of Personality and Social Psychology, 59,* 916–924.

Gagné, M., & Deci, E. L. (2005). Self-determination theory and work motivation. *Journal of Organizational Behavior, 26,* 331–362.

Garbarino, J. (1975). The impact of anticipated reward upon cross-aged tutoring. *Journal of Personality and Social Psychology, 32,* 421–428.

Gorozidis, G., & Papaioannou, A. G. (2014). Teachers' motivation to participate in training and to implement innovations. *Teaching and Teacher Education, 39,* 1–11.

Hagger, M., & Chatzisarantis, N. (2007). *Intrinsic motivation and self-determination in exercise and sport.* Leeds: Human Kinetics Europe Ltd.

Jones, R. L., Armour, K. M., & Potrac, P. (2004). *Sports coaching cultures: From practice to theory*. London: Routledge.

Lowin, A., & Craig, J. (1968). The influence of level of performance on managerial style: An experimental object-lesson in the ambiguity of correlational data. *Organizational Behavior and Human Performance, 3*, 440–458.

Mageau, G., & Vallerand, R. (2003). The coach and athlete relationship: A motivational model. *Journal of Sports Sciences, 21*, 883–904.

Maslach, C., & Jackson, S. E. (1981). The measurement of experienced burnout. *Journal of Occupational Behavior, 2*, 99–113.

Meece, J. L., Anderman, E. M., & Anderman, L. H. (2006). Classroom goal structure, student motivation, and academic achievement. *Annual Review of Psychology, 57*, 487–503.

Noels, K. A., Clement, R., & Pelletier, L. G. (1999). Perceptions of teachers' communicative style and students' intrinsic and extrinsic motivation. *Modern Language Journal, 83*, 23–34.

Pelletier, L., Fortier, M., Vallerand, R., & Brière, N. (2001). Associations among perceived autonomy support, forms of self-regulation, and persistence: A prospective study. *Motivation and Emotion, 25*, 279–306.

Pelletier, L. G., & Patry, D. (2006). Autodétermination et engagement professionnel des enseignants. In B. Galand & E. Bourgeois (Eds.), *Se motiver à apprendre* (pp. 171–182). Paris: Presses Universitaires de France.

Pelletier, L. G., Séguin-Lévesque, C., & Legault, L. (2002). Pressure from above and pressure from below as determinants of teachers' motivation and teaching behaviors. *Journal of Educational Psychology, 94*, 186–196.

Pelletier, L. G., & Sharp, E. C. (2009). Administrative pressures and teachers' interpersonal behaviour in the classroom. *Theory and Research in Education, 7*, 174–183.

Pelletier, L. G., & Vallerand, R. J. (1996). Supervisors' beliefs and subordinates' intrinsic motivation: A behavioral confirmation analysis. *Journal of Personality and Social Psychology, 71*, 331–340.

Radel, R., Sarrazin, P., Legrain, P., & Wild, T. C. (2010). Social contagion of motivation between teacher and student: Analyzing underlying processes. *Journal of Educational Psychology, 102*, 577–587.

Reeve, J. (2002). Self-determination theory applied to educational settings. In E. L. Deci & R. M. Ryan (Eds.), *Handbook of self-determination research* (pp. 183–203). Rochester, NY: University of Rochester Press.

Reeve, J., Deci, E. L., & Ryan, R. M. (2004). Self-determination theory: A dialectical framework for understanding socio-cultural influences on student motivation. In D. M. McInerney & S. Van Etten (Eds.), *Big theories revisited* (pp. 31–60). Greenwich, CT: Information Age Press.

Reeve, J., & Jang, H. (2006). What teachers say and do to support students' autonomy during a learning activity. *Journal of Educational Psychology, 98*, 209–218.

Reeve, J., Jang, H., Carrell, D., Jeon, S., & Barch, J. (2004). Enhancing students' engagement by increasing teachers' autonomy support. *Motivation and Emotion, 28*, 147–169.

Roth, G., Assor, A., Kanat-Maymon, Y., & Kaplan, H. (2007). Autonomous motivation for teaching: How self-determined teaching may lead to self-determined learning. *Journal of Educational Psychology, 99*, 761–774.

Ryan, R. (1995). Psychological needs and the facilitations of integrative processes. *Journal of Personality, 63*, 397–427.

Ryan, R. M., & Brown, K. W. (2005). Legislating competence: High-stakes testing policies and their relations with psychological theories and research. In A. J. Elliot & C. S. Dweck (Eds.), *Handbook of competence and motivation* (pp. 354–372). New York: Guilford Publications.

Ryan, R. M., & Deci, E. L. (2000). Intrinsic and extrinsic motivations: Classic definitions and new directions. *Contemporary Educational Psychology, 25*, 54–67.

Ryan, R. M., & Deci, E. L. (2009). Promoting self-determined school engagement: Motivation, learning, and well-being. In K. R. Wentzel & A. Wigfield (Eds.), *Handbook on motivation at school* (pp. 171–196). New York: Routledge.

Sarrazin, P. G., Tessier, D. P., Pelletier, L. G., Trouilloud, D. O., & Chanal, J. P. (2006). The effects of teachers' expectations about students' motivation on teachers' autonomy-supportive and controlling behaviors. *International Journal of Sport and Exercise Psychology, 4*, 283–301.

Schaufeli, W. B., Leiter, M. P., & Maslach, C. (2009). Burnout: Thirty-five years of research and practice. *Career Development International, 14*, 204–220.

Sheldon, K., Turban, D., Brown, K., Barrick, M., & Judge, Y. (2003). Applying self-determination theory to organizational research. *Volume Research in Personal and Human Resources Management, 22*, 357–393.

Sheldon, K. M., & Filak, V. (2008). Manipulating autonomy, competence and relatedness support in a game-learning context: New evidence that all three needs matter. *British Journal of Social Psychology, 47*, 267–283.

Skinner, E. A., & Belmont, M. J. (1993). Motivation in the classroom: Reciprocal effects of teacher behavior and student engagement across the school year. *Journal of Educational Psychology, 85*, 571–581.

Sørebø, Ø., Halvari, H., Gulli, V., & Kristiansen, R. (2009). The role of self-determination theory in explaining teachers' motivation to continue to use e-learning technology. *Computers & Education, 53*, 1177–1187.

Spittle, M., Jackson, K., & Casey, M. (2009). Applying self-determination theory to understand the motivation for becoming a physical education teacher. *Teaching and Teacher Education, 25*, 190–197.

Standage, M., Duda, J. L., & Ntoumanis, N. (2005). A test of self-determination theory in school physical education. *British Journal of Educational Psychology, 75*, 411–433.

Taylor, I. M., & Ntoumanis, N. (2007). Teacher motivational strategies and student self-determination in physical education. *Journal of Educational Psychology, 99*, 747–760.

Taylor, I. M., Ntoumanis, N., & Smith, B. (2009). The social context as a determinant of teacher motivational strategies in physical education. *Psychology of Sport and Exercise, 10*, 235–243.

Taylor, I. M., Ntoumanis, N., & Standage, M. (2008). A self-determination theory approach to understanding the antecedents of teachers' motivational strategies in physical education. *Journal of Sport & Exercise Psychology, 30*, 75–94.

Tessier, D., Sarrazin, P., & Ntoumanis, N. (2008). The effects of an experimental programme to support students' autonomy on the overt behaviours of physical education teachers. *European Journal of Psychology of Education, 23*, 239–253.

Tessier, D., Sarrazin, P., & Ntoumanis, N. (2010). The effect of an intervention to improve newly qualified teachers' interpersonal style, students motivation and psychological need satisfaction in sport-based physical education. *Contemporary Educational Psychology, 35*, 242–253.

Vallerand, R. J. (1997). Toward a hierarchical model of intrinsic and extrinsic motivation. In M. P. Zanna (Ed.), *Advances in experimental social psychology* (pp. 271–360). New York: Academic.

Van den Berghe, L., Soenens, B., Aelterman, N., Cardon, G., Tallir, I., & Haerens, L. (2014). Within-person profiles of teachers' motivation to teach: Associations with need satisfaction at work, need-supportive teaching, and burnout. *Psychology of Sport and Exercise, 15*, 407–417.

Van Petegem, K., Aelterman, A., Van Keer, H., & Rosseel, Y. (2008). The influence of student characteristics and interpersonal teacher behaviour in the classroom on student's wellbeing. *Social Indicators Research, 85*, 279–291.

Vansteenkiste, M., Lens, W., & Deci, E. L. (2006). Intrinsic versus extrinsic goal-contents in self-determination theory: Another look at the quality of academic motivation. *Educational Psychologist, 41*, 19–31.

Wang, C. K., & Liu, W. C. (2008). Teachers' motivation to teach national education in Singapore: A self-determination theory approach. *Asia Pacific Journal of Education, 28*, 395–410.

Wang, M. T., & Holcombe, R. (2010). Adolescents' perceptions of school environment, engagement, and academic achievement in middle school. *American Educational Research Journal, 47*, 633–662.

Wild, T., Enzle, M. E., Nix, G., & Deci, E. L. (1997). Perceiving others as intrinsically or extrinsically motivated: Effects on expectancy formation and task engagement. *Personality and Social Psychology Bulletin, 23*, 837–848.

Wilkesmann, U., & Schmid, C. J. (2014). Intrinsic and internalized modes of teaching motivation. *Evidence-Based HRM, 2*, 6–27.

Zimmerman, B. (2008). Investigating self-regulation and motivation: Historical background, methodological developments, and future prospects. *American Educational Research Journal, 45*, 166–183.

Chapter 7
Autonomy-Supportive Teaching: What It Is, How to Do It

Johnmarshall Reeve

They say that no two snowflakes are ever the same. Similarly, among teachers, no two motivating styles are ever the same. Each teacher seems to engage in autonomy-supportive teaching in a unique and personalized way. Still, the combination of a careful eye and a good theory (e.g., self-determination theory; Ryan & Deci, 2000) makes it clear that shared practices do exist among all autonomy-supportive teachers. This chapter is about those shared practices. This chapter casts a spotlight on these commonalities to pursue two goals: (1) identify what autonomy-supportive teaching is and (2) help any teacher who has a desire to do so become more autonomy supportive.

Motivating Style

If you have the opportunity to observe classroom instruction in action, you will sense a characteristic tone that is superimposed over the student-teacher interactions that take place. Sometimes the tone conveyed by the teacher is prescriptive ("Do this; do that") and is accompanied by a twist of pressure ("Hurry; now!"). Other times the tone is flexible ("What would you like to do?") and is accompanied by understanding and support. It typically takes only a thin slice of time to identify that tone, because it pervades literally everything the teacher says and does while trying to motivate and engage students.

J. Reeve (✉)
Korea University, Seoul, Korea
e-mail: reeve@korea.ac.kr

© Springer Science+Business Media Singapore 2016   129
W.C. Liu et al. (eds.), *Building Autonomous Learners*,
DOI 10.1007/978-981-287-630-0_7

Motivating Style: What It Is

All teachers face the instructional challenge to motivate their students to engage in and benefit from the learning activities they provide. For some teachers the controlling aspect of what they say and do is particularly salient. The teacher is insistent about what students should think, feel, and do, and the tone that surrounds these prescriptions is one of pressure. Implicitly, the teacher says, "I am your boss; I will monitor you; I am here to socialize and change you." These teacher-student interactions tend to be unilateral and no-nonsense. For other teachers, the supportive aspect of what they say and do is more salient. The teacher is highly respectful of students' perspectives and initiatives, and the tone is one of understanding. Implicitly, the teacher says "I am your ally; I will help you; I am here to support you and your strivings." These teacher-student interactions tend to be reciprocal and flexible. When these differences take on a recurring and enduring pattern, they represent a teacher's "orientation toward control vs. autonomy" (Deci, Schwartz, Sheinman, & Ryan, 1981) or, more simply, "motivating style" (Reeve, 2009).

Motivating style exists along a bipolar continuum that ranges from a highly controlling style on one end through a somewhat controlling style to a neutral or mixed style through a somewhat autonomy-supportive style to a highly autonomy-supportive style on the other end of the continuum (Deci et al., 1981). Because motivating style exists along a bipolar continuum, what autonomy-supportive teachers say and do during instruction is qualitatively different from, even the opposite of, what controlling teachers say and do during instruction.

Autonomy support is the instructional effort to provide students with a classroom environment and a teacher-student relationship that can support their students' need for autonomy. Autonomy support is the interpersonal sentiment and behavior the teacher provides during instruction first to identify, then to vitalize and nurture, and eventually to develop, strengthen, and grow students' inner motivational resources.

Teacher control, on the other hand, is the interpersonal sentiment and behavior the teacher provides during instruction to pressure students to think, feel, or behave in a teacher-prescribed way (Reeve, 2009). In practice, controlling teachers neglect or even thwart students' inner motivations and, instead, by-pass these motivational resources to (1) tell or prescribe what students are to think, feel, and do and (2) apply subtle or not-so-subtle pressure until students forego their own preferences to adopt the teacher's prescribed course of action.

The present paper looks carefully at the autonomy-supportive end of the motivating style bipolar continuum, but for the reader interested in a thorough analysis of the controlling motivating style, I recommend discussions on behavioral control (e.g., controlling use of rewards, negative conditional regard, intimidation, and excessive personal control; Bartholomew, Ntoumanis, Ryan, Bosch, & Thogersen-Ntoumani, 2011), psychological control (Soenens, Park, Vansteenkiste, & Mouratidis, 2012), intrusive and manipulative socialization (Barber, 2002), conditional regard (e.g., guilt induction, love withdrawal following noncompliance, love validation following compliance; Assor, Roth, & Deci, 2004; Roth, Assor, Niemiec, Ryan, & Deci, 2009; Assor), or teacher control in general (Reeve, 2009).

	Never			Occasionally			Always
Takes the Students' Perspective	1	2	3	4	5	6	7

- Invites, Asks for, Welcomes, and Incorporates Students' Input
- Is "In Synch" with Students
- Is Aware of Students' Needs, Wants, Goals, Priorities, Preferences, and Emotions

	Never			Occasionally			Always
Vitalizes Inner Motivational Resources	1	2	3	4	5	6	7

- Piques Curiosity; Provides Interesting Learning Activities
- Vitalizes and Supports Students' Autonomy, Competence, Relatedness
- Frames Learning Activities with Students' Intrinsic Goals

	Never			Occasionally			Always
Provides Explanatory Rationales for Requests, Rules, Procedures, and Uninteresting Activities	1	2	3	4	5	6	7

- Explains Why; Says, "Because,....", "The reason is..."
- Identifies the Value, Importance, Benefit, Use, Utility of a Request

	Never			Occasionally			Always
Uses Non-Pressuring, Informational Language	1	2	3	4	5	6	7

- Flexible, Open-minded, Responsive Communication
- Provides Choices, Provides Options
- Says, "You may...", "You might..."

	Never			Occasionally			Always
Acknowledges and Accepts Negative Affect	1	2	3	4	5	6	7

- Listens Carefully, Non-Defensively, with Understanding
- Acknowledges Students' Negative Affect ("Okay"; "Yes")
- Accepts Complaints as Valid ("Okay"; "Yes")

	Never			Occasionally			Always
Displays Patience	1	2	3	4	5	6	7

- Allows Students to Work at their Own Pace, in their Own Way
- Calmly Waits for Students' Signals of Initiative, Input, and Willingness

Fig. 7.1 Observer's rating sheet to score autonomy-supportive teaching

While I conceptualize motivating style within the context of a bipolar continuum, some self-determination theory researchers have begun to study autonomy-supportive and controlling instructional behaviors as two somewhat independent approaches to motivating and engaging students. That is, while some study motivating style as one single characteristic (a bipolar continuum with two opposite ends), others study autonomy-supportive teaching and controlling teaching as two distinct motivating styles (Bartholomew et al., 2011; Haerens, Aelterman, Vansteenkiste, Soenens, & Van Petegem, 2015). To illustrate how autonomy-supportive and controlling instructional behaviors can be measured separately, Figs. 7.1 and 7.2 show two rating sheets. One rating sheet is used to score six acts of autonomy-supportive teaching (Fig. 7.1), while the other is used to score six acts of controlling teaching (Fig. 7.2). This use of separate unipolar scales began because some classroom-based investigations found that autonomy-supportive and controlling instructional behaviors had negative—but not highly negative—intercorrelations (Assor, Kaplan, & Roth, 2002; Assor, Kaplan, Kanat-Maymon, & Roth, 2005). These low intercorrelations were observed because, sometimes, teachers acted in both autonomy-supportive and controlling ways (e.g., giving a command, yet offering an explanatory rationale). Complicating matters on this "one bipolar vs. two unipolar" motivating style issue is that the extent of negative correlation between ratings of autonomy-supportive teaching and ratings of controlling teaching depends on factors such as

	Never		Occasionally			Always	
Takes Only the Teacher's Perspective	1	2	3	4	5	6	7

- Attends to and Prioritizes Only the Teacher's Plans, Needs
- Teacher Is Out of Synch with Students; Unresponsive to Students' Signals
- Is Unaware of Students' Needs, Wants, Goals, Priorities, Preferences, and Emotions

Introduces Extrinsic Motivators	1	2	3	4	5	6	7

- Offers Incentives; Seeks Compliance
- Gives Consequences for Desired & Undesired Behaviors
- Utters Assignments, Directives, and Commands

Neglects to Provide Explanatory Rationales	1	2	3	4	5	6	7

for Requests, Rules, Procedures, and Uninteresting Activities

- Directives without Explanations
- Requests ("do this; do that") without Explanations

Uses Controlling, Pressuring Language	1	2	3	4	5	6	7

- Evaluative, Critical, Coercive, Inflexible; "No Nonsense"
- Prescriptive ("You *should*, you *must*, you *have to*, you've *got to*...")
- Verbally and nonverbally pressuring (raises voice, points, pushes hard, "hurry")

Counters and Tries to Change Negative Affect	1	2	3	4	5	6	7

- Counters and Argues Against Students' Negative Affect, Complaining, or "Bad Attitude"
- Tries to Change Negative Affect into Something Acceptable to the Teacher

Displays Impatience	1	2	3	4	5	6	7

- Rushes Student to Produce a Right Answer or a Desired Behavior
- Intrudes into Students' Workspace (Grabs away learning materials; Says, "Here, let me do that for you.")
- Communicates What Is Right & Pushes Students to Reproduce It Quickly

Fig. 7.2 Observers' rating sheet to score controlling teaching

the rating sheet used, the length of time the teachers are rated (e.g., 5 min teaching episode vs. 1 h classroom observation), and even who the teachers being rated are (Chua, Wong, & Koestner, 2014).

While I continue to conceptualize autonomy-supportive and controlling teaching as opposite ends of a single continuum, I recognize that there is nevertheless some wisdom and practical utility in assessing autonomy support and controlling teaching separately, and this is so for two reasons. First, SDT-based theoretical models show that autonomy-supportive teaching tends to uniquely predict students' need satisfaction, positive functioning, and well-being, while controlling teaching uniquely predicts need frustration, negative functioning, and ill-being (Bartholomew et al., 2011; Haerens et al., 2015). Second, for most teachers, developing the skill of becoming more autonomy supportive sometimes occurs over time as a two-step process in which the teacher first learns how to be less controlling and then second learns how to be more autonomy supportive.

Motivating Style: Why It Is Important

A teacher's motivating style toward students is an important educational construct for two important reasons. First, teacher-provided autonomy support benefits students in very important ways. Students who are randomly assigned to receive autonomy support from their teachers, compared to those who are not (students in a control group), experience higher-quality motivation and display markedly more positive classroom functioning and educational outcomes, including more need satisfaction, greater autonomous motivation (i.e., intrinsic motivation, identified regulation), greater classroom engagement, higher-quality learning, a preference for optimal challenge, enhanced psychological and physical well-being, and higher academic achievement (Cheon & Reeve, 2013, 2014; Cheon, Reeve, & Moon, 2012; Cheon, Reeve, Yu, & Jang, 2014; Reeve, Jang, Carrell, Jeon, & Barch, 2004; Vansteenkiste, Simons, Lens, Sheldon, & Deci, 2004; Vansteenkiste, Simons, Lens, Soenens, & Matos, 2005; Vansteenkiste, Simons, Soenens, & Lens, 2004). The general conclusion from these experimental studies is that students benefit from receiving autonomy support, and they benefit in ways that are widespread and educationally important, even vital.

Second, teacher-provided autonomy support benefits teachers themselves. Teachers who participate in workshops designed to help them learn how to become more autonomy supportive (compared to teachers in a control group) not only display greater autonomy-supportive teaching, but they further report greater need satisfaction from teaching, greater harmonious passion for teaching, greater teaching efficacy, higher job satisfaction, greater vitality during teaching, and lesser emotional and physical exhaustion after teaching (Cheon et al., 2014). Again, the general conclusion is that teachers benefit from giving autonomy support, and they benefit in ways that are widespread and professionally important.

Two Goals of Autonomy Support

At one level, the goal of autonomy support is clear and obvious—namely, to provide students with learning activities, a classroom environment, and a student-teacher relationship that will support their daily autonomy. That is, the first goal of teacher-provided autonomy support is to deliver the curriculum in a way that supports students' autonomous motivation and their autonomy need satisfaction in particular. Parenthetically, the goal of controlling teaching is also obvious—namely, to gain students' compliance with teacher-provided prescriptions ("do this") and proscriptions ("don't do that").

At another level, the second goal of autonomy support is not so obvious—namely, to become in synch with one's students (Lee & Reeve, 2012). A teacher and her students are "in synch" when they form a dialectical relationship in which the actions of one influence the actions of the other, and vice versa (e.g., the teacher makes a request, students agree but also suggest how that request might be revised or personalized, the teacher accommodates that input); a teacher and his students are "out of synch" when the relationship is unilateral in which the actions of one influence the other but not vice versa (Reeve, Deci, & Ryan, 2004).

Being in synch with one's students is an important idea to discuss, because it means that the goal of autonomy-supportive teaching is not to do something to

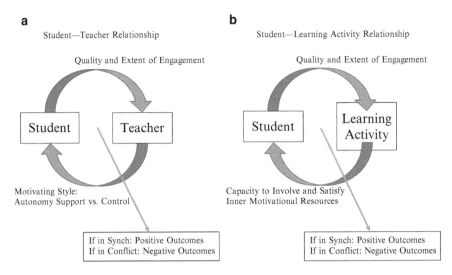

Fig. 7.3 Dialectic relationship that students have with their teachers (**a**) and learning activities (**b**)

motivate students, but, rather, it is to enter into transactional (Sameroff, 2009) and dialectical (Reeve, Deci, & Ryan, 2004) interactions so that students become increasingly able to motivate themselves (Deci, 1995). With transactional and dialectical interactions, what students do (display engagement) affects and transforms what teachers do (display a motivating style) and vice versa. As illustrated in Fig. 7.3a, when students and teachers are in synch, relationship synthesis occurs, as students' engagement affords teachers a greater opportunity to be responsive and hence more autonomy supportive toward students. Teacher-provided autonomy support, in turn, affords students a greater opportunity to be more engaged in classroom activity. Together, the teacher and student join forces to move toward a higher-quality motivation (students) and a higher-quality motivating style (teachers). When students and teachers are not in synch, however, relationship conflict occurs, as teachers are not responsive to students (because they are not engaged) and students are not responsive to teachers (because they are controlling). Apart, the teacher and students oppose each other and move toward a lower-quality motivation (students) and a lower-quality motivating style (teachers).

For years, I felt that the relations depicted in Fig. 7.3a were sufficient to capture the "in synch" goal of autonomy-supportive teaching. I continue to believe that Fig. 7.3a is likely sufficient for teachers who provide instruction to learners who do not have a long history with the learning activity (e.g., students taking a first course in social studies). In one recent study, however, we provided an autonomy-supportive intervention program to coaches of elite, lifelong, and literally Olympic-level athletes (Cheon, Reeve, Lee, & Lee, 2015). For these athletes, the sport-athlete relation was longer-lasting and more motivationally important to them than was the coach-athlete relationship. That is, athlete motivation was more closely tied to the activity than it was to the coaching relationship. We learned that one of the best ways these coaches could support their athletes' autonomy was to provide athletes with new ways to practice and train that were significantly more interesting, more need-satisfying, and more relevant to their personal goals than what the athletes were currently doing. That is, to be autonomy supportive, these coaches needed to help their athletes become more in synch with their sport (or learning activity), as shown in Fig. 7.3b. Here the question is how supportive the learning activity is of the person's inner motivational resources. Teachers can help students become more in synch with the learning activity (or subject matter) by showing students new ways of interacting with the learning activity so that need satisfaction, curiosity, interest, and goal progress become high probability occurrences while need neglect, need frustration, mere repetition, boredom, and goal stagnation become low probability occurrences.

Autonomy-Supportive Teaching in Practice

Using a laboratory procedure, Deci, Eghrari, Patrick, and Leone (1994) experimentally manipulated the presence vs. absence of three interpersonal conditions—*provide meaningful rationales*, *acknowledge negative feelings*, and *use noncontrolling language*. In the Deci et al. (1994) experiment, participants worked on a very uninteresting activity, and the instructional goal was to support students' internalization and task engagement. This research showed that providing meaningful rationales, acknowledging negative feelings, and using noncontrolling language functioned synergistically as three mutually supportive ways to support autonomy as people engage themselves in relatively uninteresting activities. In the classroom, however, the teacher's goal is expanded to include sparking engagement in interesting and personally valued activities. To support students' interest and personal goals, the following interpersonal conditions were added to the operational definition of autonomy support: *perspective taking*, *nurture inner motivational resources*, and *display patience* (i.e., allow students to work at their own pace) (Assor et al., 2002; Edmunds, Ntoumanis, & Duda, 2008; Tessier, Sarrazin, & Ntoumanis, 2008; Reeve, 2009; Reeve, Jang et al., 2004). Together, these six categories of instructional behavior rather comprehensively reveal what autonomy-supportive teachers are saying and doing during instruction.

In practice, an autonomy-supportive motivating style involves the enactment of the following six positively intercorrelated and mutually supportive instructional behaviors: (1) take the student's perspective; (2) vitalize inner motivational resources; (3) provide explanatory rationales for requests; (4) acknowledge and accept students' expressions of negative affect; (5) rely on informational, nonpressuring language; and (6) display patience (Reeve, 2009; Reeve & Cheon, 2014). In this section, I overview each of these six aspects of autonomy-supportive teaching and, in doing so, answer four questions:

- What is it?
- When is it needed?

- Why is it important?
- How is it done?

Juggling six behaviors while simultaneously delivering the curriculum is asking a lot of teachers. To help structure the teacher's effort to develop the interpersonal skill that is autonomy support, I find it useful to break down autonomy-supportive teaching into three critical moments within the instructional flow, as illustrated in Fig. 7.4. The instructional flow begins with a pre-lesson reflective period in which the teacher plans and prepares the instructional episode (e.g., learning objectives, learning activities, schedule of events). The critical aspect of autonomy-supportive teaching during this time is to take the students' perspective. Once the instructional episode has been prepared, it is then delivered. As the lesson begins, the teacher invites students to engage in the learning activity. The two critical aspects of autonomy-supportive teaching during this time are to vitalize inner motivational resources and to provide explanatory rationales. As the lesson unfolds, student problems arise (e.g., disengagement, misbehavior, poor performance) that the teacher needs to address and solve if the learning objectives are to be realized. The three critical aspects of autonomy-supportive teaching during this time are to acknowledge and accept negative affect, to use informational and nonpressuring language, and to display patience.

Pre-lesson Reflection: Preparing and Planning

During the pre-lesson reflection period, the critical aspect of autonomy-supportive teaching is to take the students' perspective, as shown on the left side of Fig. 7.4.

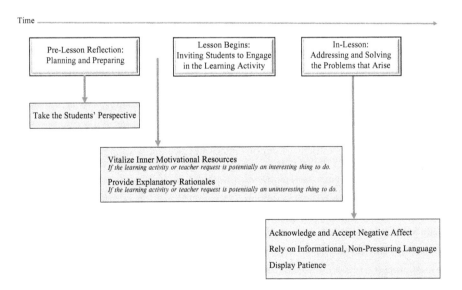

Fig. 7.4 Three critical motivational moments in the flow of autonomy-supportive teaching

Take the Students' Perspective: What Does This Mean, When Is It Needed, and Why Is It Important? Perspective taking is the teacher's seeing classroom events as if he or she were the students. With perspective taking, the teacher imagines himself or herself to be in the students' place. It is a cognitive empathic response in which the teacher first understands what students think and feel and second desires for students to think and feel better. The teacher actively monitors students' needs, wants, goals, priorities, preferences, and emotionality, and the teacher considers potential obstacles students may face that might create anxiety, confusion, or resistance. To do this, the teacher needs to partially set aside his or her own perspective to better understand the students' perspective (Davis, 2004).

It is always helpful to be mindful of the students' perspective during instruction, but it is most timely during this pre-lesson creation period. If the instruction-to-come is to align well with students' inner motivational resources, teachers need to ask, "Will students find this lesson interesting?", "Could the lesson be made more interesting, more attractive, or more relevant to students' concerns?", and "If so, how?"

Taking the students' perspective is important because the more teachers are able to design instruction to align with students' motivational assets, the more in synch the teacher and students will be during that episode of instruction. Perspective taking enables teachers to become both more willing (because of greater empathy) and more able (because of greater perspective taking) to create classroom conditions in which students' inner motivational resources guide their classroom activity. If a lesson is prepared without taking the students' perspective in mind, the odds increase dramatically that the lesson will ignore or neglect students' inner motivational resources.

Taking the Students' Perspective: How to Practice It As they prepare for instruction, teachers can tap into their experience in teaching similar students in the past and therefore somewhat anticipate the current students' likely reactions to a wide range of learning activities—and they can make instructional adjustments accordingly. The important point is to use one's classroom experience to forge new-and-improved answers to these two questions: "Will students find this lesson to be need-satisfying, curiosity-provoking, interesting, and personally important?" and "How can I make this lesson more need-satisfying, curiosity-provoking, interesting, and personally important to my students?"

To begin the lesson, teachers might start with a perspective-enabling conversation that sounds something like the following: "Here is the plan for today. Does that sound like a good use of our time? Any suggestions? Is there anything in this lesson that we might improve?" By starting a lesson in this way, the teacher shows both an openness and a willingness to welcome, ask for, encourage, and incorporate students' input and suggestions into the lesson plan and into the flow of instruction. Of course, the teacher's responsiveness to students' input and suggestions is important. So, the teacher also needs to be willing to incorporate that input and those student suggestions, assuming they are consistent with the learning objective.

During the lesson, teachers can look to students' preferences and engagement signals to gain the perspective they need to adjust instruction. As to preferences, classroom clickers might be used to solicit students' collective opinions, choices, and preferences. During instruction, if students display strong and consistent signs of engagement, this confirms that what the students are presently doing aligns well with their inner motivational resources. If students display signs of disengagement or if engagement drops off, that is confirmation that what students are presently doing is neglecting or by-passing their inner motivational resources. Teachers can use these disengagement signals as a trigger to change the flow of instruction away from that which neglects students' motivation and toward that which involves and vitalizes it.

After the lesson, teachers might conduct a formative assessment. One simple, yet highly informative, formative assessment is to hand out an index card to each student during the last 3 min of class. The index card is blank, except for the following question at the top, "Any suggestions?" If the teacher asks students not to write their names on the card and says that the purpose of the activity is only to improve everyone's experience in future classes, then students can be expected to communicate to teachers their otherwise private perspective (e.g., "Class is fine, but maybe we could have more group discussion."). In this exercise, it is important that all students hand in an index card, even if many of those cards are left blank, so that students can be assured that their individual comments will remain anonymous. Students' responses on these index cards then provide invaluable insight for teachers to incorporate into their future pre-lesson planning and preparing.

Another version of this same formative assessment strategy is to invite students to complete a "weekly reaction sheet" (Rogers, 1995). The student again receives an index card at the end of the week that is blank, except for the following invitation at the top, "Express any feeling you wish that is relevant to the course." At first, the teacher might offer suggestions, such as "the work you are doing", "what you are reading or thinking about", "a feeling about the course", or "a feeling about the instructor."

Lesson Begins: Inviting Students to Engage in the Learning Activity

When teachers present a learning activity and invite students' engagement, student participation in the lesson begins and the next two critical aspects of autonomy-supportive teaching become (1) vitalizing students' inner motivational resources and (2) providing explanatory rationales. Before inviting students to engage themselves in the learning activity, the teacher makes a judgment, based on perspective taking, whether students are likely to find the activity or behavioral request to be an interesting or an uninteresting thing to do. As shown in the middle of Fig. 7.4, if the teacher forecasts that students will likely find the activity to be a potentially interesting thing to do, then the critical autonomy-supportive instructional behavior becomes to vitalize students' inner motivational resources. This allows students to experience the activity as a more interesting and need-satisfying thing to do. If the teacher forecasts that students will likely find the activity to be a potentially uninteresting thing to do, then the critical autonomy-supportive instructional behavior becomes to provide explanatory rationales. This allows students to experience the activity as a more important or worthwhile thing to do. Notice in Fig. 7.4 that these two acts of autonomy-supportive teaching occur *before* "lesson begins." This is because the critical teaching moment occurs with the engagement invitation. It is important that students first formulate a volitional and heartfelt intention to engage in the lesson ("I want to") before they actually engage in and learn from that lesson.

Vitalize Inner Motivational Resources: What Does This Mean, When Is It Needed, and Why Is It Important? Vitalizing students' inner motivational resources entails using instruction as an opportunity to awaken (involve) and nurture (satisfy) students' psychological needs for autonomy, competence, and relatedness, as well as students' curiosity, interest, and intrinsic goals. The teacher involves the students' inner motivational resources so to make them a central part of the learning activity. Once vitalized, these inner motivational resources are fully capable of energizing, directing, and sustaining students' classroom activity in productive ways.

Vitalizing inner motivational resources is most timely when teachers introduce a learning activity or when teachers make a transition from one activity to another. It is most needed when teachers seek active engagement from students. It is particularly important because it allows students to feel like origins, rather than like pawns, during learning activities. It allows students to engage in lessons with an authentic sense of wanting to do it, because people in general freely want to do that which is need-satisfying, curiosity-satisfying, interesting, and personally important.

Vitalizing Inner Motivational Resources: How to Practice It Before teachers can vitalize students' inner motivational resources, they first need to know what inner motivational resources students possess. An inner motivational resource is an inherent energizing and directing force that all students possess, irrespective of their age, gender, nationality, or academic ability that, when supported, vitalizes engagement and enhances well-being (Ryan & Deci, 2000). Six such resources are highly classroom relevant and are summarized in Table 7.1. In a self-determination theory analysis, these inner resources represent the ultimate source of students' classroom engagement in learning activities (Reeve, Deci & Ryan, 2004).

Vitalizing inner motivational resources means building instruction around opportunities to have students' classroom engagement initiated and regulated by the six inner resources listed in Table 7.1. That is, the reason why students engage in the lesson is because it is need-satisfying (inherently enjoyable), meaningful (important), goal-relevant, curiosity-piquing, challenge inviting, etc., and not because they have to (e.g., obey a directive, earn extra credit points). Parenthetically, Table 7.1 does not list intrinsic motivation as an inner motivational resource, though it

Table 7.1 Six engagement-fostering inner motivational resources that all students possess

Autonomy	The need to be the origin of one's behavior. The inner endorsement of one's thoughts (goals), feelings, and behaviors
Competence	The need to interact effectively with one's environmental surroundings—to seek out optimal challenges, take them on, and exert persistent effort and strategic thinking to make progress in mastering them
Relatedness	The need to be involved in warm relationships characterized by mutual concern, liking, and acceptance
Curiosity	A cognitively generated emotion that occurs whenever students become aware of an unexpected gap in their knowledge that they wish to close
Interest	An engagement-fostering emotion that occurs whenever students have an opportunity to learn something new or to develop greater understanding
Intrinsic goals	Personal strivings that produce psychological need satisfaction during their pursuit. An inward focus to pursue personal growth or closer interpersonal relationships

certainly is a vital inner motivational resource that all students possess. Intrinsic motivation is omitted from Table 7.1 simply because it is defined as the motivation that arises from psychological need satisfaction (Deci & Ryan, 1985; Ryan & Deci, 2000). Teachers can certainly facilitate students' intrinsic motivation, but the way to do that is to vitalize and support students' psychological needs for autonomy, competence, and relatedness.

Autonomy Teachers can vitalize students' need for autonomy by offering them an opportunity for self-direction with the learning activity (Deci, Spiegel, Ryan, Koestner, & Kauffman, 1982; Jang, Reeve, & Halusic, 2015; Nix, Ryan, Manly, & Deci, 1999; Reeve & Jang, 2006). The autonomy need is vitalized when the student experiences a heartfelt affirmation to questions such as "Do I want to learn this?," "Do I want to do this?," and "Do I fully agree with this decision and with this course of action?" The best way to have students answer such questions in the affirmative is to ask them what they would like to do within the context of the learning activity and then allow them (and help them) to do it.

Competence Teachers can vitalize students' need for competence by offering them an optimal challenge to strive for within a failure-tolerant environment (Clifford, 1990; Keller & Bless, 2008). Teachers can offer students an optimal challenge in many different ways, such as by introducing a standard of excellence, a goal to strive for, a role model to emulate, or students' own past performance to try to surpass. In practice, teachers can start a lesson by introducing a standard of excellence (e.g., write a paragraph with only active verbs, pronounce a foreign language phrase like an audiotape of a native speaker, run a mile in 10 min or less) and then ask students, "Can you do it?" To the extent to which students perceive that they are making progress toward meeting the challenge embedded within the learning activity, they will feel competence satisfaction while doing so.

Relatedness Teachers can vitalize students' need for relatedness by offering them an opportunity to engage in communal social interaction (La Guardia & Patrick,

2008; Ryan & Powelson, 1991). Teachers can do this by giving students an opportunity to engage in face-to-face interaction with a classmate (e.g., a 2-min learning together exercise, cooperative learning). Relatedness need satisfaction occurs to the extent that teachers are able to create opportunities for students to relate their selves to others in an authentic, caring, reciprocal, and emotionally meaningful way.

Curiosity Curiosity is an emotion that occurs whenever students experience an unexpected gap in their knowledge (Loewenstein, 1994; Silvia, 2008). Curiosity is satisfied when students use exploratory behavior to acquire the information needed to remove that knowledge gap. In doing so, that exploratory behavior (i.e., engagement) generates knowledge growth, learning, and greater expertise. During instruction, teachers can vitalize students' curiosity in numerous ways, such as asking a curiosity-inducing question (Jang, 2015), introducing suspense about what comes next (Abuhamdeh, Csikszentmihalyi, & Jalal, 2015), and encouraging students to explore a new activity (Proyer, Ruch, & Buschor, 2013).

Interest Interest is an alert, positive-feeling basic emotion that creates a motivational urge to seek, explore, and investigate; it occurs whenever students have the opportunity to learn something new and to develop greater understanding (Reeve, Lee, & Won, 2015). Interest is like heart rate—it is always there but it also rises and falls; it is a constant presence that can nevertheless be either increased or decreased. It is increased during instruction by offering students new information that exposes a knowledge gap, new experiences (e.g., field trips), new stories or quotations, a brief lesson-centric video presentation, a problem to solve, a how-to demonstration, or a puzzle, riddle, or mystery to solve (Loewenstein, 1994; Schraw, Flowerday, & Lehman, 2001; Silvia, 2006, 2008).

Intrinsic Goals Teachers can vitalize students' intrinsic goals by framing the learning activity as an opportunity for personal growth, skill development, an opportunity to develop a closer relationship with others, or an opportunity to contribute constructively to one's community (Vansteenkiste, Lens, & Deci, 2006; Vansteenkiste et al., 2005). A teacher might, for instance, introduce a writing lesson not only as an exercise in writing but also as an opportunity to become a better writer, saying, "To begin, let's read this passage by the writer Philip Roth. As you read, notice how good the writing is. Ask yourself what makes this such good writing, and use your answer to discover how to become a better writer yourself." To the extent that the teacher knows that these students truly want to become better writers, that lesson will be motivating and engaging.

Provide Explanatory Rationales: What Does This Mean, When Is It Needed, and Why Is It Important? A rationale is a verbal explanation as to why putting forth effort during the activity might be a useful thing to do (Reeve, Jang, Hardre, & Omura, 2002). These verbal explanations help students understand the personal utility within the requested activity, and they therefore help students transform a perceived "worthless activity" (something not worth doing) into a potentially "worthwhile activity" (something worth doing)—something that is truly worth their time, attention, and effort.

Providing explanatory rationales is most timely when teachers request that students engage in a perceived uninteresting or unappealing learning activity, rule, or procedure. It is important because not all lessons, classroom procedures, and behavioral requests can be interesting things to do, at least from the students' point of view. In those instances, student motivation is highly fragile, as students wonder, "Why do this? Do we really need to do this?" When the teacher provides an explanatory rationale, it helps students make the motivational transition from viewing the activity or requested behavior as something that is not worth doing (because it is unimportant, trivial, or useless to the self) to something that is worth doing (because it is important, valuable, useful to the self). Satisfying explanatory rationales help students accept and begin to internalize the value of the teacher's request, and it is this perception of value that provides students with a volitional sense of "wanting to" (Jang, 2008; Koestner, Ryan, Bernieri, & Holt, 1984; Reeve et al., 2002).

Providing Explanatory Rationales: How to Practice It In the course of instruction, teachers often ask students to do things that students may perceive to be uninteresting and unimportant. Examples might include "read the book," "revise the paper," "check for spelling errors," "clean your desk," "treat others with respect," "be on time," "share with your neighbor," "wait for your turn," "participate in the group discussion," "follow the safety procedures," etc. While students do not really want to do these things, the teacher nevertheless has a good reason for asking students to undertake that particular course of action. The problem is that the teacher's very good reason is too often unknown to students. When students do not understand or appreciate why the teacher is making a request of them, they tend to view the request as arbitrary, imposed, or simply meaningless busywork. Hence, to support students' willingness to engage in the requested behavior, teachers need to reveal to students the "hidden value" (the personal utility) of the request.

Several skills are involved in communicating satisfying explanatory rationales. The first is to think reflectively, "Why am I asking students to do this?" If a teacher cannot provide an explanatory rationale, the chances tilt toward the possibility that the request really is unnecessary busywork. Of course, teachers usually have a good rationale for their requests, so there is skill in being mindful of the *why*? behind one's requests.

The second skill is to generate satisfying rationales. Rationales such as the following may sound like explanations, but they are deeply unsatisfying to students' ears: "because I said so," "because it is on the test," "because it is good for you," and "you will understand when you are older." Before teachers can provide satisfying rationales, they need to first take their students' perspective and ask if the rationale they have to offer will be well received. For instance, the teacher might believe "so that you won't bump into others and cause a lot of noise" is a good rationale for "no running in the hallway," but it is possible that students will not find this same rationale to be personally satisfying. For students, the fun and excitement of running in the hallways may trump the concern over bumping into others and causing a lot of noise. So, teachers need to explain what is truly important, useful, and worthwhile to students about walking rather than running in the hallways.

Consider the common teacher request, "clean your desk." There is skill in teachers being able to provide a rationale that their students will find to be both authentic and personally satisfying. Having a student clean his or her desk may be important, but the motivational problem to be solved is to help the student come to believe that having a clean desk is an important, useful, and valuable undertaking. In such cases, it is easy for teachers to panic and follow up an explanatory rationale with impatient pressure ("Just do it!"). Effective (satisfying) rationales, however, are those that do not have strings and hidden agendas attached to them. This is the third skill in providing effective rationales: Communicate to students what they do not yet know, which is why the teacher's request is a valuable and worthwhile thing to do.

A final skill is to provide the explanatory rationale prior to the behavioral request. Most of the time, rationales lag behind the teacher's request, as in, "After lunch, everyone needs to be sitting in their seat by 1:00, because we have a special activity that begins precisely at 1:00 and I don't want you to miss out on the fun." The order of events is "request first, rationale second." Such an order implicitly communicates primacy to the behavioral request and only supplemental concern for its underlying reason. "Request, then rationale" is better than request only (Reeve et al., 2002), and it is better than request plus a twist of pressure (Koestner et al., 1984). Still, it is motivationally odd to support motivation after, rather than before, the behavioral request. From a motivational point of view, it is more constructive to facilitate the students' acceptance, willingness, and internalization before making a behavioral request. Hence, a better order of events would be, "rationale first, request second," as in the following: "We have a special activity that begins precisely at 1:00 and I don't want you to miss out on the fun. So, after lunch, everyone needs to be sitting in their seat by 1:00."

In-Lesson: Addressing and Solving Students' Problems

Student problems can arise during any instructional episode. When they surface, these problems put at risk the quality of students' classroom motivation, the quality of their learning experience, and the quality of the teacher-student relationship. Table 7.2 lists three commonly occurring student problems: disengagement, misbehavior, and poor performance. In many ways, these problems revolve around the question of "classroom management." It is during these times in which teachers try to manage students' disengagement, behavioral problems, and poor performance that the following three aspects of autonomy-supportive teaching are most critical: acknowledge and accept negative affect, use informational and nonpressuring language, and display patience.

Acknowledge and Accept Negative Affect: What Does This Mean, When Is It Needed, and Why Is It Important? By acknowledging and accepting students'

Table 7.2 Three frequently encountered categories of students' classroom problems

Disengagement	Students show insufficient involvement to profit from the learning activity. Students are off-task, display little or no effort, use only superficial learning strategies, fail to participate, and are merely passive recipients of instruction
Misbehavior	Students act in maladaptive, immature, or antisocial ways. Students are irresponsible, unprepared, and aggressive and cheat, curse, tease, utter disrespectful language, break rules, skip class, smoke cigarettes, fail to complete their assignments, and show delinquency
Poor performance	Students perform carelessly or incompetently. Students produce sloppy, careless, or lackluster work. Students underperform standards or expectations

expressions of negative affect, the teacher shows sensitivity to and a tolerance for students' concerns, negative emotionality, and problematic self-regulation. The teacher acknowledges that his or her request may conflict with and be at odds with the students' preferences. The teacher acknowledges that negative emotionality, feelings of conflict, complaining, and resisting may be valid and legitimate reactions to the teacher's request, at least from the students' point of view.

Acknowledging and accepting negative affect is most timely when conflict arises between what teachers want students to do (e.g., read a book, revise a paper, pay attention) and what students want to do (e.g., something different, something less demanding, talk with their neighbor).

It is important because acknowledging and accepting negative affect represents the teacher's best chance of getting students' engagement-blocking negative affect out of the learning activity and out of the classroom. By considering that students' negative affect may be valid and legitimate, at least to a degree, the teacher gains an opportunity to restructure the otherwise unappealing or conflict-generating lesson so that it gains the potential to become something that is more appealing and less conflict-generating.

Students' negative affect involves complaints, resistance, protests, "bad attitude," and negative emotion and affect. Negative emotion and affect during instruction, such as anxiety, confusion, frustration, anger, resentment, stress, fear, and boredom, tends to interfere with and potentially overwhelm students' motivation and engagement in the lesson. Complaints, resistance, protests, and "bad attitude" often arise out of students' perceptions that teacher's requests, assignments, rules, demands, or expectations are unfair, are unreasonable, are asking too much of them, or simply represent things to do that are neither interesting nor important. The concern is that such negative affect, if unaddressed, will interfere with—a perhaps even poison—students' engagement and learning. Soothing these negative feelings therefore becomes a prerequisite to motivationally readying students to engage in and benefit from the lesson.

Acknowledging and Accepting Negative Affect: How to Practice It Teachers often react to students' expressions of negative affect in a defensive way. Often, teachers do not see students' resistance as valid ("You're immature; you're irresponsible.") and, hence, counter or otherwise try to change students' resistance and negative feelings into something more acceptable to the teacher (e.g., "Quit your complaining; now get to work and do what you are supposed to do."). From a motivational point of view, such teaching behavior runs the risk of replacing students' engagement-fostering inner motivational resources with engagement-thwarting negative affect and resistance to both the learning activity and to the one providing the learning activity (i.e., the teacher). In contrast, acknowledging and accepting such negative affectivity means taking to heart and even welcoming these expressions as potentially valid reactions to imposed rules, assignments, requests, and expectations.

Here is an example. When the teacher notices that students are generally uninterested in and disengaged in the lesson, the teacher might begin a conversation: "I see that you are not enthusiastic about and interested in today's lesson. Do I have that right?" These words acknowledge (address) the problem of students' negative affect (boredom). The teacher might continue: "Yes, we have practiced this same skill many times before, haven't we?" These words ("yes") accept the students' expression of negative affect as potentially valid and legitimate reactions to the instruction. The teacher might continue: "Okay. Let's see. What might we do differently this time? Any suggestions?" These words ("okay") become the teacher's starting point to find the source of the negative affect and to extinguish it. Once done, the teacher now has room to alter (to upgrade) instruction.

There is the key question of whether or not this is an effective instructional strategy. One thing is sure—namely, blaming students ("You're lazy; you're irresponsible.") and trying to change their negative affect into something acceptable to the teacher (e.g., "Quit acting like children, take responsibility for your own learning, act like an adult, and pay attention.") are a recipe for motivational and engagement disaster. Such an approach to instruction is the equivalent of throwing proverbial fuel on the fire (the problem of disengagement). It not only blocks engagement in the learning activity, but it sends a deeper message that the teacher is out of synch with the students. To solve this problem, it first needs to be addressed, which is the essence of "acknowledge and accept negative affect." But, to actually solve the problem (to actually dissipate students' negative affect), the teacher-student dialogue needs to produce fruit. This dialogue begins with something such as, "Okay. What might we do differently this time—any suggestions?" Perhaps students who are anxious, confused, frustrated, angry, stressed, etc. will voice their suggestions, but it is often the case that they first need to know the teacher is sincere in the effort to alter the flow of instruction. Hence, it is often necessary for teachers to take the first step and offer instruction-altering options. These options would be suggestions on how to transform stress-inducing, confusion-inducing, or anger-inducing instruction into instruction that is more confidence-building (de-stressing), clearer (de-confusing), or amicable (de-angering). To do so, the teacher might stop the instructional flow (put down the chalk, close the book, interrupt the discussion) and instead say something like, "Okay, how about a story? Or a demonstration? Or an example? Would you like to learn about out this in a different way? What sounds good?"

Getting negative affect out of the classroom is a difficult problem to solve, especially for emotions such as anger and resentment. But the teacher who acknowledges and accepts students' negative affect stands a chance of dissipating it. It is a vital autonomy-supportive instructional strategy not only because it helps the short-term teaching goal to extinguish students' negative affect but also because it helps the long-term teaching goal of being more in synch with one's students.

Use Informational, Nonpressuring Language: What Does This Mean, When Is It Needed, and Why Is It Important? Using informational, nonpressuring language refers to the teacher's reliance on verbal and nonverbal communications to minimize pressure while conveying choice and flexibility. Nonpressuring means avoiding messages that communicate pressure (i.e., the absences of "shoulds," "musts," "have to's," and "got to's"). Informational means providing the special insights and tips that students need to better diagnose, understand, and solve the problem they face.

Using informational and nonpressuring language is particularly needed when teachers communicate requirements, offer feedback, and address students' problems (e.g., those listed in Table 7.2). But informational and nonpressuring language is further useful during practically all teacher communications, as when teachers invite students to engage in learning activities, discuss possible strategies to try, ask students to take responsibility for their own learning and behavior, comment on progress, and generally converse with students.

It is important because it helps maintain a positive teacher-student relationship. It also helps students diagnose their engagement, behavioral, or performance problems while simultaneously maintaining students' personal responsibility for those problems.

Using Informational, Nonpressuring Language: How to Practice It Informational and nonpressuring language is communication that is diagnostic, flexible, non-evaluative, and helpful to the student. When facing a student problem such as poor performance or woeful class attendance, the teacher who uses informational and nonpressuring language might begin a discussion by communicating a noticed problem and by asking the student about it: "I've noticed that you made a surprisingly low score on the test. Do you know why that might be?" Or, the teacher might ask, "How did you feel about how you did on the test?" The idea is to address the problem while preserving students' sense of ownership and responsibility for regulating their own behavior and for solving their own problem. The temptation to avoid is to push and pressure the student verbally and nonverbally toward a teacher-specified predetermined solution or desired behavior without enlisting the students' problem-solving effort (e.g., "You must improve your grades," "Your attendance is not acceptable," "I am penalizing you 10 points"). Pressuring, controlling language is pressuring (e.g., teacher raises his or her voice, points assertively, pushes hard, and utters directives), prescriptive (e.g., "Do it this way," "Can you do it this way?," "Here, let me show you how to do it."), and laced with compliance hooks (e.g., "you should, you must, you have to, you've got to") (Assor et al., 2005; Noels, Clement, & Pelletier, 1999; Ryan, 1982).

Addressing a problem in a nonpressuring way gets the conversation off to a good start, but the teacher also needs to help the student make progress in both diagnosing the problem and actually solving it. Often the student has a good understanding of why the problem is occurring (e.g., I performed poorly because I didn't study."; "My attendance is poor because I think this class is unbelievably boring."). If the student can diagnose the underlying cause of the problem, the teacher can turn his or her effort to the students' willingness to try to cope with the problem. This is why utterances such as "Do you know why that might be?" are important. Alternatively, if the student thinks the teacher is the problem ("You are boring, you are unfair."), then the teacher might acknowledge and accept the student's negative affect and ask the student what the teacher might do to help. But if the student thinks the underlying cause of the problem lies within the self, then the teacher might provide informational insights that are outside the student's experience, such as, "Well, last year, a student had this same difficulty. She too was studying hard but still making poor test scores. One day, she decided to work with a partner. She and a classmate studied together, and this really worked for her. Perhaps you might want to consider a strategy like this too."

Display Patience: What Does This Mean, When Is It Needed, and Why Is It Important? Displaying patience means to wait calmly for students' input, initiative, and willingness. Displaying patience means giving students the time and space they need during learning activities to overcome the inertia of inactivity, to explore and manipulate the learning materials, to ask questions, to retrieve information, to make plans and set goals, to evaluate data and feedback, to formulate and test hypotheses, to monitor and revise their work, to recognize that they are not making progress and need to start anew, to change problem-solving strategies, to revise their thinking, to monitor their progress, to go in their own direction, to reflect on their learning and progress, and to work at their own pace and natural rhythm.

It is timely when students are trying to learn something new, unfamiliar, or complex or trying to develop or refine a skill.

It is important because learning and understanding take time, even if teachers feel that they do not have the class time to give to students.

Displaying Patience: How to Practice It Giving students the time and space they need to work at their own pace typically means, in practice, that teachers listen, watch, be responsive, and postpone their help and assistance until it is needed and wanted. Teachers watch and observe, but they do not interfere, intrude, or intervene. Patience is the calmness a teacher shows as students struggle to start, to understand, or to adjust their behavior. It often means putting one's hands in the lap, taking the time to listen and to observe, providing encouragement for effort and initiative, offering hints when students seem stuck, postponing advice until first understanding what the student is trying to do, and waiting for a signal that one's help, scaffolding, or feedback would be appreciated (Reeve & Jang, 2006). Of course, circumstances such as time constraints and high-stakes testing make it easy to understand why teachers are not patient, but the reason to be patient (motivationally speaking) comes from a deep valuing for the student's autonomy and an understanding that cognitive engagement (e.g., elaborating, paraphrasing, organizing) and learning (e.g., conceptual change, cognitive accommodation, and deep information processing) are processes that take time.

While patience comes in many flavors, impatience is pretty straightforward and easy to recognize. The impatient teacher pushes and pressures students to go faster, using both verbal (e.g., two-word utterances, such as "hurry up" and "let's go") and nonverbal (e.g., clap, clap, clap the hands; snap, snap, snap the fingers; standing over students to communicate that time is up; turning the page before the student is ready) communications. The impatient teacher rushes students to finish what they are doing (e.g., literally grabbing the learning materials out of students' hands, such as the student's pencil, keyboard, musical instrument, or worksheet). And they bring the learning activity to a quick close by showing or telling students the right answer (e.g., "Here, let me do this for you."). The two key problems with impatience are that it shuts down students' inner motivational resources (to give way to compliance with the teacher's commands) and it by-passes the actual learning opportunity.

How Do I Know If I Am Becoming More Autonomy Supportive?

In the effort to become significantly more autonomy supportive toward one's students, it helps to know how one is doing. Becoming more autonomy supportive is a skill, and that skill can be developed and refined. Toward that end, I can suggest three sources of feedback.

First, you can ask your students to report their perceptions of your motivating style. To assess students' perceptions of autonomy-supportive teaching, it is fairly common to use the Learning Climate Questionnaire (LCQ; Williams & Deci, 1996). The LCQ asks questions such as, "I feel understood by my teacher" and "My teacher tries to understand how I see things before suggesting a new way to do things."

Second, you can ask a trained rater to visit your classroom, observe your motivating style, and score your autonomy-supportive teaching using the rating scale shown in Fig. 7.1. It may be difficult to arrange for a trained rater to visit your classroom, but a trusted colleague may take on this same role. Or you might videotape or audiotape your own instruction and use the rating sheet in Fig. 7.1 to self-score your autonomy-supportive teaching.

Third, you can monitor students' engagement signals during your instruction. When teachers are more autonomy supportive, students' engagement rises, and when teachers are less autonomy supportive, students' engagement falls (Reeve, Deci, & Ryan, 2004; Reeve & Cheon, 2014). To the extent that you utilize autonomy-supportive teaching, then students should react by showing large and immediate engagement spikes during instruction. This engagement spike should be so large as to be an obvious (easily noticed) classroom event.

These are three reliable sources of feedback. I can also suggest a fourth, though indirect, way of knowing. As teachers become more autonomy supportive, they experience many personal and professional benefits, such as gains in teaching efficacy and job satisfaction (e.g., Cheon et al., 2014). So, the fourth way of knowing would be to ask, "Are these same benefits occurring for me?"

Conclusion

I introduced six empirically validated autonomy-supportive instructional behaviors. Each of these acts of instruction is highly positively intercorrelated with the other five, so it is best to think about a teacher's overall motivating style. When used in isolation from the other five, none of the individual autonomy-supportive instructional behaviors seems able to produce the classroom conditions and teacher-student relationship that students experience as autonomy support (Deci et al., 1994). Instead, an experience of autonomy support emerges when teachers use the instructional behaviors synergistically. The purpose of this chapter was to help the interested reader learn how to do this.

References

Abuhamdeh, S., Csikszentmihalyi, M., & Jalal, B. (2015). Enjoying the possibility of defeat: Outcome uncertainty, suspense, and intrinsic motivation. *Motivation and Emotion, 39*, 1–10.

Assor, A., Kaplan, H., Kanat-Maymon, Y., & Roth, G. (2005). Directly controlling teacher behaviors as predictors of poor motivation and engagement in girls and boys: The role of anger and anxiety. *Learning and Instruction, 15*, 397–413.

Assor, A., Kaplan, H., & Roth, G. (2002). Choice is good, but relevance is excellent: Autonomy-enhancing and suppressing teaching behaviors predicting students' engagement in schoolwork. *British Journal of Educational Psychology, 27*, 261–278.

Assor, A., Roth, G., & Deci, E. L. (2004). The emotional costs of perceived parental conditional regard: A self-determination theory analysis. *Journal of Personality, 72*, 47–89.

Barber, B. K. (2002). *Intrusive parenting: How psychological control affects children and adolescents*. Washington, DC: American Psychological Association.

Bartholomew, K. J., Ntoumanis, N., Ryan, R. M., Bosch, J. A., & Thogersen-Ntoumani, C. (2011). Self-determination theory and diminished functioning: The role of interpersonal control and psychological need thwarting. *Personality and Social Psychology Bulletin, 37*, 1459–1473.

Cheon, S. H., & Reeve, J. (2013). Do the benefits from autonomy-supportive PE teacher training programs endure?: A one-year follow-up investigation. *Psychology of Sport & Exercise, 14*, 508–518.

Cheon, S. H., & Reeve, J. (2014). A classroom-based intervention to help teachers decrease student amotivation. *Contemporary Educational Psychology, 40*, 99–111.

Cheon, S. H., Reeve, J., & Moon, I. S. (2012). Experimentally based, longitudinally designed, teacher-focused intervention to help physical education teachers be more autonomy supportive toward their students. *Journal of Sport & Exercise Psychology, 34*, 365–396.

Cheon, S. H., Reeve, J., Yu, T. H., & Jang, H. R. (2014). Teacher benefits from giving students autonomy support during physical education instruction. *Journal of Sport and Exercise Psychology, 36*, 331–346.

Cheon, S. H., Reeve, J., Lee, J., & Lee, Y. (2015). Giving and receiving autonomy support in a high-stakes sport context: A field-based experiment during the 2012 London Paralympic Games. *Psychology of Sport and Exercise, 19*, 1–11.

Chua, S. N., Wong, N., & Koestner, R. (2014). Autonomy and controlling support are two sides of the same coin. *Personality and Individual Differences, 68*, 48–52.

Clifford, M. M. (1990). Students need challenge, not easy success. *Educational Leadership, 48*, 22–26.

Davis, M. H. (2004). Empathy: Negotiating the border between self and other. In L. Z. Tiedens & C. W. Leach (Eds.), *The social life of emotions* (pp. 19–42). New York: Cambridge University Press.

Deci, E. L. (1995). *Why we do what we do: Understanding self-motivation.* New York: Penguin Books.

Deci, E. L., Eghrari, H., Patrick, B. C., & Leone, D. R. (1994). Facilitating internalization: The self-determination theory perspective. *Journal of Personality, 62*, 119–142.

Deci, E. L., & Ryan, R. M. (1985). *Intrinsic motivation and self-determination in human behavior.* New York: Plenum.

Deci, E. L., Schwartz, A., Sheinman, L., & Ryan, R. M. (1981). An instrument to assess adult's orientations toward control versus autonomy in children: Reflections on intrinsic motivation and perceived competence. *Journal of Educational Psychology, 73*, 642–650.

Deci, E. L., Spiegel, N. H., Ryan, R. M., Koestner, R., & Kauffman, M. (1982). Effects of performance standards on teaching styles: Behavior of controlling teachers. *Journal of Educational Psychology, 74*, 852–859.

Edmunds, J., Ntoumanis, N., & Duda, J. L. (2008). Testing a self-determination theory-based teaching style intervention in the exercise domain. *European Journal of Social Psychology, 38*, 375–388.

Haerens, L., Aelterman, N., Vansteenkiste, M., Soenens, B., & Van Petegem, S. (2015). Do perceived autonomy-supportive and controlling teaching relate to physical education students' motivational experiences through unique pathways? Distinguishing between the bright and dark side of motivation. *Psychology of Sport and Exercise, 16*, 26–36.

Jang, H. (2008). Supporting students' motivation, engagement, and learning during an uninteresting activity. *Journal of Educational Psychology, 100*, 798–811.

Jang, H. (2015). *Three empirical illustrations of a teacher's use of curiosity-inducing strategies to promote students' motivation, engagement, and learning.* Manuscript under review.

Jang, H., Reeve, J., & Halusic, M. (2015). *A new autonomy-supportive instructional strategy that increases conceptual learning: Teaching in students' preferred ways.* Manuscript submitted for publication.

Keller, J., & Bless, H. (2008). Flow and regulatory compatibility: An experimental approach to the flow model of intrinsic motivation. *Personality and Social Psychology Bulletin, 34*, 196–209.

Koestner, R., Ryan, R. M., Bernieri, F., & Holt, K. (1984). Setting limits on children's behavior: The differential effects of controlling versus informational styles on intrinsic motivation and creativity. *Journal of Personality, 52*, 233–248.

La Guardia, J. G., & Patrick, H. (2008). Self-determination theory as a fundamental theory of close relationships. *Canadian Psychology, 49*, 201–209.

Lee, W., & Reeve, J. (2012). Teacher's estimates of their students' motivation and engagement: Being in synch with students. *Educational Psychology, 32*, 727–747.

Loewenstein, G. (1994). The psychology of curiosity: A review and reinterpretation. *Psychological Bulletin, 116*, 75–98.

Nix, G. A., Ryan, R. M., Manly, J. B., & Deci, E. L. (1999). Revitalization through self-regulation: The effects of autonomous and controlled motivation on happiness and vitality. *Journal of Experimental Social Psychology, 35*, 266–284.

Noels, K. A., Clement, R., & Pelletier, L. G. (1999). Perceptions of teachers' communicative style and students' intrinsic and extrinsic motivation. *Modern Language Journal, 83*, 23–34.

Proyer, R. T., Ruch, W., & Buschor, C. (2013). Testing strengths-based interventions: A preliminary study on the effectiveness of a program targeting curiosity, gratitude, hope, humor, and zest for enhancing life satisfaction. *Journal of Happiness Studies, 14*, 275–292.

Reeve, J. (2009). Why teachers adopt a controlling motivating style toward students and how they can become more autonomy supportive. *Educational Psychologist, 44*, 159–178.

Reeve, J., & Cheon, H. S. (2014). An intervention-based program of research on teachers' motivating styles. In S. Karabenick & T. Urdan's (Eds.), *Advances in motivation and achievement* (Vol. 18, pp. 297–343). Bingley: Emerald Group Publishing.

Reeve, J., Deci, E. L., & Ryan, R. M. (2004). Self-determination theory: A dialectical framework for understanding the sociocultural influences on student motivation. In D. McInerney & S. Van Etten (Eds.), *Research on sociocultural influences on motivation and learning: Big theories revisited* (Vol. 4, pp. 31–59). Greenwich, CT: Information Age Press.

Reeve, J., & Jang, H. (2006). What teachers say and do to support students' autonomy during learning activities. *Journal of Educational Psychology, 98*, 209–218.

Reeve, J., Jang, H., Carrell, D., Jeon, S., & Barch, J. (2004). Enhancing high school students' engagement by increasing their teachers' autonomy support. *Motivation and Emotion, 28*, 147–169.

Reeve, J., Jang, H., Hardre, P., & Omura, M. (2002). Providing a rationale in an autonomy-supportive way as a motivational strategy to motivate others during an uninteresting activity. *Motivation and Emotion, 26*, 183–207.

Reeve, J., Lee, W., & Won, S. (2015). Interest as emotion, as affect, and as schema (Chapter 5). In K. A. Renninger, M. Nieswandt, & S. Hidi (Eds.), *Interest in mathematics and science learning* (pp. 79–92). Washington, DC: American Educational Research Association.

Rogers, C. R. (1995). What understanding and acceptance mean to me. *Journal of Humanistic Psychology, 35*, 7–22.

Roth, G., Assor, A., Niemiec, C. P., Ryan, R. M., & Deci, E. L. (2009). The emotional and academic consequences of parental conditional regard: Comparing conditional positive regard, conditional negative regard, and autonomy support as parenting practices. *Developmental Psychology, 45*, 1119–1142.

Ryan, R. M. (1982). Control and information in the intrapersonal sphere: An extension of cognitive evaluation theory. *Journal of Personality and Social Psychology, 43*, 450–461.

Ryan, R. M., & Deci, E. L. (2000). Self-determination theory and the facilitation of intrinsic motivation, social development, and well-being. *American Psychologist, 55*, 68–78.

Ryan, R. M., & Powelson, C. L. (1991). Autonomy and relatedness as fundamental to motivation and education. *Journal of Experimental Education, 60*, 49–66.

Sameroff, A. (Ed.). (2009). *The transactional model of development: How children and contexts shape each other*. Washington, DC: American Psychological Association.

Schraw, G., Flowerday, T., & Lehman, S. (2001). Increasing situational interest in the classroom. *Educational Psychology Review, 13*, 211–224.

Silvia, P. J. (2006). *Exploring the psychology of interest*. New York: Oxford University Press.

Silvia, P. J. (2008). Interest: The curious emotion. *Current Directions in Psychological Science, 17*, 57–60.

Soenens, B., Park, S. Y., Vansteenkiste, M., & Mouratidis, A. (2012). Perceived parental psychological control and adolescent depressive experiences: A cross-cultural study with Belgian and South-Korean adolescents. *Journal of Adolescence, 35*, 261–272.

Tessier, D., Sarrazin, P., & Ntoumanis, N. (2008). The effects of an experimental programme to support students' autonomy on the overt behaviours of physical education teachers. *European Journal of Psychology of Education, 23*, 239–253.

Vansteenkiste, M., Lens, W., & Deci, E. L. (2006). Intrinsic versus extrinsic goal contents in self-determination theory: Another look at the quality of academic motivation. *Educational Psychologist, 41*, 19–31.

Vansteenkiste, M., Simons, J., Lens, W., Sheldon, K. M., & Deci, E. L. (2004). Motivated learning, performance, and persistence: The synergistic role of intrinsic goals and autonomy-support. *Journal of Personality and Social Psychology, 87*, 246–260.

Vansteenkiste, M., Simons, J., Lens, W., Soenens, B., & Matos, L. (2005). Examining the motivational impact of intrinsic versus extrinsic goal framing and autonomy-supportive versus internally controlling communication style on early adolescents' academic achievement. *Child Development, 2*, 483–501.

Vansteenkiste, M., Simons, J., Soenens, B., & Lens, W. (2004). How to become a persevering exerciser? Providing a clear, future intrinsic goal in an autonomy supportive way. *Journal of Sport and Exercise Psychology, 26*, 232–249.

Williams, G. C., & Deci, E. L. (1996). Internalization of biopsychosocial values by medical students: A test of self-determination theory. *Journal of Personality and Social Psychology, 70*, 767–779.

Chapter 8
An Instruction Sequence Promoting Autonomous Motivation for Coping with Challenging Learning Subjects

Avi Assor

Teachers often feel that many of their students show very little enthusiasm and interest in their studies and are not willing to cope with challenging subjects. Many students also try to invest as little effort as possible and sometimes actively avoid opportunities to develop new skills and knowledge. In self-determination theory (SDT, Ryan & Deci, 2000, and see also Chap. 2 in this volume), these students are conceived as lacking intrinsic motivation, and as externally motivated, A-motivated, or defiant. And, as explained by several chapters in this volume and documented in past research (e.g., Assor, Kaplan, Kanat-Maymon, & Roth, 2005; Assor, Vansteenkiste, & Kaplan, 2009; Deci, Ryan, & Williams, 1996; Vansteenkiste, Simons, Lens, Soenens, & Matos, 2005), external motivation and amotivation often lead to low levels of engagement and processing, diminished capacity to apply what is learnt in other domains, and lack of creativity. In addition, external motivation or amotivation also appears to result in withdrawal from challenging subjects, especially in the domains of mathematics and the exact sciences.

In this chapter, I present a sequence or structure of teaching and learning that is based on SDT, as well as on some other motivation theories, which can strengthen autonomous motivation for learning and coping with challenging tasks among students. This sequence was applied, on a small scale, in some schools in Israel. Interviews with teachers and classroom observations suggest that it can indeed enhance autonomous motivation. I will start with an analysis of potential reasons for lack of autonomous student motivation for learning a specific subject. Then, based on this analysis, I will present an instruction and work structure including four stages. To assist application I will also present an observation form that enables teachers to examine how well they apply some of the stages or actions suggested.

A. Assor (✉)
Ben Gurion University of the Negev, Be'er Sheva, Israel
e-mail: assor@bgu.ac.il

© Springer Science+Business Media Singapore 2016
W.C. Liu et al. (eds.), *Building Autonomous Learners*,
DOI 10.1007/978-981-287-630-0_8

Why Do Students Avoid Coping with Challenging Subjects?

Based on SDT, students' amotivation and avoidance of challenging tasks can be viewed as resulting from their experience of these subjects as threatening three basic psychological needs: competence, autonomy, and relatedness. In my experience, the major reason many students avoid coping with challenging tasks is that they experience these tasks as threatening their need for competence. In addition, lack of sufficient support for the two other needs may further undermine this students' willingness to cope with difficult tasks. Accordingly, I will devote considerable attention to the threats posed by challenging tasks to students' need for competence and then discuss the two other needs more briefly.

The Need to Feel Competent It appears that students feel that a given task or subject threatens their need for competence due to three major factors: (a) frequent past failures, (b) exposure to verbal comments or nonverbal behaviors implying low ability, and (c) belief in a harmful naïve theory of success. The first factor is almost self-evident: students who have suffered many past failures or were exposed to messages implying low ability are likely to fear that their attempts to cope with a new task would only further augment their sense of low competence. The third factor – belief in a harmful naïve theory of success – requires some explanation. This notion is derived from Nicholls' work on achievement goals (e.g., Nicholls, 1984) and Dweck's work on naïve theories of intelligence (e.g., Dweck, 1999). A similar view is presented by Skinner, Wellborn, and Connell (1990).

Figure 8.1 summarizes the main components of harmful versus constructive naïve theories of success, as well as some major outcomes of these theories in terms of students' goals, feelings, and mode of coping with challenges.

When students hold a harmful success theory, they believe that a major reason for their lack of success in coping with academic challenges, across many situations, is their lack of inborn capacity (talent). In addition, they also believe that this capacity cannot be developed and increased as a function of practice and instruction provided by skilled helpers. This theory ignores the fact that, often, lack of success is a result of lack of necessary prior knowledge or skills, not knowing or not using appropriate learning strategies, not using social and emotional strategies to achieve success and cope with failure, or simply not investing enough effort. This theory is termed "harmful" because it leads students to suspect that if they invest a lot and still fail, this would cause them and others to believe that they are stupid or not as smart as they feel they have to be. Because failure following considerable investment is interpreted as indicating poor inborn capacity, students feel ashamed and unworthy when they fail, try to hide their difficulties and failures, and are reluctant to seek help. In addition, because they believe that the investment of much effort indicates lack of capacity, they avoid investing much effort in public.

Finally, because they are so concerned that failure or lack of great success following effort will disclose their limited inborn and unchangeable capacity, they mainly focus on trying to impress others that they have high ability (or making sure

Student's Naïve Theory of Success

Student's Goals, Feelings and Mode of Coping with Challenge:

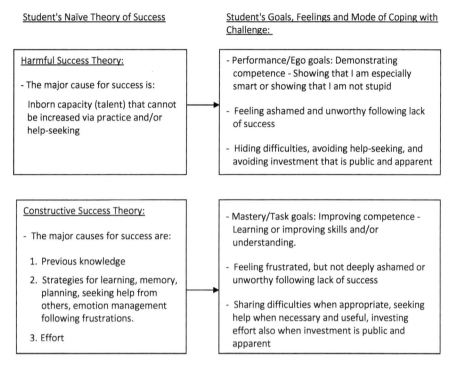

Harmful Success Theory:

- The major cause for success is:

Inborn capacity (talent) that cannot be increased via practice and/or help-seeking

- Performance/Ego goals: Demonstrating competence - Showing that I am especially smart or showing that I am not stupid

- Feeling ashamed and unworthy following lack of success

- Hiding difficulties, avoiding help-seeking, and avoiding investment that is public and apparent

Constructive Success Theory:

- The major causes for success are:

1. Previous knowledge
2. Strategies for learning, memory, planning, seeking help from others, emotion management following frustrations.
3. Effort

- Mastery/Task goals: Improving competence - Learning or improving skills and/or understanding.

- Feeling frustrated, but not deeply ashamed or unworthy following lack of success

- Sharing difficulties when appropriate, seeking help when necessary and useful, investing effort also when investment is public and apparent

Fig. 8.1 Harmful versus constructive naïve theories of success and their outcomes in terms of students' goals, feelings, and modes of coping with challenges

they do not appear incapable) rather than improving their ability. In short, they focus on ability demonstration rather than on ability improvement. In the relevant literature, this focus or orientation is termed performance goal (e.g., Dweck, 1999) or ego goal orientation (Nicholls, 1984). Martin Covington (1992) described a similar orientation in his perceptive descriptions of students' desperate attempts to protect their sense of self-worth.

In contrast to students holding a harmful success theory, those holding a constructive success theory believe that the major causes for success are previous knowledge, appropriate strategies, and/or effort rather than limited and unchangeable inborn capacity. Therefore, when these students fail, they do not feel ashamed, they do not hide their failure, they try to understand what strategies or knowledge they need to acquire in order to cope better, and they are willing to put more effort and/or seek help. In addition, because failure simply implies lack of sufficient knowledge, effort, or strategies, they focus on ability improvement and hold mastery goals (Dweck, 1999) or task orientation (Nicholls, 1984).

The Need to Feel Autonomous As already noted, in my opinion, the major reason students often avoid challenges is that these challenges threaten their need for competence. However, students can be amotivated or reluctant to cope with certain tasks also because these tasks threaten their need for autonomy (e.g., Assor, 2012; Assor, Kaplan, & Roth, 2002). The need for autonomy involves the desire to feel that one is able to self-regulate and self-organize one's actions. Thus, students feel that their need for autonomy is supported when others allow and help them to handle themselves in ways they find most valuable and useful for themselves. In contrast, students feel that their need for autonomy is frustrated when others coerce and pressure them to do things they do not value or are not interested in. Consistent with this view, students may avoid investing in difficult tasks when they feel that teachers are too controlling and not allowing them to do things in the pace and manner they find useful. In contrast, they may be willing to work harder when teachers allow them to choose subjects, ways of working, and ways of being evaluated. These aspects of autonomy supported are emphasized in the instruction sequence to be presented.

The Need for Relatedness Another reason why students sometimes avoid working hard is that investing effort may hurt their social standing, since "cool" students are not supposed to work hard. In addition, some students may feel that excelling in some subjects may cause envy, which may cause some of their classmates to be less affectionate and friendly. More generally, students need to feel that serious attempts to cope with challenging and difficult tasks are not likely to undermine the affection they get from other classmates. The proposed instruction sequence tries to incorporate this need in some of the activities and procedures it includes.

A Detailed Description of an Instruction Sequence Promoting Autonomous Motivation for Learning and Coping with Challenging Tasks

Figure 8.2 provides a detailed description of the instruction sequence. The sequence is designed for regular (often crowded) classrooms aimed at helping teachers to provide at least some support for students' needs as part of their regular instruction process. The sequence is especially relevant and more feasible and workable for instruction and learning conducted in small groups or for individualized instruction. However, major aspects of it are also relevant for large classrooms, provided that teachers are willing to reduce the amount of "material" (concepts, facts, skills) they try to cover. As noted somewhere in this volume, the notion that "less is more" is a beneficial practice, since it allows students to have time to digest things at their own pace and minimize the risk of creating a pressuring class atmosphere. As I describe the specific components and practices comprising the sequence, I will also point to the way they are likely to support students' needs. However, readers are encouraged to make their own speculations on how different components and practices may affect students' and teachers' needs. This is important because we sometimes cannot predict how a certain well-intentioned procedures will be experienced by students and teachers.

An Instruction Sequence Promoting Autonomous Motivation for Learning
and Coping with Challenging Tasks

(I) **Classroom Preparation**: Creating a class culture supporting a constructive theory of success and autonomous adherence to classroom rules while teacher is not paying attention.

(II) **Application of the Sequence in Individual and Group Work**:

    (**a**) Joint student-teacher setting of a general learning objective.

    (**b**) Joint formation of a work and evaluation plan.

    (**c**) Structured ongoing student work. Students work according to the plan they have formulated, while receiving three types of competence supports:

        (1) Informational teacher feedback: Specific, frequent, non-comparative, focusing first on positive aspects, and supporting a constructive success theory.

        (2) Teacher support for coping with non-success: (a) Helping students to identify potential reasons for their non-success in a way that supports a constructive success theory; (b) Helping students to identify missing strategies and supporting strategy development (only when relevant); (c) Helping to acquire missing basic knowledge; (d) Changing or modifying the objective and the plan; (e) Ongoing emotional and moral support

        (3) Peer Support: Working with student and class-mates on assisting each other and perhaps also providing informational feedback.

    (**d**) Bi-directional Summary: Student and teacher summarize their attainments, and identify strengths and difficulties in their collaboration.

    (**e**) Joint setting of a new general goal.

(III) **All-classroom interim activities and summary discussions:** Aimed at (a) identifying classroom processes that undermine or enhance students' coping with Challenges, (b) fostering a constructive theory of success, and (c) cultivating classroom behaviors and atmosphere that enhance autonomous motivation.

Fig. 8.2 An instruction sequence promoting autonomous motivation for learning and coping with challenging tasks

Classroom Preparation: Creating a Class Culture Supporting a Constructive Theory of Success and Autonomous Adherence to Classroom Rules While Teacher Is Not Paying Attention

In this phase, students learn concepts and start to internalize values that teachers can later refer to when students cope (or fail to cope) with various challenges. Student knowledge and internalization of such concepts and values are essential to mobilize students' understanding and cooperation when students show amotivation, external motivation, or defiance and when students are unwilling to work quietly without supervision when the teachers' attention turns to one student who needs feedback or assistance. It is possible to distinguish between a narrow focus and a wide focus.

The narrow-focus approach includes two components:

Class Discussions and Activities Promoting Learning and Valuing of the Notions of Constructive and Harmful Success Theories

The goal of these learning activities is to promote understanding of and identification with a constructive theory of success and a culture of ability improvement, which in turn leads to the development of a class and school culture of ability improvement, in contrast to ability demonstration. This culture includes a system of expectations, symbols, and interpretive dispositions reflecting and expressing a constructive theory of success and a nonchalant problem-solving approach to lack of success.

It is possible to create such an ability-improvement culture in classrooms via class activities, discussions, movies, and stories focusing on the two theories and their consequences. **Personal demonstration by teachers is especially helpful**. In such demonstrations, teachers may share with their students how they held a harmful success theory, which created feelings of shame, and prevented them from investing effort or seeking help. It is also useful to expose students to people they can easily identify with, who tell students how they avoided coping with certain subjects and how they overcome their difficulties by changing the way they interpret their lack of success, and focusing on ability improvement rather than demonstration. It is also very important to illustrate the theories via visual and physical artifacts such as posters on the classroom walls, graphic displays in notebooks and activity calendars, etc. Following a more distant and less personal discussion of the concepts, it is often useful to sensitively conduct activities in which children start sharing how they respond to difficult challenges, including sharing feelings of shame, fears that failure may affect their social standing, and worries about the consequences of disclosing difficulties and seeking help.

Class Discussions and Activities Promoting Autonomous Internalization of and Adherence to Norms of Consideration for Others and Acceptance of Class Rules and Procedures

As will be shown later, the sequence requires students to internalize values of consideration of others and respect for class rules rather than rely on external regulation by the teacher. In order to attain internalization of these norms and rules, teachers have to discuss these issues with their class, explain the rationale, and have students participate in the formation of rules and procedures ensuring that the teacher can work with several students while the rest of the class does not disturb and keeps working. After the rules are applied, any deviation from them should be dealt with immediately, in autonomy-supportive ways, that is, via discussion, non-vindictive but firm limit setting, and joint decision-making. These procedures can be expected to minimize future violations of the jointly formed rules.

The wide focus includes a third component:

Activities Promoting the Learning of SDT-Based Concepts of Four Motivation Types (Autonomous, Controlled, Amotivation, and Defiance) and the Needs Underlying Them

These concepts are learnt in a simplified way. The understanding and learning of these concepts may help to create a classroom culture that is sensitive to students and teacher needs and may enhance students' understanding of what is stopping them from studying or from cooperating with the teacher. A description of classroom features and activities that help to create a need-supporting classroom appears in Assor, Kaplan, Feinberg, and Tal (2009) and in Feinberg, Assor, Kaplan, and Kanat-Maymon (2014). It should be noted that the inclusion of this type of activities demands considerable time and effort, and from my experience, it can be added at later stage. Moreover, many aspects of the sequence already include components supporting students' and teachers' needs without explicitly talking about it.

Application of the Sequence in Individual and Group Work

Joint Student-Teacher Setting of a General Learning Objective

This part starts with an individual conversation with each child, in which the teacher explains the rationale for the joint objective-setting and the entire sequence. Essentially, teachers explain that they apply the sequence so that each student can develop knowledge and ability in an area that is important for her/him. Then, the teacher asks the child to share subjects, concepts, or skills she/he would like to develop or learn. The teacher may also present some goals for the child and ask for the child thoughts and preferences regarding these goals. Often, one meeting would not be enough and students would need to meet for one or two more sessions. The teacher may also help the child find what is of special importance or interest to her/him by suggesting various activities that may help to discover such interests and priorities.

Joint Formation of a Work and Evaluation Plan

Teacher and student would collaboratively formulate a work plan aimed at attaining the learning objective they set jointly. The plan usually includes short-term, realistic objectives (specific concepts and skills) constituting benchmarks (and necessary steps) in the way to the more distant and general learning objectives. The plan should also include ways of evaluating the extent to which the benchmarks were attained. To set up such a plan, it is important to assess student's mastery of knowledge (and sometimes also strategies) necessary to attain the general learning objectives. It is important to emphasize that this assessment should be carried out only after the rationale for it was explained and accepted by the students, so they do not experience it as a controlling act. It should also be noted that people are often unaware of their difficulties and how much effort they would have to invest to acquire missing knowledge (see Zimmerman, 2002, and personal communication). As a result, teachers may sometimes have to insist, quite firmly, that an initial assessment should be carried out even when students do not see a need for it. Of course, in negotiating this issue, sensitivity to students' emotions and needs is extremely important, as is an attempt to attribute the considerable lack of knowledge or skills to factors other than limited inborn capacity (i.e., use terms reflecting a constructive theory of success). There is considerable research suggesting that the setting of short-term optimal objectives (and specific, timely, and informative feedback on the extent to which these objective are met) is essential to the maintenance of students' sense of efficacy, competence, and motivation (e.g., Schunk, 1996).

Importantly, in order for teachers to conduct an informative assessment of knowledge and skills required to attain various learning objectives, they need to know the relevant knowledge domain quite well. That is, the have-to-be knowledge and pedagogy experts in that domain and the application of the instruction sequence may in fact help them to further develop their expertise, thus supporting teacher's sense of competence as well.

Following Zimmerman (2002), the initial objectives may focus on successful mastery of important strategies and not on performance in the tasks the strategies are supposed to help with. For example, if students learn strategies for extracting the main concepts from a written text, this is what they should receive feedback on, rather than how they write and organize a text based on these concepts. We should also be very careful to emphasize to both teachers and students that strategies are only tools for mastery knowledge and skills, so it is very important to assess if students really need them, as some students may have their own ways of learning and do not need to be formally introduced to various strategies.

Structured Ongoing Student Work

In this phase, students work according to the plan they have formulated, while receiving three types of competence supports. These supports are described below:

1. **Informational teacher feedback**. To support student's sense of competence and autonomous motivation as they try to reach the objectives they set up, it is absolutely essential that students receive frequent informational feedback. It is desirable that at least some of the feedback will not be formal or written, but rather a part of a nonchalant verbal interchange that occurs as the teacher moves around the classroom or stops briefly to see how a student is doing. There is considerable research suggesting that such feedback should *be specific, non-comparative, focusing first on positive aspects*, and *supporting a constructive success theory* (e.g., Butler, 1987; Hattie & Timperley, 2007; Madjar & Assor, 2013). From this perspective, teachers would do well to give specific comments pointing to areas of improvement and aspects that need to be improved and are not yet mastered.

It is also important to try to avoid giving numerical grades that can easily encourage comparisons between students. Another option is a within-student grading reflecting rate of improvement relative to the student's past performance. In order to strengthen students' constructive theory of success, it is important to avoid trait-oriented feedback such as "you are talented and have a high potential" because when students do not succeed, they may attribute their non-success to lack of talent and potential (i.e., unchangeable inborn capacity). In contrast, feedbacks pointing to knowledge/skill components that can be improved, and potential strategies for reaching such improvements, strengthen a constructive success theory by implicitly implying that success is a product of strategies and effort.

2. **Teacher support for coping with non-success**. When students do not succeed or fail, it is, of course, important that the teacher will address this issue and help students cope with the failure. In this section, we describe five components of teacher support following student failure. These components are presented in the order they often appear in practice.

2a. **Helping students to identify potential reasons for their non-success in a way that supports a constructive success theory**. When students do not succeed or fail, it is extremely important that teachers will, promptly, address their experience and the way they interpret it. If teachers do not intervene, students may very quickly interpret their non-success in ways that only further consolidate the harmful success theory they already hold. To prevent such early unfortunate consolidation, teachers may invite students to collaborate with them in an attempt to identify which of the causes of success and non-success that were already discussed in the preparation phase (and may also appear on nearby poster) may account for their (temporary) non-success. Whether they are using inappropriate strategies? Perhaps they do not possess some necessary concepts or skills that are required to master the task? Did they put enough effort or leave enough time to practice?

As students might feel rather upset by their non-success, teachers need to be quite sensitive in these kinds of interventions. For example, it appears important to respect students' negative feelings following non-success, rather than try to quickly comfort them or provide simple practical solutions. Often, attempts to somehow quickly help students feel better may be interpreted as lack of understanding or as an invalidation of students' experiences. There are several useful books and training programs providing guides for sensitive listening in such incidents, including the identification of useful and non-useful teacher responses (e.g., Faber & Mazlish 1996; Gordon, 1975). In my experience, such training programs often help teachers to create more empathic and open relationships with students, which then allow teachers to work together with students as they try to understand the reasons for lack of success and as they plan ways of overcoming difficulties.

Finally, it appears that students' failure experiences, while clearly unpleasant for all involved, may create an opportunity to understand whether students' hold a harmful success theory, how deeply they adhere to it, and how destructive it is for them. To the extent that this is the case, teachers' responses to the way students interpret the failure may help students to start shifting toward a more constructive success theory. As teachers work with students, it often helps if they give personal examples showing how changing their naïve theories helped them to cope effectively with failure or avoidance of challenges. In addition, as teachers work with students in analyzing the reasons for failure, it is important that they convey a matter-of-fact problem-solving approach, viewing lack of success as a natural phase of learning.

2b. **Helping students to identify missing strategies and supporting strategy development** (only when relevant). Often, lack of success in a learning task is caused by lack of reliance on useful strategies or deficient use of such strategies. Roughly, it is possible to distinguish between learning and organization strategies and socio-emotional strategies. The category of learning strategies includes methods for enhancing reading comprehension (e.g., Duffy, 2009; Dole, Nokes, & Drits, 2009; Pressley, Woloshyn, & Associates, 1995), summarizing materials, memory strategies, conceptual mapping, methods for sequential organization of numerical data, efficient time planning, etc. (e.g., Weinstein, 1994; Weinstein & Hume, 1998; Zimmerman, Bonner, & Kovach, 1996). Socio-emotional strategies include, for example, various emotion-management skills and help-seeking skills.

While the importance of learning and organization skills is clear and well known, teachers often are not sufficiently aware of the potential contribution of emotion-management skills. Failures, especially those perceived as unfair, often arouse strong feelings of anger, envy, sadness, or anxiety. In coping with these feelings, students often use strategies that may reduce the painful emotions in the short run, but are fairly destructive in the long run. For example, students may devalue the merit of the subject they failed in, deny the failure or its implications, unjustly accuse others for their failure, destroy helpful teachers' comments, etc. (e.g., Rijavec & Brdar, 1997; Skinner & Wellborn, 1997). In such cases, teachers may try to help students learn more constructive coping strategies adapted from cognitive-behavioral approaches such as acceptance and commitment (e.g., Hayes, Strosahl, & Wilson, 1999) and/or mindfulness training (e.g., Greenberg & Harris, 2012; Kabat-Zinn, 2003). These methods strive to enhance people's ability to accept their negative emotions and observe them without becoming fully identified with these emotions and controlled by them. Of course using these practices requires training and personal maturity. However, it appears that training teachers to use these methods can be beneficial to both teachers and students.

2c. **Helping to acquire missing basic knowledge**. As was already noted, failure can often be a product of missing concepts and vocabulary that is essential for understanding the task and/or coping with the task successfully. In such cases, teachers need to help students to bridge the gap. Often, teachers do not have to do it themselves. They can connect the student with other teachers, tutors, other students, etc. In some cases, they can provide useful Internet tutorials or library resources. In all these cases, it is extremely important that teachers follow up and examine to what extent students really start to close the knowledge gap. In cases students do not take any responsibility, teachers may try to enhance student motivation by trying to understand what is stopping them and by helping to create a structure that enhances student motivation to invest in acquiring the missing knowledge.

2d. **Changing or modifying the objective and the plan**. At times, it may become clear that the original distal learning objective is too ambitious, is not feasible, or is clearly not meaningful or interesting for the student. In such cases, it is necessary to choose another objective and reorganize the plan accordingly.

2e. **Ongoing emotional and moral support**. Throughout the whole process of coping with failures, it is important that teachers will, at times, transmit messages conveying their belief that the student can effectively use the feedback they get and the strategies they are exposed to, as well as learn missing knowledge and skills. The emphasis is not on trait-like compliments such as "you are smart" or "talented," but more on messages such as "I am sure that you can learn the concepts you missed in an earlier grade," "I am convinced that you can find the kind of strategies that would work for you," and more generally "if you work hard and use the suitable strategies, you would meet the objective you set up for yourself." It is advisable to use these statements only sporadically, and they cannot substitute the various practices and acts described before.

3. **Peer Support**. After the instruction sequence is applied and running fairly well, it is desirable to add the peer support component. This involves learning of ways of asking and giving feedback, when to ask for feedback, and how to give feedback and assistance in ways that contribute to learning and do not undermine the recipient's self-esteem or social standing. The feedback given should, of course, be a constructive theory of success and an ability-improvement culture. Methods for promoting constructive peer feedback and assistance appear in publications focusing on the promotion of cooperative learning in classrooms (e.g., Sharan, 1994; Slavin, 1995).

Bidirectional Summary

Following a period of collaborative work, it is important to set up a review and evaluation of the joint work process and its products. It is advisable to do this evaluation after there was some progress toward the attainment of the general learning objective or a significant interim objective. However, such summary may also be called for if there is very little progress. The review can address questions such as: Did students develop the knowledge or skills they wanted to develop (a product focus)? Did they develop useful strategies as part of the process? How did the student and the teacher feel throughout the process and presently? In discussing the last question, it is advisable to use the motivational concepts specified in SDT (i.e., intrinsic motivation, identified/integrated motivation, amotivation, etc.). Such discussion would be easier if those terms were learnt as part of the preparation phase (third component). However, it is possible to use these terms using everyday language referring to the same phenomena. Other important review questions include: What aspects of the sequence or the teacher's behaviors or reactions were helpful for students and what aspects hindered their progress and how? Similarly, what aspects of students' behaviors or reactions were helpful for the teacher and what aspects hindered her/his capacity or motivation to help? Often, the school, teachers, students, or parents may want to present the knowledge or skills students developed to parents or other people in the school community. In this case, students and teacher may discuss how they feel about it and what kind or presentation they prefer.

Joint Setting of a New General Learning Objective

After the learning goal was attained (or mostly attained) and the summary and review process is over, the teacher and the student would discuss the next general learning objective. Often, because of lack of various constraints or other preferences, there would be a break and a new sequence (and learning goal) would only be initiated only after several months of break. In such cases it is useful to go back to the bidirectional so as to refresh what was learnt about the most effective and motivating ways of working together.

All-Classroom Interim and Summary Activities and Discussions

These activities and discussions are aimed at maintaining and supporting the values, norms, and class culture and atmosphere that the preparation phase has started to establish. As such, they refresh and expand the students' understanding of naïve theories of success and their consequences and class rules that allow the teacher to work with individual students while others work quietly on their tasks. More generally, such discussions may enable teachers to foster a sense of shared class responsibility for ability improvement of all students, as well as a general feeling of the class as a caring community. The discussions also aim at early identification of classroom processes that undermine the motivation and progress of individual children, as well as creating motivationally sound ways of coping with such impediments. As part of this process, teachers may expose students to the motivation concepts of SDT, so their understanding of what may account for progress or stagnation in individual learning and/or in caring among classmates may be deepened.

Summary Comments

This chapter presented an instruction structure that is likely to strengthen students' motivation to cope with challenging subjects they have previously avoided, mainly because they believe that they do not possess the required inborn talent. I believe that sensitive, high-quality implementation of this sequence is likely to help students to discover that their self-sabotaging beliefs are not valid. It is important to note that the implementation of the proposed sequence should be supported by a system of professional, organizational, and moral support within the school, a system that provides space for trial and error and provides continual guidance and opportunities for consultation when difficulties emerge. One area where the proposed sequence may be especially relevant and useful is the domain of special education. In many special education classes, there are enough teachers or teacher aides to allow individualized and small-group instruction. In addition, the challenges faced by many special education students are similar to those described in this chapter. Alfi, Katz, and Assor (2004) described a mode of working with special education settings that can be integrated with the sequence presented in this chapter.

It is extremely important to note that the proposed learning sequence, of course, is not the only way to promote autonomous motivation to study challenging subjects. One limitation of this structure is that it fits small-group or individual instruction more than a whole-classroom instruction. In heterogonous, large-size classrooms, it may be quite different to implement such individualized learning sequences. Reeve and Halusic (2009) have described a structure such as this. Bar Ziv, Assor, and Feinberg (2012) have described an in-service process and an observational system providing teachers with brief and clear guidelines on how to promote autonomous motivation in large classrooms.

A second, and very serious, limitation of the proposed sequence is that it may not fit students who already have intrinsic motivation and considerable knowledge in the relevant subject. For them, the meticulous setting of a series of short-term concrete objectives and assignments and the frequent evaluations may actually be experienced as pressuring interferences that only undermine their intrinsic motivation, flexibility, and creativity. When teachers spot such students, they may well want to allow them to work in ways that these students find most beneficial. Yet, for these students too, continual teachers' interest and availability are still important.

A third limitation of the proposed sequence is that it is based mainly on enhancing students' feeling that they are able to cope well with difficult challenges; that is, it augments students' sense of competence. However, it is possible that to reach a highly intrinsic motivation and great pleasure from studying a certain subject, it is not enough to feel that studying the subject contributes to our sense of competence. Thus, a real sense of enchantment and fascination with a certain subject may be based, to a large extent, on sensing the "beauty" of that subject, the surprising aspects of it, its contribution to new important understandings, and its capacity to expand our emotional experience or to connect more deeply to oneself or the world around us. In short, highly intrinsic engagement with a given subject may be, in part, due to its strong contribution to our intellectual, aesthetic, and/or emotional experiences, experiences that go beyond the sense of enhanced personal competence. The type of learning process proposed by Boaler (2009) may perhaps promote a type of learning characterized by such fascination and intrinsic motivation.

The last limitation refers to the type of knowledge and skills the sequence promotes. I believe that the proposed sequence fits mainly to the acquisition of skills and knowledge in what can be termed "basic languages": math, language, computers, grammar, and maybe some basic concepts and procedures in various subjects, especially the exact natural sciences. This is because in these domains there is a relatively accepted knowledge structure, in which certain concepts and skills serve as a necessary foundation for more advanced ones. Because such knowledge structure exists, it is possible to create a relatively logical instruction sequence in which more basic aspects are acquired before more complex ones are presented. However, there are knowledge and thinking domains that are very important, but do not have clear knowledge structure beyond a few basic concepts and skills. In fact, many topics in the domains of the humanities, the arts, and the social studies fall into this category. For example, how do we develop critical thinking regarding important social issues? How do we form interesting personal interpretations regarding the meaning of literary or artistic works? How do we foster a creative approach to the solution of various social or personal problems? It is evident that the highly structured sequence proposed in this chapter is mostly irrelevant to the nurturing of these capacities. In these domains too, it may, at times, be important to define concepts and skills students need to acquire, as well as establish criteria for evaluating creative or scholarly products. But, unlike in the proposed sequence, such definitions and criteria should not be introduced frequently, may be less precise, and are clearly be secondary to the more open and flexible critical and creative processes they are expected to serve.

In sum, despite some serious limitations, it appears that high-quality implementation of the proposed sequence may provide students with empowering experiences that enhance their capacity to cope with challenging subjects, at least in domains where there is a clear structure of basic concepts and skills. Importantly, the enhancement of students' motivation and capacity can also constitute a meaningful and motivating formative experience in the professional and personal development of the teachers working with the sequence.

References

Alfi, O., Katz, I., & Assor, A. (2004). Supporting teachers' willingness to allow temporary, competence-supporting, failure. *Journal of Education for Teaching, 30*, 27–41.

Assor, A. (2012). Allowing choice and nurturing an inner compass: Educational practices supporting students' need for autonomy. In S. L. Christenson, A. L. Reschly, & C. Wylie (Eds.), *The handbook of research on student engagement* (pp. 421–438). New York: Springer Science.

Assor, A., Kaplan, H., Feinberg, O., & Tal, K. (2009). Combining vision with voice A learning and implementation structure promoting teachers' internalization of practices based on self-determination theory. *Theory and Research in Education, 7*(2), 234–243.

Assor, A., Kaplan, H., Kanat-Maymon, Y., & Roth, G. (2005). Directly controlling teacher behaviors as predictors of poor motivation and engagement in girls and boys: The role of anger and anxiety. *Learning and Instruction, 15*(5), 397–413.

Assor, A., Kaplan, H., & Roth, G. (2002). Choice is good, but relevance is excellent: Autonomy-enhancing and suppressing teacher behaviors predicting students' engagement in schoolwork. *British Journal of Educational Psychology, 72*, 261–278.

Assor, A., Vansteenkiste, M., & Kaplan, A. (2009). Identified versus introjected approach and introjected avoidance motivations in school and in sports: The limited benefits of self-worth strivings. *Journal of Educational Psychology, 101*(2), 482–497.

Bar Ziv, N., Assor, A., & Feinberg, O. (2012). *Observation based consultation as a tool for promoting teachers support for students' autonomy.* Paper presented in the international research workshop on self determination theory perspective on parenting, emotion regulation and education. Beer Sheva, Israel: Ben Gurion University.

Boaler, J. (2009). *What's math got go do with it? How parents and teachers can help children learn to love their least favorite subject.* New York: Penguin.

Butler, R. (1987). Task-involving and ego-involving properties of evaluation: Effects of different feedback conditions on motivational perceptions, interest and performance. *Journal of Educational Psychology, 78*, 210–216.

Covington, M. V. (1992). *Making the grade.* New York: Cambridge University Press.

Deci, E. L., Ryan, R. M., & Williams, G. C. (1996). Need satisfaction and the self-regulation of learning. *Learning and Individual Differences, 8*, 165–183.

Dole, J. A., Nokes, J. D., & Drits, D. (2009). Cognitive strategy instruction. In S. E. Israel & G. Duffy (Eds.), *Handbook of research on reading comprehension* (pp. 347–372). New York: Routledge.

Duffy, G. G. (2009). *Explaining reading: A resource for teaching concepts, skills, and strategies.* New York: Guilford Press.

Dweck, C. S. (1999). *Self-theories: Their role in motivation, personality, and development.* Philadelphia, PA: Psychology Press.

Faber, A., & Mazlish, E. (1996). *How to talk so kids can learn.* New York: Scribner.

Feinberg, O., Assor, A., Kaplan, H., & Kanat-Maymon, Y. (2014). Reducing violence and promoting caring in non-controlling ways: An educational change program based on self determination theory. *The Elementary School Journal* (Manuscript under review).

Gordon, T. (1975). *Teacher effectiveness training.* New York: Crown Publishers.

Greenberg, M. T., & Harris, A. R. (2012). Nurturing mindfulness in children and youth: Current state of research. *Child Development Perspectives, 6*(2), 161–166.

Hattie, J., & Timperley, H. (2007). The power of feedback. *Review of Educational Research, 77*(1), 81–112.

Hayes, S. C., Strosahl, K. D., & Wilson, K. G. (1999). *Acceptance and commitment therapy: An experiential approach to behavior change.* New York: Guilford Press.

Kabat-Zinn, J. (2003). Mindfulness-based interventions in context: Past, present, and future. *Clinical Psychology: Science and Practice, 10*(2), 144–156.

Madjar, N., & Assor, A. (2013). Two types of perceived control over learning perceived efficacy and perceived autonomy. In J. A. C. Hattie & E. M. Anderman (Eds.), *The international handbook of student achievement* (pp. 439–441). New York: Rutledge.

Nicholls, J. G. (1984). Achievement motivation: Conceptions of ability, subjective experience, task choice, and performance. *Psychological Review, 91*, 328–346.

Pressley, M., Woloshyn, V. E., & Associates. (1995). *Cognitive strategy instruction that really works with children* (2nd ed.). Cambridge, MA: Brookline.

Reeve, J., & Halusic, M. (2009). How K-12 teachers can put self-determination theory principles into practice. *Theory and Research in Education, 7*(2), 145–154.

Rijavec, M., & Brdar, I. (1997). Coping with school failure: Development of the school failure coping scale. *European Journal of Psychology of Education, 12*(1), 37–49.

Ryan, R. M., & Deci, E. R. (2000). Self-determination theory and the facilitation of intrinsic motivation, social development and well being. *American Psychologist, 55*(1), 68–78.

Schunk, D. H. (1996). Goal and self-evaluative influences during children's cognitive skill learning. *American Educational Research Journal, 33*(2), 359–382.

Sharan, S. (1994). *Handbook of cooperative learning methods.* New York: Greenwood Publishing Group.

Skinner, E. A., & Wellborn, J. G. (1997). Children's coping in the academic domain. In S. Wolchik & I. N. Sandler (Eds.), *Handbook of children's coping with common stressors: Linking theory and intervention* (pp. 387–422). New York: Springer.

Skinner, E. A., Wellborn, J. G., & Connell, J. P. (1990). What is takes to do well in school and whether I've got it: The role of perceived control in children's engagement and school achievement. *Journal of Educational Psychology, 82,* 22–32.

Slavin, R. E. (1995). *Cooperative learning: Theory, research and practice.* Boston, MA: Allyn & Bacon.

Vansteenkiste, M., Simons, J., Lens, W., Soenens, B., & Matos, L. (2005). Examining the motivational impact of intrinsic versus extrinsic goal framing and autonomy-supportive versus internally controlling communication style on early adolescents' academic achievement. *Child Development, 76*(2), 483–501.

Weinstein, C. E. (1994). Strategic learning/strategic teaching: Flip sides of a coin. In P. R. Pintrich, D. R. Brown, C. E. Weinstein, & W. J. McKeachie (Eds.), *Student motivation, cognition, and learning: Essays in honor of Wilbert J. McKeachie* (pp. 257–273). Hillsdale, NJ: L. Erlbaum.

Weinstein, C. E., & Hume, L. M. (1998). *Study strategies for lifelong learning.* Washington, DC: American Psychological Association.

Zimmerman, B. J. (2002). Becoming a self-regulated learner: An overview. *Theory Into Practice, 41*(2), 64–70.

Zimmerman, B. J., Bonner, S., & Kovach, R. (1996). *Developing self-regulated learners: Beyond achievement to self-efficacy.* Washington, DC: American Psychological Association.

Chapter 9
Parental Involvement and Children's Academic Motivation and Achievement

Wendy S. Grolnick

In the effort to increase children's achievement and promote educational equality, parent involvement in children's schooling has become a key focus of both researchers and practitioners. There is now strong evidence that parent involvement in children's schooling is associated with children's achievement and that this relation holds across diverse populations and contexts (e.g., for reviews, see Fan & Chen, 2001; Hill & Taylor, 2004; Jeynes, 2005, 2007; Pomeranz, Grolnick, & Price, 2005). With this knowledge in mind, increasing parent involvement has become a goal within many educational contexts.

While pursuing this goal should be applauded, it is important that key stakeholders do so with knowledge of the complexities of this important resource. In particular, it is important to consider (1) what types of involvement are most effective, (2) why parent involvement facilitates children's achievement so that its effects can be maximized, (3) whether the way in which parents are involved makes a difference, and (4) what factors predict how involved parents become in their children's schooling. It is also important to consider parents' viewpoints to understand why they are involved, in that their own motivations may impact not only their levels of involvement but the way they become involved. This chapter takes up each of these issues. Using a Self-Determination Theory (SDT) perspective (Deci & Ryan, 1985, 2000), we explore how using a motivational model can help us to understand when, how, and why parent involvement is effective so as to maximize its impact for student motivation, achievement, and adjustment.

W.S. Grolnick (✉)
Clark University, Worcester MA, USA
e-mail: WGrolnick@clarku.edu

© Springer Science+Business Media Singapore 2016
W.C. Liu et al. (eds.), *Building Autonomous Learners*,
DOI 10.1007/978-981-287-630-0_9

A Self-Determination Theory Perspective on Parental Involvement

From an SDT perspective, children, as all humans, have three needs: those for autonomy, or to feel volitional and agentic; for competence, or to feel effective in their environments; and for relatedness, or to feel loved and valued. Given that parents are the primary socializing agents in children's lives, whether children's needs are satisfied within their day-to-day contexts is highly dependent on the degree to which parents create need-satisfying contexts. While parents affect children in a number of domains including social development, household responsibilities, and behavioral adjustment, they also play a key role in children's school experience.

Parent involvement, defined as parents' dedication of resources within a domain (Grolnick & Ryan, 1989; Grolnick & Slowiaczek, 1994), can be considered from the perspective of these three needs. First, when parents dedicate resources such as time, warmth, and more tangible resources such as books and assistance, children feel important and valued, thus fulfilling their need for relatedness. Parent involvement, however, needs to be provided in a way that supports children's needs for autonomy and competence. In particular, parents can be involved in an autonomy-supportive or a controlling manner. When autonomy supportive, parents take children's perspectives, help them solve their own problems, and encourage their initiatives. By contrast, when parents are controlling, they act from their own perspectives, solve problems for the children, and direct and pressure them to achieve in particular ways. Given children's need for autonomy, parents' involvement should be most beneficial when it is enacted in an autonomy-supportive manner. Second, involvement should be most effective when parents support children's competence by providing a structured environment including clear guidelines, expectations, and information about how to be successful.

Another important tenet of SDT concerns the idea that individuals are active with respect to their environments. They develop beliefs and motives in response to their experiences in their environments, which then shape their behaviors. Thus, academic contexts, including those created by parents and teachers, impact children's beliefs about their abilities and their motives, i.e., why they engage in school behaviors. In particular, when contexts support autonomy, children will be more likely to engage in school behaviors because they see value in these behaviors, rather than because they feel pressure to do so. With regard to competence, when contexts provide structure, children will be more likely to feel competent and to understand how to be successful and to avoid failure or have a sense of perceived control.

Having delineated the SDT framework, we now explore data on particular issues relevant to parent involvement. Across these issues, the extant data support the usefulness of an SDT perspective.

Types of Parent Involvement: Not All Behaviors Are Equally Effective

Parent involvement in children's schooling has included a variety of activities and resources. Many researchers distinguish between two major types of involvement, that at school and that at home. Involvement at school includes activities such as going to school meetings, attending parent-teacher conferences, talking with teachers, and volunteering at school. Parent involvement outside of school includes helping children with homework, discussing school activities, and exposing children to intellectual activities that help to bring school and home together. Interestingly, when examining the effects of different types of involvement, several researchers have shown that it is the types of involvement that involve parent-child interaction, rather than those that focus on involvement at school, that are most effective. For example, McWayne, Hampton, Fantuzzo, Cohen, and Sekino (2004) showed that only supportive home learning (including talking to children about school activities and organizing the home to facilitate learning), but not direct involvement with the school, facilitated reading and math achievement. Hill and Tyson (2009) differentiated between school-based involvement, home-based involvement, and academic socialization, including providing support for children's own educational and vocational aspirations, conveying the value of learning, and helping to make clear to children how learning activities connect to their interests. There were no effects of school-based involvement, modest effects of home involvement, and strong effects of academic socialization. These findings are in line with three meta-analyses: two conducted by Jeynes (2005, 2007), one involving studies of elementary-age children and one involving secondary schools, and one conducted by Fan and Chen (2001). In all three meta-analyses, there were stronger effects for academic socialization than for other practices, including assistance with homework, parental reading, and at-school participation.

Why would academic socialization-type behaviors have stronger effects than at-school behaviors and help with homework? One explanation is that parent involvement may have its most potent effects not by helping children with specific skills (e.g., math skills) or by changing teachers' behaviors or attitudes but, rather, by facilitating children's school-related motivation. In other words, through their involvement, parents may help children develop the beliefs and motives that would translate into higher levels of engagement in school activities and ultimately higher achievement. From an SDT viewpoint, these would be the very self-related beliefs and motives tied to the satisfaction of the needs for autonomy, competence, and relatedness. More specifically, parent involvement would facilitate perceptions of competence and control tied to the need for competence, autonomous self-regulation tied to the need for autonomy, and feelings of connection tied to the need for relatedness.

Consistent with this reasoning, Grolnick and Slowiaczek (1994) proposed two models for understanding the effects of parental involvement, a direct effects model, in which parent involvement helps children by providing them specific academic skills, and a motivational model, in which parent involvement facilitates children's success by helping them to build key motivational resources. They tested the motivational model in a study of 302 seventh grade children and their mothers and fathers. Three types of involvement were measured. School involvement concerned involvement in school activities and events, such as parent-teacher conferences and volunteering at school. Cognitive/intellectual involvement included parents exposing children to stimulating events such as museums and current events. Personal involvement was parents' display of interest and expectations for their children in school. In this study, children's motivational resources were also measured, and grades and achievement scores were obtained. Path analyses supported the indirect effects model for both mothers and fathers whereby involvement facilitated the motivational resources of perceived competence and perceived control which then predicted school grades. Marchant, Paulson, and Rothlisberg (2001) similarly measured fifth and sixth grade children's perceptions that their parents were involved by valuing doing well in school and by participating in school activities and events. Only perceptions that parents valued school performance and effort were associated with children's perceiving that ability, effort, and grades were important as well as their perceptions of competence in school. These motivational variables were then associated with children's grades. In a sample of younger children (7 years old), Topor, Keane, Shelton, and Calkins (2010) found that teachers' perceptions of parent involvement (that they showed a value for and interest in school) predicted children' academic perceived competence, which then predicted their achievement.

How Involvement Is Conveyed Matters

While research clearly attests to its positive effects, parent involvement can be conveyed in different ways, and this may influence how it affects children. Importantly, parents can be more autonomy supportive or more controlling in the way they are involved in school endeavors. In addition, they can be involved in a way that does or does not include providing the structure that would increase feelings of competence. We take up each of these issues, beginning with autonomy support.

Involvement: Autonomy Supportive vs. Controlling

Whether it is the way they discuss and deal with children's grades or how they help with homework, parents can convey attitudes and behaviors that either support children's initiations and encourage them to solve problems or ones that pressure children and solve problems for them. SDT would suggest that more controlling involvement should undermine children's experience of autonomy. In this case, children's motivation would tend to be external, with children engaging in schoolwork and homework because of contingencies (rewards and punishments) or introjects (engaging in behaviors to avoid negative self-related affects such as guilt). Controlling behaviors should prevent children from internalizing the value of their own learning and thus engaging in behaviors because they see them as important for their own self-valued goals (identified motivation). Further, during interactions, controlling parental behaviors may prevent children from internalizing the information that is being conveyed. When children are directed and pressured to learn, they are less likely to process information deeply and have it available later (Grolnick & Ryan, 1987).

To address the issue of autonomy-supportive versus controlling involvement, several researchers have examined parental styles during homework-like tasks. Grolnick, Gurland, DeCourcey, and Jacob (2002) had 60 third grade students and their mothers engage together in homework-like tasks – a map task where children had to describe how to get to locations on a map and a poem task, where children had to identify different forms of quatrains (four-lined rhyming poems). Mothers' behavior during the tasks was rated from videotapes for how controlling (e.g., directing the child when he or she was progressing well; providing answers to the children) versus autonomy supportive (providing needed information; giving feedback) their behavior was. After the parent-child interaction, children were asked, unbeknownst to the children and the parents, to do similar map and poem tasks on their own. Results suggested that, controlling for children's school grades as a measure of academic competence, the more controlling the mothers, the less accurate the children were on the quatrain and map tasks when on their own. Further, children of mothers who were more controlling and less autonomy supportive during the interactive poem task wrote less creative poems when asked to write a poem on their own relative to children whose mothers were more autonomy supportive. In analyzing these poems, the children of the more controlling mothers tended to repeat the themes of the poem they wrote with their mothers.

The results of the Grolnick et al. (2002) study suggest the importance of an autonomy-supportive style during interactions around school work. While parents who are controlling may try to help their children by giving them answers and solving problems for them, such behaviors seem to prevent the deep processing and internalization of information such that it can be used independently. By contrast, autonomy-supportive interactions appear to help children internalize information so that it can be readily used when necessary. We explore another aspect of this study – different instructions that do or do not provide pressure on parents to have their children do well – on mothers' behavior. This aspect of the study helps us to understand why some parents may adopt a more controlling style, even when they may not endorse such behaviors.

A study by Kenney-Benson and Pomerantz (2005) also examined parent-child interactions during homework-like tasks in a sample of 7–10-year-olds. Mothers' behavior was rated on a scale from controlling to autonomy supportive. Children also completed questionnaires about perfectionism and depression. Findings showed that the more controlling parents were, the more children reported perfectionism and depression. Further, path analyses showed that the effects of controlling maternal behavior on depression were mediated by children's perfectionism. Thus, parent control seemed to translate into children's developing controlling standards for their own performance, something that had negative implications for their well-being.

There is also some evidence from field studies that parent involvement has more positive effects when conveyed in an autonomy-supportive style. Steinberg, Lamborn, Dornbusch, and Darling (1992) had 14–18-year-olds report on their parents' involvement in school, which included helping with homework, attending school activities and events, and helping with choosing classes. They also measured children's perceptions of their parents' overall styles, dividing them into more authoritative (autonomy supportive and structured), authoritarian (controlling and structured), and permissive (unstructured). They found that parent involvement had its most positive effects when combined with an authoritative style. The positive effects of parent involvement were attenuated when parents were either authoritarian or permissive.

Given the importance of how parents are involved, we later address what may make parents more controlling in interacting with their children, focusing on pressures parents may feel to have their children perform well. We also address how teachers may help to decrease the level of pressure parents feel. But next, we discuss how parents can provide structure at home to help their children succeed.

When Parents Provide Structure

While autonomy support has received some attention in the literature, parental structure has been studied less. Within an SDT framework, structure concerns the organization of the environment to facilitate competence. Parents provide structure for their children when they make clear their expectations and rules, provide feedback about how children are doing in meeting these expectations, and provide consistent consequences for action. When these aspects of structure are in place, children know how to be successful and should feel competent to do so.

Farkas and Grolnick (2010) studied the effects of parental structure within the academic domain. In particular, they interviewed seventh and eighth graders about studying and homework and, in particular, whether their parents provide rules and expectations, feedback about how they are doing, consistent consequences for rule-breaking behavior, rationales for why they implement rules and expectations, and, in general, whether they act as authorities in the home. Raters coded the interviews and ratings of these different aspects of structure were combined. These authors found that the more parents provided structure, the higher were children's perceptions of control of their school successes and failures and the more competent they felt in school.

Building on this work, Grolnick et al. (2014b) measured both parents' provision of structure and whether they provide structure in an autonomy-supportive or controlling manner with their children in three areas: academics, unstructured time, and responsibilities. Providing structure in an autonomy-supportive manner involves jointly establishing rules and expectations (versus parents dictating rules and expectations without child input), allowing for open exchange about rules and expectations, providing empathy about the child's viewpoint on the rules/expectations, and providing choice in how the rules were to be followed. Within the academic domain, how structure was provided was more important than the level of structure itself. More specifically, when parents provided structure in an autonomy-supportive manner, children felt most competent (and parents perceived them as most competent), felt more in control of school outcomes, and evidenced higher levels of engagement and school grades.

In another study (Grolnick et al. 2014a), the importance of parental structure was examined at the transition to middle school. The authors reasoned that the transition to middle school involves a series of changes including a new and larger school, a move from one teacher and classroom to multiple teachers and classrooms, higher expectations from teachers, and more controlling classrooms. Such changes would challenge children's perceptions of how to succeed and their sense of their own competence and autonomy. We reasoned that parental structure would buffer children from declines in such motivation and self-beliefs at this transition. One-hundred and thirty-six 6th grade students were interviewed about parental structure at sixth grade and then followed into seventh grade as they made the transition to middle school. Results showed that children in homes with higher level of structure were buffered from declines in perceived competence, intrinsic motivation, and English grades relative to those in homes with lower levels of structure. Further, the more autonomy supportive the structure provided, the higher children's perceived competence, autonomous motivation, and English grades. Thus, it appears that, by providing autonomy-supportive structure, parents can help their children weather the challenges of this important transition.

Predictors of Involvement

If educators are to increase parent involvement, it is important to understand the factors that are associated with differing levels of parent involvement. Further, it is important to know why parents become involved. We take up each of these in turn.

Factors Affecting Parents' Level of Involvement

Several studies have shown that demographic factors such as parent education, income, and single-parent status predict parent involvement (e.g., Bogenschneider, 1997; Stevenson & Baker, 1987). However, this may be more the case for some forms of involvement than others. For example, Grolnick, Benjet, Kurowski, and Apostoleris (1997) found that SES was more strongly related to parents' school and cognitive/intellectual involvement than their personal involvement. Undoubtedly, the time and resources one needs to be involved in these ways make it more difficult for less advantaged families to be involved. Parents from disadvantaged backgrounds may want to be involved but are able to do so in only certain ways. This point will be discussed later as we consider the implications of research findings for educators hoping to increase parent involvement in their schools.

Beyond these background factors, however, researchers have looked at contextual and attitudinal factors that impact levels of involvement. For example, in one study, controlling for SES, parents who reported more stressful life events and lower levels of social support were less likely to be involved, especially for mothers of boys (Grolnick et al., 1997). Taking the view that parents are active in determining how they distribute their time and resources, several studies have examined how parents see their role in children's learning and achievement as predictors of involvement. For example, Grolnick et al. found that parents who saw their role as that of their children's teachers were more likely to get involved in cognitive activities with their children relative to those who were less likely to endorse this role. Green, Walker, Hoover-Dempsey, and Sandler (2007) showed that parents who believed that parents should be active in children's educations showed higher levels of home and school involvement relative to those who did not have these beliefs. Finally, Walker, Ice, Hoover-Dempsey, and Sandler (2011) measured three types of role constructions – one where parents thought they had primary responsibility for their children's school performance, one where they believed they had shared responsibility with the school for children's school performance, and one where the school had primary responsibility for children's school performance. In a study of 147 Latino parents, these authors found that parents who endorsed the shared responsibility role construction were more likely to be involved at home, whereas those who believed the school had primary responsibility were less involved at home.

Taking parents' viewpoints even more seriously, we have focused on parents' own motivation for being involved as a factor that may affect their behavior. Just as we have shown that whether children's participation in school endeavors is more autonomous or more controlled has implications for their school functioning and adjustment, we wondered whether parents whose involvement behaviors were experienced as more versus less autonomous would have different experiences and levels of involvement. Thus, in a diverse sample of 178 mothers and their third through sixth grade children (Grolnick, 2015), we asked mothers why they were involved in three types of activities: talking to your child's teacher (e.g., conferences and meetings), participating in events at your child's school (e.g., fund-raisers or volunteering), and helping your child with his or her schoolwork. Parents then rated their reasons for being involved in each of these activities. Reasons were associated with the four types of motivation: external (e.g., because I am supposed to), introjected (e.g., because I would feel guilty if I didn't), identified (e.g., because I think it is important to talk with the teacher), and intrinsic (e.g., because it is fun to go to the events). Parents also reported on their affect when involved (i.e., interested, relaxed, calm, nervous, strained, bored) and their levels of school, cognitive/intellectual, and personal involvement. Finally, children reported on their perceptions of competence and children's grades were obtained. Results showed that mothers' motivation for involvement had both affective and behavioral concomitants. In particular, mothers' external and introjected motivation for involvement were associated with lower levels of positive affect when involved, while mothers' identified and intrinsic motivation were positively associated with positive affect. In addition, identified and intrinsic motivations were associated with higher levels of school, cognitive/intellectual, and personal involvement. Introjected motivation was negatively associated with school and personal involvement, and external motivation was negatively associated with personal involvement. Finally, the results supported a pathway in which more identified motivation for involvement was associated with higher levels of cognitive/intellectual involvement, which then predicted children's perceived competence and reading grades. In addition, identified motivation was associated with children's self-worth through increased personal involvement.

The results of the study on mothers' motivation for involvement underscore the importance of considering why parents are involved for both their level of involvement and for parents' experience. That the strongest results were for identified motivation suggests that it is crucial for parents to be involved because they see their involvement as important for their own goals vis-a-vis their children rather than because of regulations and contingencies. Pushing parents to be involved through contingencies or guilt evoking may result in some increases in involvement, but if this results in more external and introjected motivation, these increases are unlikely to be sustained. Further, they may result in parents feeling unhappy when involved, and this may translate into uncomfortable interactions with children. Since positive affect during homework has been found to moderate children's feelings of helplessness on tasks (Pomerantz, Wang, & Ng, 2005), facilitating motivation in parents that is likely to be more autonomous needs to be a goal in efforts to involve parents.

Though not examining levels of involvement per se, a study by Katz, Kaplan, and Buzukashvily (2011) assessed parents' autonomous versus controlled motivation for homework involvement by asking parents to respond to questions about why they help their children with homework. These authors found that the more autonomous parents' motivation for helping their children with homework, the more they showed need-supportive behavior (i.e., were perceived by students and reported themselves as providing support for autonomy (i.e., understanding students' perspectives, offering choice, allowing for criticism), support for children's competence (e.g., helping students to plan, offering feedback), and support for relatedness (i.e., providing acceptance and empathy). In turn, the more need-supportive behavior parents displayed, the more students reported autonomous motivation for completing their homework. Thus, again, parents' motivation for involvement must be considered if involvement is to be most facilitative.

What Affects the How *of Involvement?*

Results described earlier showed that higher levels of involvement were positive for school achievement but also that more autonomy-supportive involvement had the most robust effects on motivation and performance. Therefore, it is important to study what predicts whether parents are more or less autonomy supportive in their school-related involvement.

Within our framework, pressure is a key factor in predicting parental autonomy support versus control. Pressure, whether it is from external demands, internal pressures to have children succeed, or a result of the children themselves pushing parents, narrows one's focus on the outcome and would thus lead parents to make the quickest and most expedient response to assure it. Oftentimes, this involves controlling children's behavior, since autonomy-supportive behaviors, such as taking children's perspectives and engaging in joint problem-solving, take time and require a focus on the process of the interaction not just the outcome.

Consistent with this reasoning, in our lab, we have examined how pressure on parents to have their children succeed influences the degree to which parents interact with their children in more autonomy-supportive versus controlling ways. In one study (Grolnick et al., 2002), 60 mothers worked on map and poem tasks with their third grade children. Mothers completed questionnaires about their orientations toward being controlling or supporting autonomy in children. Then half of the mothers received pressure to have their child perform by being told "Your role is to ensure that your child learns to give directions [write a poem]. We will be testing him/her after to make sure that he/she performs well enough." The other half received a non-pressuring orientation, "Your role is to help your child learn how to give directions [write a poem]. We will be asking him/her some questions after but there is no particular level at which he/she needs to perform." Mothers' behavior during the tasks was coded for level of autonomy support versus control. For the poem task, mothers in the pressuring condition were more controlling than those in the non-pressuring condition, directing the children and solving problems for them. For the map task, there was an interesting statistical interaction in which mothers who displayed highly autonomy-supportive attitudes toward working with children were not affected by the pressuring condition. On the other hand, mothers who believed strongly in control were much more controlling in the high-pressure condition than in the low-pressure condition. These results show how pressure can "roll downhill" and affect interactions with others. It also shows that some parents may be more vulnerable to pressure to have their children do well. The implications of these findings for helping parents work with their children in a motivation-enhancing manner are discussed at the end of the chapter.

Another factor that may predict parents' autonomy-supportive versus controlling school-related interactions concerns parents' ideas about their children's intelligence. A body of work suggests that children who believe intelligence is fixed and not changeable (i.e., have an entity theory of intelligence) show decrements in their performance on tasks when work gets difficult (e.g., Dweck & Leggett, 1988). The interpretation of this is that, when children believe their intelligence is unchangeable, difficulties and setbacks would be an indication that they are not "smart" and there is nothing they can do about it. They become helpless – giving up and denigrating their capacities. By contrast, those who have an incremental theory, seeing intelligence as changeable and able to be increased, show more effort when faced with setbacks. Pomerantz and her colleagues have examined parents' ideas about children's intelligence. They reasoned that parents who have an entity mind-set regarding their children's intelligence would see children's mistakes and setbacks as indicative of a permanent deficit in their competence. They would thus try to ensure that they perform well. This might lead to unconstructive interactions with parents more controlling and negative in their affect. On the other hand, mothers with an incremental mind-set would see difficulties as signs only that their children need to display more effort to master tasks. They would be less concerned about performance. In one study (Moorman & Pomerantz, 2010), these authors induced 79 parents to have either an entity mind-set by telling them that the task their child was about to complete measured innate intelligence and children's performance on the task was stable or an incremental mind-set, by telling them that children's performance on the task measured potential and was highly changeable through practice and learning. Mothers then worked on the tasks with their children, helping them as much as they wanted. The researchers coded mothers' behaviors for whether they were pressuring and intrusive or encouraging of mastery. They also coded children's responses to challenge for level of helplessness (i.e., frustration) versus engagement. Results showed that mothers induced to have an entity mind-set were more unconstructive in their involvement. In addition, when children showed signs of helplessness, mothers in the entity condition engaged in more unconstructive involvement. The results of the study show that parents' beliefs about children's intelligence may play a role in how they interact with their children on school-related tasks.

Consistent with the idea of pressure from below, investigators have found that the lower children's achievement, the more parents are controlling in their assistance with their children's homework. For example, Dumont, Trautwein, Nagy, and Nagengast (2014) measured how controlling parents were in helping their children with their homework when children were in fifth and seventh grades. They found that children with lower levels of reading achievement at fifth grade received more control from their parents 2 years later relative to children with higher levels of achievement. In a further aspect of the study looking at reciprocal relations between parents' and children's behavior, lower levels of achievement led to more parental control which in turn led to children procrastinating more on their homework and then in turn to lower levels of achievement. Such results refute the often stated idea that children performing poorly require more controlling styles. Findings of the study indicate that, though they may elicit them, unfortunately, controlling interventions do not appear to help them move toward greater self-regulation and academic performance.

Pomerantz and Eaton (2001) explored the mechanisms through which children's achievement might elicit more controlling behaviors on the part of mothers. These authors had mothers complete a checklist of behaviors they used when assisting their children with homework. Some of these behaviors, such as helping with or checking homework when their child did not request it, were labeled intrusive support. The authors found that the lower children's achievement, the more mothers used intrusive support behaviors. Further, they found that children's achievement elicited parental worry and signals of uncertainty from children which were then associated with intrusive support. Thus, parental worry and concern, which may be well meant, may result in pressuring their children.

In sum, there are a variety of factors that influence both the level and the quality of involvement parents display in their children's academic lives. These factors need to be addressed in efforts to involve parents as they can be the difference between involvement that it is facilitative and undermining of children's motivation and adjustment.

Implications and Recommendations

The research on parent involvement is extensive and makes it clear that enhancing parent involvement should be a goal for all schools. The research provides key information on how to maximize efforts to harness this key resource for children's motivation and learning. Some ideas and suggestions are described below.

1. Encourage diverse ways to be involved
   When people think about parent involvement, they most likely imagine parents coming to school for open school night or being active in fund-raising or volunteering. Not all parents, however, are able to attend activities at school given work schedules, other responsibilities, lack of transportation, or language barriers. Given that research evidence suggests that the most potent forms of involvement are those that involve parent-child interaction, teachers and schools can involve parents in other ways. Frequent communication through e-mails and newsletters helps parents to be able to know what is going on in school so that they can discuss it with their children. Schools can also provide information to parents so that they might help their children manage their time, select courses, and engage in activities related to school topics. As described in the Teachers Involve Parents in Schoolwork (TIPS) project (Epstein & Van Voorhis, 2001), teachers may assign homework involving family members such as interviewing them about earlier times. Finally, schools can invite parents to the classroom to see their children present their work or share their own interests and cultural activities. Given that parent involvement has its largest effects through children's motivation, all parents can be involved in ways that will support their children.
2. Help parents create meaningful and facilitative roles
   Research shows that parents who believe their role is that of their child's teacher and who believe they share responsibility for their children's learning with the school are more likely to be involved. Schools may expect that parents know

they have a crucial role in their children's school success but may not convey this expectation. Thus, schools may interpret parents' lack of involvement as evidence that they are not interested in being involved. It is crucial, therefore, that schools convey their expectations and the value that they have for families. Teachers and principals can do this by sharing their philosophy via communications such as newsletters and explicitly addressing how important parents are during parent-teacher conferences and school events.

Beyond knowing that they are part of the home-school partnership team in helping their children, parents need to know what role teachers expect them to play in their children's homework and studying. Parents have a strong stake in their children doing well in school. They may become highly invested in children's performance outcomes, especially if they see intelligence as a fixed entity and feel that their performance reflects this highly valued trait. This situation may lead parents to push and pressure their children when working with them at home, which may lead to negative homework interactions that are quite prevalent among families (Xu & Corno, 2003). Teachers can prevent this situation by helping parents to see their role as to support children's initiations and provide needed resources rather than ensuring that their homework makes them look "smart." When parents receive the message that their children's mistakes and questions do not reflect on them or on their children's potential, they may be more likely to have positive interactions around schoolwork in which children feel supported to convey their misconceptions and their struggles as well as successes.

3. Meet Parents' Needs

Our research, reviewed previously, showed that parents' own motivation for being involved plays a role in their levels of and experience of involvement. When parents have more autonomous motivation for being involved, in particular, when they are involved because they see the importance of their behaviors rather than because they feel they are supposed to or would feel guilty if they didn't, they have more positive experiences and higher levels of involvement. Just as parents can set up facilitative conditions for their children's motivation, schools can help to set up situations that may lead to parents' more autonomous involvement. In particular, in asking parents to be involved, schools can provide clear rationales for how parents' actions will be helpful to the school and to their children. They can also provide clear expectations so that parents know how to be most helpful to their children. These actions can help parents to feel competent in working with their children and with the school. Second, to support parents' sense of autonomy, schools can provide choices for how parents can be involved so that they can engage in the activities that fit them best. Finally, establishing mutual relationships at the start of the school year can provide a context within which requests and opportunities for involvement are welcomed. While many school-to-parent communications occur when children are experiencing problems, some schools initiate contact with parents when something is positive or just to establish a working relationship. While touching base with parents before problems arise may be time-consuming, it may ultimately result in a stronger school-home alliance that will pay off many times in the long run. Of course, parent-school interactions are a two way street. Parents can help to meet teachers' basic needs by valuing and respecting them, communicating their expectations, and establishing a context of joint problem-solving and partnership.

In sum, our review of work on parent involvement supports the usefulness of an SDT framework in understanding how parent involvement exerts its effects on children's achievement. The theory highlights the important role that parents play in facilitating children's motivation and the factors, including pressures from various sources that undermine parents' own motivation to be involved. Schools can play an important role in creating contexts that welcome and encourage parents' support of their children's learning. Our hope is that schools will increasingly prioritize and nurture this crucial resource.

References

Bogenschneider, K. (1997). Parental involvement in adolescent schooling: A proximal process with transcontextual validity. *Journal of Marriage and the Family, 59*, 718–733.

Deci, E. L., & Ryan, R. M. (1985). *Intrinsic motivation and self-determination in human behavior.* New York: Plenum Press.

Deci, E. L., & Ryan, R. M. (2000). The "what" and "why" of goal pursuits: Human needs and the self-determination of behavior. *Psychological Inquiry, 11*, 319–338.

Dumont, H., Trautwein, U., Nagy, G., & Nagengast, B. (2014). Quality of parental homework involvement: Predictors and reciprocal relations with academic functioning in the reading domain. *Journal of Educational Psychology, 106*, 144–161.

Dweck, C. S., & Leggett, E. L. (1988). A social-cognitive approach to motivation and personality. *Psychological Review, 95*, 256–273.

Epstein, J. L., & Van Voorhis, F. L. (2001). More than minutes: Teachers' roles in designing homework. *Educational Psychologist, 36*, 181–193.

Fan, X., & Chen, M. (2001). Parental involvement and students' academic achievement: A meta-analysis. *Educational Psychology Review, 13*, 1–22.

Farkas, M. S., & Grolnick, W. S. (2010). Examining the components and concomitants of structure in the academic domain. *Motivation and Emotion, 34*, 266–279.

Green, C. L., Walker, J. M. T., Hoover-Dempsey, K. V., & Sandler, H. M. (2007). Parents' motivations for involvement in children's education: An empirical test of a theoretical motel of parental involvement. *Journal of Educational Psychology, 9*, 532–544.

Grolnick, W. S. (2015). Mothers' motivation for involvement in their children's schooling: Mechanisms and outcomes. *Motivation and Emotion, 39*, 63–73.

Grolnick, W. S., Benjet, C., Kurowski, C. O., & Apostoleris, N. (1997). Predictors of parent involvement in children's schooling. *Journal of Educational Psychology, 89*, 538–548.

Grolnick, W. S., Gurland, S., DeCourcey, W., & Jacob, K. (2002). Antecedents and consequences of mothers' autonomy support. An empirical investigation. *Developmental Psychology, 38*, 143–155.

Grolnick, W. S., Raftery-Helmer, J. N., Flamm, E. S., Marbell, K., Cardemil, E. V. (2014a). Parental provision of academic structure and the transition to middle school. *Journal of Research on Adolescence.* doi:10.1111/jora.12161

Grolnick, W. S., Raftery-Helmer, J. N., Marbell, K., Flamm, E. S., Cardemil, E. V., & Sanchez, M. (2014b). Parental provision of structure: Implementation, correlates, and outcomes in three domains. *Merrill-Palmer Quarterly, 60*, 335–384.

Grolnick, W. S., & Ryan, R. M. (1987). Autonomy in children's learning: An experimental and individual difference investigation. *Journal of Personality and Social Psychology, 52*, 890–898.

Grolnick, W. S., & Ryan, R. M. (1989). Parent styles associated with children's self-regulation and competence in school. *Journal of Educational Psychology, 81*, 143–154.

Grolnick, W. S., & Slowiaczek, M. L. (1994). Parents' involvement in children's schooling: A multidimensional conceptualization and motivational model. *Child Development, 65*, 237–252.

Hill, N. E., & Tyson, D. F. (2009). Parental involvement in middle school: A meta-analytic assessment of the strategies that promote achievement. *Developmental Psychology, 45*, 740–763.

Hill, N. E., & Taylor, L. C. P. (2004). Parental school involvement and children's academic achievement: Pragmatics and issues. *Current Directions in Psychological Science, 13*, 161–164.

Jeynes, W. H. (2005). A meta-analysis of the relation of parental involvement to urban elementary school student academic achievement. *Urban Education, 40*, 237–269.

Jeynes, W. H. (2007). The relationship between parental involvement and urban secondary school student academic achievement: A meta-analysis. *Urban Education, 42*, 82–110.

Katz, I., Kaplan, A., & Buzukashvily, T. (2011). The role of parents' motivation in students' autonomous motivation for doing homework. *Learning and Individual Differences, 21*, 376–386.

Kenney-Benson, G. A., & Pomerantz, E. M. (2005). The role of mothers' use of control in children's perfectionism: Implications for the development of children's depressive symptoms. *Journal of Personality, 73*, 23–46.

Marchant, G. J., Paulson, S. E., & Rothlisberg, B. A. (2001). Relations of middle school students' perceptions of family and school contexts with academic achievement. *Psychology in the Schools, 38*, 505–519.

McWayne, C., Hampton, V., Fantuzzo, J., Cohen, H. L., & Sekino, Y. (2004). A multivariate examination of parent involvement and the social and academic competencies of urban kindergarten. *Psychology in the Schools, 41*, 363–377.

Moorman, E. A., & Pomerantz, E. M. (2010). Ability mindsets influence the quality of mothers' involvement in children's learning: An experimental investigation. *Developmental Psychology, 46*, 1354–1362.

Pomerantz, E. M., & Eaton, M. M. (2001). Maternal intrusive support in the academic context: Transactional socialization processes. *Developmental Psychology, 37*, 174–186.

Pomerantz, E. M., Wang, Q., & Ng, F. Y. (2005). Mothers' affect in the homework context: The importance of staying positive. *Developmental Psychology, 41*, 414–427.

Pomeranz, E. M., Grolnick, W. S., & Price, C. E. (2005). The role of parents in how children approach school: A dynamic process perspective. In A. J. Elliot & C. S. Dweck (Eds.), *The handbook of competence and motivation* (pp. 259–278). New York: Guilford.

Steinberg, L., Lamborn, S. D., Dornbusch, S. M., & Darling, N. (1992). Impact of parenting practices on adolescent achievement: Authoritative parenting, school involvement, and encouragement to succeed. *Child Development, 63*, 1266–1281.

Stevenson, D. L., & Baker, D. P. (1987). The family-school relation and the child's school performance. *Child Development, 58*, 1348–1357.

Topor, D. R., Keane, S. P., Shelton, T. L., & Calkins, S. D. (2010). Parent involvement and student academic performance: A multiple mediational analysis. *Journal of Prevention and Intervention in the Community, 38*, 183–197.

Walker, J. M. T., Ice, C. L., Hoover-Dempsey, K. V., & Sandler, H. M. (2011). Latino parents' motivations for involvement in their children's schooling. *The Elementary School Journal, 111*, 409–429.

Xu, J., & Corno, L. (2003). Family help and homework management reported by middle school students. *Elementary School Journal, 103*, 503–536.

Chapter 10
Parental Influence and Students' Outcomes and Well-Being

Wai Cheong Eugene Chew

If you ask parents how they can positively influence the development of their children, they may conjure various notions in their minds. Some may tell you that parents need to spend enough time with their children, and if that is not possible, then quality time with their children is critical. Others may say that parental control is vital and that the parenting style that exerts such control over the children can foster the desired development outcomes such social socio-psychological well-being or educational achievements. Or some may maintain that it is about their parenting practices that are aimed at steering their children towards socialisation goals in the various domains such as studies, sports or character development. Most will probably insist that parents must be involved in the lives of their children in order that they can make a difference in how their children turn out to be or what they can accomplish. Are they correct? Does the research evidence support their claims?

One of the key questions that this chapter seeks to answer is: "Are there some aspects of parental influence that have been found consistently to be important to predicting positive child outcomes?" Studies on parenting which were largely conducted in the context of socialisation and academic achievements have looked at various aspects of parental influence. We will consider some notable studies that offer some indications of convergence towards characteristic patterns of parental behaviours that are associated with positive child outcomes. These are contrasted with those that are linked to negative child outcomes. With sports pursuits being an integral aspect of the educational experience of students in schools, it then begs the question as to whether these identified beneficial forms of parental influence are also associated with positive child outcomes in the sports domain. This chapter will also seek to offer some insights into this question.

W.C.E. Chew (✉)
National Institute of Education, Nanyang Technological University, Singapore, Singapore
e-mail: eugene.chew@nie.edu.sg

© Springer Science+Business Media Singapore 2016
W.C. Liu et al. (eds.), *Building Autonomous Learners*,
DOI 10.1007/978-981-287-630-0_10

Importance of Sports Pursuits in the Education Process

Traditionally, academic achievements have been the focus of educational outcomes. However, from a holistic development standpoint, sports pursuits are part and parcel of the educational process that a student goes through. Very often, they form part of the co-curricular activities in schools. Particularly, in Singapore, in line with the emphasis on a well-rounded education, sports and other aspects of co-curricular activities are an integral part of the students' holistic education. Students participate in intramural sports activities, inter-school sports competitions or both. Some of them also compete in sports competitions at the national or international level. Doing well in sports and studies is valued by the stakeholders, and it places the student in an advantageous position to secure better educational opportunities. Parents in Asian societies such as Singapore, Hong Kong, Japan and South Korea recognise the utility of a good education in securing coveted career paths that help ensure a bright future for their children. The pathway to a good educational outcome is often equated with students doing well in their early years of education, gain admission to top schools and then continue to achieve good academic grades. Increasingly, this is not enough. Parents focus their effort and resources in providing their children the competitive advantage in their educational pursuit. In Singapore, performing well in sports improves the chance of students gaining admission to choice schools through admission schemes that favour students with sports achievements. Also, organisations offering scholarships to students to pursue further studies in higher educational institutions often seek out candidates who are well-rounded individuals.

Key Patterns of Parental Behaviours

Various conceptualisations and terminologies have been used to describe or define parental influence. In some ways they were associated with the methods used to analyse the data. Researchers sometimes examined specific parental behaviours such as presence, praise and providing feedback or parental characteristics such as goal orientations, beliefs or socio-demographics (e.g. Duda & Hom, 1993; Ebbeck & Becker, 1994; Fredricks & Eccles, 2005; White, Kavussanu, Tank, & Wingate, 2004). Other researchers statistically analysed specific parental behaviours and formed clusters of related behaviours such as *democracy, acceptance or warmth, indulgence* (Baldwin, Kalhorn, & Breese, 1945), *acceptance* versus *rejection, firm control* versus *lax control* and *psychological autonomy* versus *psychological control* (Schaefer, 1965b). These clusters are also termed syndromes or dimensions, and according to Baldwin and colleagues, they can be viewed as patterns of parental behaviours variables that reflect underlying attitudes, philosophies or personality traits. Researchers sometimes further aggregate these syndromes or dimension to form classifications (e.g. acceptant-democratic, acceptant-democratic-indulgent;

Baldwin et al., 1945) or configurations (e.g. authoritarian, authoritative, permissive; Baumrind, 1971) of parental behaviours. Hence, different researchers may examine parental behaviours at different levels of complexity. The two latter approaches are more commonly used by researchers to see whether such patterns of parental behaviours are linked to various child outcomes. Studies employing the dimensional and configurational approaches suggest that certain parenting dimensions and parenting style, respectively, are associated with positive child outcomes. We first consider parenting styles.

Parenting Styles

In looking through the literature on parental influence, one cannot ignore the various research findings based on Baumrind's (1966) conceptualisation of patterns of parental control. Baumrind described three prototype configurations of parental behaviours—*authoritarian, authoritative* and *permissive*. The authoritarian parent is characterised as one who shapes, controls and evaluates the attitudes and behaviours of the child with a specific standard of conduct, values obedience and uses punitive measures to align the child's beliefs and actions with those of the parent. The authoritarian parent highly values work, tradition and preservation of order and does not encourage bidirectional communication. The authoritative parent adopts a rational and issue-oriented approach to directing the child's actions, encourages open communication and verbal give and take, provides reasons for directives and policies, values autonomous self-will and disciplined conformity to set standards of conduct and exerts firm control at points of conflicts but also allows for individual expressions and interests. The third pattern is the permissive parent who is non-punitive, acceptant and affirmative towards the child's impulses and actions and lax in instilling responsibility and orderly behaviour, allows considerable self-regulation and avoids the exercise of control but tries to use reason and manipulation to achieve the desired objectives. The permissive parent does not encourage obedience to externally defined standards and sees herself as a resource but not a role model or an active socialisation agent. Consistent with previous studies (Baumrind, 1966, 1967), in a subsequent study (1971) that used a different methodology in analysing parental behaviours, Baumrind also found three prototype configurations (authoritarian, authoritative and permissive) and added a fourth configuration, *rejecting-neglecting*. However, the earlier three prototype configurations of parental authority remained prominent and were widely used in literature in parenting. While Baumrind initially did not use the term "parenting style", she subsequently employed this term to describe the patterns of parental authority (Baumrind, 1991b).

Often parenting styles and parenting practices are used interchangeably. However, some researchers distinguished between parenting styles and parenting practices in which the former refers to global attitudes and emotional stances, while the latter are specific types of parental behaviours with specific socialisation content and goals (Darling & Steinberg, 1993). Darling and Steinberg asserted that parenting style changes the efficacy of parental influence by transforming the nature and affective quality of the parent-child interactions and by changing the child's personality to being more open to parental influence. Parenting style, therefore, is posited to moderate the influence of parenting practices on the child's development. Some evidence supports this proposition. Studies have found that the relationship between parental involvement practices and adolescent school achievement is strongest for students with authoritative parenting (Paulson, Marchant, & Rothilsberg, 1998; Steinberg, Lamborn, Dornbusch, & Darling, 1992).

The authoritative parenting style has been shown to be the optimal parenting style across different cultures and is linked to better academic performance, adaptive social behaviours and other positive child outcomes (e.g. Baumrind, 1991a; Baumrind & Black, 1967; Chen, Dong, & Zhou, 1997; Dornbusch, Ritter, Leiderman, Roberts, & Fraleigh, 1987; Maccoby, 1992; Steinberg et al., 1992). Researchers continue to be drawn to the salutary effects of authoritative parenting on child development. More recent studies have continued to employ the parenting styles conceptualised by Baumrind either in their study designs or in the way data analyses are conducted. For example, some of these studies provided further evidence of the beneficial effects of authoritative parenting relative to other parenting styles, linking authoritative parenting to greater psychological well-being in adolescence (Milevsky, Schlechter, Klem, & Kehl, 2008; Slicker & Thornberry, 2002), and in adulthood (Rothrauff, Cooney, & An, 2009), and showing that perceived authoritative parenting was positively related to both higher autonomous motivation and mastery goal orientation in adolescents' achievement motivation in mathematics (Gonzalez & Wolters, 2006).

Parenting Dimensions of Authoritative Parenting Style

Although studies based on parenting styles provided descriptive characteristics of parenting attitudes and behaviours that are associated with each parenting style's differential influence on child outcomes, the psychological mechanisms and processes by which a child is influenced are not fully understood when individual differences in child outcomes are examined at this aggregated level. For example, when investigating the influence of authoritative parenting style on a particular child outcome, neither the independent effects of a specific dimension (e.g. firm enforcement) nor the relative effects of other dimensions (e.g. encourage independence and individuality, passive-acceptance) of this style can be examined. To address this shortcoming, researchers have advocated the dimensional approach which disaggregates the components of parenting style and looking at specific dimensions of parenting in relation to child correlates (Barber, 1997; Barber, Stolz, Olsen, Collins, & Burchinal, 2005; Grolnick & Ryan, 1989; Roberts & Steinberg, 1999). Since authoritative parenting style has been shown to be beneficial to child development, it will be instructive to understand how the components of this style are linked to child outcomes.

In Baumrind's (1991a) subsequent study, she conceptualised parenting styles as a combination of two orthogonal dimensions: responsiveness and demandingness. "*Demandingness* refers to the claims parents make on the child to become integrated into the family whole by their maturity demands, supervision, disciplinary efforts and willingness to confront the child who disobeys. *Responsiveness* refers to actions which intentionally foster individuality, self-regulation and self-assertion by being attuned, supportive and acquiescent to the child's special needs and demands" (pp. 61–62). Authoritative parenting is classified as high in responsiveness and high in demandingness. It is also described as having the elements of high warmth, autonomy support and behavioural control (Baumrind, 2005). Authoritarian parenting is classified as low in responsiveness and high in demandingness. Permissive parents are highly responsive but are not demanding, and rejecting-neglecting or disengaged parents are neither responsive nor demanding. Baumrind stated that the notion of adolescents' optimal competence was relevant to how parents interact with their adolescents. Optimal competence was defined as the integration of agency and communion, where "... communion refers to the need to be of service and be included and connected, whereas agency refers to the drive for independence, individuality, and self-aggrandizement" (p. 61). Alluding to salutary effects of the authoritative parenting style, Baumrind argued that when parents are both highly demanding and highly responsive, adolescents are most likely to be optimally competent.

Using the dimensional approach to further understand the beneficial effects of authoritative parenting on child correlates, Roberts and Steinberg (1999) unpacked Baumrind's configuration of authoritative parenting into three core dimensions, i.e. *acceptance-involvement, behavioural control* and *psychological autonomy granting*, and examined their separate and joint effects on adolescent behaviour problems, psychosocial development, internal distress and academic competence. Their study with adolescents (N = 10,000) examined the independent and joint interactive contributions of these dimensions to four areas of adolescent adjustments. Their results showed that acceptance-involvement, behavioural control and psychological autonomy granting each contributes in unique and independent ways to the four areas of adolescent development. As expected, behavioural control, acceptance-involvement and psychological autonomy granting were negatively related to behaviour problems and internal distress and were positively related to psychosocial development and academic competence. Behavioural control demonstrated the strongest relation to behaviour problems. Acceptance-involvement and psychological autonomy granting were more strongly associated than behavioural control with adolescent psychosocial development as well as with internal distress. All three parenting dimensions were significantly and positively related to academic competence. Curvilinear and interactive relations between the parenting dimensions were also present; however, their specific patterns vary depending on the area of adolescent adjustment analysed. More importantly, the researchers were able to examine the variations due to each specific dimension.

Parenting Dimensions Based on SDT

Thus far, we note that the dimensional approach further shed light on the how the authoritative parenting style is linked to more positive child outcomes. Can we explain why it is so? The dimensional approach also offers a way for researchers to study specific parenting dimensions that are theoretically based, and thereby facilitating theoretical explanations for understanding the effects of the studied parenting dimensions on the associated outcomes. One notable development in this area of research is the deployment of the self-determination theory (SDT; Deci & Ryan, 1985) as the theoretical framework by researchers in the investigation of parental influence to better understand the dynamics involved in the parent-child relationship (e.g. Assor, Roth, & Deci, 2004; Grolnick & Ryan, 1989; Grolnick, Ryan, & Deci, 1991; Grolnick & Slowiaczek, 1994; Silk, Morris, Kanaya, & Steinberg, 2003; Soenens, Duriez, Vansteenkiste, & Goossens, 2007; Soenens & Vansteenkiste, 2010; Soenens, Vansteenkiste, & Sierens, 2009). It offers perspectives on how parents can influence their child's motivational processes and its related outcomes.

In discussing the complexities of parental involvement, Wendy Grolnick, in the earlier chapter of this book, provided insightful evidence on how the SDT-based parenting dimensions of autonomy support and structure can enhance the quality of parental involvement. She presented research evidence indicating that the way (e.g. in a controlling or autonomy-supportive manner) in which parents are involved has important implications on children's achievements. The subsequent sections will look beyond parental involvement, elaborate on the dimensions of autonomy and structure and consider other SDT-based parenting dimensions examined by researchers. We will briefly discuss the key findings associated with some notable studies in these areas and observe some convergence in what researchers consider to be important parenting dimensions. Also, we will consider the similarity between these SDT-based dimensions and those that are of the authoritative parenting style, thereby providing a way for understanding the reason why beneficial effects on child development are linked to this parenting style:

Autonomy Support One of the key tenets of SDT is that it distinguishes between autonomous and controlled motives for one's reason to act. And that the satisfaction of one's innate needs of autonomy, competence and relatedness conduces one towards more autonomous motivation. Autonomy support is therefore expected to be beneficial to child development. Numerous SDT-based studies have collectively maintained that parents who are autonomy supportive promote adaptive and favourable child outcomes. For example, Grolnick and Ryan (1989) showed that children who perceived that their parents were more autonomy supportive were positively related to the children's self-determined motivation, academic achievement and grades, competence and school behavioural adjustments. Chirkov and Ryan (2001) also demonstrated that students of autonomy-supportive parents tended to be more autonomously motivated and were better adjusted. Soenens and Vansteenkiste (2005) found evidence showing that higher autonomous motivation in three different life domains (school, social competence, job-seeking behaviours) were associated with autonomy-supportive parenting of adolescents. Other aspects of individual growth and development were also linked to autonomy-supportive parenting. For instance, Smits, Soenens, Vansteenkiste, Luyckx and Goosens (2010) when investigating the identity styles of adolescents in relation to their autonomous or controlled forms of motivation, and how these motives in turn were linked to adolescent developmental, also examine parenting dimensions as antecedents of these motives. They found that autonomy-supportive parenting was positively related to autonomous motives which were positively linked to commitment and psychological well-being.

Joussemet, Landry and Koestner's (2008) extensive review of studies on parental autonomy support employing parent observations, parent interviews and children's reports of parental behaviours clearly showed that children from as young as 1 year to college-age adolescents derived positive and healthy development from parental autonomy support. Parental autonomy support was positively associated with child outcomes such as competence, self-regulation, control understanding (i.e. children's understanding of who or what controls outcomes in their lives) at school and school performance in elementary school children (Grolnick & Ryan, 1989; Grolnick et al., 1991); young children's reading achievement and social and academic adjustment (Joussemet, Koestner, Lekes, & Landry, 2005); and adolescents' self-regulation, adjustment and school success (Guay, Ratelle, & Chanal, 2008; Vallerand, Fortier, & Guay, 1997).

More recently, Soenens and colleagues (Soenens, Vansteenkiste, et al., 2007) further refined the conceptualisation of autonomy support by differentiating between conceptualising autonomy support as promotion of independence (PI) and as promotion of volitional functioning (PVF). Grounded on separation-individuation theory (Blos, 1979), PI is assessed by tapping on parents' promotion of independent view and expression and decision-making (Silk et al., 2003). On the other hand, PVF is in sync with how autonomy is defined as volitional functioning in SDT. Consistent with SDT, the results in Soenens and colleagues' study showed that PVF is a stronger predictor of well-being and that adolescents' tendency to act in a volitional manner mediated the link between perceived parental and adolescent psychosocial functioning.

Structure In Grolnick and Ryan's (1989) study examining the three parenting dimensions of structure, involvement and autonomy support provided by parents to elementary school children, structure was operationally defined as clarity and consistency in rules, expectations and limits. Parental provision of structure was positively related to children's (third to sixth grade) understanding of how to control their successes and failures. Structure, autonomy support and involvement were maintained by Grolnick and colleagues (1997), from SDT's perspective, to be three important social-contextual dimensions for promoting internalisation as a developmental process. Also, Grolnick (2003) associated the construct of structure to Steinberg's (1990) behavioural control and Baumrind's (1967) construct of firm control which is a characteristic feature of authoritative parenting: a parenting style associated with positive child and adolescent development. These conceptualisations are also in sync with Barber and colleagues' (2005) notion of behavioural control. Recent studies show that structure is independent of autonomy support and that it makes a unique contribution to motivation and performance in the academic domain (Farkas & Grolnick, 2010) and that structure and autonomy support are two complementary instructional support features that foster greater engagement behaviours (Jang, Reeve, & Deci, 2010).

Warmth The construct warmth is usually associated with, or used synonymously with, involvement. Grolnick and colleagues (see Grolnick et al., 1997), in identifying autonomy support, involvement and structure as key parenting dimensions for the positive development of children, included "providing warmth and caring" (p. 147) as one of the characteristic features of interpersonal involvement. Steinberg and colleagues (1992) reiterated that parental warmth, apart from psychological autonomy granting and firm control, contributes to adolescent psychological health and better school performance. In Baumrind's (1965) conceptualisation, warmth is part of nurturance along with involvement. She defined warmth as:

> the parents' personal love and compassion for the child expressed by sensory stimulation of the child, verbal approval, and tenderness of expression. By *involvement* is meant by identification by the parent with the behavior and feelings of the child, her pride and pleasure with the child's accomplishments, and her conscientious protection of the child's welfare. (p. 231)

Baumrind's (1967, 1971) authoritative parenting style combines warmth with firm control and communication. Other early studies have also examined warmth as a parenting dimension that is related to individual differences in children. As mentioned earlier, Schaefer (1959, 1965a) identified warmth versus hostility and control versus autonomy as two orthogonal variables, while Becker (1964) looked at two similar variables, warmth (acceptance) versus hostility (rejection) and restrictive versus permissive. Maccoby and Martin (1983) suggested that the role that parental warmth plays in the parent-child relationship goes beyond encouraging children's willing acceptance of parental directive to establishing positive affects between parent and child. Therefore, parental warmth is seen to be an important factor that impacts on the psychosocial outcome of the child and contributes to a sense of relatedness between parent and child. Relatedness, one of the three primary psychological needs according to SDT, is analogous to what Harlow (1958) contends to be necessary for optimal development of the individual—the need to experience warmth and affection in their interpersonal contact. This sense of relatedness (Ryan, Deci, & Grolnick, 1995) allows intrinsic motivation to thrive and bolsters healthy psychological growth. Studies have found that adolescents who reported strong relatedness to their parents were associated with being autonomously motivated and engaged in school, as well as having a greater sense of well-being (Learner & Kruger, 1997; Ryan, Stiller, & Lynch, 1994).

Psychological Control Parenting is often thought of in terms of controlling the child. Hence, it is not surprising that psychological control has been investigated by various researchers including those examining parental influence from the perspective of the SDT. In addition, within SDT, autonomy support is often contrasted with control. Before we consider psychological control from the SDT perspective, a brief look at key conceptualisations of this construct by other researchers (Barber, 1996; Barber, Olsen, & Shagle, 1994; Barber et al., 2005; Schaefer, 1965b) allows us to understand it better. Barber and colleagues (2005) referred to Schaefer's three parenting dimensions (acceptance versus rejection, firm control versus lax control and autonomy versus psychological control) as key dimensions of parenting but re-labelled them as *parental support, behavioural control* and *psychological control*, respectively, to better represent the essence of constructs (Barber et al., 2005). According to them, parental support includes the degree to which parents exhibit nurturance, warmth and affection towards their children. Importantly, they distinguished behavioural control from psychological control. Behavioural control concerns the degree to which parents supervise and monitor their child's behaviour and activities. Psychological control refers to parental control that intrudes on the thoughts and emotions of the child through such parental behaviours as invalidation of the child's feelings, constraining verbal expression, withdrawal of love and induction of guilt. Barber and colleagues found that parental support was positively associated with social initiative; behavioural control was associated primarily with lower antisocial behaviour; psychological control was associated primarily with depression. In addition, it was found that parental support was also associated with lower levels of adolescent depression and that parental psychological control was also associated with higher levels of antisocial behaviour.

Based on SDT, Assor and colleagues' (2004) work on parental conditional regard (PCR) further investigated aspects of psychological control and child correlates. Conditional regard is practiced when parents react positively by showing their children with more care and affection when children behave in ways the parents want them to and react negatively by withdrawing their care and affection when children do not behave accordingly (Roth, Assor, Niemiec, Ryan, & Deci, 2009). The latter aspect is said to be aligned to love withdrawal which is one of the parental behaviours in Barber and colleagues' (2005) definition of psychological control. Grounded on the conceptual distinction between contingent self-esteem and true self-esteem made by Deci and Ryan (1995) from the perspective of SDT, PCR represents forms of psychological control associated with contingent self-esteem. Contingent self-esteem refers to one's feelings about oneself, and sense of worthiness, that results from and is "dependent on matching some standard of excellence or living up to some interpersonal or intrapsychic expectations" (Deci & Ryan, 1995, p. 32). One of the main findings of the Assor and colleagues' (2004) study was that adolescents' perceptions of their mothers' and fathers' use of PCR were significantly associated with parentally expected behavioural enactment in the emotion-control, prosocial and sports domains, but was not significantly correlated with behavioural enactment in the academic domain. Introjected regulation (i.e. sense of internal compulsion and a less self-determined form of self-regulation) was found to mediate between PCR and these behavioural enactments. The use of PCR was associated with affective cost—adolescents felt resentment towards their parents. Assor, Roth and colleagues (Assor & Tal, 2012; Roth & Assor, 2010; Roth, Assor, Niemiec, Ryan, & Deci, 2009) more recently distinguished between two forms of parental conditional regard vis-à-vis parental conditional positive regard (PCPR) and parental conditional negative regard (PCNR). In PCPR, "parents are perceived to provide more affection and esteem than usual when the child meets parents' expectations", and for PCNR, "parents are perceived to provide less affection and esteem than they usually do when the child does not meet parents' expectations" (Assor & Tal, 2012, p. 250). According to these researchers, PCPR is akin to conditional love, and PCNR is similar to love withdrawal. The use of both forms of conditional regard is negatively associated with emotional and academic consequences (Roth et al., 2009) and the emotional skills of sadness recognition, awareness of sadness and emphatic response (Roth & Assor, 2010). The use of PCPR to promote academic achievement was associated with an unstable self-esteem, maladaptive emotions and coping responses (Assor & Tal, 2012).

Soenens and colleagues also shed light on parents' use of psychological control from the SDT perspective. In one study that was based on Barber's (1996) conceptualisation of parental control, they examined the relations between parenting dimensions (responsiveness, behavioural control, psychological control), adolescent self-disclosure and adolescent problem behaviours (Soenens, Vansteenkiste, Luyckx, & Goossens, 2006). Psychological control, defined as parental behaviours that intrude on the child's psychological world, was found to negatively predict adolescent self-disclosure which in turn predicted parental knowledge which was linked to adolescent problem behaviours. Soenens and colleagues, employing the distinction made within SDT between externally and controlling types of socialisation pressure, further contended that psychological control is more akin to the use of internally controlling strategies such as guilt-induction, shaming, love withdrawal and manipulation of the attachment bond (Soenens & Vansteenkiste, 2010). Externally controlling parenting involves open and overt parental behaviours such as shouting, hitting and rewarding.

Core Parenting Dimensions

The importance of the above-mentioned SDT-based parenting dimensions is further underscored by the work of Skinner, Johnson and Snyder (2005). In the historical review of research on parenting and using a motivational conceptualisation of parental influence, core parenting dimensions important for facilitating positive child outcomes were identified. In line with SDT, the positive features of the core parenting dimensions are autonomy support, structure and warmth. The identified corresponding negative features are coercion, chaos and rejection, respectively (see Table 10.1 for their definitions and descriptions). Besides the support for the importance of the core parenting dimensions discussed by Skinner and colleagues, converging evidence points to the relevance of the three positive parenting dimensions.

First, from the SDT perspective, the positive parenting dimensions (autonomy support, structure, warmth) and the corresponding negative parenting dimensions (coercion, chaos, rejection) are said to be relevant to the fulfilment or non-fulfilment

Table 10.1 Definitions and descriptions of core parenting dimensions

Parenting dimensions	Definitions/descriptions
Warmth	"refers to the expression of affection, love, appreciation, kindness, and regard; it includes emotional availability, support, and genuine caring." (Skinner et al., 2005, p. 185)
Rejection	"parents are rejecting when they actively dislike their children. Expressions of rejection include aversion, hostility, harshness, overreactivity, irritability, and explosiveness; they also include overt communication of negative feelings for the child, such as criticism, derision, and disapproval." (Skinner et al., 2005, p. 185)
Autonomy support	"was defined as the degree to which parents value and use techniques which encourage independent problem solving, choice, and participation in decisions …" (Grolnick & Ryan, 1989, p. 144)
	"allow freedom of expression and action. Encourage child to attend to, accept, and value genuine preferences and opinions" (Skinner et al., 2005, p. 186)
Coercion	Degree to which parents "… externally dictating outcomes, and motivating achievement through punitive disciplinary techniques, pressure, or controlling rewards." (Grolnick & Ryan, 1989, p. 144)
	"Restrictive, overcontrolling, intrusive autocratic style. Strict obedience is demanded" (Skinner et al., 2005, p. 186)
Structure	"… the extent to which parents provide clear and consistent guidelines, expectations, and rules for child behaviors…" (Grolnick & Ryan, 1989, p. 144)
	"Provision of information about pathways to reach desired outcomes. Predictable, consistent. Clear expectations, firm maturity demands" (Skinner et al., 2005, p. 186)
Chaos	"Interferes with or obscures the pathways from means to ends. Noncontingent, inconsistent, erratic, unpredictable, arbitrary, or, undependable." (Skinner et al., 2005, p. 186)

of the child's basic psychological needs of autonomy, competence and relatedness, respectively, which in turn are linked to the child's motivational, psychosocial or behavioural outcomes (Skinner et al., 2005). In their study, Skinner and colleagues found correlations between the six dimensions of adolescent report of parenting and adolescent outcomes in the expected directions. For example, the perceived positive parenting dimensions correlate positively with adolescents' reports of positive academic outcomes such as academic competence, commitment to school, mastery, social competence and self-worth, and they correlated negatively with adolescent substance abuse and problem behaviour. Also, as expected, for the negative parenting dimensions, the opposite patterns of correlations with the adolescent outcomes were observed.

Second, the three positive parenting dimensions (autonomy support, structure, warmth) align with those (autonomy support, structure, involvement) maintained by Grolnick (2003) to be critical in enhancing positive child outcomes. Grolnick indicated that it is important to distinguish between the level (i.e. amount) of involvement and the quality (i.e. "the how") of involvement. The quality of involvement includes parental autonomy support and warmth. Grolnick, Deci and Ryan (1997) posited that the dimensions of optimal parenting that facilitate greater intrinsic motivation are those that promote a greater autonomy and competence in the child and also where relational support is present. Previous studies showed that parental autonomy support, structure and involvement are central dimensions of parenting that facilitate both intrinsic motivation and internalisation (e.g. Grolnick & Ryan, 1989; Grolnick et al., 1991; Grolnick & Slowiaczek, 1994; Ryan & Grolnick, 1986; Ryan et al., 1994).

Third, the three positive parenting dimensions—warmth, autonomy support and structure—are closely akin to aspects of Baumrind's authoritative parenting style which has been described as the optimal parenting style and has been shown consistently to be associated with positive child outcomes (Maccoby, 1992; Steinberg, 2001). Baumrind (2005), in referring to the salutary effect of authoritative parenting on adolescent development, described authoritative parenting as having a "... unique configuration of high warmth, autonomy support and behavioural control, and minimal use of psychological control" (p. 67). As we discussed earlier, behavioural control is liken to structure (Grolnick, 2003; Soenens et al., 2006). Similarly, these positive parenting dimensions are also analogous to the disaggregated components (acceptance-involvement, psychological autonomy granting, behavioural control) of the authoritative parenting style identified by Steinberg and colleagues that have been shown to facilitate adolescents' academic success (Roberts & Steinberg, 1999; Steinberg, Elmen, & Mounts, 1989). As noted earlier, warmth is often labelled as acceptance by researchers (Baldwin et al., 1945; Becker, 1964) and is usually associated with involvement (Baumrind, 1965; Grolnick et al., 1997).

Parental Influence and Child Outcomes in the Sports Domain

In view of the relevance and importance of sports pursuits as part of the holistic development of students, we turn our attention to the study of parental influence in the sports domain. Vallerand's (2007) work on the hierarchical model of intrinsic and extrinsic motivation (HMIEM), explaining how the influence of social factors on motivation can take place at varying levels of interaction, is relevant to the discussion of how parental influence can be studied. According to the HMIEM, global social factors such as parents operate at a global level of generality and affect almost all aspects of the child's life and hence can exert influence over the global motivation of the child. The child's motivation at the contextual level such as motivation in the sports domain is postulated to be influenced by the top-down effects of motivation from this higher-level global motivation. Various studies in the educational and socialisation settings, such as those discussed earlier, have employed the approach of examining parenting dimensions at the global level of generality in relation to child outcomes. It has provided empirical support and added understanding on the influence of parents with respect to the studied child outcomes. Yet, studies in the sports domain do not seem to have taken a similar approach. Adopting this approach is consistent with the call by Horn and Horn (2007) for future research in the sports domain to assume a more global perspective on the measurement of parental influences.

Although previous reviews have shown there has been an increasing number of studies examining parental influence and child outcomes in the sports domain (see Horn & Horn, 2007; Partridge, Brustad, & Stellino, 2008), a review on studies investigating parental influence from a more global perspective, and in terms of the identified parenting dimensions based on SDT, showed that this area of research is still relatively scarce when compared to those conducted in the other domains (Chew, 2011). Some of the findings from recent sports-related studies (Chew, 2011; Chew & Wang, 2010) on the influence of SDT-based parenting dimensions on adolescent student-athletes' motivational and other psychological outcomes are highlighted here. In one study (Chew & Wang, 2010), the relationships between parenting dimensions (autonomy support, involvement, warmth) and various psychosocial variables (i.e. basic psychological needs satisfaction, sports motivation, self-constructs and life aspirations) of adolescent student-athletes were examined. Cluster analysis yielded three distinct groups with characteristic perceived parenting dimensions and psychological needs satisfaction. The results from the analyses of the effect of the three clusters on the key variables showed that student-athletes with high perceived parental involvement, autonomy support and warmth and who reported that their basic psychological needs are highly met, when compared to the other two clusters, had significantly higher autonomous motivation and higher self-perceptions (global self-worth and physical self-worth) and rated the importance of, and the likelihood of achieving, intrinsic aspirations higher. On the whole, findings in this study suggest that student-athletes with perceived parental autonomy support that were also characterised by involvement and warmth facilitated a more autonomously motivated, positive and congruent self. In sync with SDT, such individuals were also less likely to seek extrinsic forms of recognition or worth such as wealth or fame as they tended to pursue intrinsic life aspirations.

In another study that aimed to better understand how parents can influence student-athletes' sports motivation, the relationships among the core parenting dimensions (autonomy support, structure, warmth, coercion, chaos, rejection), psychological needs satisfaction and sports motivation were examined (Chew, 2011). Profiles of parenting dimensions as perceived by secondary school student-athletes were derived using latent profile analysis (LPA). Maternal and paternal variables of the six identified SDT-based parenting dimensions were used as clustering variables in the analyses which yielded a four-group solution (see Fig. 10.1). Further multivariate analysis showed that the four LPA groups were distinctive. The relations between the four LPA groups and psychological needs satisfaction and sports motivation (together with other motivational variables) were examined using multivariate analysis of variance. As hypothesised, one of the key findings showed that student-athletes belonging to the LPA group (LPA Group 2) with highest scores in the positive parenting dimensions and lowest scores in negative parenting dimensions recorded the highest scores in psychological needs satisfaction and sports motivation and lowest level of amotivation, thus demonstrating the beneficial effects of this parenting profile. In contrast, student-athletes belonging to the LPA group (LPA Group 1) with lowest scores in the positive parenting dimensions and highest scores in negative parenting dimensions recorded the lowest scores in psychological

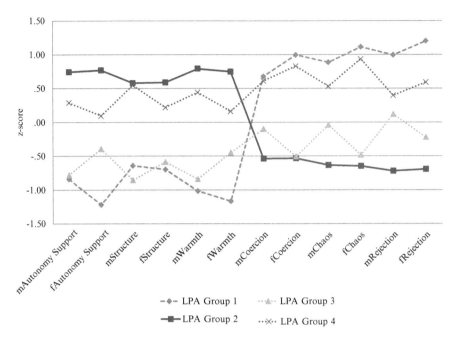

Fig. 10.1 Profiles of group means (z-scores) for the four-group solution from the latent profile analysis. Note. Maternal parenting variables and paternal parenting variables are denoted by the prefixes "m" and "f", respectively

needs satisfaction and sports motivation and highest level of amotivation. The tenets of SDT provide explanation for the above findings for LPA Group 1 and LPA Group 2 by way of the psychological processes related to the fulfilment of basic psychological needs. It is postulated in SDT that a social environment that supports psychological needs satisfaction facilitates an individual's basic psychological needs to be met, which in turn lead to higher autonomous motivation (Deci & Ryan, 1985, 2000). The positive parenting dimensions (autonomy support, structure, warmth) were expected to be supportive of psychological needs satisfaction, while the negative features of parenting (coercion, chaos, rejection) are not conducive to the satisfaction of needs. Consistent with SDT, the student-athletes in LPA Group 2 registered the highest level of psychological needs satisfaction, as well as the highest level of self-determined sports motivation and the lowest level of amotivation. Conversely, and as theorised in SDT, the student-athletes in LPA Group 1 had the lowest scores for psychological needs satisfaction and self-determined sports motivation, and their scores on amotivation were the highest among all groups.

In relation the authoritative parenting style, the above explanation from the SDT perspective also provides insights into the salutary effects of the authoritative parenting style. The profile of LPA Group 2 can be likened to the configuration of parenting dimensions of high warmth, autonomy support, behavioural control and low psychological control that is characteristic of the authoritative parenting style

(Baumrind, 2005). The findings suggest that the beneficial parental influence of the authoritative style stems from the satisfaction of the basic psychological needs which in turn lead to positive motivational consequences.

In a follow-up qualitative study (Chew, 2011) that further dwelled into the nature of the parent-child relationship by interviewing purposefully selected participants from each of the four LPA groups found in the previous study, it yielded findings that not only provided richer descriptions of the LPA group profiles but also provided support for the existence of the four LPA groups. For example, being like a friend, open communication and the sharing of fun and laughter between the parent and the student-athlete characterised the parent-child relationships in LPA Group 2. It was also found that a relaxed, light touch and non-pressuring approach is adopted by the parents in the way they relate to the student-athletes concerning their sports, studies and friends. Parents of the student-athletes in this LPA Group 2 are sensitive to the emotional state of their child and are mindful to relate to their child in an appropriate manner and at an opportune time. Not only are these characteristics reminiscent of the authoritative parenting style, they are instructive for guiding parents in how they should relate to their children.

In another subsequent study (Chew, 2011), the question as to whether psychological needs satisfaction indeed mediates between the relations between the core parenting dimensions (autonomy support, structure, warmth, coercion, chaos, rejection) and student-athletes' subjective well-being was examined using structural equation modelling. All three positive parenting dimensions were positively correlated with psychological needs satisfaction and with subjective well-being, while all three negative parenting dimensions were negatively associated with these two outcomes. Using mediation analyses, the hypothesised multiple-steps, multiple-mediators model was tested. In this model, psychological needs satisfaction was posited as a key proximal intervening variable between perceived parenting dimensions and student-athletes' subjective well-being and where intrinsic aspirations and extrinsic aspirations were the more distal intervening variables that further mediate the effects of these parenting dimensions on subjective well-being. One of the findings was that the effects of all of the identified positive parenting dimensions on subjective well-being were fully mediated by psychological needs satisfaction. However, it was found that the direct effects of all three negative parenting dimensions were statistically significant and that psychological needs satisfaction only partially mediates the effects of the coercion and rejection, but not chaos, on subjective well-being. The findings provide an insight into the psychological processes underlying how parents can better meet the needs of student-athletes and enhance their well-being. Clearly, the results show that parental autonomy support, structure and warmth enhance the subjective well-being of student-athletes through satisfaction of their basic psychological needs. The findings did not fully support the importance of psychological needs satisfaction as a mediator for the negative parenting dimension (coercion, chaos, rejection). These dimensions negative links with both psychological needs satisfaction and subjective well-being indicate their debilitating effects on these student-athlete outcomes.

Implications for Parents and School Leaders

The overwhelming evidence pointing to the salutary effects of authoritative parenting in relation to the child's achievement and psychosocial outcomes clearly suggest that parents adopt such a stance in their parent-child interactions. This entails one being mindful to embrace a host of parenting behaviours such as adopting a rational approach guiding the child's actions, encouraging open communication, valuing autonomous self-will and disciplined conformity to standards of conduct and exerting firm control at points of conflicts but also allowing for individual expressions and interests. Alternatively, in terms of parenting dimensions which are characteristic of authoritative parenting, parents should adopt a combination of high warmth, autonomy support and behavioural control if they hope to promote better achievements and more positive psychosocial outcomes in their children. Parents should note that parental control is not necessarily bad for child development if it is of the sorts as mentioned above. However, a form of parental control—psychological control—that intrudes on the thoughts and emotions of the child has been shown detrimental to the child (Barber & Harmon, 2002). Parents should therefore eschew controlling behaviours such as invalidating the child's feelings, giving the child the "cold shoulder", withdrawal of love and inducing guilt. Parents should also avoid the use of conditional regard (and its bifurcated forms of PCNR and PCPR), a variant of psychological control, as it has been shown to be associated with negative child consequences such as feeling resentment towards parents, deficient emotional skills, unstable self-esteem and coping responses. If parents desire self-disclosure from their child, psychological control should be avoided.

The application of SDT as the theoretical framework in examining the identified parenting dimensions that are associated with authoritative parenting style in the series of studies conducted by Chew (2011) offered a theoretical basis for the understanding of the efficacy of authoritative parenting style in promoting positive adolescent motivational outcomes. These studies demonstrated that psychological needs satisfaction as the key psychological process underlying the influence of parenting dimensions on student-athletes' motivational outcomes and subjective well-being. Parents should focus on meeting their children basic psychological needs of autonomy, competence and relatedness through honing their patterns of parental behaviours to be autonomy supportive, expressing warmth and providing structure. Listening and understanding the child's perspectives, enabling the child to feel a sense of volition in his/her actions, having a firm but light touch approach in supervising and guiding the child, being like a friend to the child, sharing of fun and laughter, having open communication, being sensitive to the emotional state of the child and providing financial, emotional and other forms of support to meet the needs of the child as he/she seeks to gain competency in various pursuits (e.g. academic, sports) are aspects that parents should pay attention to. To do all these, parents require ample time spent with their children, and concerted effort from parents is also needed. Providing a familial climate that is conducive for optimal development of the child in terms of their psychosocial and motivational outcomes and well-being is in sync with the desires of most, if not all, parents.

A key practical implication for school leaders interested in enhancing young adolescent athletes' sports motivation and well-being is that they should engage these young athletes' parents to heighten their awareness of the effects of parenting dimensions on motivational outcomes and gain their cooperation to foster a familial climate conducive for optimal satisfaction of the young athletes' basic psychological needs of autonomy, competence and relatedness. Not only should attention be paid to helping parents provide higher levels of parental autonomy support, structure and warmth, but consideration should also be given to diminishing the negative parenting dimension. Such efforts to generate awareness can be achieved either formally, such as through letters to the parents, or through some existing school-parent communication channel such as a newsletter. Information relevant to helping parents know how to support their child can also be communicated to them through informal conversations which the teacher-in-charge may have with parents.

This learning regarding working in partnership with parents to promote positive motivational consequences and well-being in student-athletes can be implemented on a school-wide basis for the holistic development of all students. In Singapore, support for such an initiative is provided by the policy statement of the Ministry of Education: "Every parent a supportive partner". Intervention programmes could also be designed to teach parents how they can provide better support to meet their children's psychological needs. Studies have shown that managers and teachers can be taught to behave in more autonomy-supportive ways and that their behavioural change is associated with positive effects on their employees and students, respectively (Hardré & Reeve, 2009; Reeve, Jang, Carrell, Jeon, & Barch, 2004).

Conclusion

Since the advent of SDT as a theoretical framework for research on parental influence, a number of the studies have concentrated on examining parental autonomy support and psychological control, which in SDT are posited to be important to the psychological needs satisfaction of the child, and the associated motivational consequences. By focusing the study of parental influence on pertinent constructs that are based on theory, this line of research is at the nexus of theory and practice and holds strong potential in advancing our understanding of the subject area as well as in translating research findings into interventions that can enhance the positive influence of parents in relation to child outcomes. However, it seems that research on parental influence in the sports domain is only beginning to take a similar approach.

From the perspective of SDT, further research on parental influence focusing on investigating the relations between the quality of the parent-child relationship and child outcomes that have bearing on the extent in satisfaction of the need for relatedness holds promise in illuminating greater understanding on the motivational processes leading to enhanced child outcomes. Thus far, only some researchers have alluded to the importance of warmth in contributing to a sense of relatedness between parent and child and to the psychosocial outcome of the child. After all, the importance of the social environmental factors to the development of individuals is well recognised by social psychologists.

References

Assor, A., Roth, G., & Deci, E. L. (2004). The emotional costs of parents' conditional regard: A self-determination theory analysis. *Journal of Personality, 72*, 47–88. doi:10.1111/j.0022-3506.2004.00256.x.

Assor, A., & Tal, K. (2012). When parents' affection depends on child's achievement: Parental conditional positive regard, self-aggrandizement, shame and coping in adolescents. *Journal of Adolescence, 35*(2), 249–260. http://dx.doi.org/10.1016/j.adolescence.2011.10.004.

Baldwin, A. L., Kalhorn, J., & Breese, F. H. (1945). Patterns of parent behavior. *Psychological Monographs, 58*(3), i–75. doi:10.1037/h0093566.

Barber, B. K. (1996). Parental psychological control: Revisiting a neglected construct. *Child Development, 67*, 3296–3319. doi:10.1111/1467-8624.ep9706244861.

Barber, B. K. (1997). Introduction: Adolescent socialization in context-the role of connection, regulation, and autonomy in the family. *Journal of Adolescent Research, 12*, 5–11.

Barber, B. K., & Harmon, E. L. (2002). Violating the self: Parental psychological control of children and adolescents. In B. K. Barber (Ed.), *Intrusive parenting: How psychological control affects children and adolescents* (pp. 15–52). Washington, DC: American Psychological Association.

Barber, B. K., Olsen, J. E., & Shagle, S. C. (1994). Associations between parental psychological and behavioral control and youth internalized and externalized behaviors. *Child Development, 65*, 1120–1136.

Barber, B. K., Stolz, H. E., Olsen, J. A., Collins, A., & Burchinal, M. (2005). Parental support, psychological control, and behavioral control: Assessing relevance across time, culture, and method: Abstract. *Monographs of the Society for Research in Child Development, 70*(4), 125–137.

Baumrind, D. (1965). Parental control and parental love. *Children, 12*, 230–234.

Baumrind, D. (1966). Effects of authoritative parental control on child behavior. *Child Development, 37*, 887–907.

Baumrind, D. (1967). Child care practices anteceding three patterns of preschool behavior. *Genetic Psychology Monographs, 75*, 43–88.

Baumrind, D. (1971). Current patterns of parental authority. *Developmental Psychology Monographs, Part 2, 4*, 1–103.

Baumrind, D. (1991a). The influence of parenting style on adolescent competence and substance abuse. *Journal of Early Adolescence, 11*, 56–95.

Baumrind, D. (1991b). Parenting styles and adolescent development. In J. Brooks-Gunn, R. Lerner, & A. C. Peterson (Eds.), *The encyclopedia of adolescence* (pp. 746–758). New York: Garland.

Baumrind, D. (2005). Patterns of parental authority and adolescent autonomy. *New Directions for Child and Adolescent Development, 108*, 61–69.

Baumrind, D., & Black, A. E. (1967). Socialization practices associated with dimensions of competence in preschool boys and girls. *Child Development, 38*, 291–327.

Becker, W. C. (1964). Consequences of different kinds of parental discipline. In M. L. Hoffman & L. W. Hoffman (Eds.), *Review of child development research* (Vol. 1, pp. 169–208). New York: Russell Sage.

Blos, P. (1979). *The adolescent passage*. Madison, CT: International Universities Press.

Chen, X., Dong, Q., & Zhou, H. (1997). Authoritative and authoritarian parenting practices and social and school performance in Chinese children. *International Journal of Behavioral Development, 21*, 855–873.

Chew, W. C. E. (2011). Perceptions of parenting dimensions: Its relations to motivation, life aspirations, and subjective well-being among adolescent athletes (Doctoral thesis, Nanyang Technological University, Singapore). Retrieved from http://hdl.handle.net/10497/4615

Chew, E., & Wang, J. (2010). Perceptions of parental autonomy support and control, and aspirations of student athletes in Singapore. In M. Chia & J. Chiang (Eds.), *Sport science & studies in Asia: Reflection, issues and emergent solutions* (pp. 231–248). Singapore, Singapore: World Scientific.

Chirkov, V. I., & Ryan, R. M. (2001). Parent and teacher autonomy-support in Russian and U.S. adolescents: Common effects on well-being and academic motivation. *Journal of Cross-Cultural Psychology, 32*, 618–635.

Darling, N., & Steinberg, L. (1993). Parenting style as context: An integrative model. *Psychological Bulletin, 113*, 487–496.

Deci, E. L., & Ryan, R. M. (1985). *Intrinsic motivation and self-determination in human behaviour.* New York: Plenum.

Deci, E. L., & Ryan, R. M. (1995). Human autonomy: The basis for true self-esteem. In M. Kemis (Ed.), *Efficacy, agency, and self-esteem* (pp. 31–49). New York: Plenum.

Deci, E. L., & Ryan, R. M. (2000). The "what" and "why" of goal pursuits: Human needs and the self-determination of behavior. *Psychological Inquiry, 11*, 227–268.

Dornbusch, S. M., Ritter, P. L., Leiderman, P. H., Roberts, D. F., & Fraleigh, M. J. (1987). The relation of parenting style to adolescent school performance. *Child Development, 58*, 1244–1257.

Duda, J. L., & Hom, J. H. L. (1993). Interdependencies between the perceived and self-reported goal orientations of young athletes and their parents. *Pediatric Exercise Science, 5*, 234–241.

Ebbeck, V., & Becker, S. L. (1994). Psychosocial predictors of goal orientations in youth soccer. *Research Quarterly for Exercise and Sport, 65*, 355–358.

Farkas, M. S., & Grolnick, W. S. (2010). Examining the components and concomitants of parental structure in the academic domain. *Motivation and Emotion, 34*, 266–279. doi:10.1007/s11031-010-9176-7.

Fredricks, J. A., & Eccles, J. S. (2005). Family socialization, gender, and sport motivation and involvement. *Journal of Sport & Exercise Psychology, 27*, 3–31.

Gonzalez, A., & Wolters, C. A. (2006). The relation between perceived parenting practices and achievement motivation in mathematics. *Journal of Research in Childhood Education, 21*, 203–217.

Grolnick, W. S. (2003). *The psychology of parental control: How well-meant parenting backfires.* Mahwah, NJ: Lawrence Erlbaum Associates.

Grolnick, W. S., & Ryan, R. M. (1989). Parent styles associated with children's self-regulation and competence in school. *Journal of Educational Psychology, 81*, 143–154. doi:10.1037/0022-0663.81.2.143.

Grolnick, W. S., & Slowiaczek, M. L. (1994). Parents' involvement in children's schooling: A multidimensional conceptualization and motivational model. *Child Development, 64*, 237–252.

Grolnick, W. S., Ryan, R. M., & Deci, E. L. (1991). The inner resources for school achievement: Motivational mediators of children's perceptions of their parents. *Journal of Educational Psychology, 83*, 508–517.

Grolnick, W. S., Deci, E. L., & Ryan, R. M. (1997). Internalization within the family: The self-determination theory perspective. In J. E. Grusec & L. Kuczynski (Eds.), *Parenting and children's internalization of values: A handbook of contemporary theory* (pp. 135–161). New York: Wiley.

Guay, F., Ratelle, C. F., & Chanal, J. (2008). Optimal learning in optimal contexts: The role of self-determination in education. *Canadian Psychology, 49*, 233–240.

Hardré, P. L., & Reeve, J. (2009). Training corporate managers to adopt a more autonomy-supportive motivating style toward employees: An intervention study. *International Journal of Training and Development, 13*, 165–184. doi:10.1111/j.1468-2419.2009.00325.x.

Harlow, H. F. (1958). The nature of love. *American Psychologist, 13*, 673–685.

Horn, T. S., & Horn, J. L. (2007). Family influences on children's sport and physical activity participation, behaviour, and psychosocial responses. In G. Tenenbaum & R. C. Eklund (Eds.), *Handbook of sport psychology* (3rd ed., pp. 685–711). New York: Wiley.

Jang, H., Reeve, J., & Deci, E. L. (2010). Engaging students in learning activities: It is not autonomy support or structure but autonomy support and structure. *Journal of Educational Psychology, 102*, 588–600. doi:10.1037/a0019682.

Joussemet, M., Koestner, R., Lekes, N., & Landry, R. (2005). A longitudinal study of the relationship of maternal autonomy support to children's adjustment and achievement in school. *Journal of Personality, 73*, 1215–1236.

Joussemet, M., Landry, R., & Koestner, R. (2008). A self-determination theory perspective on parenting. *Canadian Psychology Psychologie Canadienne, 49*, 194–200. doi:10.1037/a0012754.

Learner, D. G., & Kruger, L. J. (1997). Attachment, self-concept, and academic motivation in high-school students. *American Journal of Orthopsychiatry, 67*, 485–492.

Maccoby, E. E. (1992). The role of parents in the socialization of children: An historical overview. *Developmental Psychology, 28*, 1006–1017. doi:10.1037/0012-1649.28.6.1006.

Maccoby, E. E., & Martin, J. A. (1983). Socialization in the context of the family: Parent-child interaction. In E. M. Hetherington (Ed.), *Handbook of child psychology: Vol. 4. Socialization, personality, and social development* (4th ed., pp. 1–102). New York: Wiley.

Milevsky, A., Schlechter, M., Klem, L., & Kehl, R. (2008). Constellations of maternal and paternal parenting styles in adolescence: Congruity and well-being. *Marriage & Family Review, 44*, 81–98. doi:10.1080/01494920802185447.

Partridge, J. A., Brustad, R. J., & Stellino, M. B. (2008). Social influence in sport. In T. S. Horn (Ed.), *Advances in sport psychology* (3rd ed., pp. 270–291). Champaign, IL: Human Kinetics.

Paulson, S. E., Marchant, G. J., & Rothilsberg, B. A. (1998). Early adolescents' perceptions of patterns of parenting, teaching, and school atmosphere: Implications for achievement. *Journal of Adolescence, 18*, 5–26.

Reeve, J., Jang, H., Carrell, D., Jeon, S., & Barch, J. (2004). Enhancing students' engagement by increasing teachers' autonomy support. *Motivation and Emotion, 28*, 147–169.

Roberts, M., & Steinberg, L. (1999). Unpacking authoritative parenting: Reassessing a multidimensonal construct. *Journal of Marriage and the Family, 61*, 574–587.

Roth, G., & Assor, A. (2010). Parental conditional regard as a predictor of deficiencies in young children's capacities to respond to sad feelings. *Infant and Child Development, 19*(5), 465–477. doi:10.1002/icd.676.

Roth, G., Assor, A., Niemiec, C. P., Ryan, R. M., & Deci, E. L. (2009). The emotional and academic consequences of parental conditional regard: Comparing conditional positive regard, conditional negative regard, and autonomy support as parenting practices. *Developmental Psychology, 45*(4), 1119–1142.

Rothrauff, T. C., Cooney, T. M., & An, J. S. (2009). Remembered parenting styles and adjustment in middle and late adulthood. *The Journals of Gerontology, 64B*, 137–146.

Ryan, R. M., Deci, E. L., & Grolnick, W. S. (1995). Autonomy, relatedness, and the self: Their relation to development and psychopathology. In D. Cicchetti & D. J. Cohen (Eds.), *Developmental psychopathology* (Theory and Methods, Vol. 1, pp. 618–655). New York: Wiley.

Ryan, R. M., & Grolnick, W. S. (1986). Origins and pawns in the classroom: Self-report and projective assessments of individual differences in children's perceptions. *Journal of Personality and Social Psychology, 50*, 550–558. doi:10.1037/0022-3514.50.3.550.

Ryan, R. M., Stiller, J. D., & Lynch, J. H. (1994). Representations of relationships to teachers, parents, and friends as predictors of academic motivation and self-esteem. *The Journal Early Adolescence, 14*, 226–249. doi:10.1177/027243169401400207.

Schaefer, E. S. (1959). A circumplex model for maternal behavior. *Journal of Abnormal and Social Psychology, 59*, 226–235.

Schaefer, E. S. (1965a). Children's reports of parental behavior: An inventory. *Child Development, 36*, 413–424.

Schaefer, E. S. (1965b). A configurational analysis of children's reports of parent behavior. *Journal of Consulting Psychology, 29*, 552–557.

Silk, J. S., Morris, A. S., Kanaya, T., & Steinberg, L. (2003). Psychological control and autonomy support: Opposite ends of a continuum or distinct constructs? *Journal of Research on Adolescence, 13*, 113–128.

Skinner, E., Johnson, S., & Snyder, T. (2005). Six dimensions of parenting: A motivational model. *Parenting Science Practice, 5*, 175–235. doi:10.1207/s15327922par0502_3.

Slicker, E. K., & Thornberry, I. (2002). Older adolescent well-being and authoritative parenting. *Adolescent and Family Health, 3*, 9–19.

Smits, I., Soenens, B., Vansteenkiste, M., Luyckx, K., & Goossens, L. (2010). Why do adolescents gather information or stick to parental norms? Examining autonomous and controlled motives behind adolescents' identity style. *Journal of Youth and Adolescence, 39*, 1343–1356.

Soenens, B., Duriez, B., Vansteenkiste, M., & Goossens, L. (2007). The intergenerational transmission of empathy-related responding in adolescence: The role of maternal support. *Personality and Social Psychology Bulletin, 33*, 299–311.

Soenens, B., & Vansteenkiste, M. (2005). Antecedents and outcomes of self-etermination in 3 life domains: The role of parents' and teachers' autonomy support. *Journal of Youth and Adolescence, 34*, 589–604. doi:10.1007/s10964-005-8948-y.

Soenens, B., & Vansteenkiste, M. (2010). A theoretical upgrade of the concept of parental psychological control: Proposing new insights on the basis of self-determination theory. *Developmental Review, 30*, 74–99. doi:10.1016/j.dr.2009.11.001.

Soenens, B., Vansteenkiste, M., Lens, W., Luyckx, K., Goossens, L., Beyers, W., et al. (2007). Conceptualizing parental autonomy support: Adolescent perceptions of promotion of independence versus promotion of volitional functioning. *Developmental Psychology, 43*(3), 633–646. doi:10.1037/0012-1649.43.3.633.

Soenens, B., Vansteenkiste, M., Luyckx, K., & Goossens, L. (2006). Parenting and adolescent problem behavior: An integrated model with adolescent self-disclosure and perceived parental knowledge as intervening variables. *Developmental Psychology, 42*(2), 305–318. doi:10.1037/0012-1649.42.2.305.

Soenens, B., Vansteenkiste, M., & Sierens, E. (2009). How are parental psychological control and autonomy-support related? A cluster-analytic approach. *Journal of Marriage and Family, 71*, 187–202. doi:10.1111/j.1741-3737.2008.00589.x.

Steinberg, L. (1990). Autonomy, conflict, and harmony in the family relationship. In S. Feldman & G. Elliot (Eds.), *At the threshold: The developing adolescent* (pp. 255–276). Cambridge, MA: Harvard University Press.

Steinberg, L. (2001). We know some things: Parent-adolescent relationships in retrospect and prospect. *Journal of Research on Adolescence, 11*, 1–19.

Steinberg, L., Elmen, J. D., & Mounts, N. S. (1989). Authoritative parenting, psychosocial maturity, and academic success in adolescents. *Child Development, 60*, 1424–1436. doi:10.1111/1467-8624.ep9772457.

Steinberg, L., Lamborn, S. D., Dornbusch, S. M., & Darling, N. (1992). Impact of parenting practices on adolescent achievement: Authoritative parenting, school involvement, and encouragement to succeed. *Child Development, 63*, 1266–1281. doi:10.1111/1467-8624.ep9301210142.

Vallerand, R. J. (2007). Intrinsic and extrinsic motivation in sport and physical activity: A review and a look at the future. In G. Tenenbaum & R. C. Eklund (Eds.), *Handbook of sport psychology* (3rd ed., pp. 59–83). New York: Wiley.

Vallerand, R. J., Fortier, M. S., & Guay, F. (1997). Self-determination and persistence in a real-life setting: Toward a motivational model of high school dropout. *Journal of Personality and Social Psychology, 72*, 1161–1176. doi:10.1037/0022-3514.72.5.1161.

White, S. A., Kavussanu, M., Tank, K. M., & Wingate, J. M. (2004). Perceived parental beliefs about the causes of success in sport: Relationship to athletes' achievement goals and personal beliefs. *Scandinavian Journal of Medicine & Science in Sports, 14*, 57–66. doi:10.1111/j.1600-0838.2003.00314.x.

Chapter 11
Creating an Autonomy-Supportive Physical Education (PE) Learning Environment

Yew Meng How and John Chee Keng Wang

Introduction

Physical activity (PA) has beneficial effects on many bodily systems, with strong epidemiological evidence showing that PA is associated with reduced risk of coronary heart disease, obesity, type 2 diabetes and other chronic diseases and conditions (Department of Health, 2009; World Health Organisation, 2010). As healthy PA habits developed early in life may continue into adulthood (Telama, Yang, Laakso, & Vilkari, 1997), adequate participation in PA during childhood and adolescence is critical in the prevention of obesity-related diseases in later life. Research has shown that as children grow older into adolescents, their level of PA decreases (Yli-Piipari, Wang, Jaakkola, & Liukkonen, 2012). In view of the age of this identified cohort, it should come as no surprise that physical education (PE) has been advanced as an avenue in which to mitigate the reported decreases in PA participation (Lonsdale et al., 2013).

PE teachers' behaviours, practices and motivational styles have a substantial impact on students' feelings about and engagement in learning and can influence children to adopt physically active lifestyles as adults (Wright, Patterson, & Cardinal, 2000). Students differ in many aspects such as learning domains, learning styles, physical growth and development, as well as social and emotional development (Jenkins, 1986). Hence, PE teachers are constantly exploring effective teaching strategies to meaningfully engage and motivate students. To motivate students, an effective PE teacher needs to not only be familiar with unpredictable student behaviour but also be well aware of the challenges to meet the diverse needs of their students. Importantly, they must understand how their students learn and how they learn best (Siedentop & Tannehill, 2000).

Y.M. How (✉) • J.C.K. Wang
National Institute of Education, Nanyang Technological University, Singapore, Singapore
e-mail: yewmeng.how@gmail.com; john.wang@nie.edu.sg

© Springer Science+Business Media Singapore 2016
W.C. Liu et al. (eds.), *Building Autonomous Learners*,
DOI 10.1007/978-981-287-630-0_11

This chapter traces the trend in motivational research in PE teaching and aims to understand the "what", "why" and "how" of motivation in PE. Firstly, we will look at "what" are the features of an effective PE lesson, with the purpose of providing a background on understanding the influence of learning environments on students' motivation towards PA and learning in PE. Secondly, we will examine at the learning environment through the theoretical framework of SDT and understand "why" it is crucial to students' motivation and learning in PE. We will also specifically present a case for autonomy support and structure as particularly important factors in an effective PE learning environment. Finally, we will suggest some practical ideas "how" PE teachers can implement an autonomy-supportive style in their teaching of PE.

"What" Makes a Good PE Lesson: The Learning Environment in Effective PE Teaching

PE is important in equipping students with knowledge, skills and attitudes to pursue a physically active and healthy lifestyle. Sallis and colleagues (Sallis, Prochaska, & Taylor, 2000) believe that positive PE experiences can influence children to adopt physically active lifestyles as adults, and PE teachers play an important role in facilitating these processes. However, due to ineffective instructional strategies and a lack of effort to constantly engage students, some PE teachers find it difficult to motivate their students towards participating in PA (Bycura & Darst, 2001). Likewise, Bryan and Solmon (2007) posit that the structuring of PE programmes to achieve this larger intent of PE can be improved.

Past research identifies several key factors within the PE social context that play a major role in determining the degree to which students are motivated to lead a physically active lifestyle. Firstly, shared decision-making in PE lessons with students and providing students with levels of choices regarding activity or equipment selection results in desirable outcomes such as higher self-concepts (Schempp, Cheffers, & Zaichkowsky, 1983) and greater future participation (Ferrer-Caja & Weiss, 2000). Additionally, a PE learning environment with high student perceptions of choice in PE was associated with high perceptions of autonomy (Ntoumanis, 2005).

A second factor is competence at performing and confidence in using motor skills, both of which are established through early experiences in PA and sport (Solmon, 2003). Deci and Ryan (1985) posit a close relationship between a sense of competence and intrinsic motivation, such that the more able a person believes himself/herself to be at some activity, the more intrinsically motivated they will be at that activity. Specifically in PE, teaching effectiveness is perceived as a hierarchy of pedagogical practices in which organisations, management, discipline and control form the base, and student success is situated at the top (Parker, 1995). According to Rink (2002), teacher effectiveness is maximised by engaging students at a high level of appropriate activities incorporating some form of student choice for a prolonged period of time.

Deci and Ryan (1985) further suggest that for classroom environments to ener-gise students' natural curiosity and learning, optimal challenges must be provided. Students have to be engaged at a high level and be successful at an appropriate task for a sufficient amount of time if they are to gain competence in complex motor skills, such as those most frequently taught in PE lessons (Silverman, Devillier, & Ramirez, 1991). However, the research evidence also suggests that a very high level of success rate during the acquisition phase of learning does not always lead to increased retention or learning and that "errorless practice and rote repetition are poor learning strategies" (Lee, Swinnen, & Serrien, 1994, p. 338). In fact, high per-ceptions of challenge have been associated with high perceived competence (Koka & Hein, 2003). Hence, effective teachers will find ways to challenge the students optimally by manipulating the demands of motor tasks and matching student effort against the degree of success (Solmon, 2003).

A third important motivating factor in the social context is in the provision of structure in the PE learning environment. Structure describes the extent to which a social context is structured, predictable, contingent and consistent (Skinner & Belmont, 1993). When a teacher provides challenging tasks, negotiates clear and short-term goals, delivers contingent feedback related to students' endeavours and encourages their effort and progress, he/she tends to nurture the students' need for competence and their self-determined motivation (Tessier, Sarrazin, & Ntoumanis, 2010). Particularly important for PE, structure creates a positive learning climate in which students are focused and motivated to learn (Evertson & Emmer, 1982). A well-structured learning environment allows teachers to effectively manage student behaviour, develop systems and methods of holding students accountable for their work, present information clearly and organise instruction so that students spend more time on related tasks rather than non-related tasks (Evertson & Emmer, 1982). Additionally, a structured environment also allows students to know what to expect, which can in turn enhance their sense of control (Blankenship, 2008).

A fourth important factor in PE is the students' relationship with their teachers and classmates, specifically the degree in which they feel socially connected with them. Teachers may influence these perceptions of connectedness in PE through the type of learning climate they establish daily interactions and communication via feedback. Feedback can occur in numerous fashions, and individuals can interpret the feedback in a number of ways. Positive or negative verbal statements or a system of rewards all constitute kinds of feedback. If the individual senses that the feedback is intended to be instructive and helpful, then the advice is likely to promote intrin-sic motivation (i.e. pursuing an activity out of interest and due to the inherent enjoy-ment that it provides) (Bryan & Solmon, 2007). If, on the other hand, the feedback is viewed as calculating, in an attempt to manipulate performance, then intrinsic motivation will decrease (Bryan & Solmon, 2007). At worst, the feedback may be become amotivational (i.e. a lack of motivation characterised by a belief that suc-cess is not possible and that the activity is not valuable), promoting a sense of incompetence or helplessness (Deci & Ryan, 1985). Sport-related research has shown considerable increases in intrinsic motivation for individuals who receive positive feedback and are in circumstances that allow them a level of autonomy by providing choice in situations (Thill & Mouanda, 1990).

Furthermore, an effective PE programme targets the development of a physically active lifestyle directly, focusing on the acquisition of the skills, knowledge and dispositions that encourage students' volitional engagement in PA (Rink & Hall, 2008). PA has been identified as a key factor in avoiding premature mortality and morbidity (Bouchard, Shephard, & Stephens, 1994). Regular involvement in PA improves the health status of children and adults (Berkey, Rockett, Gillman, & Colditz, 2003); however, there is a need to examine the factors that promote motivation and engagement in PE and to better understand the determinants of PA in children and youth (Taylor & Lonsdale, 2010). While some individuals participate in regular PA simply for the enjoyment of exercising, others appear to exercise to attain intrinsic or extrinsic rewards such as losing weight, being more attractive or obtaining recognition from significant others (Deci & Ryan, 2000). Previous research has shown that individuals who exercise out of enjoyment rather than being motivated by external rewards are more likely to adhere to a specified exercise programme (Deci & Ryan, 2008a).

Motivation is an important determinant of sustained participation in PA, and Deci and Ryan's (1985, 2000) self-determination theory (SDT) allows examination of the motives underpinning individuals' engagement in certain behaviours and activities (Ntoumanis, 2001). According to SDT, motivation may exist in various forms, ranging from a complete absence of motivation at one end of the spectrum (i.e. amotivation) through to engagement in activities for the inherent pleasure and interest they hold (i.e. intrinsic motivation). From the most self-determined to the least, the motivational regulations outlined within SDT are: (a) intrinsic motivation (i.e. pursuing an activity out of interest and due to the inherent enjoyment that it provides), (b) extrinsic motivation (i.e. the performance of an activity to attain some separate outcome, comprising integrated, identified, introjected and external regulation) and (c) amotivation (i.e. a lack of motivation characterised by a belief that success is not possible and that the activity is not valuable). One key principle of SDT is that individuals are more likely to continually engage in behaviours for which they feel autonomously motivated (Deci & Ryan, 2000). That is, those activities that individuals initiate of their own volition rather than feeling controlled to do so.

In additional, research in the exercise domain show that social conditions that support the satisfaction of basic psychological needs has been related to autonomous forms of motivation from the perceived locus of causality consistent with SDT (Edmunds, Ntoumanis, & Duda, 2007). Additionally, interventions supporting autonomous motivation were found to increase psychological need satisfaction as well as motivational regulations (Edmunds et al., 2007).

"Why" the Learning Environment Is Important (Part 1): Creating a Facilitating Environment Through the Satisfaction of Psychological Needs in PE

Deci and Ryan (2008b, 2000) proposed that social conditions that allow greater satisfaction of the basic psychological needs for autonomy, relatedness and competence can lead to more autonomous or self-determined motivation. The PE teacher plays an important role in influencing students' motivational orientations and behaviours through the learning environment they create. The social context established in PE (e.g. autonomy support, structure, cooperation) influences a student's perceptions of competence, autonomy and relatedness. These perceptions in turn influence the student's motivational orientation (e.g. intrinsic, extrinsic and amotivation), which consequently brings about affective (e.g. enjoyment, happiness), cognitive (e.g. engagement) and behavioural (e.g. increased PA) outcomes. Studies examining the learning environment in PE and PA settings found that students' perceptions of teachers' needs support positively predicted students' perceptions of needs satisfaction (Ntoumanis, 2005; Standage, Duda, & Ntoumanis, 2005).

Competence or "effectance-focused motivation" (Deci & Ryan, 2000, p. 231) is based on the need to have an impact on our surroundings, which is shown in the degree to which a person can make changes effectively in an environment (Deci & Ryan). Competence, as conceptualised as a nutriment in SDT, has a direct influence on intrinsic motivation. When an individual feels responsible for proficiently executing a task or other undertaking, intrinsic motivation can be enhanced (Deci & Ryan). When positive results do occur, it is critical that the individual perceive that he/she had a direct impact on the desirable outcome through feedback. Feelings of competence can be enhanced or negated by episodes of feedback. If an individual experiences negative feedback, intrinsic motivation will often decrease (Deci & Ryan).

Studies in PA settings generally support the notion that greater levels of perceived competence yield increases in self-determination and intrinsic motivation (Ntoumanis, 2001; Wang, Liu, Lochbaum, & Stevenson, 2009), although some indicate that the effect of perceived competence on intrinsic motivation is indirect (Goudas, Biddle, Fox, & Underwood, 1995). Perceived competence is particularly pertinent for PE, where most if not all of the skill performance is within public view (Whitehead & Corbin, 1991).

The benefits of competence needs satisfaction in PE also extend beyond the lesson. Taylor, Ntoumanis, Standage and Spray (2010) found that PE students' who were higher in competence need satisfaction showed more effort in PE, intended to be more physically active and reported more leisure-time PA, as compared with students who reported lower levels of competence need satisfaction. In addition, students who reported higher levels of competence need satisfaction experienced a greater acceleration in leisure-time PA over the school trimester, compared with students who reported lower levels of competence need satisfaction.

According to SDT, relatedness is characterised by a state of loving and caring for others, with the reciprocal being true, where love and care is also received by the individual, and is important in us flourishing as human beings (Deci & Ryan, 2000). In a school environment, when teachers are sympathetic, warm and affectionate with their students, when they dedicate psychological resources, such as attention, energy and affection (Reeve, Deci, & Ryan, 2004), they tend to nurture their students' relatedness and self-determined motivation. Relatedness in the classroom maybe conceptualised as interpersonal involvement by teachers in creating opportunities for students to feel related and belonging when they interact within a social environment that offers affection, warmth, care and nurturance (Skinner, Furrer, Marchand, & Kindermann, 2008).

Research in PE has demonstrated a positive relationship between relatedness in PE and more self-determined levels of motivation (identified regulation, integrated regulation and intrinsic motivation). It is not uncommon for individuals to report that a main reason they participate in PA is for the social interaction it provides (Ntoumanis, 2001). Studies with students from 11 to 19 years of age have shown that high perceptions of relatedness in PE were linked to higher levels of self-determined motivation (Standage et al., 2006), identified regulation and intrinsic motivation in females (Ntoumanis, 2001). Conversely, low perceptions of relatedness were associated with high levels of amotivation (Ntoumanis, 2005; Standage et al., 2006).

In PE, a students' relationship with his/her classmates is also important in contributing to their perception of relatedness, and positive relationships with peers can positively impact intrinsic motivation in sport and PE (Ulrich-French & Smith, 2006). Perceptions of cooperation or actual participation in cooperative learning activities are also linked with high perceived relatedness (Ntoumanis, 2001).

The concept of autonomy that is central within SDT has long been recognised as a fundamental factor in the promotion of optimal motivation. When individuals feel that their opinions are valued, their feelings are taken into account, and they have the opportunity to make choices and be self-managers, autonomy is enhanced (Ryan & Deci, 2000). School-based research has provided evidence that intrinsic motivation flourishes when students perceive that they are in an autonomy-supportive environment, where they have some level of control (Jang, Reeve, & Deci, 2010; Reeve, 2009). In PE, when students are able to make informed choices, engagement in PA is expected to follow (How, Whipp, Dimmock, & Jackson, 2013). In a study of middle school girls, when students were allowed to make choices regarding the activity in which they wanted to participate, situational motivation was increased, and amotivation was decreased, with additional beneficial effects of higher PA levels (Ward, Wilkinson, Graser, & Prusak, 2008). As such, when looking into PA intentions and adherence issues, investigating the construct of autonomy is essential.

Studies also show that students who report high perceptions of autonomy support in PE are more likely to be physically active in their leisure time. Chatzisarantis and Hagger (2009) developed a 5-week intervention programme involving 10 PE teachers and 215 pupils and examined its effects on students' PA intentions and self-reported leisure-time activity behaviour. The study employed two conditions, an autonomy-supportive one in which teachers were trained to provide rationale, feedback, choice and acknowledge difficulties and a less autonomy-supportive one in which teachers provided rationale and feedback only. Results indicated that students who were taught by more autonomy-supportive teachers reported stronger intentions to exercise during leisure time and participated more frequently in leisure-time physical activities than students taught by less autonomy-supportive teachers. This study further demonstrates the usefulness of SDT for the development of school-based interventions to increase PA participation.

When students are involved in a PE task that is appropriately self-determined, off-task behaviour should be minimised. Teachers must make use of strategies in PE lessons that help elicit autonomous behaviours from students. SDT is well suited to be an appropriate framework as insights into how PE teachers can influence students' motivation-related outcome variables can be gained by understanding how teachers' motivational styles affect the learning environment that supports the satisfaction of these needs. One key point repeatedly emerges in the literature that is especially relevant to the practitioner in PE, and that is students must perceive that their PE classes provide some form of autonomy. There is clear evidence suggesting that an autonomy-supportive environment is preferable to a controlling environment in PE (Hagger, Chatzisarantis, Culverhouse, & Biddle, 2003; Standage et al., 2006).

"Why" the Learning Environment Is Important (Part 2): Autonomy Support in Learning Environments

Autonomy support refers to the interpersonal connection and behaviour one person provides to identify, nurture and develop the other's inner motivational resources — such as the need for autonomy, intrinsic motivation, personal interests, intrinsic goals and self-endorsed values (Reeve, 2009). As opposed to autonomy support, controlling is the interpersonal feeling and behaviour one person provides to another to pressure them to think, feel or behave in a specific way (Assor, Kaplan, Kanat-Maymon, & Roth, 2005). SDT posits that when people experience autonomy need satisfaction from nurturing environmental conditions, they function more positively and experience greater psychological well-being (Deci & Ryan, 2008a; Kee, Wang, Lim, & Liu, 2012). Conversely, a controlling environment undermines positive functioning and outcomes because it elicits in individuals an external perceived locus of causality, a sense of pressure and a sense of obligation to others or to one's own negative emotion (Reeve, Nix, & Hamm, 2003).

Autonomy-Support Versus Controlling Motivational Style

Controlling and autonomy support represent a single bipolar continuum to conceptualise the quality or learning climate of a teacher's motivating style towards students (Deci, Schwartz, Sheinman, & Ryan, 1981). This concept is an important educational construct because students of autonomy-supportive teachers display more markedly positive classroom functioning and educational outcomes than do students of controlling teachers (Lim & Wang, 2009; Reeve & Jang, 2006; Ryan & Deci, 2000). There is strong empirical evidence showing that the degree to which teachers are autonomy supportive versus controlling is significantly linked with students' need satisfaction and motivations (Liu et al., 2013). Studies on autonomy-supportive motivating styles suggest that teachers who support autonomy by listening, allowing time for independent work and asking questions about what they want to do as they teach enhance students' intrinsic motivation and internalisation

(Reeve, Bolt, & Cai, 1999). Sierens, Vansteenkiste, Goossens, Soenens and Dochy (2009) further suggest that when help, instructions and expectations are provided in an autonomously supportive way to the students, there is a greater chance that they would self-reflect, plan their study activity and perceive themselves as learners.

On the other hand, teachers who are controlling use characteristically more directives, give more solutions to the students, criticise them more and put more pressure on them using rewards, threats and deadlines (Reeve, 2009). When teachers are controlling, students' engagement becomes lacking in the important motivational underpinnings of personal interest, valuing, task involvement, positive feelings, self-initiative, self determination and persistence (Reeve, 2009). It is this contrast between engaging in a task with and without these autonomous sources of motivation that differentiates the positive functioning and outcomes of autonomy-supported students from the negative functioning and outcomes of controlled students.

Effectiveness of Autonomy Support in PE

To date, there are a number of studies that examined the effectiveness of autonomy-supportive interventions in secondary school PE (Chatzisarantis & Hagger, 2009; Cheon, Reeve, & Moon, 2012; Tessier, Sarrazin, & Ntoumanis, 2008). These studies are important in adding to the understanding of the causal relationships between autonomy-supportive interventions and subsequent student outcomes.

A study by Tessier and colleagues (2008) involved five PE teachers (i.e. three males and two females) randomly assigned to a control or an autonomy-supportive training group over an 8-week teaching cycle. Results showed that compared to the teachers in the control group, those in the experimental group used an autonomy-supportive style with greater frequency. In a follow-up study to address the effects of the teacher training on students' engagement and motivation, Tessier and colleagues (2010) developed an intervention to test the effects of a training programme for three newly qualified PE teachers on teachers' overt behaviours and students' psychological needs satisfaction, self-determined motivation and engagement in sport-based PE. Results revealed that from pre- to post-intervention: (1) teachers managed to improve their teaching style in terms of all three dimensions, and (2) students were receptive to these changes, as shown by increases in their reported need satisfaction, self-determined motivation and engagement in the class.

Cheon and his colleagues (2012) designed, implemented and assessed the effectiveness of an intervention to help physical education (PE) teachers be more autonomy supportive during instruction. Nineteen secondary school PE teachers in Seoul were randomly assigned into either an experimental or a delayed-treatment control group, and their 1,158 students self-reported their PE-related psychological need satisfaction, autonomous motivation, amotivation, classroom engagement, skill development, future intentions and academic achievement at the beginning, middle and end of the semester. Observers' ratings and students' self-report confirmed that the intervention was successful.

Overall, strong recent evidence has emerged suggesting that PE teachers can learn to better support students' psychological needs through provision of autonomy support.

Structure and Engagement in the Learning Environment

Structure refers to how much information and how clearly teachers provide instruction to students about expected behaviour and the means whereby desired educational outcomes can be effectively achieved (Skinner & Belmont, 1993). Structure has been examined thoroughly within the classroom management literature as introducing procedures (Emmer, Evertson, & Anderson, 1980), establishing order (Doyle, 1986), communicating instructions about how to complete work (Carter & Doyle, 2006) and reducing to a minimum poor behaviour while promoting achievement and engagement (Brophy, 2006). The opposite of structure is chaos, whereby teachers are confusing or contradict themselves, unable to articulate clear expectations and directions and ask for results without communicating how to get them (Jang et al., 2010). From a SDT perspective, structure further facilitates students' development of a sense of an internal locus of control, perceived competence, mastery motivation, self-efficacy and a positive attribution style (Skinner et al., 2008).

Teachers sometimes equate control with structure. Controlling strategies are often inappropriately associated with a structured learning environment, whereas autonomy-supportive strategies are often wrongly associated with a disorderly or helter-skelter one (Reeve, 2009). Teachers do not want to risk losing control over their classrooms, so they sometimes believe that a controlling style will provide them with the classroom structure they seek. Similarly, they may fear that an autonomy-supportive style will lead to students be lax in learning or chaos in the classroom. It is a mistake to equate control with structure, however, because information can be provided by teachers in *either* controlling or autonomy-supportive ways (Deci & Ryan, 1985). Although structure tells students what they need to do (e.g. goals, expectancies), it is a teacher's motivating style that sets the tone as to how students make progress towards those objectives. A classroom that has objectives is typically a structured one, whereas a classroom without objectives is typically a chaotic one. The key difference is that a teacher who pushes and pressures students towards those objectives is controlling, whereas a teacher who supports students' movement towards those objectives is autonomy supportive (Reeve, 2009).

The Role of Autonomy Support and Structure in Fostering Engagement in PE

When teachers' naturally occurring styles are scored by raters, providing structure is actually *positively* correlated with the provision of autonomy support and *negatively* correlated with the provision of control (Jang et al., 2010). Hence autonomy-supportive teachers provide more, not less, classroom structure than do controlling teachers (Sierens, Goossens, Soenens, Vansteenkiste, & Dochy, 2007). Students too rate their autonomy-supportive teachers as providing them with greater structure than do their controlling teachers (Jang et al., 2010; Sierens et al., 2009). Findings such as these show that a controlling style in which teachers take charge and push hard does not afford students the structured learning environment they seek. In a nutshell, teachers need to find ways to administer elements of classroom structure that not only structure the lessons but also support students' autonomy while doing so.

More recently, Jang and colleagues (2010) investigated the impact of autonomy support and structure on students' engagement and found that students' engagement was highest when teachers provided high levels of both. They also found that (a) autonomy support and structure were positively correlated, (b) autonomy support and structure both predicted students' behavioural engagement and (c) autonomy support was a unique predictor of students' self-reported engagement.

In PE lessons, the emphasis is on the presentation of motor skills. Demonstration, or modelling, often with the teacher in front of the class, is recognised as a critical aspect of presenting information to learners (McCullagh, Stiehl, & Weiss, 1990). Prior research on classroom climate and teacher behaviour offers a potential insight as to how autonomy support and structure might combine during the ongoing flow of instruction to enhance students' engagement. Researchers found that providing structure at central moments in the lesson (e.g. when the teacher was in front of the class and introducing a new learning activity) was crucial to predicting students' subsequent classroom engagement (Brekelmans, Sleegers, & Fraser, 2000).

Structure is especially important in PE because teachers who have not developed a sound structure cannot progress onto developing learning environments that maintains a high level of student engagement in practice (Rink, 2002). Teachers who do develop a structured learning environment that support students' autonomy can employ effective teaching strategies (such as working in cooperation or independently) critical to the development of students in PE (Hellison, 1995). To set the conditions under which students could later regulate their own learning in an autonomous and responsible way—especially during less supervised group and individual work—it will be helpful for a teacher to first display a strong sense of leadership (i.e. high structure) during central lesson segments (Jang et al., 2010).

With autonomy support and structure functioning as important predictors of students' collective classroom engagement, teachers struggling with the daily goal of supporting students' engagement during learning activities need not choose between providing autonomy support or structure but, instead, can focus their instructional energies on providing autonomy support and structure.

However, there are limited intervention studies examining the role of structure together with autonomy support in PE. Past research (Skinner & Belmont, 1993) conceptualises autonomy support and structure as a comprehensive framework. However, Jang et al. (2010) recognise that conceptual and operational definitions might capture only the essential elements of autonomy support and structure. To understand the comprehensive elements of autonomy support and structure, further experimental and longitudinal designs that are subject specific (in this case PE) are warranted.

"How" to Create an Autonomy-Supportive Learning Environment: Five Instructional Behaviours to Support Students' Autonomy

In the first article to operationally define autonomy support as a construct that could be manipulated within the context of an experiment, Deci and colleagues (Deci, Eghrari, Patrick, & Leone, 1994) used a laboratory procedure to vary the presence versus absence of three interpersonal conditions—provide meaningful rationales, acknowledge negative feelings and use non-controlling language. This three-condition operational definition of autonomy support was applied to a task in which participants worked on a very uninteresting activity. From the study, they found that none of the conditions by itself created an experience in which participants felt their autonomy was supported. Rather, it was only when all three conditions were provided together that participants felt their autonomy was supported.

As experimental and intervention-based research was extended into naturally occurring applied settings (e.g. the classroom), researchers necessarily expanded the operational definition so that it applied equally well to supporting people's autonomy as they engaged in interesting and personally valued activities. In doing so, researchers added "offer choices" (Williams, Cox, Kouides, & Deci, 1999) and "nurture inner motivational resources" (Reeve, Jang, Carrell, Jeon, & Barch, 2004) as additional theory-based elements (or interpersonal conditions) of autonomy support. Another contemporary expansion has been to recognise the importance of taking the other person's perspective, as many researchers now integrate "acknowledge negative feelings," "acknowledge perspective" and "perspective taking," into a single supportive condition—namely, "acknowledge perspective and feelings" (Tessier et al., 2008).

Research conducted on the constructs of autonomy support provides substantial empirical support for the validity of each interpersonal condition. (A) In "providing meaningful rationales", participants provided with a rationale that explained why task engagement was a personally beneficial thing to do self-reported greater perceived autonomy and task importance and showed greater task engagement than did participants who worked on the same task or lesson without an explanatory rationale (Jang, 2008). (B) In "acknowledging negative feelings", participants who had others acknowledge, accept and even welcome their expressions of negative affect (e.g. "this is boring") self-reported greater perceived autonomy and showed greater engagement than did participants who had their expression of negative affect criticised or suppressed (Assor et al., 2005; Reeve & Jang, 2006). (C) In "using non-controlling language", participants exposed to flexible communications ("you may…"), and non-evaluative comments self-reported greater perceived autonomy and greater task engagement than did participants exposed to language that pushed and pressured them towards specific predetermined products, solutions, answers and desired behaviours (Assor et al., 2005; Reeve & Jang, 2006; Vansteenkiste, Simons, Lens, Sheldon, & Deci, 2004). (D) In "offering choices", participants offered choices among options and invitations to self-direct their own task engagements self-reported greater perceived autonomy and task engagement than did participants given assigned tasks (Assor et al., 2002; Reeve et al., 2003). (E) In "nurturing inner motivational resources", participants showed greater constructive motivation and task engagement when others built their requested task engagements around their interests (Schraw & Lehman, 2001), intrinsic motivation (Gottfried, Fleming, & Gottfried, 1994), autonomy (Reeve & Jang, 2006), competence (Ryan & Grolnick, 1986), relatedness (Furrer & Skinner, 2003), sense of challenge (Clifford, 1990) and intrinsic goals (Vansteenkiste, Zhou, Lens, & Soenens, 2005).

In view of the evidence provided by literature, teachers should be encouraged to promote autonomy support through providing choice, initiative and decision-making in the classroom. Reeve (2009) proposes five instructional behaviours that teachers can adopt to be more autonomy supportive: (1) foster intrinsic motivation, (2) offer rationale for tasks, (3) use informational/non-controlling language, (4) display patience for student learning and (5) acknowledge and accept students' expressions of negative affect. In the following sections, we will highlight some of the practical ways in which teachers can operationalise autonomy support in their classes.

1. Fostering Intrinsic Motivation

To foster intrinsic motivation in students, teachers must find ways to coordinate the instructional activities with students' preference, interests, sense of enjoyment, sense of challenge, competencies and choice-making (Reeve, Jang et al., 2004). For example, the PE teacher could allow the class to design interesting learning activities of their choice, as well as allow students to have some time to read up or research more on the current topic that is being taught. To challenge students optimally, the teacher may also set differentiated levels of difficulty that the students may choose from, instead of a once-size-fit-all approach. These practices are particularly useful when introducing or making a transition to a new learning activity. They encourage students' active engagement in lessons by allowing students to feel a sense of freedom with respect to their actions, since what they do is aligned with their genuine interests.

2. Offer Rationale for Tasks

When asking students to engage in potentially uninteresting activities or rule following, teachers could support students' autonomy by offering a rationale (or a steady stream of rationales) (Reeve, 2009). For example, a teacher who wishes to teach orienteering to students can highlight the real-life importance of angles in map reading and other cross-disciplinary applications. The teacher can also focus on framing these skills towards intrinsic contexts (Vansteenkiste et al., 2004) and how they would be personally useful and of significance and value to the students. For example, map reading help the students in navigation when they go on a holiday. In both cases (explanatory rationales, intrinsic goal framing), the teacher supports students' appreciation, understanding and internalisation for why the otherwise uninteresting activity is actually a personally useful thing to do (Assor et al., 2002; Vansteenkiste & Lens, 2006). Providing rationale is important in internalisation of the learning activity, by changing the perception of what is not worth doing into something worth doing.

3. Use Informational/Non-controlling Language

Teachers could rely on informational and non-controlling language to support autonomy when communicating requirements. For example, a PE teacher may notice in a lesson that a student is off-task, low in motivation and intentionally disruptive to other students' learning. Instead of telling the student off right away, the teacher can support the student's autonomy and encourage volitional engagement by relying on non-controlling language through flexible messages that are non-evaluative and information rich (Vansteenkiste et al., 2004). The teacher could help the student become aware of his actions and that his actions are not helping with the objective of learning. The teacher could further remind the student the rules of the classroom behaviour and the objectives of the lesson. The use of informational and non-controlling language is beneficial when communicating requirements, responsibilities and feedback. It is also effective in addressing motivational and behavioural problems in the classroom. Beyond promoting positive teacher-student relationships, informational and non-controlling language also helps students be more aware of their motivational, behavioural and performance issues while maintaining their personal responsibility for these problems.

4. Display Patience for Student Learning

When students are developing skills on tasks that are unfamiliar or complex, teachers should display patience for students' learning. They can do so by taking the time to listen, providing encouragement for initiative and effort, providing time for students to work in their own way, offering helpful hints when students seem stuck, praising signs of progress, postponing advice until they first understand the students' goals and perspective and providing scaffolding when it is needed and invited (Reeve & Jang, 2006). For example, a teacher may notice her students in a PE class facing difficulties in understanding the concepts taught. Instead of saying, "Here, let me show you how to do it", the teacher could ask guiding questions to direct students towards focusing on the concept and allow students the space to think and figure it out for themselves as they continue to engage in the lesson. Teachers often feel that they do not have the "luxury" to let students learn at their own pace. However, when students have time and space to explore and manipulate materials, make plans, set goals, formulate and test hypothesis, monitor and revise their work and change problem-solving strategies, they are better able to accommodate knowledge, understand conceptual change and integrate deeper information processing.

5. Dealing with Negative Affect/Misbehaviour

How teachers deal with students' off-task and non-engaged behaviour also has implications for students' motivation. Sometimes in lessons, students' preferences are at odds with teacher's requests and requirements. For example, a teacher may want her PE class to practise dribbling a basketball. She has designed a series of progressive tasks for her class to help them. However some of her students may perceive the tasks to be boring and irrelevant. A controlling teacher would brush off these negative affects and impose her demands on the class. Alternatively, after listening to her students' comments, an autonomy-supportive teacher could decide to make the lesson more interesting by using games to teach skills rather than using drills and tasks. When teachers acknowledge, accept and even welcome expressions of negative feelings, they communicate an understanding of the students' perspectives and give voice to that perspective. By opening themselves to receiving students' negative emotionality as constructive information, it creates opportunities to enhance students' engagement by restructuring an otherwise unappealing lesson.

Conclusion

Teachers' behaviours and practices have a substantial impact on student engagement in PE. When students learn out of curiosity and are intrinsically motivated, they are more engaged in and satisfied with their learning. They better understand the material they are trying to learn and are happier in PE lessons. The practical SDT framework discussed in this chapter allows teachers to work through the steps of becoming less controlling, wanting to support autonomy and learning the practical "how-to" of classroom autonomy support.

One of the key goals of PE is to provide students with a supportive and highly active environment, which also facilitates the skills, knowledge and attitudes that are necessary to pursue an active, healthy lifestyle beyond the school environment. The motivating style that best facilitates students' engagement is an autonomy-supportive one. Reviews from the previous studies showed that PE teachers might not need to spend substantial amounts of time designing an autonomy supportive PE environment. The provision of autonomy support in PE could be achieved with minimal modification to a traditional teacher-centred PE pedagogy. Allowing time in PE lessons for students to plan and execute their own activities could enhance their engagement in PA and perceptions about PE within the classroom, as well as better enable them to make informed choices and sustain their PA levels outside school.

References

Assor, A., Kaplan, H., & Roth, G. (2002). Choice is good, but relevance is excellent: Autonomy enhancing and suppressing teacher behaviours predicting students' engagement in schoolwork. *British Journal of Educational Psychology, 72*, 261–278.

Assor, A., Kaplan, H., Kanat-Maymon, Y., & Roth, G. (2005). Directly controlling teacher behaviors as predictors of poor motivation and engagement in girls and boys: The role of anger and anxiety. *Learning and Instruction, 15*, 397–413.

Berkey, C. S., Rockett, H. R. H., Gillman, M. W., & Colditz, G. A. (2003). One-year changes in activity and in inactivity among 10 to 15 year old boys and girls: Relationship to change in body mass index. *Pediatrics, 111*, 836–843.

Blankenship, B. T. (2008). *The psychology of teaching physical education: From theory to practice*. Scottsdale, AZ: Holcomb Hathaway.

Bouchard, C., Shephard, R. J., & Stephens, T. (1994). *Physical activity, fitness and health: International proceedings and consensus statement*. Champaign, IL: Human Kinetics.

Brekelmans, M., Sleegers, P., & Fraser, B. J. (2000). Teaching for active learning. In R. J. Simons, J. Van der Linden, & T. Duffy (Eds.), *New learning* (pp. 227–242). Dordrecht, the Netherlands: Kluwer Academic.

Brophy, J. (2006). Observational research on generic aspects of classroom teaching. In P. A. Alexander & P. H. Winne (Eds.), *Handbook of educational psychology* (2nd ed., pp. 755–780). Mahwah, NJ: Erlbaum.

Bryan, C. L., & Solmon, M. A. (2007). Self-determination in physical education: Designing class environments to promote active lifestyles. *Journal of Teaching in Physical Education, 26*(3), 260–278.

Bycura, D., & Darst, P. W. (2001). Motivating middle school students: A health-club approach. *Journal of Physical Education, Recreation & Dance, 72*, 24–29.

Carter, K., & Doyle, W. (2006). Classroom management in early childhood and elementary classrooms. In C. M. Evertson & C. S. Weinstein (Eds.), *Handbook of classroom management: Research, practice, and contemporary issues* (pp. 373–406). Mahwah, NJ: Erlbaum.

Chatzisarantis, N. L., & Hagger, M. S. (2009). Effects of an intervention based on self-determination theory on self-reported leisure-time physical activity participation. *Psychology and Health, 24*, 29–48.

Cheon, S. H., Reeve, J., & Moon, I. S. (2012). Experimentally based, longitudinally designed, teacher-focused intervention to help physical education teachers be more autonomy supportive toward their students. *Journal of Sport & Exercise Psychology, 34*, 365–396.

Clifford, M. M. (1990). Students need challenge, not easy success. *Educational Leadership, 48*, 22–26.

Deci, E. L., Eghrari, H., Patrick, B. C., & Leone, D. (1994). Facilitating internalization: The self determination theory perspective. *Journal of Personality, 62*, 119–142.

Deci, E. L., & Ryan, R. M. (1985). *Intrinsic motivation and self-determination in human behavior* (2nd ed.). New York: Plenum Press.

Deci, E. L., & Ryan, R. M. (2000). The "what" and "why" of goal pursuits: Human needs and the self-determination of behavior. *Psychological Inquiry, 11*, 227–268.

Deci, E. L., & Ryan, R. M. (2008a). Facilitating optimal motivation and psychological well-being across life's domains. *Canadian Psychology, 49*, 14–23.

Deci, E. L., & Ryan, R. M. (2008b). Self-determination theory: A macrotheory of human motivation, development, and health. *Canadian Psychology/Psychologie Canadienne, 49*, 182–185.

Deci, E. L., Schwartz, A., Sheinman, L., & Ryan, R. M. (1981). An instrument to assess adult's orientations toward control versus autonomy in children: Reflections on intrinsic motivation and perceived competence. *Journal of Educational Psychology, 73*, 642–650.

Department of Health. (2009). *Be active, be healthy: A plan for getting the nation moving*. London: DoH.

Doyle, W. (1986). Classroom organisation and management. In M. Wittrock (Ed.), *Handbook of research on teaching* (3rd ed., pp. 392–441). New York: Macmillan.

Edmunds, J., Ntoumanis, N., & Duda, J. L. (2007). Perceived autonomy support and psychological need satisfaction in exercise. In M. S. Hagger & N. L. D. Chatzisarantis (Eds.), *Intrinsic motivation and self-determination in exercise and sport* (pp. 35–53). Champaign, IL: Human Kinetics.

Emmer, E., Evertson, C., & Anderson, L. (1980). Effective classroom management at the beginning of the school year. *The Elementary School Journal, 80*, 219–231.

Evertson, C., & Emmer, E. (1982). Effective management at the beginning at the beginning of the year in junior high school classes. *Journal of Educational Psychology, 74*, 485–498.

Ferrer-Caja, E., & Weiss, M. R. (2000). Predictors of intrinsic motivation among adolescent students in physical education. *Research Quarterly for Exercise and Sport, 71*, 267–279.

Furrer, C., & Skinner, E. A. (2003). Sense of relatedness as a factor in children's academic engagement and performance. *Journal of Educational Psychology, 95*, 148–162.

Gottfried, A. E., Fleming, J. S., & Gottfried, A. W. (1994). Role of parental motivational practices in children's academic intrinsic motivation and achievement. *Journal of Educational Psychology, 86*, 104–113.

Goudas, M., Biddle, S., Fox, K., & Underwood, M. (1995). It ain't what you do, it's the way that you do it! Teaching style affects children's motivation in track and field. *The Sport Psychologist, 9*, 254–264.

Hagger, M. S., Chatzisarantis, N. L. D., Culverhouse, T., & Biddle, S. J. H. (2003). The processes by which perceived autonomy support in physical education promotes leisuretime physical activity intentions and behavior: A trans-contextual model. *Journal of Educational Psychology, 95*, 784–795.

Hellison, D. (1995). *Teaching responsibility through physical activity*. Champaign, IL: Human Kinetics.

How, Y. M., Whipp, P., Dimmock, J., & Jackson, B. (2013). The effects of choice on autonomous motivation, perceived autonomy support, and physical activity levels in high school physical education. *Journal of Teaching in Physical Education, 32*, 131–148.

Jang, H. (2008). Supporting students' motivation, engagement, and learning during an uninteresting activity. *Journal of Educational Psychology, 100*, 798–811.

Jang, H., Reeve, J., & Deci, E. L. (2010). Engaging students in learning activities: It is not autonomy support or structure but autonomy support and structure. *Journal of Educational Psychology, 102*, 588–600.

Jenkins, C. P. (1986). Brain research leads to new teaching methods. *BYU Today, 40*(1), 4–5.

Kee, Y. H., Wang, C. K. J., Lim, B. S. C., & Liu, W. C. (2012). Secondary students' motivation and learning strategies profiles: The importance of an autonomy-supportive classroom structure. In J. N. Franco & A. E. Svensgaard (Eds.), *Handbook on psychology of motivation: New research* (pp. 271–282). New York: Nova Publisher.

Koka, A., & Hein, V. (2003). The impact of sports participation after school on intrinsic motivation and perceived learning environment in secondary school physical education. *Kinesiology, 35*(1), 5–13.

Lee, T., Swinnen, S., & Serrien, D. (1994). Cognitive effort and motor-learning. *Quest, 46*, 328–344.

Lim, B. S. C., & Wang, C. K. J. (2009). Perceived autonomy support, behavioural regulations in physical education and physical activity intention. *Psychology of Sport and Exercise, 10*, 52–60.

Liu, W. C., Wang, C. K. J., Kee, Y. H., Koh, C., Lim, B. S. C., & Chua, L. (2013). College students' motivation and learning strategies profiles and academic achievement: A self-determination theory approach. *Educational Psychology, 34*(3), 338–353.

Lonsdale, C., Rosenkranz, R. R., Peralta, L. R., Bennie, A., Fahey, P., & Lubans, D. R. (2013). A systematic review and meta-analysis of interventions designed to increase moderate-to-vigorous physical activity in school physical education lessons. *Preventive Medicine, 56*, 152–161.

McCullagh, P., Stiehl, J., & Weiss, M. (1990). Developmental modeling effects on the quantitative and qualitative aspects of motor performance. *Research Quarterly for Exercise and Sport, 61*, 344–350.

Ntoumanis, N. (2001). A self-determination approach to the understanding of motivation in physical education. *British Journal of Educational Psychology, 71*, 225–242.

Ntoumanis, N. (2005). A prospective study of participation in optional school physical education using a self-determination theory framework. *Journal of Educational Psychology, 97*, 444–453.

Parker, J. (1995). Secondary teachers' views of effective teaching in physical education. *Journal of Teaching in Physical Education, 14*, 127–139.

Reeve, J. (2009). Why teachers adopt a controlling motivating style toward students and how they can become more autonomy supportive. *Educational Psychologist, 44*, 159–175.

Reeve, J., Bolt, E., & Cai, Y. (1999). Autonomy-supportive teachers: How they teach and motivate students. *Journal of Educational Psychology, 91*, 537–548.

Reeve, J., Deci, E. L., & Ryan, R. M. (2004). Self-determination theory: A dialectical framework for understanding the sociocultural influences on student motivation. In D. McInerney & S. Van Etten (Eds.), *Research on sociocultural influences on motivation and learning: Big theories revisited* (Vol. 4, pp. 31–60). Greenwich, UK: Information Age Press.

Reeve, J., & Jang, H. (2006). What teachers say and do to support students' autonomy during a learning activity. *Journal of Educational Psychology, 98*, 209–218.

Reeve, J., Jang, H., Carrell, D., Jeon, S., & Barch, J. (2004). Enhancing students' motivation by increasing teachers' autonomy support. *Motivation and Emotion, 28*, 147–169.

Reeve, J., Nix, G., & Hamm, D. (2003). Testing models of the experience of self determination in intrinsic motivation and the conundrum of choice. *Journal of Educational Psychology, 95*, 375–392.

Rink, J. E. (2002). *Teaching physical education for learning*. St. Louis, MO: Mosby Year Book.

Rink, J. E., & Hall, T. J. (2008). Research on effective teaching in elementary school physical education. *The Elementary School Journal, 108*, 207–218.

Ryan, R. M., & Deci, E. L. (2000). Self-determination theory and the facilitation of intrinsic motivation, social development, and well-being. *American Psychologist, 55*(1), 68–78.

Ryan, R. M., & Grolnick, W. S. (1986). Origins and pawns in the classroom: Self-report and projective assessments of individual differences in children's perceptions. *Journal of Personality and Social Psychology, 50*, 550–558.

Sallis, J. F., Prochaska, J. J., & Taylor, W. C. (2000). A review of correlates of physical activity of children and adolescents. *Medicine and Science in Sports and Exercise, 32*(5), 963–975.

Schempp, P. G., Cheffers, J. T. F., & Zaichkowsky, L. D. (1983). Influence of decision-making on attitudes, creativity, motor skills, and self-concept in elementary children. *Research Quarterly for Exercise and Sport, 54*, 183–189.

Schraw, G., & Lehman, S. (2001). Situational interest: A review of the literature and directions for future research. *Educational Psychology Review, 13*, 23–52.

Siedentop, D., & Tannehill, D. (2000). *Developing teaching skills in physical education* (4th ed.). Mountain View, CA: Mayfield Publishing Company.

Sierens, E., Goossens, L., Soenens, B., Vansteenkiste, M., & Dochy, F. (2007). The interactive effect of perceived autonomy support and structure in the prediction of self-regulated learning. Paper presented at the 3rd International Conference on Self-determination Theory, Toronto, Ontario

Sierens, E., Vansteenkiste, M., Goossens, L., Soenens, B., & Dochy, F. (2009). The synergistic relationship of perceived autonomy support and structure in the prediction of self-regulated learning. *British Journal of Educational Psychology, 79*, 57–68.

Silverman, S., Devillier, R., & Ramirez, T. (1991). The validity of academic learning time-physical education (ALT-PE) as a process measure of student achievement. *Research Quarterly for Exercise and Sport, 62*, 319–325.

Skinner, E. A., & Belmont, M. J. (1993). Motivation in the classroom: Reciprocal effects of teacher behavior and student engagement across the school year. *Journal of Educational Psychology, 85*, 571–581.

Skinner, E. A., Furrer, C., Marchand, G., & Kindermann, T. (2008). Engagement and disaffection in the classroom: Part of a larger motivational dynamic? *Journal of Educational Psychology, 100*, 765–781.

Solmon, M. A. (2003). Student issues in physical education classes: Attitudes, cognition and motivation. In S. J. Silverman & C. D. Ennis (Eds.), *Student learning in physical education: Applying research to enhance instruction* (pp. 147–163). Champaign, IL: Human Kinetics.

Standage, M., Duda, J. L., & Ntoumanis, N. (2005). A test of self-determination theory in school physical education. *British Journal of Educational Psychology, 75*, 411–433.

Standage, M., Duda, J. L., & Ntoumanis, N. (2006). Students' motivational processes and their relationship to teacher ratings in school physical education: A self-determination theory approach. *Research Quarterly for Exercise and Sport, 77*, 100–110.

Taylor, I. M., & Lonsdale, C. (2010). Cultural differences in the relationships among autonomy support, psychological need satisfaction, subjective vitality, and effort in British and Chinese physical education. *Journal of Sport & Exercise Psychology, 32*, 655–673.

Taylor, I. M., Ntoumanis, N., Standage, M., & Spray, C. M. (2010). Motivational predictors of physical education students' effort, exercise intentions, and leisure-time physical activity: A multilevel linear growth analysis. *Journal of Sport & Exercise Psychology, 32*, 99–120.

Telama, R., Yang, X., Laakso, L., & Vilkari, J. (1997). Physical activity in childhood and adolescence as predictor of physical activity in young adulthood. *American Journal of Preventive Medicine, 13*, 317–323.

Tessier, D., Sarrazin, P., & Ntoumanis, N. (2008). The effects of an experimental programme to support students' autonomy on the overt behaviours of physical education teachers. *European Journal of Psychology of Education, 23*, 239–253.

Tessier, D., Sarrazin, P., & Ntoumanis, N. (2010). The effect of an intervention to improve newly qualified teachers' interpersonal style, students motivation and psychological need satisfaction in sport-based physical education. *Contemporary Educational Psychology, 35*, 242–253.

Thill, E., & Mouanda, J. (1990). Autonomy or control in the sports context: Validity of the cognitive evaluation theory. *International Journal of Sport Psychology, 21*, 1–20.

Ulrich-French, S., & Smith, A. L. (2006). Perceptions of relationships with parents and peers in youth sport: Independent and combined prediction of motivational outcomes. *Psychology of Sport and Exercise, 7*, 193–214.

Vansteenkiste, M., & Lens, W. (2006). Intrinsic versus extrinsic goal contents in self-determination theory: Another look at the quality of academic motivation. *Educational Psychologist, 41*(1), 19–31.

Vansteenkiste, M., Simons, J., Lens, W., Sheldon, K. M., & Deci, E. L. (2004). Motivating learning, performance, and persistence: The synergistic role of intrinsic goals and autonomy support. *Journal of Personality and Social Psychology, 87*, 246–260.

Vansteenkiste, M., Zhou, M., Lens, W., & Soenens, B. (2005). Experiences of autonomy and control among Chinese learners: Vitalizing or immobilizing? *Journal of Educational Psychology, 97*, 468–483.

Wang, C. K. J., Liu, W. C., Lochbaum, M. R., & Stevenson, S. J. (2009). Sports ability beliefs, 2 × 2 achievement goals, intrinsic motivation: The moderating role of perceived competence in sport and exercise. *Research Quarterly for Exercise & Sport, 80*(2), 303–312.

Ward, J., Wilkinson, C., Graser, S. V., & Prusak, K. A. (2008). Effects of choice on student motivation and physical activity behavior in physical education. *Journal of Teaching in Physical Education, 27*, 385–398.

Whitehead, J. R., & Corbin, C. B. (1991). Youth fitness testing: The effect of percentile based evaluative feedback on intrinsic motivation. *Research Quarterly for Exercise and Sport, 62*, 225–231.

Williams, G. C., Cox, E. M., Kouides, R., & Deci, E. L. (1999). Presenting the facts about smoking to adolescents: The effects of an autonomy supportive style. *Pediatrics and Adolescent Medicine, 153*, 959–964.

World Health Organisation. (2010). Global strategy on diet, physical activity and health. Retrieved form, January 20, 2013, http://www.who.int/dietphysicalactivity/en/

Wright, M. T., Patterson, D. L., & Cardinal, B. J. (2000). Increasing children's physical activity. *Journal of Physical Education Recreation & Dance, 71*, 26–29.

Yli-Piipari, S., Wang, C. K. J., Jaakkola, T., & Liukkonen, J. (2012). Examining the growth trajectories of physical education students' motivation, enjoyment, and physical activity: A person-oriented approach. *Journal of Applied Sport Psychology, 24*, 401–417.

Chapter 12
Can Being Autonomy-Supportive in Teaching Improve Students' Self-Regulation and Performance?

John Chee Keng Wang, Betsy L.L. Ng, Woon Chia Liu, and Richard M. Ryan

Introduction

Within self-determination theory (SDT; Deci & Ryan, 1985), learners' intrinsic motivation is said to be facilitated and enhanced by nurturing their innate psychological needs for autonomy, competence and relatedness. These three basic needs relate to choice, feeling of effectiveness and connectedness. Satisfaction of the needs within a context will promote intrinsic motivation for doing a task or activity. Through experiencing a sense of choice in learning, a sense of competence as well as a sense of connectedness, learners feel self-determined (autonomous) and motivated.

Studies in the SDT literature have provided the benefits associated with learners' need satisfaction and teacher's autonomy support (Gagne, 2003; Jang, Kim, & Reeve, 2012). Satisfaction of needs provides the condition for optimal learning by yielding an energizing effect in which learners can get more fully immersed in the learning process and predicts positive learning outcomes (Reeve, Deci, & Ryan, 2004). Despite the documented existence of SDT-based intervention research, little is known about the inclusion of motivational-cognitive variables. The aim of this study was to test the effects of the autonomy-supportive classroom intervention on student learning outcomes in terms of needs satisfaction, motivational-cognitive factors and academic achievement in the Singapore context.

J.C.K. Wang • B.L.L. Ng (✉) • W.C. Liu
National Institute of Education, Nanyang Technological University, Singapore, Singapore
e-mail: john.wang@nie.edu.sg; n_betsy@hotmail.com; woonchia.liu@nie.edu.sg

R.M. Ryan
Institute for Positive Psychology and Education, Faculty of Health Sciences,
Australian Catholic University, Strathfield, NSW, Australia
e-mail: richard.ryan@acu.edu.au

© Springer Science+Business Media Singapore 2016   227
W.C. Liu et al. (eds.), *Building Autonomous Learners*,
DOI 10.1007/978-981-287-630-0_12

SDT-Based Educational Research

SDT is a macro-theory on human motivation, in particularly autonomous motivation, controlled motivation and amotivation which are used as predictors of academic performance (Deci & Ryan, 2008). Recent empirical studies support the associations of autonomous motivation with achievement and engagement (De Naeghel et al., 2012; Reeve, 2013), the positive impact of teacher need support on motivation and learning (Diseth, Danielsen, & Samdal, 2012; Jang et al., 2012) as well as the relationship between student need satisfaction and intrinsic motivation (Brooks & Young, 2011; Otoshi & Heffernan, 2011).

From the SDT perspective, autonomy-supportive teachers permit students to act upon their personal interests and values, to provide students with the desired amount of choice and to give a meaningful rationale when choice is constrained (Soenens et al., 2007). Such teachers are effective in supporting students' need for autonomy as they can empathetically adopt learners' internal frame of reference (i.e. autonomy support). Autonomy-supportive teachers also satisfy students' needs for competence; thereby students might be more engaged in self-regulated learning (Sierens et al., 2009). Autonomy support is likely to allow a more student-attuned learning environment as it acts in accordance with students' goals.

According to Deci and his colleagues (Deci, Eghari, Patrick, & Leone, 1994), an autonomy-supportive environment is when the leader provides rationale, acknowledgement of conflict and choice. Autonomy-supportive environment facilitates more self-determined forms of motivation in students as opposed to controlling behaviours. Controlling behaviours arise in a controlled environment whereby two of the three critical abovementioned factors are absent. Therefore, the utility of applying SDT to educational settings is evident whereby students thrive in both academic and developmental domains.

Determinants of Motivation and Self-Regulated Learning

Perceived autonomy support can facilitate autonomous learning, which will lead to self-determined behaviours and greater well-being (Levesque, Zuehlke, Stanek, & Ryan, 2004). To measure the extent to which individuals are relatively autonomous versus controlled in performing a task or activity, the Academic Self-Regulation Questionnaire (SRQ-A) was developed by Ryan and Connell (1989). This self-report questionnaire provides statements asking the rationale in engaging specific behaviours that vary along the autonomy-control continuum. By combining the ratings based on the degree of each regulatory style, a summary score called the relative autonomy index (RAI) can then be computed. High RAI scores in educational settings related to more autonomous learning but also predicted positive educational outcomes including competence and enjoyment of school (Miserandino, 1996; Williams & Deci, 1996).

Two other tenets that contribute to autonomous learning are motivational beliefs and self-regulatory strategies. More specifically, positive motivational beliefs such as high self-efficacy and task value and low level of test anxiety can aid in engagement of deep processing and metacognitive regulation (Pintrich, Smith, Garcia, & McKeachie, 1993). Conversely, self-regulatory strategies help students focus on planning, monitoring and controlling their cognition (Pintrich, 2000). In accordance with the active learner's beliefs and cognition, the Motivated Strategies for Learning Questionnaire (MSLQ) was developed (Pintrich et al., 1993) to evaluate self-regulatory skills and to predict academic performance. In relation to this, MSLQ can be used to measure students' motivational beliefs and self-regulated learning in academic context.

A recent local research study (Wang, Liu, Koh, Tan & Ee, 2011) demonstrated students' perceived basic psychological needs, motivational factors and achievement in project work across a three-point period. The context of project work had facilitated the psychological needs of students as well as enhanced students' motivation, learning strategies and achievement in project work. Their findings highlighted the nature of a learning context (i.e. project work) could foster optimal learning in students. However, other social factors such as autonomy-supportive interpersonal behaviours are also important.

Several studies used the MSLQ and Intrinsic Motivation Inventory (McAuley, Duncan, & Tammen, 1989) to measure students' perceived self-regulatory skills and their enjoyment, respectively (Ee, Wang, Koh, Tan, & Liu, 2009; Van Nuland, Dusseldorp, Martens, & Boekaerts, 2010). Their findings revealed that self-regulatory skills (i.e. metacognition) and enjoyment had positive influence on academic performance. Besides the importance of self-regulatory skills, the learning climate may support or thwart students' learning. As proposed by Vallerand, Pelletier and Koestner (2008), there is a need to study the effect of social factors on individuals' needs and motivational orientations in education. Such research is necessary as previous studies reported high self-determined forms of motivation (i.e. intrinsic motivation) versus low levels of extrinsic motivation from undergraduates.

In this study, some of the motivational and self-regulated learning constructs of MSLQ were selected to examine students' beliefs and use of learning strategies in their academic subjects. By understanding their motivational beliefs and learning strategies, the MSLQ can be used to predict students' grades in academic subjects such as mathematics and science.

Autonomy-Supportive Interventions

Su and Reeve's (2011) recent meta-analysis supported the effectiveness of autonomy-supportive intervention in terms of helping people to support the autonomy of others. In these 19 studies, the unit of analysis in most autonomy-supportive trainings is the individual teacher, parent, manager, coach or clinician. In contrast to practice, interventions are often carried out at a macro-level such as at the level of the school, corporation or hospital. Results from these intervention studies indicated that laboratory settings were more effective and relatively consistent than authentic settings such as schools had more diverse results. In this vein, it is necessary to test the effectiveness of teacher's autonomy-supportive instructional behaviours on student motivation and learning.

Based on existing knowledge, limited empirical studies have examined the effects of autonomy-supportive teaching style on student motivation and self-regulated learning in academic contexts. Most school-based intervention studies focused on leisure-time physical activities and physical education. For instance, Chatzisarantis and Hagger (2009) evaluated the utility of school-based intervention to increase student physical activity participation over a 5-week interval of time. Their study employed two conditions: (1) teachers in the treatment condition were trained to adopt an autonomy-supportive teaching style during physical education classes, and (2) teachers in the control condition were instructed to adopt a less autonomy-supportive teaching style. Results indicated that students in the treatment condition exhibited stronger intentions and higher frequency to exercise during leisure time than those in the control condition. According to a recent intervention study in a physical education setting (Tessier, Sarrazin, & Ntoumanis, 2010), teacher interpersonal involvement (i.e. interactions with students) was salient in autonomy-supportive behaviours, thus promoting students' psychological need satisfaction in relatedness, but not in autonomy and competence. This calls for the potential research to examine how students perceived autonomy-supportive teaching behaviours that may influence their needs satisfaction.

In regard to autonomy-supportive intervention in classroom settings, Reeve and colleagues (2004) observed how trained teachers in autonomy-supportive behaviours engage their students' learning in an experimental group versus the untrained teachers in a control group. Their findings demonstrated enhanced engagement in students through classroom observations. Likewise, Furtak and Kunter (2012) conducted an autonomy-supportive intervention through a reform-based science lesson on motion. It was a small-scale research evaluating the effect of procedural and cognitive autonomy-supportive teaching on student motivation and learning. Enhanced motivation and improved achievement test score demonstrated the effect of cognitive autonomy-supportive teaching.

The Present Study

The abovementioned evidence indicated that teachers being autonomy-supportive can better facilitate students' psychological needs and autonomous learning behaviours. However, further research is needed to address the research gaps in previous studies. The purpose of this study is to test the effectiveness of an autonomy-supportive intervention that provide rationale, feedback, choice and acknowledgement of personal conflicts versus a control group whereby the teachers will conduct their lessons per se. The following hypotheses were formulated:

H1 Autonomy-supportive intervention would have a positive effect on perceived autonomy support, basic psychological needs and relative autonomy.

H2 Autonomy-supportive teaching style would have a positive effect on the students' motivational beliefs and learning strategies.

H3 Students with perceived autonomy support would have enhanced effort exertion, intrinsic interest and grades in the academic context.

Method

Participants

Eight local schools from Singapore with 393 secondary school students ($M = 15.3$, $SD = 1.25$, age range from 13 to 17 years) participated in the present study. Of these, 213 were males whereas 175 were females. With a total of 16 classes, each school had two intact classes, namely, one control group and one intervention group. Permission was granted to the researchers to conduct the research in the classroom setting of each school and confidentiality of the participants' responses was assured. The pre- and post-intervention questionnaires were administered in a quiet classroom condition. Note that English was the medium of instruction for all participating schools.

Procedure

This study adopted a 5-week intervention design from Chatzisarantis and Hagger (2009). At pre-intervention, eight teachers in the treatment condition (i.e. intervention) were trained to adopt an autonomy-supportive interpersonal style according to Reeve's (2009) five acts of instructional behaviour: (1) offering choices and options, (2) providing explanatory rationales, (3) giving feedback through informational, non-controlling language, (4) allowing time for self-paced learning to occur as well as (5) acknowledging students' expressions of negative affect.

The training was conducted on four sessions with 3 h per session, over a month by an expert in SDT. The trained teachers implemented their autonomy-supportive teaching style during the 5 weeks of intervention. The control group comprised of the remaining eight teachers whose classes had no implementation of the treatment condition. These teachers were not randomly assigned to experimental conditions to avoid any class disruption in schools. At pre- and post-intervention, data collection was based on the students' responses from the self-report measures in terms of mathematics, science as well as design and technology (D&T) contexts.

Measures

The pre- and post-intervention questionnaires contained all the following self-report measures (except for grades). A 7-point scale format, ranging from 1 (not true at all) to 7 (very true of me), was used for all measures (except grades).

Learning Climate Questionnaire (LCQ)

Perceived teacher's autonomy support was measured using the 15-item LCQ (Williams & Deci, 1996). An example of the items was "I feel that my teacher provides me choices and options". Students responded the questionnaire in accordance with the degree to which they perceived their teacher's autonomy-supportive interpersonal style. The mean scores of students' responses were then computed.

Academic Self-Regulation Questionnaire (SRQ-A)

The Academic Self-Regulation Questionnaire (SRQ-A; Ryan & Connell, 1989) was used to measure the motivational orientations in the context of academic subjects. The adapted fourteen items represented an autonomous motivational style (identified regulation, intrinsic motivation) and a controlling motivational style (external regulation, introjection). An example of the items that measured identified regulation was "because I want to improve in project work", intrinsic motivation was "because project work is fun", for external regulation included "because I'll get into trouble if I don't" and, lastly, introjection was "because I'll feel bad about myself if I didn't". The relative autonomy index (RAI) was computed to evaluate students' autonomous motivation in the academic contents. RAI was calculated by external regulation $\times$ (−2) + introjection $\times$ (−1) + identification + intrinsic motivation $\times$ (2). Higher RAI score indicates a more autonomous motivational orientation of the individual.

Basic Psychological Needs Scale

To measure students' autonomy, competence and relatedness need satisfaction, the Basic Psychological Needs Scale (Liu et al., 2009) was used. It comprised of 12 items, namely, 6 items for autonomy (e.g. "I feel that my teacher provides me with choices and options in school"), 3 items for competence (e.g. "In school, I feel pretty competent") as well as 3 items for relatedness (e.g. "I feel close to my school mates").

Motivated Strategies for Learning Questionnaire

In this study, 28 items were selected from the 44-item MSLQ (Pintrich & De Groot, 1990) to measure junior high students' motivational beliefs and their learning strategies. As the intention of the study was to test if autonomy-supportive teaching style would have a positive effect on the students' motivational beliefs and learning strategies, the selected items included the following six scales: self-efficacy (e.g. "Compared with other students in this class I expect to do well"; five items), task value (e.g. "I prefer class work that is challenging so I can learn new things"; six items), test anxiety (e.g. "I am so nervous during a test that I cannot remember facts I have learned"; four items), rehearsal (e.g. "When I study for a test I practice saying the important facts over and over to myself"; four items), elaboration (e.g. "When reading I try to connect the things I am reading about with what I already know"; five items) and metacognitive self-regulation (e.g. "When I am studying a topic, I try to make everything fit together"; four items).

Intrinsic Motivation Inventory (IMI)

The measurement of the students' learning outcome in terms of enjoyment and effort was represented by "intrinsic value" and "effort exertion". To measure students' intrinsic value (i.e. enjoyment) and effort exertion, two relevant subscales from the IMI (McAuley et al., 1989) were used. Intrinsic value was assessed by the four items from the IMI interest/enjoyment subscale (e.g. "I would describe school as very interesting") and effort was measured by three items (e.g. "I put a lot of effort into my school work").

Grades

At pre- and post-intervention, students' term test grades for mathematics, science as well as D&T were collected.

Data Analysis

Data analyses were performed using IBM SPSS Statistics 20. In the main analysis, three repeated-measures MANOVA and follow-up ANOVAs were conducted, followed by post hoc tests using Bonferroni. A separate ANOVA was conducted for academic grades between groups. As the sample sizes for classes and teachers were considered small, the student participants were used as the unit of analysis and multilevel analysis was not conducted.

Results

Perceived Autonomy Support, Basic Needs and RAI

Repeated-measures MANOVA with perceived autonomy support, basic needs and RAI as dependable variables, time of measurement as the within-subjects factor (within group) and group as the between-subjects factor was performed on the two groups (i.e. control versus intervention). The results revealed significant between-group effect, Wilk's $\Lambda=0.959$, $F(5, 365)=3.10$, $p<0.01$ and $\eta^2=0.04$; within-group effect, Wilk's $\Lambda=0.942$, $F(5, 365)=4.46$, $p<0.01$ and $\eta^2=0.06$; as well as time × group interaction effect, Wilk's $\Lambda=0.946$, $F(5, 365)=4.20$, $p<0.01$ and $\eta^2=0.05$.

Subsequent univariate tests showed significant within-group effects for perceived autonomy support, $F(1, 359)=5.93$, $p<0.05$ and relatedness, $F(1, 359)=2.92$, $p<0.05$; significant interaction effects for perceived autonomy support, $F(1, 359)=14.9$, $p<0.01$ and RAI, $F(1, 359)=8.49$, $p<0.01$; as well as between-group effect for competence, $F(1, 359)=7.41$, $p<0.01$. The ANOVA results demonstrated that students' perceived autonomy support, autonomy, competence and RAI increased from the pre- to post-intervention, as compared to those in the control group. However, the change for autonomy was not significant. Table 12.1 shows the means, standard deviations and effects for the outcome measures in the two groups.

MSLQ Variables

Repeated-measures MANOVA with MSLQ variables (i.e. intrinsic value, self-efficacy, learning strategies, lack of self-regulation and anxiety) as dependable variables, time of measurement as the within-subjects factor (within group) and group as the between-subject factor was performed on the two groups (i.e. control versus intervention). The multivariate results for MSLQ variables showed significant effects of group, Wilk's $\Lambda=0.968$, $F(5, 373)=2.43$, $p<0.05$ and $\eta^2=0.032$, and

Table 12.1 Repeated-measures MANOVA for perceived autonomy support, basic needs and RAI

Variables	Control group				Intervention group				Effect
	Pre		Post		Pre		Post		
	Mean	SD	Mean	SD	Mean	SD	Mean	SD	
Autonomy support	4.55	1.14	4.45	1.05	4.38	1.05	4.75	1.19	*T/*I
Autonomy	4.50	1.03	4.45	0.93	4.52	0.89	4.69	1.01	–
Competence	4.43	1.15	4.36	1.06	4.60	1.04	4.73	1.13	*G
Relatedness	4.90	1.05	4.68	0.94	4.87	1.01	4.84	1.04	*T
RAI	1.58	4.53	0.66	3.77	2.17	4.62	2.40	4.29	*I

*T, time effect; *I, interaction effect; *G, group effect; –, no effect

Table 12.2 Repeated-measures MANOVA for MSLQ subscale measures

| | Control group | | | | Intervention group | | | | |
| | Pre | | Post | | Pre | | Post | | Effect |
Variables	Mean	SD	Mean	SD	Mean	SD	Mean	SD	
Intrinsic values	4.77	1.23	4.74	1.11	4.94	1.07	5.15	1.13	–
Self-efficacy	4.11	1.21	4.19	1.14	4.11	1.09	4.47	1.20	*T/*I
Learning strategies	4.62	1.12	4.64	1.02	4.65	1.07	4.83	1.04	–
Lack of self-regulation	4.28	1.22	4.09	1.12	4.55	1.26	4.23	1.29	*T
Anxiety	4.04	1.20	4.05	1.23	3.92	1.26	4.08	1.33	–

*T, time effect; *I, interaction effect; –, no effect

within-group effects, Wilk's $\Lambda = 0.940$, $F(5, 373) = 4.81$, $p < 0.05$ and $\eta^2 = 0.061$, but no significant effect on time × group interaction.

It was hypothesized that the autonomy-supportive intervention would have a positive effect on the MSLQ variables. Subsequent univariate tests revealed significant within-group effects for self-efficacy, $F(1, 357) = 15.18$, $p < 0.01$ and lack of self-regulation, $F(1, 357) = 8.18$, $p < 0.01$, as well as interaction effect for self-efficacy, $F(1, 357) = 7.81$, $p < 0.01$. The main effect of teacher's autonomy support on self-efficacy was significant such that students scored higher level of self-efficacy for the intervention, compared to those in control condition. The ANOVA results demonstrated that students' intrinsic value, learning strategies and anxiety increased from the pre- to post-intervention, as compared to those in the control group. However, the change for these variables was not significant. Table 12.2 shows the means, standard deviations and effects for the outcome measures in the two groups.

IMI Variables and Grade

Repeated-measures MANOVA with two dependent variables on IMI was conducted. There was a significant multivariate effect of group for effort and interest, Wilk's $\Lambda = 0.960$, $F(2, 370) = 7.70$, $p < 0.01$ and $\eta^2 = 0.04$. However, the within-group differences and time × group interaction had no significant effect. Subsequent univariate ANOVA also yielded no significant effects.

It was hypothesized that the autonomy-supportive intervention would have a positive effect on perceived effort, interest and grades. A mixed-method ANOVA results conducted for grades showed that students in the intervention group scored higher ($F(1, 280) = 13.08$, $p < 0.01$, $\eta^2 = 0.05$) than those in control group. In addition, there was a significant interaction effect, $F(1, 280) = 4.76$, $p < 0.05$ and $\eta^2 = 0.02$. However, there was no significant effect for within-group grades. Table 12.3 shows the descriptive statistics and effects for the outcome measures in the two groups.

Table 12.3 Repeated-measures MANOVA for IMI subscale measures/mixed-method ANOVA for grades

	Control group				Intervention group				
	Pre		Post		Pre		Post		Effect
Variables	Mean	SD	Mean	SD	Mean	SD	Mean	SD	
Effort exertion	4.81	0.98	4.69	0.91	4.93	1.09	4.92	1.08	–
Intrinsic interest	4.61	1.28	4.55	1.15	5.01	1.21	4.99	1.23	–
Grade	61.05	16.99	57.98	20.72	65.46	13.81	66.62	16.69	*G/*I

*I, interaction effect; *G, group effect; –, no effect

Discussion

The purpose of the present study was to assess the effectiveness of the autonomy support intervention in enhancing perceived autonomy support, students' motivational orientations and learning strategies. This study also evaluates the perceptions of students' needs of satisfaction, effort and interest in studying mathematics, science and D&T. In line with the research studies that emphasized the centrality of autonomy support for students' higher levels of psychological needs (Reinboth & Duda's, 2006; Vansteenkiste et al., 2009), the 5-week intervention had significant positive effects on students' perceived autonomy support, competence and relatedness. In addition, there were significant interaction effects on students' perceived autonomy support, RAI, self-efficacy and achievement. Results are discussed in light of the three aforementioned hypotheses.

Changes in Students' Perceived Autonomy Support, Needs and Relative Autonomy

The autonomy-supportive intervention was successfully implemented, as indicated by the significant increase in perceived autonomy support. Despite the positive change in perceived autonomy support, this may not be sufficient to propel students' autonomy emanating from being in a classroom setting, as indicated by the insignificant change in perceived autonomy. When students feel that doing schoolwork is due to some external coercion, they do not experience the need for autonomy (Urdan & Schoenfelder, 2006), suggesting that an internal perceived locus of causality is more relevant to the need of autonomy towards academic learning.

On the other hand, when students perceive the need for competence, they will experience efficacy upon completion of a learning task (Sierens et al., 2009). This corresponds with the increased level of students' reported competence in this intervention study. Autonomy-supportive teachers provide structure that will provide competence-relevant feedback and express confidence in students' abilities towards completion of tasks (Reeve et al., 2004). Research on SDT applied in educational settings supported that autonomy-supportive teachers facilitate students' need for competence and nurture students' need for relatedness, which are beneficial in both academic and development domains. The significant increased level of students' relatedness suggests that students could relate to teacher's effortful engagement. When teachers support students' autonomy in classroom learning, such engagement provided students with information about teachers' commitment to students' well-being (McHugh, Horner, Colditz, & Wallace, 2013). These perceptions may relate to students' fulfilment of need for relatedness.

Previous studies (Deci et al., 1994; Williams & Deci, 1996) advocated that autonomy demonstrated increased autonomous learning and greater relative autonomy. Within the SDT framework, the positive impact of autonomy support is when children self-regulated in an integrated manner such that they acted in accord to their feelings and thoughts of the task (Joussemet, Koestner, Lekes, & Houlfort, 2004). This explains the overall significant effect of the autonomy-supportive teaching approach on students' relative autonomy. This might be explained by the students' perceived autonomy support from their teachers, resulting in students being more autonomous and self-regulated in their learning.

Changes in Student Motivational-Cognitive Measures

Regarding the MSLQ variables, the results partially confirmed the second hypothesis, as shown by the significant positive and interaction effects of self-efficacy. On the contrary, there was no significant effect on students' intrinsic value, use of learning strategies and anxiety between the autonomy-supportive teaching approach and control condition. One possible explanation could be due to the routine school tasks. The perception of task value is similar to that of intrinsic value which assesses students' perceptions that the content of their classes is interesting, relevant and important to them (Anderman, 2003). Likewise, when the task is perceived as being closely connected to individuals' values and interests, they portray stronger feelings of autonomy (Katz & Assor, 2007). However, only one significant interaction effect between the teaching approach and students' self-efficacy was found. This suggests that autonomy-supportive teachers could affect changes in students' self-efficacy beliefs in terms of enhancing their self-efficacy with regard to classroom activities and subjects (Wigfield, Guthrie, Tonks, & Perencevich, 2004). Previous research by Williams et al. (2004) proposed that autonomy may have an indirect effect on outcomes through self-efficacy beliefs. However, further research is needed to test this relationship.

Research studies (Sierens et al., 2009; Vansteenkiste et al., 2009) have shown that autonomy-supportive teaching style was associated with students' management of their classroom learning and self-regulated learning strategies. In contrast to this study, the insignificant effect on the learning strategies variable suggests that students in both control and intervention groups could control and apply effective learning strategies. Such strategies can be constructed from experience or facilitate by teachers and peers (Paris & Newman, 1990). Consequently, the significant decrease for lack of self-regulation between groups demonstrated an improvement in self-regulation of students from the intervention group. Recent empirical findings (Jang, Reeve, & Deci, 2010; Soenens et al., 2012) confirmed that students became more self-regulated learners when the learning climate was autonomy-supportive. Nonetheless, students still experienced anxiety in both control and intervention groups. As stated by Pajares (2005), students can feel a fairly good sense of their confidence as they contemplate an action. Although negative feelings provide cues that something is amiss, one may not be aware of such case. Hence, negative feelings such as anxiety still exist in students and teachers can help to decrease anxiety by increasing a student's attention to the task at hand (Britner & Pajares, 2006). When a mind is well-focused on the dynamics of the task, the shift of focus to apprehension can be avoided, hence reducing the level of anxiety.

Changes in Student Effort, Interest and Achievement

An important finding arose in this study is that the autonomy-supportive teaching style did not affect students' effort regulation and intrinsic interest in their school-work. This phenomenon confirms the view advocated by Legault et al. (2006) in which students are amotivated in schools based on their effort beliefs, value placed on academic tasks and characteristics of the academic tasks. Alternatively, by fostering relevance of school tasks to students, autonomy-supportive teachers can help students to become autonomous and discover how extrinsically motivated academic tasks can become relevant to their interests (Assor, Kaplan, & Roth, 2002). In addition, students' enjoyment and valuing of their academic subject may be related to their perceived needs satisfaction (Liu et al., 2009). Findings reported in this study suggest that the lack of enjoyment (i.e. intrinsic interest) and effort in the school work could relate to students' perceived autonomy. Next, the significant interaction effect between the teaching approach and grades might be explained by students who endorsed autonomy support at the beginning of the 5-week benefit most from the intervention. This is consistent with previous research findings (Blackwell, Trzesniewski, & Dweck, 2007).

Overall, there was a significant time × group interaction effect for each variable – perceived autonomy support, RAI, self-efficacy and grades. Findings of this study indicated that the intervention was successful in terms of significant changes in the desired learning outcomes. Specifically, individuals in the intervention group were more autonomous and self-efficacious as well as more autonomy support than individuals in the control group. Subsequently, the intervention group had significantly improved students' grades of academic subjects. Evidently, the findings of this study suggest that feeling of self-efficacy is facilitated by autonomy-supportive contexts. Nevertheless, there are still implications and limitations to be considered when implementing future intervention studies.

Practical Implications

This present study examined the effects within groups and between groups. The rationale of within-group effects is that students' perceptions of the classroom climate are key factors in predicting the students' motivation and learning outcomes (Jang et al., 2010). Hence, the students' perceptions of their teachers' interpersonal behaviours and their own learning behaviours are important variables. By examining the between-group effects, the emphasis is on classroom climate and teacher's interpersonal behaviour. The findings of between-group effects can be considered as an important socio-contextual contribution which adds on to the current literature of autonomy support.

As the control groups comprised of students from eight schools, the interpretation of the learning context may be divergent. Previous studies have shown that students in the same grade will often interpret classroom goal structures or teacher's expectations in divergent way (Urdan & Midgley, 2003). It should be noted that students may interpret the challenges or requirements of specific contexts to be more important than actual learning context. This implies that students' learning in the classroom environment may be more influenced by a variety of factors (interpersonal, emotional and cultural) than the cognitive factors associated with classroom learning. This conjecture seems to be in line with an earlier finding by effectiveness of teacher's behaviour (Den Brok, Brekelmans, & Wubbels, 2004), suggesting that certain teacher's behaviour might have different effects in one subject sample or one outcome measure as compared to another. In addition, there was a strong association between proximity and students' subject-specific motivation but no association with students' cognitive test scores was found.

Based on current findings, autonomy-supportive training programme is likely to influence teachers' teaching style. However, it is important to consider teachers' beliefs before the training, as teachers' beliefs may affect their autonomy-supportive teaching styles. Understanding teachers' beliefs about the utility of autonomy-supportive teaching may predict how effective and how easy-to-implement autonomy-supportive teaching styles.

Limitations and Conclusion

There are several limitations in the present study. First, the absence of the effects for students' reported autonomy, intrinsic values and effort may reflect the constraints of the nature and choice of school tasks. The task and learning context might lack of motivational components such that students did not endorse interest and enjoyment. Furthermore, sense of autonomy may be enhanced through choice of tasks and use of neutral language during teacher-student communication. For future study, adequate measures of the learning context may be included to overcome this limitation.

Another limitation is the lack of random assignment of teachers to experimental conditions. It is difficult to employ random assignment due to period of implementation and school contextual issues that could not controlled for in this study. Future intervention research should consider random assignment as the results are likely to be much more interpretable.

Finally, the present study did not include any classroom observation to look out for treatment fidelity during the intervention period. It is noted, however, that the absence of classroom observation is to minimize any elemental intrusion into classrooms. Still, future studies may utilize the classroom observations to examine the consistency of autonomy-supportive teaching style.

In conclusion, results of this study herein suggest the important role of autonomy-supportive teachers in establishing the positive interpersonal climate to increase self-determination in schools. Despite the extensive SDT-based research, the present study expands upon previous classroom-based interventions and sheds light on the inclusion of MSLQ-based variables. The current findings also contribute to the understanding of autonomy-supportive teaching style and its effects on student motivational-cognitive learning. Besides the importance of teaching style, further research may look at other social factors such as classroom structure and culture in similar academic contexts.

References

Anderman, L. H. (2003). Academic and social perceptions as predictors of change in middle school students' sense of school belonging. *The Journal of Experimental Education, 72*(1), 5–22.

Assor, A., Kaplan, H., & Roth, G. (2002). Choice is good, but relevance is excellent: Autonomy-enhancing and suppressing teacher behaviours predicting students' engagement in schoolwork. *British Journal of Educational Psychology, 72*(2), 261–278.

Blackwell, L. S., Trzesniewski, K. H., & Dweck, C. S. (2007). Implicit theories of intelligence predict achievement across an adolescent transition: A longitudinal study and an intervention. *Child Development, 78*(1), 246–263.

Britner, S. L., & Pajares, F. (2006). Sources of science self-efficacy beliefs of middle school students. *Journal of Research in Science Teaching, 43*(5), 485–499.

Brooks, C. F., & Young, S. L. (2011). Are choice-making opportunities needed in the classroom? Using self-determination theory to consider student motivation and learner empowerment. *International Journal of Teaching & Learning in Higher Education, 23*(1), 48–59.

Chatzisarantis, N. L. D., & Hagger, M. S. (2009). Effects of an intervention based on self-determination theory on self-reported leisure-time physical activity participation. *Psychology & Health, 24*(1), 29–48.

De Naeghel, J., Van Keer, H., Vansteenkiste, M., & Rosseel, Y. (2012). The relation between elementary students' recreational and academic reading motivation, reading frequency, engagement, and comprehension: A self-determination theory perspective. *Journal of Educational Psychology, 104*(4), 1006–1021.

Deci, E. L., Eghrari, H., Patrick, B. C., & Leone, D. R. (1994). Facilitating internalization: The self-determination theory perspective. *Journal of Personality, 62*(1), 118–142.

Deci, E. L., & Ryan, R. M. (1985). *Intrinsic motivation and self-determination in human behavior.* New York: Plenum.

Deci, E. L., & Ryan, R. M. (2008). Facilitating optimal motivation and psychological well-being across life's domains. *Canadian Psychology, 49*(1), 14–23.

Den Brok, P., Brekelmans, M., & Wubbels, T. (2004). Interpersonal teacher behaviour and student outcomes, school effectiveness and school improvement. *An International Journal of Research, Policy & Practice, 15*(3–4), 407–442.

Diseth, Å., Danielsen, A. G., & Samdal, O. (2012). A path analysis of basic need support, self-efficacy, achievement goals, life satisfaction and academic achievement level among secondary school students. *Educational Psychology, 32*(3), 335–354.

Ee, J., Wang, C. K. J., Koh, C., Tan, O. S., & Liu, W. C. (2009). Goal orientations and metacognitive skills of normal technical and normal academic students on project work. *Asia Pacific Education Review, 10*(3), 337–344.

Furtak, E. M., & Kunter, M. (2012). Effects of autonomy-supportive teaching on student learning and motivation. *The Journal of Experimental Education, 80*(3), 284–316.

Gagne, M. (2003). Autonomy support and need satisfaction in the motivation and well-being of gymnasts. *Journal of Applied Sport Psychology, 15*(4), 372–390.

Jang, H., Kim, E. J., & Reeve, J. (2012). Longitudinal test of self-determination theory's motivation mediation model in a naturally occurring classroom context. *Journal of Educational Psychology, 104*(4), 1175–1188.

Jang, H., Reeve, J., & Deci, E. L. (2010). Engaging students in learning activities: It is not autonomy support or structure but autonomy support and structure. *Journal of Educational Psychology, 102*(3), 588–600.

Joussemet, M., Koestner, R., Lekes, N., & Houlfort, N. (2004). Introducing uninteresting tasks to children: A comparison of the effects of rewards and autonomy support. *Journal of Personality, 72*(1), 139–166.

Katz, I., & Assor, A. (2007). When choice motivates and when it does not. *Educational Psychology Review, 19*(4), 429–442.

Legault, L., Green-Demers, L., & Pelletier, L. (2006). Why do high school students lack motivation in the classroom? Toward an understanding of academic amotivation and the role of social support. *Journal of Educational Psychology, 98*(3), 567–582.

Levesque, C., Zuehlke, A. N., Stanek, L. R., & Ryan, R. M. (2004). Autonomy and competence in German and American university students: A comparative study based on self-determination theory. *Journal of Educational Psychology, 96*(1), 68–84.

Liu, W. C., Wang, C. K. J., Tan, O. S., Koh, C., & Ee, J. (2009). A self-determination approach to understanding students' motivation in project work. *Learning & Individual Differences, 19*(1), 139–145.

McAuley, E., Duncan, T., & Tammen, V. V. (1989). Psychometric properties of the intrinsic motivation inventory in a competitive sport setting: A confirmatory factor analysis. *Research Quarterly for Exercise & Sport, 60*(1), 48–58.

McHugh, R. M., Horner, C. G., Colditz, J. B., & Wallace, T. L. (2013). Bridges and barriers: Adolescent perceptions of student-teacher relationships. *Urban Education, 48*(1), 9–43.

Miserandino, M. (1996). Children who do well in school: Individual differences in perceived competence and autonomy in above-average children. *Journal of Educational Psychology, 88*(2), 203–214.

Otoshi, J., & Heffernan, N. (2011). An analysis of a hypothesized model of EFL students' motivation based on self-determination theory. *Asian EFL Journal, 13*(3), 66–86.

Pajares, F. (2005). Self-efficacy beliefs during adolescence: Implications for teachers and parents. In F. Pajares & T. Urdan (Eds.), *Adolescence & education: Self-efficacy beliefs of adolescents* (Vol. 5, pp. 339–366). Greenwich, CT: Information Age Publishing.

Paris, S. G., & Newman, R. S. (1990). Development aspects of self-regulated learning. *Educational Psychologist, 25*(1), 87–102.

Pintrich, P. R. (2000). The role of goal orientation in self-regulated learning. In M. Boekaerts, P. R. Pintrich, & M. Zeidner (Eds.), *Handbook of self-regulation: Theory, research, and applications* (pp. 451–502). San Diego, CA: Academic Press.

Pintrich, P. R., & De Groot, E. V. (1990). Motivational and self-regulated learning components of classroom academic performance. *Journal of Educational Psychology, 82*(1), 33–40.

Pintrich, P. R., Smith, D., Garcia, T., & McKeachie, W. J. (1993). Reliability and predictive validity of the motivated strategies for learning questionnaire (MSLQ). *Educational & Psychological Measurement, 53*(3), 801–813.

Reeve, J. (2009). Why teachers adopt a controlling motivating style toward students and how they can become more autonomy supportive. *Educational Psychologist, 44*(3), 159–175.

Reeve, J. (2013). How students create motivationally supportive learning environments for themselves: The concept of agentic engagement. *Journal of Educational Psychology, 105*(3), 579–595.

Reeve, J., Deci, E. L., & Ryan, R. M. (2004). Self-determination theory: A dialectical framework for understanding socio-cultural influences on student motivation. In M. McInerney & E. Shawn Van (Eds.), *Big theories revisited: Research on sociocultural influences on motivation and learning* (Vol. 4, pp. 31–60). Greenwich, CT: Information Age Publishing.

Reinboth, M., & Duda, J. L. (2006). Perceived motivational climate, need satisfaction and indices of well-being in team sports: A longitudinal perspective. *Psychology of Sport & Exercise, 7*(3), 269–286.

Ryan, R. M., & Connell, J. P. (1989). Perceived locus of causality and internalization: Examining reasons for acting in two domains. *Journal of Personality & Social Psychology, 57*(5), 749–761.

Sierens, E., Vansteenkiste, M., Goossens, L., Soenens, B., & Dochy, F. (2009). The synergistic relationship of perceived autonomy support and structure in the prediction of self-regulated learning. *British Journal of Educational Psychology, 79*(1), 57–68.

Soenens, B., Sierens, E., Vansteenkiste, M., Dochy, F., & Goossens, L. (2012). Psychologically controlling teaching: Examining outcomes, antecedents, and mediators. *Journal of Educational Psychology, 104*(1), 108–120.

Soenens, B., Vansteenkiste, M., Lens, W., Luyckx, K., Goossens, L., Beyers, W., et al. (2007). Conceptualizing parental autonomy support: Adolescent perceptions of promotion of independence versus promotion of volitional functioning. *Developmental Psychology, 43*(3), 633–646.

Su, Y., & Reeve, J. (2011). A meta-analysis of the effectiveness of intervention programs designed to support autonomy. *Educational Psychology Review, 23*(1), 159–188.

Tessier, D., Sarrazin, P., & Ntoumanis, N. (2010). The effect of an intervention to improve newly qualified teachers' interpersonal style, students' motivation and psychological need satisfaction in sport-based physical education. *Contemporary Educational Psychology, 35*(4), 242–253.

Urdan, T., & Midgley, C. (2003). Changes in the perceived classroom goal structure and pattern of adaptive learning during early adolescence. *Contemporary Educational Psychology, 28*(4), 524–551.

Urdan, T., & Schoenfelder, E. (2006). Classroom effects on student motivation: Goal structures, social relationships, and competence beliefs. *Journal of School Psychology, 44*(5), 331–349.

Vallerand, R. J., Pelletier, L. G., & Koestner, R. (2008). Reflections on self-determination theory. *Canadian Psychology, 49*(3), 257–262.

Van Nuland, H. J. C., Dusseldorp, E., Martens, R. L., & Boekaerts, M. (2010). Exploring the motivation jungle: Predicting performance on a novel task by investigating constructs from different motivation perspectives in tandem. *International Journal of Psychology, 45*(4), 250–259.

Vansteenkiste, M., Sierens, E., Soenens, B., Luyckx, K., & Lens, W. (2009). Motivational profiles from a self-determination perspective: The quality of motivation matters. *Journal of Educational Psychology, 101*(3), 671–688.

Wang, C. K. J., Liu, W. C., Koh, C., Tan, O. S., & Ee, J. (2011). A motivational analysis of project work in Singapore using self-determination theory. *The International Journal of Research & Review, 7*(1), 45–66.

Wigfield, A., Guthrie, J. T., Tonks, S., & Perencevich, K. C. (2004). Children's motivation for reading: Domain specificity and instructional influences. *The Journal of Educational Research, 97*(6), 299–309.

Williams, G. C., & Deci, E. L. (1996). Internalization of biopsychosocial values by medical students: A test of self-determination theory. *Journal of Personality & Social Psychology, 70*(4), 767–779.

Williams, G. C., McGregor, H. A., Zeldman, A., Freedman, Z. R., & Deci, E. L. (2004). Testing a self-determination theory process model for promoting glycemic control through diabetes self-management. *Health Psychology, 23*(1), 58–66.

Chapter 13
Translating Motivational Theory into Application of Information Technology in the Classroom

Caroline Koh

Introduction

In his book, The Road Ahead, Bill Gates (1996, p. 234) had this to say about the future of education:

> I can imagine a middle school science teacher a decade or so from now working on a lecture...When she wants to show a still picture or a video...the net will allow her to select from a comprehensive catalog of images...The teacher will have organized the links to servers on the global network in advance, and she'll make the list of links available to her students...

Generally, what he predicted in 1996 has materialized two decades later. In schools across Europe, North America and many parts of Australasia, the computer commonly features as standard classroom equipment. Teachers, digital natives and migrants alike, are downloading 'apps' aplenty and using them as teaching and learning tools. They are using social media platforms such as Facebook and Twitter to communicate with their students within and outside school walls. Students are whipping out their smart phones and i-gadgets to make records of their observations and findings during field trips and are relaying them within seconds to their teachers. Mr Gates would be pleased with the extent to which technology has permeated social and educational arenas.

Many studies have shown that the positive outcomes of ICT application in education are derived from an enhancement of student motivation on their assigned tasks. This is particularly true of Web 2.0 technology, defined as 'a new generation of web software that embraces the power of user participation, collective intelligence, and knowledge sharing' (Deng & Yuen, 2012, p. 48; Brown & Adler, 2008; Harrison &

C. Koh (✉)
National Institute of Education, Nanyang Technological University, Singapore, Singapore
e-mail: caroline.koh@nie.edu.sg

© Springer Science+Business Media Singapore 2016
W.C. Liu et al. (eds.), *Building Autonomous Learners*,
DOI 10.1007/978-981-287-630-0_13

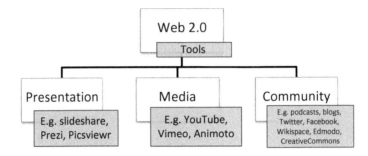

Fig. 13.1 Web 2.0 tools and their usage

Barthel, 2009; McLoughlin & Lee, 2007; O'Reilly, 2007). In essence, Web 2.0 tools allow users to create and edit online content, to collaborate with others in this endeavor and to share what they have produced with the wider web community. Figure 13.1 shows the types of Web 2.0 tools that are most relevant in the educational context and their applications in teaching and learning.

Generally, these tools can be classified into three broad categories: (i) presentation tools allow the production, editing and sharing of presentations, (ii) media tools allow the production, editing and/or sharing of online audio and video recordings, and (iii) community tools allow communication, collaboration and sharing amongst users. Since Web 2.0 tools are specifically designed to promote interaction between web users and sites, there is considerable overlap between the three categories. For example, a podcast serves the dual purpose of a media and social networking tool. Thus, in so doing, Web 2.0 has the effect of motivating students towards higher engagement and participation in online activities (Deng & Yuen, 2012).

However, the use of ICT has spread so fast globally that formal research on its effectiveness has had a hard time playing catch-up. Many authors have explored the use of specific Web 2.0 tools in education, but there is scant information on the collective influence of these applications on student engagement and motivation. A review of the literature reveals that the use of ICT in education is not without any challenges, but when used appropriately, the benefits derived far outweigh the drawbacks.

The aim of this chapter is thus to provide an overview of the application of the more common ICT tools in education. This is followed by an exploration of the extent to which these have achieved their purpose in motivating students towards autonomous learning and the theoretical constructs underlying these effects.

Theoretical Constructs

Self Determination

Recent trends in motivational research in education have focused on factors influencing learner motivation. Alm (2006) argues that internet-based learning environments are able to motivate learners because they have the potential to fulfill the latter's needs. She proposes that the Self-Determination Theory/SDT (Deci & Ryan, 1985) provides a relevant theoretical framework to explain how ICT creates a motivating learning environment for learners by supporting the three basic psychological needs of relatedness (the sense of connectedness and belonging to a group), competence (the sense of self-efficacy and high effectiveness) and autonomy (sense of ownership and control over one's behavior).

The SDT explains how behavior, such as adoption and usage of new technologies and Web 2.0 tools, is initiated, moderated, modified and sustained with the aim of achieving positive growth and development of a coherent sense of identity. The theory posits that the degree of self-determined motivation increases with a heightened perception of basic needs satisfaction. Motivational regulation thus ranges across a spectrum, with the total lack of motivation (amotivation) at one end, and at the other, intrinsic motivation (self-initiated and arising from personal satisfaction). Between the two extremes is a range of motivational regulations, deemed extrinsic, that describe an activity undertaken as a means to an end. In SDT, extrinsic motivation is defined as a multidimensional construct, comprising different types of external motivational regulations, each reflecting a different causal attribution for the chosen behaviour. They are termed external, introjected and identified forms of regulation. External regulation refers to behaviour that is controlled by external means, such as rewards, penalties/punishments or external authority. Introjected regulation refers to behaviour that is internally controlled, self-imposed, and ego-protective, such as acting out of guilt or in an attempt to avoid guilt, and is characterised by feelings of internalised pressure, such as 'I ought to ...'. For identified regulation, the behaviour is self-determined and according to what one values as important. It is characterised by feelings of 'want' rather than 'ought'. The motivational regulations thus form a continuum that characterises the degree of internalisation of the behaviour.

Self-Regulation

Self-regulated learners are active participants in their own learning (Zimmerman, 1990). They show a high degree of self-determined motivation, are known to adopt a metacognitive approach to learning, and demonstrate a cycle of disciplined and effective learner behaviors. The metacognitive approach involves knowledge of one's cognitive processes and the ability to control and make adjustments to these in order to attain specific goals. The metacognitive and behavioral processes interplay to optimize learning through a cycle of planning, implementation and evaluation of learning strategies and procedures. E-learning systems should thus facilitate learners' self-regulation by incorporating scaffolding features and functionalities that prompt users to apply metacognitive and self-regulation processes.

Using Technology to Enhance Autonomous Learning

Through the years, several authors have attempted to define autonomous learning. Holec (1981) viewed autonomy in learning as taking charge and being responsible for all decisions with regards to one's learning own learning – a view that seems to absolve the teacher of all interference with the student. Dam (2000) agrees with the notion that the learner should be responsible for his/her own learning, but emphasizes the role played by the teacher in creating a supportive environment that facilitates autonomy, which Little (1991, p. 4) defines as a capacity "…for detachment, critical reflection, decision making, and independent action". Gonzalez and St. Louis (2008) concur that autonomous learning involves both the teacher and the learner working together towards greater awareness of the latter's academic ability, learning preferences and needs such that the appropriate plans and learning approaches could be devised. The aim therefore is to nurture autonomous learners with "a desire to learn…a positive self-image along with metacognitive capacity and the ability to handle change and to negotiate with others" (Gonzalez & St. Louis, p. 28; Breen & Mann, 1997).

A review of the literature shows that a number of Web 2.0 tools have the potential to promote learner motivation and autonomous learning by offering learning platforms that support basic psychological needs satisfaction and by facilitating self-regulatory learning processes. The ensuing sections explore how this is achieved in three Web 2.0 applications, namely weblogs, e-portfolios and YouTube. This is followed by a discussion on how the concerted use of these and other Web 2.0 tools in computer assisted learning programs may promote autonomous learning.

Blogs

A blog is a personal website consisting of a series of entries that may include the user's comments, daily entries, video and audio recordings, as well as other readers' comments and feedback. A number of authors have reported the educational benefits of well-designed blogs (Clyde, 2005; Ellison & Wu, 2008; Goktas, 2009; Holzberg, 2003; Wassell & Crouch, 2008). There has been an upward trend in the use of blogs as teaching and learning tools. The growing pervasiveness of blogs was indicated in a study involving 197 undergraduate students in the UK, where 51 % of those surveyed perceived that blogs/wikis could be useful in promoting learning and about 30 % claimed to have used blogs or wikis (Sandars & Morrison, 2007). For instance, Goktas and Demirel (2012), in a study involving 339 pre-service teachers, found that blogs helped the prospective teacher by familiarizing them with new technologies, improving their perceptions of ICT, promoting their motivation to use ICT and in so doing, their knowledge and competencies in teaching and in ICT, as well as the provision of opportunities to apply and practice what they have learned.

Poling (2005) identified the various types of blogs and their respective uses. Individual blogs, for instance, serve as personal on-line journals enabling users to record and publish their daily reflections. They present opportunities for students to carry out self-reflection and evaluation of their own learning, and to invite peers and tutors to provide comments and feedback on their posts. Classroom blogging, whereby students set up group blogs and participate in the group discussions and activities, have the added advantage of promoting collaboration and communication amongst group members within the same class. The collaborative blogs can be further extended to allow between-class interactions, whereby students from a particular class are given the opportunity to work with those from another class within the same school or in a different school.

The use of blogs in teaching and learning English as a Foreign Language (EFL) has been investigated in a number of studies (Pinkman, 2005; Ward, 2004; Zhang, 2009). In one such study, the researchers explored the use of blogs as collaborative tools for EFL students at the University of Chile (Trajtemberg & Yiakoumetti, 2011). This research was initiated as an attempt to boost student motivation in learning English, in a context where proficiency in the language was generally poor. The investigators believed that since the blogs were visible in the public domain, they provided the necessary scaffolding to facilitate learning, since the students were able to view other bloggers' posts and to learn from them. In addition, the blogs provided a collaborative learning environment, while offering sufficient autonomy for the learner to experience improved confidence and motivation in mastering the language. For instance, participation and interaction in the blogs, while purely voluntary, were fuelled by the teacher's feedback which served to engage the students in discussion. Thus, blogs were likely to promote student motivation as they satisfied the basic psychological needs for autonomy, relatedness and competence necessary for autonomous motivation, in accordance with the Self-Determination Theory.

With the emergence of Web 2.0 applications, there has been a growing need to provide a "scaffolding structure that encourages student motivation and facilitates advanced thinking with integration of enriched learning resources" (March, 2007, p. 2). The solution may reside in updated versions of WebQuests, originally conceived as a scaffold for guiding novice users in decision making and experiences when navigating through the expansive World Wide Web. March (2007) provided a refined definition of the WebQuest as "a scaffolded learning structure that uses links to essential resources on the World Wide Web and an authentic task to motivate students' investigation of an open-ended question, development of individual expertise, and participation in a group process that transforms newly acquired information into a more sophisticated understanding" (p. 2). He further claimed that Web 2.0 technologies embedded in WebQuests hold the potential to motivate students intrinsically by promoting satisfaction of the three psychological needs of autonomy, relatedness and competence as professed by the Self-Determination Theory (Deci & Ryan, 1985). For instance, WebQuests may provide opportunities for satisfaction of competence by chunking learning and measuring student attainment through the learning process, enable learners to experience relatedness through collaborative group tasks, promote autonomy support by allowing students to select their own roles and/or offer students a range of options to choose from.

In support of the above claims, a study by Mason (2006) on the impact of learning technologies on adult continuing education showed that some of the adult learners who were initially averse to blogging, eventually became 'converts' and continued using blogs in their professional domains. Knowles (1990) established that adult learners subscribe to a self-directed, problem-based approach to learning, use their own life and work experiences as prior knowledge, and value the social aspect of learning. Wenger (1998) viewed adults as belonging to 'communities of practice', whereby individuals come together as a group and learn through interaction with one another. In this respect, blogs seem to provide a framework that is closely aligned to the learning needs of adults. They provide platforms for setting up learning communities, where members benefit from a sense of relatedness. In addition, blogs provide the avenue for autonomy in terms of flexible learning, self-expression and choice. It is not surprising therefore, that even the so-called 'digital migrants' have taken the plunge into blogging. One adult learner thus commented: "I didn't like blogging, but was interested to do it and see what people put in their logs" (Mason, 2006, p. 127).

E-portfolios

In its electronic form, the portfolio is a virtual repository enabling information to be stored in a variety of formats such as word documents, presentation slides, media files and even blogs. E-portfolios thus provide their users with numerous benefits, namely the provision of a personalized learning environment and opportunities for social networking within Web 2.0 technologies (Gerbic, Lewis, & Northover, 2009).

Abrami and his co-workers (2009) attributed the growing interest in e-portfolios to their ability to engage learners, especially those whose competencies are best reflected through authentic tasks. E-portfolios may scaffold learning by offering a repertoire of tools that facilitate self-regulation processes, such as reflective practice, knowledge consolidation, task refinement as well as communication with tutors and peers. They provide students with an expansible 'space' for safekeeping and organizing their resources, as well as a platform for sharing and discussion that is accessible from anywhere and at any time. Students thus have the opportunity to develop self-regulation in their learning, leading to an enhancement of their self-efficacy (Abrami & Barrett, 2005).

A number of researchers have focused their investigations on student motivation in the adoption and usage of e-portfolios. They found, for instance, that students were more motivated towards the use of web-based portfolios than paper-based portfolios (Driessen, Muijtjens, van Tartwijk, & van der Vleuten, 2007). The implementation of the e-portfolio assessment system was found to have a greater influence on low motivation students, in terms of the effect on their self-evaluated learning and perceived usefulness of the system (Chang, 2009). In their study on the possible determinants of individual's adoption of e-portfolios, M. Y. Chen, F. Chang,

C. C. Chen, M. J. Huang, and J. W. Chen (2012) found that perceived usefulness of the e-portfolio had a significant and more positive effect on user's attitude towards usage than perceived ease of use. In addition, their findings also revealed that attitude towards e-portfolio adoption had the most significant and highest direct influence on learner's intent to use the e-portfolio.

In line with the above findings, a study conducted by McLeod and Vasinda (2009) explored the perspectives of students, teachers and parents on the use of e-portfolios as a tool to promote elementary pupils' learning and to communicate with parents. When interviewed, the majority of the student participants enjoyed setting up and using their digital portfolio, qualifying their views with statements such as "...I worked really hard on it and it was fun to do" and "...it is something that you need to do good because it will be shown to the whole world and the whole world will see it when you get done" (p. 35). This showed that the elementary school pupils were intrinsically motivated and understood the value of their work and the need to do it well. Focus group interviews of some of the pupils indicated that one of the possible reasons for their enjoyment of the experience was the provision of choice at a personal level (they could choose whatever artifacts they wanted to include) and within the e-portfolio process (they could adopt their own approaches to constructing the e-portfolios). Although McLeod and Vasinda's article did not focus specifically on any motivational theories, their findings seem to corroborate with the tenets of the SDT, on the premise that motivation is enhanced when individuals perceive the provision of autonomy support when carrying out an assigned task. On their part, the teachers were satisfied with their pupils' work with the e-portfolio and with the fact that their pupils took their work seriously. Parents, when given access to the website on which their children's e-portfolio entries were posted, enjoyed the rare opportunity of getting a glimpse of classroom life and being part of their children's learning. Thus, McLeod and Vasinda's study showed that the use of the e-portfolio in elementary school was generally well received. However, is this observation equally applicable to adult learning?

In Mason's (2006) study on the effect of new learning technologies on adult learners, the graduate student participants found the use of the e-portfolio in their final course assessment a challenge, although they understood its purpose and value in their learning. This indicates that although adult learners may not be intrinsically motivated in using an e-portfolio approach to assessment, they demonstrated a relatively high degree of self-determination in their use of the new technology since they could appreciate its importance. This suggests, in SDT terms, that the adult learners were likely to show identified regulation in their behavioural regulation (Deci & Ryan, 1985). Mason (2006) viewed the e-portfolio as of particular value to adult learners, since it is 'a form of multimedia, ever-developing CV' and thus 'has obvious benefits for the pursuit of lifelong learning' in that it 'builds independence and learning-to-learn skills' (p. 129), thus incorporating elements of self-regulation. Furthermore, the e-portfolio has the added advantage over its hard-copy counterpart in that it is expansible and allows ease of collection, organization and selection, thus facilitating fast retrieval for the purpose of assignments or job interviews.

YouTube

YouTube is an open access Web 2.0 application which allows users to view and share videos. It is one of the fastest-growing and one of the most accessed Internet sites, with more than one billion unique users visiting the site on a monthly basis (YouTube, n.d.). YouTube is particularly attractive as it allows users to interact socially through its community tools. Thus, aside video sharing and viewing, users are able to rate videos by indicating their likes/dislikes, and by posting comments. As Duffy (2008) suggested, YouTube has the potential "to create a learning community where everyone has a voice, anyone can contribute, and the value lies equally within the creation of the content and the networks of learners" (p. 125).

Despite its pervasiveness, there are relatively few studies on the use of YouTube videos to promote learning, although teachers often search for videos to illustrate and substantiate their teaching. For instance, Herreid and Schiller (2013) wrote on the adoption of the flipped classroom model in teaching, whereby students read up on the course content and watch the relevant videos on YouTube before coming to class, and then attempt their 'homework' or assigned tasks. In their study on the use of YouTube to provide feedback to students, Ng and Hussain (2009) found YouTube highly effective in providing autonomy support by empowering students to give authentic feedback to their peers. Students also perceived their level of competence and sense of relatedness to be improved as they learned from one another. In addition, in the move towards self-regulation, learners were prompted to reflect on their own practices and to think of ways of refining and improving their work. For instance, one student shared the following about the use of YouTube: "it gives me the chance to see other people's view, see what I'm lacking in…I realize that other's work is far better than mine. So I can learn from them" (p. 282). It appears from such comments, that YouTube provides a platform that satisfies the three basic psychological needs forming the basis of students' intrinsic motivation to learn.

YouTube videos have also proven to be valuable as tools to liven up language teaching. Mullen and Wedwick (2008) described the use of YouTube clips to introduce songs that could serve as mnemonics to help pupils remember grammar rules. Mullen was a language teacher in the middle school where the research was conducted. Her efforts spurred students to access the videos outside the classroom, and even to attempt writing their own songs to facilitate language learning. From Mullen's observations, one may infer that the students were motivated to carry out the tasks triggered by the viewing of a single video clip. In addition, the authors' report suggests that the students had the autonomy to design their own songs, acquired increased competence in vocabulary learning and experienced relatedness as they worked together creating and performing new songs. Adam and Mowers (2007) shared the view that YouTube videos can be used to motivate students by offering them a platform to hone their creative skills (competence building) and to allow their voices to be heard (autonomy support).

In a study by Sun (2014), pre-service teachers, enrolled in a second language writing course, were required to work in groups to develop micro-teaching videos on YouTube. The researcher then investigated the pre-service teachers' views on their experience with using YouTube. The findings showed that the pre-service teachers felt that their knowledge on how to teach writing and how to integrate technology into teaching improved, indicating a perceived increase in competence in these areas. However, they encountered challenges in the process, namely technical issues such as computer-related problems, hitches in the filming process and in the recruitment of students as viewers for their videos. The pre-service teachers also shared about how the sense of relatedness within their team kept them going during the challenging times, and about the sense of accomplishment they felt at the end of the project. This study showed that getting pre-service teachers to develop teaching videos on YouTube provided authentic learning experiences in integrating technology with pedagogy and practice. Teacher motivation could however be improved by providing adequate support with regards to video recording and the use of computer technologies.

Integrating Web 2.0 Tools in Computer Assisted Learning

Daintith (2004) defined Computer Assisted Learning (CAL) as any use of computers to help or assist the education or training of people. Since its inception, CAL has been applied in diverse settings, ranging from medicine and health care, to education, language learning, and science (Greenhalgh, 2001; Levy, 1997; Maor & Fraser, 1996; Teh & Fraser, 1994). CAL is usually implemented in several phases, each involving the introduction and application of different Web 2.0 tools.

Although authors such as Benson (2001, p. 140) have cautioned against jumping blindly into the bandwagon of computer applications without due consideration of the fact that "a great deal depends on the ways in which technologies are made available to the learners and the kinds of interaction that takes place around them", the views of those who embarked on CAL have, so far, been encouraging. For instance, Gonzales and St. Louis (2008, p. 29) found that "students do develop the necessary skills to work with technological tools and that the use of technology can, indeed, foster learner autonomy". These authors further discussed how this was achieved in their work on CAL in language learning.

Earlier in this chapter, it was established that an autonomous learner shows five main attributes: a desire (intrinsic motivation) to learn, self-perceived competence (positive self-image and self-efficacy), relatedness (ability to communicate and collaborate with others), autonomy (adaptability and independent learning), and meta-cognitive capacity (for self-regulation). To assist novice web users, Salmon (2000) and Greenhalgh (2001) outlined a step-wise process for cultivating *competence* in online learning. These stages are presented in Fig. 13.2.

Gonzalez and St. Louis (2008) were able to further demonstrate how autonomous learning could be fostered through a CAL program. To promote motivation and *desire to learn*, they suggested the design of a meaningful, student-centered syllabus catering to the needs, interests and learning styles of the students, and made

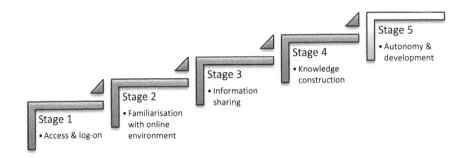

Fig. 13.2 Competence levels in online learning

available to students through virtual community platforms such as blogs or wikis. Having access to the course information and content would then give students the flexibility to plan, carry out and monitor their work in their own time and at their own pace, thus enabling them to be *self-regulated* in their learning. To foster perceived autonomy and a sense of relatedness, students were able to *learn independently* by making use of available online resources (e.g. search engines, data bases), and to *communicate and collaborate* with peers. Social networking and communication platforms (such as Facebook, Twitter, Google+ and Skype) allow synchronous interaction between team members, while online forums, blogposts and chat logs are asynchronous tools that enable students to view inputs at their own convenience. Hence, students are able to communicate with peers at any time and any place, and using a multitude of web tools.

Challenges and Concerns

Despite the many benefits that Web 2.0 tools can potentially offer to improve classroom teaching and promote learner motivation, there are concerns raised with regards to the misuse of these applications and the danger that this might present to young users. For instance, many are wary of the offensive nature of some of the videos constantly surfacing in YouTube. Mesch (2009) warned against the dangers of internet pornography and the potential risks to the psychological and social development to youths who subscribe to it. There are also issues regarding the antagonistic behavior of some users when posting comments on YouTube, especially when there is the option of retaining anonymity. Campbell (2005) and Snider and Borel (2004) warned against the threat of cyberbullying which, on its own, can take various forms. These include abusive mobile phone text messages, email threats and humiliation, and the emergence of denigratory websites, blogs and videos, all of which could potentially undermine the sense of relatedness, autonomy and competence within online learner communities. While mobile phone and video bullying was less pronounced than bullying through text or instant messaging, the former were perceived to be more detrimental and subversive to the victim (Smith et al., 2008).

Netizens, however, respond to online hostility in different ways (Lange, 2007). While it may be highly disturbing to some, others are able to rationalize that 'haters' and 'flamers' will always surface, and that one can simply obliterate the hate posts or block the insurgents from the site. Yet others feel that one should not overlook the positive comments, and that a single positive remark is enough to compensate for the many hostile ones.

Thus, rather than banishing YouTube and other social network applications as having a negative influence on pupils, a better option is for teachers to create a safe learning environment within the video-sharing site, whereby pupils could freely support one another through online learning and collaboration.

Conclusion

This chapter discusses the extent to which Web 2.0 applications such as blogs, e-portfolios and YouTube affect self-determined motivation and self-regulation in learning. A review of the literature shows that these three tools, amongst many others, provide the necessary framework for the support of the three basic psychological needs for autonomy, relatedness and competence, the satisfaction of which leads to heightened self-determined motivation. In addition, these three digital tools provide the necessary scaffolds for the various stages of self-regulated learning. A summary of how this is achieved is given in Fig. 13.3.

Despite earlier reservations against computer assisted learning, the proliferation of Web 2.0 tools and mobile applications in recent years has reaffirmed that given adequate technical support and provision for competence building, the integration of ICT in learning offers valuable opportunities for promoting autonomous learning.

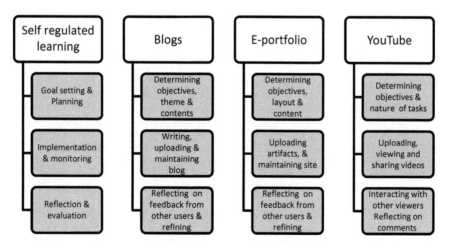

Fig. 13.3 Self-regulation using blogs, e-portfolio and YouTube

References

Abrami, P. C., & Barrett, H. (2005). Directions for research and development on electronic portfolios. *Canadian Journal of Learning and Technology, 31*(3), 1–15.

Abrami, P., Wade, A., Pillay, V., Aslan, O., Bures, E., & Bentley, C. (2009). Encouraging self-regulated learning through electronic portfolios. *Canadian Journal of Learning and Technology/La Revue Canadienne De L'Apprentissage Et De La Technologie, 34*(3). Retrieved from http://www.cjlt.ca/index.php/cjlt/article/view/507

Adam, A., & Mowers, H. (2007). YouTube comes to the classroom. *School Library Journal, 53*(1), 22. Retrieved from, http://search.proquest.com/docview/211824700?accountid=28158.

Alm, A. (2006). CALL for autonomy, competence and relatedness: Motivating language learning environments in Web 2.0. *The JALT CALL Journal, 2*(3), 29–38.

Benson, P. (2001). *Teaching and researching autonomy in language learning.* Harlow, UK: Pearson Education.

Breen, M. P., & Mann, s J. (1997). Shooting arrows at the sun: Perspectives on a pedagogy for autonomy. In P. Benson & P. Voller (Eds.), *Autonomy & independence in language learning* (pp. 132–149). Harlow, UK: Addison Wesley Longman Ltd.

Brown, J. S., & Adler, R. P. (2008). Minds on fire: Open education, the long tail, and learning 2.0. *Educause Review, 43*(1), 16–32. http://www.educause.edu/EDUCAUSE+Review/EDUCAUSEReviewMagazineVolume43/MindsonFireOpenEducationtheLon/162420.

Campbell, M. A. (2005). Cyber bullying: An old problem in a new guise? *Australian Journal of Guidance and Counselling, 15*(1), 68–76.

Chang, C. (2009). Self-evaluated effects of web-based portfolio assessment system for various student motivation levels. *Journal of Educational Computing Research, 41*(4), 391–405.

Chen, M.-Y., Chang, F. M.-T., Chen, C.-C., Huang, M.-J., & Chen, J.-W. (2012). Why do individuals use e-portfolios. *Educational Technology & Society, 15*(4), 114–125.

Clyde, L. A. (2005). Educational blogging. *Teacher Librarian, 32*(3), 43–45.

Daintith, J. (2004). Computer-assisted learning. In *A Dictionary of computing.* Retrieved from Encyclopedia.com: http://www.encyclopedia.com/doc/1O11-computerassistedlearning.html

Dam, L. (2000). Evaluating autonomous learning. In B. Sinclair, I. McGrath, & T. Lamb (Eds.), *Learner autonomy, teacher autonomy: Future directions* (pp. 48–59). Harlow, UK: Pearson Education Limited.

Deci, E. L., & Ryan, R. M. (1985). *Intrinsic motivation and self-determination in human behaviour.* New York: Plenum Press.

Deng, L., & Yuen, H. K. (2012). Understanding student perceptions and motivation towards academic blogs: An exploratory study. *Australasian Journal of Educational Technology, 28*(1), 48–66.

Driessen, E. W., Muijtjens, A. M., van Tartwijk, J., & van der Vleuten, C. P. (2007). Web- or paper-based portfolios: Is there a difference. *Medical Education, 41*(11), 1067–1073.

Duffy, P. (2008). Engaging the YouTube Google-eyed generation: Strategies for using Web 2.0 in teaching and learning. *The Electronic Journal of e-Learning, 6*(2), 119–130.

Ellison, N. B., & Wu, Y. (2008). Blogging in the classroom: A preliminary exploration of student attitudes and impact on comprehension. *Journal of Educational Multimedia and Hypermedia, 17*(1), 99–122.

Gates, B., Myhrvold, N., & Rinearson, P. (1996). *The road ahead.* New York: Viking.

Gerbic, P., Lewis, L., & Northover, M. (2009). Student perspectives of eportfolios: A longitudinal study of growth and development. In *Same places, different spaces.* Proceedings of ascilite Auckland 2009. Retrieved from: http://www.ascilite.org.au/conferences/auckland09/procs/gerbic.pdf

Goktas, Y. (2009). Incorporating blogs and the seven principles of good practice into preservice teacher ICT courses: A case study. *The New Educational Review, 19*(3–4), 29–44.

Goktas, Y., & Demirel, T. (2012). Blog-enhanced ICT courses: Examining their effects on prospective teachers' ICT competencies and perceptions. *Computers & Education, 58*(3), 908–917.

Gonzalez, D., & St Louis, R. (2008). The use of Web 2.0 tools to promote learner autonomy. *Independence, 43*, 28–32. Retrieved from http://peoplelearn.homestead.com/MEdHOME2/Technology/WebToos.2.0.autonomy.pdf.

Greenhalgh, T. (2001). Computer assisted learning in undergraduate medical education. *British Medical Journal, 322*, 40–44.

Harrison, T. M., & Barthel, B. (2009). Wielding new media in Web 2.0: Exploring the history of engagement with the collaborative construction of media products. *New Media & Society, 11*(1–2), 155–178. doi:10.1177/1461444808099580.

Herreid, C. F., & Schiller, N. A. (2013). Case studies and the flipped classroom. *Journal of College Science Teaching, 42*(5), 62–66.

Holec, H. (1981). *Autonomy in foreign language learning.* Oxford: Pergamon.

Holzberg, C. S. (2003). Educational web logs. *Techlearning, 24*(1), 52.

Knowles, M. S. (1990). *The adult learner: A neglected species* (4th ed.). Houston, TX: Gulf Publishing.

Lange, P. G. (2007, March). *Commenting on comments: Investigating responses to antagonism on YouTube.* Paper presented at the Society for Applied Anthropology Conference, Florida.

Levy, M. (1997). *Computer-assisted language learning: Context and conceptualization.* New York: Oxford University Press.

Little, D. (1991). *Learner autonomy 1: Definitions, issues and problems.* Dublin, Ireland: Authentik.

Maor, D., & Fraser, B. J. (1996). Use of classroom environment perceptions in evaluating inquiry-based computer-assisted learning. *International Journal of Science Education, 18*(4), 401–421.

March, T. (2007). Revisiting WebQuests in a Web 2 World. How developments in technology and pedagogy combine to scaffold personal learning. *Interactive Educational Multimedia, 15*, 1–17.

Mason, R. (2006). Learning technologies for adult continuing education. *Studies in Continuing Education, 28*(2), 121–133. doi:10.1080/01580370600751039.

McLeod, J. K., & Vasinda, S. (2009). Electronic portfolios: Perspectives of students, teachers and parents. *Education and Information Technologies, 14*(1), 29–38.

McLoughlin, C. & Lee, M. (2007). Social software and participatory learning: Pedagogical choices with technology affordances in the Web 2.0 era. In ICT: Providing choices for learners and learning. Proceedings ascilite Singapore 2007. http://www.ascilite.org.au/conferences/singapore07/procs/mcloughlin.pdf

Mesch, G. S. (2009). Social bonds and Internet pornographic exposure among adolescents. *Journal of Adolescence, 32*(3), 601–618.

Mullen, R., & Wedwick, L. (2008). Avoiding the digital abyss: Getting started in the classroom with YouTube, digital stories, and blogs. *The Clearing House, 82*(2), 66–69. Retrieved from http://search.proquest.com/docview/196844606?accountid=28158.

Ng, H. Z., & Hussain, R. M. R. (2009). Empowering learners as the owners of feedback while YouTube-ing. *Interactive Technology and Smart Education, 6*(4), 274–285.

O'Reilly, T. (2007). What is Web 2.0: Design patterns and business models for the next generation of software. *Communications & Strategies, 65*, 17–37. http://www.oreillynet.com/lpt/a/6228.

Pinkman, K. (2005). Using blogs in the foreign language classroom: Encouraging learner independence. *The JALT CALL Journal, 1*(1), 12–24.

Poling, C. (2005). Blog on: Building communication and collaboration among staff and students. *Learning & Leading with Technology, 32*(6), 12–15.

Salmon, G. (2000). *E-moderating: A guide to tutoring and mentoring online.* London: Kogan Page.

Sandars, J., & Morrison, C. (2007). What is the Net generation? The challenge for future medical education. *Medical Teacher, 29*(2–3), 85–88.

Smith, P. K., Mahdavi, J., Carvalho, M., Fisher, S., Russell, S., & Tippett, N. (2008). Cyberbullying: Its nature and impact in secondary school pupils. *Journal of Child Psychology and Psychiatry, 49*(4), 376–385.

Snider, M., & Borel, K. (2004). Stalked by a cyberbully. *Maclean's, 117*(21/22), 76–77.

Sun, Y. (2014). Microteaching writing on YouTube for pre-service teacher training: Lessons learned. *CALICO Journal, 31*(2), 179–200. doi:10.11139/cj.31.2.179-200.

Teh, G. P., & Fraser, B. J. (1994). An evaluation of computer-assisted learning in terms of achievement, attitudes and classroom environment. *Evaluation & Research in Education, 8*(3), 147–159.

Trajtemberg, C., & Yiakoumetti, A. (2011). Weblogs: A tool for EFL interaction, expression, and self-evaluation. *ELT Journal*, ccr015. Retrieved from, http://www.vnseameo.org/zakir/ELT%20J-2011.pdf

Ward, J. M. (2004). Blog assisted language learning (BALL): Push button publishing for the pupils. *TEFL Web Journal, 3*(1), 1–16.

Wassell, B., & Crouch, C. (2008). Fostering connections between multicultural education and technology: Incorporating weblogs into preservice teacher education. *Journal of Technology and Teacher Education, 16*(2), 211–232.

Wenger, E. (1998). *Communities of practice: Learning, meaning and identity*. Cambridge, UK: Cambridge University Press.

YouTube. (n.d.). About YouTube. Retrieved from https://www.youtube.com/yt/about/

Zhang, D. (2009). The application of blog in English writing. *Journal of Cambridge Studies, 4*(1), 64–72.

Zimmerman, B. J. (1990). Self-regulated learning and academic achievement: An overview. *Educational Psychologist, 25*(1), 3–17.

Chapter 14
Focus on Competing for Performance or Mastering New Knowledge? Insights from Discovering the Relations Between Classroom Goal Structures and Students' Learning in Singapore Secondary Schools

Youyan Nie

Ranking based on academic performance is a common educational practice in some Asian countries such as Singapore and China (e.g., Liu & Wang, 2008; Wei, 2003). Due to ranking's far-reaching consequences resulting from high-stake assessments, as well as year-end school examinations (i.e., placement to different schools, classes, and streams), teachers may face challenges in adopting the appropriate teaching strategy. In particular, should they create a competitive climate, mirroring the reality in society, in classroom learning or should they encourage students to focus on their own learning and improvement? The current study aims to address this question by examining the differential relations of these two classroom climates to students' learning motivational beliefs, behaviors, and academic achievements.

Classroom Goal Structures: Classroom Climate from Achievement Goal Theory Perspective

In the last three decades, research on the effects of competitive classroom climate on students' learning motivation has contributed to the development of achievement goal theory (e.g., Ames, 1984, 1992, Ames & Ames, 1984); in turn, the development of achievement goal theory has also shed light on research in classroom climate (e.g., Bong, 2008; Lau & Nie, 2008; Murayama & Elliot, 2009; Roeser, Midgley, & Urdan, 1996; Urdan, 2004). According to achievement goal theory, two types of classroom climate were described, i.e., classroom performance goal structure and classroom mastery goal structure. Classroom performance goal structure refers to classrooms in which instructional practices, task assignments, and

Y. Nie (✉)
Psychological Studies Academic Group, National Institute of Education, Nanyang Technological University, Singapore, Singapore
e-mail: youyan.nie@nie.edu.sg

© Springer Science+Business Media Singapore 2016
W.C. Liu et al. (eds.), *Building Autonomous Learners*,
DOI 10.1007/978-981-287-630-0_14

evaluation procedures are structured to emphasize students competing with each other and demonstrating competence. In contrast, classroom mastery goal structure refers to classrooms in which instructional practices, task assignments, and evaluation procedures are structured to emphasize students' learning, task mastery, and striving to improve one's skills.

Studies on classroom goal structures and student learning outcomes have flourished due to its important implications for educational practices. Many research on this topic used structural equation modeling to study the perceived classroom goal structures and their relations to student learning outcomes at the student level (e.g., Bong, 2008; Roeser et al., 1996; Urdan, 2004). These generally found that perceived classroom goal structures were related to students' learning outcomes either directly or indirectly through the mediation of personal goal orientation. However, due to wordings similarity between classroom goal structures measures and personal goal orientation measures as well as common method bias, the correlations may be inflated. Multilevel analyses have been recommended and used in recent years to study classroom goal structures (e.g., Lau & Nie, 2008; Murayama & Elliot, 2009; Turner et al., 2002). Therefore, the current study will adopt the multilevel approach to construct, measure, analyze, and infer classroom goal structures at the classroom level in relation to students' learning.

Conduct Classroom Goal Structure Research in Asian's Competitive Educational Contexts

Research conducted in the West has shown that classroom performance goal structure is related to many maladaptive outcomes (e.g., self-handicapping, low self-efficacy) and classroom mastery goal structure related to adaptive outcomes (e.g., interest and enjoyment, deep learning), though the relationship between classroom goal structure and student learning outcomes could be both direct or indirect (see Kaplan, Middleton, Urdan, & Midgley, 2002; Meece, Anderman, & Anderman, 2006; for reviews). More achievement goal studies conducted in Asian countries have been reported in the last 10 years and these have attracted the attention of many researchers and teachers. For example, Lau and Nie's (2008) large-scale survey research found that classroom performance goal structure showed negative relations to students' engagement and achievement but positive relations to effort withdrawal and avoidance coping in Singapore's Grade 9 mathematics classrooms. Murayama and Elliot (2009) reported that classroom performance goal structure showed negative relations to students' intrinsic motivation and self-concept but classroom mastery goal structure showed positive relations with students' intrinsic motivation and self-concept in Japanese junior high schools and high school students. However, some Asian research found that competitive environment may have certain positive effect. For example, Lam, Yim, Lau, and Cheung (2004) conducted an experimental study and found that Hong Kong's Grade 7 students, under competitive conditions, performed better in essay tasks. The findings from this Asian research which differ in some aspects to those from research conducted in the Western contexts and other Asian contexts highlight the importance of reexamining the application of Western motivation theories and research findings in an Asian context.

Children in many Asian countries are expected to work very hard and succeed in a highly competitive education system (e.g., China, Singapore, South Korea, and Japan). The norm-referenced high-stake examinations immensely impact teaching and assessment practices in school and thus affect students' learning styles, motivations, and achievements. Streaming and ranking are common practices in schools and classrooms. Comparisons of students' achievements are highlighted either formally or informally. Will students be able to adapt to the competitive environment if they study in this competitive system for an extended time? This is an important question on practices in the Asian education context, especially for secondary school students who are at that critical age in developing their concept of ability (either as fix or incremental) but where motivation showed a decreased pattern in comparison to primary school stage (Nicholls, 1989; Yeung, Lau, & Nie, 2011). The current study was conducted in Singapore mathematics and English classrooms at the Grade 9 level, based on the trend of studying classroom goal structures in the Asian education context.

Need to Link Classroom Goal Structures with Multiple Student Outcomes

Many studies which examined the relations between classroom goal structures and students' learning outcomes included only limited motivational outcomes, such as intrinsic motivation and self-concept (Murayama & Elliot, 2009), self-handicapping, avoidance help-seeking, and avoiding novelty (Turner et al., 2002). To enable a comprehensive description of students' motivation, five adaptive and four maladaptive motivational constructs were examined in the current study. In addition, we also linked classroom goal structures with students' academic achievement in both mathematics and English classes.

Self-efficacy is one of the most important adaptive motivational constructs in students' learning. Bandura (1997) defined self-efficacy as "beliefs in one's capabilities to organize and execute the courses of action required to produce given attainments" (p. 3). According to Bandura (1997), self-efficacy is the essence of personal control, and school can be an agency for cultivating self-efficacy. Numerous empirical studies in educational psychology have also suggested that students with high self-efficacy are more inclined to invest effort and engage in learning tasks to achieve better performance (e.g., Lau, Liem, & Nie, 2008; Lau & Roeser, 2002; Liem, Lau, & Nie, 2008; Schunk, Pintrich, & Meece, 2008). However, more studies are needed to provide teachers with information on how to promote self-efficacy in classrooms.

Interest is considered as an important adaptive motivation because it demonstrates the quality of motivation (Ryan & Deci, 2000). Students' interest and enjoyment is a crucial factor that provides a driving force that enables them to persist in learning tasks and activities in the long term (Elliot & Church, 1997). Therefore, interest and enjoyment cannot be overlooked in the examination of students' motivation.

Engagement is considered as another important adaptive motivation because it demonstrates the quality of motivation and is frequently listed as a teaching objective. In the current study, we focused on behavioral engagement such as students' attention and participation in the learning tasks and classroom activities.

Mastery goal orientation and performance approach goal orientation have become the most important constructs in current motivation research. Mastery approach goal orientation emphasizes learning new knowledge and improving skills, while performance approach goal orientation emphasizes the demonstration of one's superiority over others. A major review by Moller and Elliot (2006) suggested that cognitive and motivational consequences of mastery approach goals are generally positive. Although it is not always the case that performance approach goal is adaptive, performance approach goals are also adaptive in many instances (Moller & Elliot, 2006). Therefore, they were included in the current study as adaptive motivational outcomes.

In addition to the five adaptive motivational constructs, we also examined four maladaptive motivational constructs, i.e., performance avoidance goal, effort withdrawal, avoidance coping, and test anxiety. Performance avoidance goal orientation emphasizes the avoidance of looking incompetence relative to others. Moller and Elliot (2006) review suggested that performance avoidance goal orientation is typically inimical. Effort withdrawal refers to students' tendency to hold back or minimize effort in their academic work (Meece, Blumenfeld, & Hoyle, 1988; Nicholls, Patashnick, & Nolen, 1985). Avoidance coping refers to students' tendency to give up when the work is difficult or boring. A number of experimental studies found that these two constructs were most significant in examining students' motivation in that they were sensitive measures in detecting students' amotivation in Singapore schools samples (e.g., Lau & Nie, 2008, Yeung et al., 2011). Test anxiety refers to a situation-specific form of anxiety that accompanies concern about possible negative consequences or poor performance in a test. Test anxiety has drawn increasing attention in research because it has become a universal experience in competitive societies (e.g., Stankov, 2010).

Academic achievements for two major subjects, i.e., mathematics and English, were also included in the current study as it is a key concern of schools, teachers, and parents.

The Present Study

The purpose of the current study is to examine the multilevel relations between classroom goal structures (i.e., performance goal structure and mastery goal structure) and students' multiple learning outcomes, including adaptive motivation, maladaptive motivation, and academic achievement. The current study advances the existing literature in two ways. First, it measured and analyzed classroom goal structures at the classroom climate level rather than students' perception level, thus matching the level of inferences if recommendations are suggested to classroom teachers. Second, the current study includes multiple outcome measures (five adaptive motivational outcomes, four maladaptive motivational outcomes and academic achievements) which are considered as very important in teaching and learning. Thus, it advances previous studies by providing more comprehensive information on how classroom mastery goal structure and classroom performance goal structure are related to multiple outcomes.

Method

Sampling Design and Participants

In this study, we sampled a large number of students and classrooms using a stratified random sampling technique. Schools were divided into three strata based on their prior aggregate school achievement and 13 schools were randomly selected from each stratum. About half of the Secondary 3 classrooms in each participating school were randomly selected to do the mathematics survey and assessment and another half of the Secondary 3 classrooms in each participating school did the English survey and assessment. In total, 8011 Secondary 3 students in 247 classes across 39 schools in Singapore participated in this study. Our sampling design ensured that we tapped sufficient "natural variance" in classroom characteristics and student demography by selecting schools and classrooms that covered a broad spectrum of achievement levels.

The procedure consisted of two parts. Part 1 was an online survey conducted in the eighth month from the beginning of the school year. The online survey included two forms. Half of the students in each class were randomly selected to complete survey form 1 in which they reported their motivational beliefs and behaviors in either their mathematics or English classrooms. The other half of the students in the same class completed survey form 2 in which they reported their perceived classroom goal structures of either their mathematics or English classrooms. In other words, half of the students provided student-level (or level-1) data and the other half provided classroom-level (or level-2) data. In effect, half of the students served as independent raters of classroom goal structures. Because different groups of students provided data at different levels, potential inflation of cross-level correlations would be reduced. Such inflation could occur, for example, as a result of similar item wordings of the personal goal and classroom goal structures measures. In Part 2 of the study, which was conducted about 1 month after the initial survey administration, an achievement test (either mathematics or English) was administered to the students who had completed either form 1 or form 2 of the survey. The students who participated in the mathematics-related survey took the mathematics test, and the students who participated the English-related survey took the English test.

The mathematics survey and assessment sample included 4164 students from 130 classes. About half of the students (2094) did the mathematics survey form 1 and mathematics test, including 1494 Chinese (71.3 %), 417 Malays (19.9 %), 130 Indians (6.2 %), and 53 students of other ethnic origins (2.5 %). There were 983 (46.9 %) boys and 1111 (53.1 %) girls. The mean age of the participants was 15.5 years and the standard deviation was 0.57. Other half students (2070) did the mathematics survey form 2 and mathematics test, including 1473 Chinese (71.2 %), 411 Malays (19.9 %), 146 Indians (7.1 %), and 40 students of other ethnic origins (1.9 %). There were 988 (47.7 %) boys and 1082 (52.3 %) girls. The mean age of the participants was 15.5 years and the standard deviation was 0.64.

The English survey and assessment sample included 3847 students from 117 classes. About half students (1941) did the English survey form 1 and English test, including 1425 Chinese (73.4 %), 353 Malays (18.2 %), 107 Indians (5.5 %), and 56 students of other ethnic origins (2.9 %). There were 931 (48.0 %) boys and 1010 (52.0 %) girls. The mean age of the participants was 15.5 years and the standard deviation was 0.58. The other half students (1906) did the English survey form 2 and English test, including 1387 Chinese (72.8 %), 340 Malays (17.8 %), 128 Indians (6.7 %), and 51 students of other ethnic origins (2.7 %). There were 946 (49.6 %) boys and 960 (50.4 %) girls. The mean age of the participants was 15.5 years and the standard deviation was 0.67.

Measures

All the items on the survey were rated on a 5-point Likert scales (1 = strongly disagree to 5 = strongly agree or 1 = never to 5 = always). Sample items of self-report scales are provided in the Appendix.

Classroom Goal Structures Classroom mastery and classroom performance goal structure were assessed in the current study. The classroom mastery goal structure describes an environment in which the teacher emphasizes that learning and task mastery are important. The classroom performance goal structure describes an environment in which the teacher emphasizes that demonstrating high ability and getting better grades compared to other students are important. The measures of classroom mastery and classroom performance goal structure were adapted from the Patterns of Adaptive Learning Survey (PALS, Midgley et al., 2000).

A confirmatory factor analysis was conducted to examine the factor structure of the constructs. For the mathematics sample, a two-factor structure provided a good fit for the data, χ^2 (19, $N = 2070$) = 288.33, TLI = 0.91, CFI = 0.95, and RMSEA = 0.08. Each scale showed adequate internal consistency ($\alpha = 0.88$ for classroom mastery goal structure and $\alpha = 0.70$ for classroom performance goal structure). For the English sample, a two-factor structure provided a good fit for the data, χ^2 (19, $N = 1906$) = 269.17, TLI = 0.91, CFI = 0.95, and RMSEA = 0.08. Each scale showed adequate internal consistency ($\alpha = 0.87$ for classroom mastery goal structure and $\alpha = 0.70$ for classroom performance goal structure).

Classroom-level measures of classroom goal structures were derived from aggregating individual students' perceptions of classroom goal structures into class-level (class-mean) aggregated measures (Karabenick, 2004; Ryan, Gheen, & Midgley, 1998). ICC was 16.3 % for mathematics classroom mastery goal structures and 14.5 % for English classroom mastery goal structures. ICC was 12.3 % for mathematics classroom performance goal structures and 9.9 % for English classroom performance goal structures. Chi-square test results showed that all the class-level variances were significant at $p < 0.001$ level. The aggregated measures used reflected the between-class component and thus were used as level-2 predictors in HLM. At the classroom level, the correlation between classroom mastery goal structure and classroom performance goal structure was −0.11 ($p = 0.20$) for mathematics classrooms and 0.03 ($p = 0.70$) for English classrooms.

Achievement   A multiple-choice mathematics achievement test was developed for this study because a standardized test at Secondary 3 level was not available in Singapore. The internal consistency reliability scores were 0.851 for the mathematics test (28 items) and 0.934 for the English test (70 items).

Motivation   To provide a comprehensive view of how classroom goal structures are related to a variety of motivational outcomes, nine motivational criterion variables were selected in this study, including five adaptive motivational criterion variables and four maladaptive motivational variables. The five adaptive motivational constructs included students' engagement, self-efficacy and interest in mathematics classes, as well as mastery approach goal orientation and performance approach goal orientation. Our measure of engagement was based on students' report of their attention, effort, and participation in their mathematics classes (Steinberg, Lamborn, Dornbusch, & Darling, 1992; Wellborn & Connell, 1987). Our measure of self-efficacy was based on students' report of their beliefs on how confident they are of mastering the lessons and skills taught in class (Midgley, et al., 2000). Our measure of interest and enjoyment was based on students' reports of their intrinsic motivation and enjoyment in learning (Elliot & Church, 1997). Mastery approach goal scale measured the extent to which students are focused on learning new things and improving skills (Midgley, et al., 2000). Mastery performance approach goal scale measured the extent to which students are focused on demonstrating that they were more capable than others (Midgley, et al., 2000).

The four maladaptive motivational outcomes included avoidance coping, effort withdrawal, performance avoidance goal orientation, and test anxiety. The avoidance coping scale assessed students' tendency to give up when the work is difficult or boring. It was adapted from the Motivated Strategies for Learning Questionnaire (MSLQ; Pintrich, Smith, Garcia, & McKeachie, 1993). The effort withdrawal scale assessed students' tendency to hold back or minimize effort in their mathematics work (Meece et al., 1988; Nicholls et al., 1985). Performance avoidance goal scale measured the extent to which students' aim in studying was to avoid being perceived as less competent than others in the class (Midgley, et al., 2000). Test anxiety scale measured students' negative affective reactions to performing mathematics/English activities and their worries about their performance in mathematics/English (Pintrich et al., 1993).

A confirmatory factor analysis was conducted to examine the factor structure of the constructs. A second-order factor model, in which adaptive factors loaded onto the higher-order factor and maladaptive factors onto another higher-order factor, provided a good fit for the data for both the mathematics and English samples. For the mathematics sample, χ^2 (686, $N=2094$) = 4132.79, TLI=0.92, CFI=0.93, and RMSEA=0.05. Each scale showed adequate to high internal consistency ($\alpha=0.86$ for self-efficacy, $\alpha=0.94$ for interest, $\alpha=0.82$ for engagement, $\alpha=0.89$ for mastery approach goal, $\alpha=0.88$ for performance approach goal, $\alpha=0.79$ for effort withdrawal, $\alpha=0.81$ for avoidance coping, $\alpha=0.77$ for performance avoidance goal, and $\alpha=0.90$ for test anxiety). For the English sample, χ^2 (686, $N=1941$) = 3903.56, TLI=0.92, CFI=0.93, and RMSEA=0.05. Each scale showed adequate to high internal consistency ($\alpha=0.86$ for self-efficacy, $\alpha=0.94$ for interest, $\alpha=0.82$ for engagement, $\alpha=0.89$ for mastery approach goal, $\alpha=0.88$ for performance approach goal, $\alpha=0.79$ for effort withdrawal, $\alpha=0.81$ for avoidance coping, $\alpha=0.77$ for performance avoidance goal, and $\alpha=0.90$ for test anxiety).

Results

Descriptive Statistics and Zero-Order Correlations

Descriptive statistics and zero-order correlations among the student-level variables used in this study are presented in Table 14.1. Descriptive statistics and zero-order correlations among the class-level variables used in this study are presented in Table 14.2.

Hierarchical Linear Modeling

All predictors were standardized before running HLM. Outcome variables remained as original values. Standardized level-2 predictors were derived by first aggregating level-1 scores to level 2 and then standardizing the level-2 scores at level 2.

The HLM analysis was performed to evaluate cross-level predictive relations between classroom goal structures and student outcome variables. Classroom goal structures were level-2 variables, whereas student motivational and achievement outcome variables were level-1 variables. The results are presented in Table 14.3.

The results from both English and mathematics classrooms showed consistent findings: classroom mastery goal structure was positively related to students' academic self-efficacy, interest and enjoyment, personal mastery goal orientation, and engagement, whereas classroom performance goal structure was positively related to personal performance avoidance goal orientation and negatively related to academic achievement. Results specific to either English or mathematics classrooms were also found. In English classrooms, classroom performance goal structure was positively related to avoidance coping and negatively related to engagement. In the mathematics sample, the classroom mastery goal positively predicted personal performance goal and classroom performance goal also positively predicted personal mastery goal, but these findings were not observed in the English sample.

Discussion

Classroom Mastery Goal Structure and Classroom Performance Goal Structure

Based on the descriptive statistics, students reported that teachers generally created more classroom mastery goal structure than performance goal structure. This suggests that teachers focused more on learning even the educational system is very competitive. In addition, there was neither positive nor negative correlation between classroom mastery goal structure and performance goal structure, thus suggesting a distinction between the two types of classroom structures. It also suggests that teachers who emphasized more classroom mastery goal structure may not mean that they used less classroom performance goal structure.

Classroom Goal Structures and Students' Learning Outcomes

Previous studies have shown the relations between classroom goal structures and some students' learning outcomes. For example, Murayama and Elliot (2009) included intrinsic motivation and self-concept as outcome variables and found classroom mastery goal structure positively related to intrinsic motivation and self-concept but classroom performance goal structure negatively related to intrinsic motivation and self-concept in Japanese high school students. Turner et al. (2002) reported that classroom mastery goal structure was a negative predictor of self-handicapping and avoiding help-seeking in Grade 6 classrooms in the USA. Lau and Nie (2008) found classroom mastery goal structure positively related to mathematics achievement and negatively related to effort withdrawal and avoidance coping. However performance goal structure was negatively related to achievement and engagement but positively related to effort withdrawal and avoidance coping in Grade 5 mathematics classrooms in Singapore. Consistent with previous multilevel studies on classroom goal structures, the current study showed convergent conclusions on the adaptive roles of classroom mastery goal structure and adaptive roles of classroom performance goal structure. However, previous studies only examined limited learning outcomes in each single study. Therefore, the current study advanced the previous research by linking classroom goal structures with ten important students' learning outcomes and showed comprehensive and convincing conclusions that classroom mastery goal structure showed adaptive roles in

Table 14.1 Descriptive statistics and zero-order correlations among student-level variables

	M	SD	1	2	3	4	5	6	7	8	9	10
English sample												
1. Academic achievement	37.76	14.32	–									
2. Self-efficacy	3.77	0.67	0.16**	–								
3. Interest	3.53	0.89	-0.02	0.52**	–							
4. Engagement	3.88	0.69	0.15**	0.46**	0.37**	–						
5. Personal mastery goal	3.55	0.76	-0.09**	0.58**	0.70**	0.44**	–					
6. Personal performance goal	3.06	1.00	-0.04	0.26**	0.26**	0.15**	0.28**	–				
7. Work avoidance	2.56	0.87	0.00	-0.19**	-0.26**	-0.31**	-0.31**	0.10**	–			
8. Avoidance coping	2.52	0.91	-0.22**	-0.23**	-0.23**	-0.23**	-0.19**	0.05	0.44**	–		
9. Personal avoidance goal	2.65	0.86	-0.21**	-0.09**	-0.03	-0.10**	0.03	0.42**	0.34**	0.28**	–	
10. Test anxiety	3.37	0.99	-0.27**	-0.21**	-0.08**	-0.01	0.01	0.07**	0.06*	0.24**	0.26**	–

Math sample			1	2	3	4	5	6	7	8	9	10
1. Academic achievement	12.95	5.70	–									
2. Self-efficacy	3.74	0.72	0.19**	–								
3. Interest	3.44	0.99	0.14**	0.57**	–							
4. Engagement	3.76	0.73	0.14**	0.42**	0.40**	–						
5. Personal mastery goal	3.55	0.79	0.10**	0.64**	0.79**	0.46**	–					
6. Personal performance goal	3.09	0.99	-0.05*	0.26**	0.20**	0.17**	0.26**	–				
7. Work avoidance	2.57	0.86	-0.07**	-0.21**	-0.31**	-0.29**	-0.32**	0.10**	–			
8. Avoidance coping	2.79	0.95	-0.07**	-0.21**	-0.24**	-0.14**	-0.21**	0.06**	0.37**	–		
9. Personal avoidance goal	2.58	0.89	-0.19**	-0.06**	-0.05*	-0.05*	-0.01	0.44**	0.36**	0.26**	–	
10. Test anxiety	3.55	0.95	-0.14**	-0.15**	-0.10**	0.07**	-0.09**	0.09**	0.10**	0.23**	0.25**	–

$^*p<0.05$; $^{**}p<0.01$

Table 14.2 Descriptive statistics and zero-order correlations among class-level variables

	M	SD	1	2
Mathematics sample[*]				
1. Classroom mastery goal structure	3.82	0.40	–	
2. Classroom performance goal structure	2.84	0.41	−0.11	–
English sample[**]				
1. Classroom mastery goal structure	3.78	0.37	–	
2. Classroom performance goal structure	2.72	0.32	0.03	–

[*]$n = 129$ [**]$n = 117$

Table 14.3 Results from HLM analyses predicting motivational outcomes

	Math sample				English sample			
	Classroom mastery goal		Classroom performance goal		Classroom mastery goal		Classroom performance goal	
	γ	SE	γ	SE	γ	SE	γ	SE
1. Academic achievement	−0.029	0.057	−0.265[***]	0.069	−0.027	0.076	−0.417[***]	0.065
2. Self-efficacy	0.083[**]	0.025	−0.003	0.027	0.087[**]	0.028	−0.043	0.029
3. Interest	0.143[***]	0.029	0.045	0.034	0.125[***]	0.030	0.036	0.029
4. Engagement	0.092[**]	0.029	−0.047	0.030	0.112[**]	0.032	−0.092[**]	0.031
5. Personal mastery goal	0.155[***]	0.026	0.089[**]	0.032	0.137[***]	0.033	0.066	0.032
6. Personal performance goal	0.069[**]	0.022	0.045	0.021	0.011	0.023	0.033	0.026
7. Work avoidance	−0.026	0.022	0.063	0.024	−0.067	0.027	−0.010	0.033
8. Avoidance coping	0.007	0.030	0.031	0.034	−0.052	0.029	0.113[**]	0.032
9. Personal avoidance goal	0.000	0.028	0.172[***]	0.023	0.009	0.023	0.098[***]	0.025
10. Test anxiety	−0.043	0.025	−0.015	0.026	0.073	0.034	0.082	0.033

[**]$p < 0.01$; [***]$p < 0.001$

students' learning motivation and achievement in both mathematics and English learning at the Grade 9 level in Singapore due to its positive relations with academic achievement, self-efficacy, interest, engagement, and personal mastery goal, whereas classroom performance goal structure showed maladaptive roles in student learning due to its negative relations with engagement and positive relations with avoidance coping and avoidance goal.

Even though Singapore students are used to ranking, banding, and streaming from the primary to secondary school level in this competitive education system, the negative effects of highlighting performance competition in classroom are still significant and Grade 9 students cannot adaptively response to such environment in classrooms.

A significant strength of the current study is that the cross-level relations unveiled will not be inflated because class-level data and student-level data are provided by different participants. The use of HLM also ensures the degree of freedom in statistical tests at the class level is correctly calculated. Therefore, there is more confidence in the significant conclusions drawn at the class level, especially when the message was delivered to classroom teachers and used to guide classroom practices.

Limitations

Several limitations in this study should be noted. First, the correlational nature of the current study does not allow us to infer causal relations between classroom goal structures and student outcomes. We hoped that our research could stimulate more longitudinal studies or quasi-experimental/experimental studies to fully understand the relations between classroom goal structures and student learning outcomes. Second, our measures of classroom goal structures were based on students' self-reports, which were their subjective interpretations of goal messages conveyed by their teachers. Experimental and quasi-experimental studies of manipulations of objective goal-related features in the classroom may be considered in future research. Third, to fully understand the dynamic relations among classroom goal structures and students' learning outcomes, potential interaction effects may be considered. Some research has addressed the interaction between classroom goal structure and personal goal orientations (Lau & Nie, 2008; Murayama & Elliot, 2009); however the interaction between two types of classroom goal structures needs to be considered in future research. This is particularly important when removing classroom performance goal structure is not realistic in a competitive education context. For example, could mastery goal structure buffer the negative effects of classroom performance goal structure in students learning? Could student self-beliefs (e.g., self-efficacy, self-concept) buffer the negative effects of classroom performance goal structure? Future studies may consider exploring more buffering factors if it is not possible to reduce the negative effects through the removal of antecedent variables like performance goal structure.

Implications for Classroom Practices

The findings from the current study suggest that teachers should de-emphasize performance goals in their classrooms, even if teachers' goal messages are meant to encourage students to demonstrate superior ability and to get grades higher than their peers. As our findings indicated, classroom performance goal structure showed maladaptive roles with multiple student learning outcomes, i.e., negatively related to academic achievements and positive relations with personal avoidance goal orientation. In addition, the maladaptive roles are even more noteworthy in English classrooms due to its negative relations with engagement and positive relations with avoidance coping. In addition, given the convergence of evidence from the current study and prior research (e.g., Kaplan, Gheen, & Midgley, 2002; Karabenick, 2004; Lau & Nie; 2008; Murayama & Elliot, 2009) regarding the positive relations between classroom mastery goal structures and students learning outcomes, it is advisable for teachers to place greater emphasis on mastery goals in their classrooms.

Appendix

Sample Items for Self-Report Scales

Classroom Mastery Goal Structure (*Four Items*)

1. My math teacher wants us to really understand the subject, not just to remember facts or rules.
2. My math teacher really wants us to enjoy learning new things in math.
3. My math teacher tells us that it is very important to try hard.
4. My math teacher gives us time to learn new ideas.

Classroom Performance Goal Structure (*Four Items*)

1. My math teacher tells the class which pupils are doing poorly in their work.
2. My math teacher calls on smart pupils more than other pupils.
3. My math teacher emphasizes that we do better than pupils in other classes.
4. My math teacher thinks that it is more important to do well in math tests than to learn new things.

Engagement (*Five Items*)

1. In my math class, I pay attention well.
2. In my math class, I try my best to complete class work.
3. In my math class, I try my best to contribute during small group discussions.
4. In my math class, I share my ideas during group work.
5. In my math class, I try my best to contribute to group work.

Self-Efficacy (*Five Items*)

1. I am sure I can learn the skills taught in math class well.
2. I can do almost all the work in math class if I do not give up.

3. If I have enough time, I can do a good job in all my math work.
4. Even if the work in math is hard, I can learn it.
5. I am sure I can do difficult work in my math class.

Interest (Four Items)

1. I enjoy doing math.
2. I am really interested in math.
3. I think it's great that I learn all sorts of things in math class.
4. I find math interesting.

Personal Mastery: Approach Goal (Five Items)

1. An important reason I do my math work is that I like to learn new things.
2. I like the work in my math class best when it challenges me to think.
3. An important reason I do my work in math class is because I want to get better at it.
4. An important reason I do my math work is that I enjoy it.
5. An important reason I do my math work is that I want to learn challenging ideas well.

Personal Performance-Approach Goal (Four Items)

- I want to show pupils in my math class that I am smart.
- I like to show my teacher that I am smarter than the other pupils in my math class.
- It is important to me that the other pupils in my math class think I am smart.
- I feel successful in math if I get better marks than most of the other pupils.

Avoidance Coping (Three Items)

1. When the work in math is dull and boring, I stop doing it even if it is incomplete.
2. When the work in math is difficult, I give up.
3. When the work in math is difficult, I only study the easy parts.

Effort Withdrawal (Four Items)

1. I wait until the last minute to study for a math test/exam.
2. I like math class best when I do not have to work hard.
3. I do not work hard on my math homework.
4. I try to put in the least effort in my math class.

Personal Performance-Avoidance Goal (Four Items)

1. I do not participate in math class because I do not want to look stupid.
2. It is important that the other pupils in my math class do not think I am stupid.
3. I do my math work because I do not want the teacher to think that I am stupid.
4. I try to avoid answering questions because I am afraid of giving wrong answers.

Test Anxiety (*Five Items*)

1. I worry a lot about math tests.
2. When taking math tests, I worry about doing poorly.
3. I feel uneasy when taking math tests.
4. I think a lot about how poorly I am doing when taking math tests.
5. I am nervous when taking math tests.

References

Ames, C. (1984). Achievement attributions and self-instructions under competitive and individualistic goal structures. *Journal of Educational Psychology, 76*, 478–487.

Ames, C. (1992). Classrooms: Goals, structures, and student motivation. *Journal of Educational Psychology, 84*, 261–271.

Ames, C., & Ames, R. (1984). Systems of student and teacher motivation: Toward a qualitative definition. *Journal of Educational Psychology, 76*, 535–556.

Bandura, A. (1997). *Self-efficacy: The exercise of control*. New York: W.H. Freeman.

Bong, M. (2008). Effects of parent-child relationships and classroom goal structures on motivation: Help-seeking avoidance, and cheating. *Journal of Experimental Education, 76*, 191–217.

Elliot, A. J., & Church, M. (1997). A hierarchical model of approach and avoidance achievement motivation. *Journal of Personality and Social Psychology, 72*, 218–232.

Kaplan, A., Gheen, M., & Midgley, C. (2002). Classroom goal structure and student disruptive behavior. *British Journal of Educational Psychology, 72*, 191–211.

Kaplan, A., Middleton, M. J., Urdan, T., & Midgley, C. (2002). Achievement goals and goal structures. In C. Midgley (Ed.), *Goals, goal structures, and patterns of adaptive learning* (pp. 21–53). Mahwah, NJ: Erlbaum.

Karabenick, S. A. (2004). Perceived achievement goal structure and college student help seeking. *Journal of Educational Psychology, 96*, 569–581.

Lam, S. F., Yim, P. S., Law, J. S., & Cheung, R. W. (2004). The effects of competition on achievement motivation in Chinese classrooms. *British Journal of Educational Psychology, 74*, 281–296.

Lau, S., Liem, A. D., & Nie, Y. (2008). Task- and self-related pathways to deep learning: The mediating role of achievement goals, classroom attentiveness, and group participation. *British Journal of Educational Psychology, 78*, 639–662.

Lau, S., & Nie, Y. (2008). Interplay between personal goals and classroom goal structures in predicting student outcomes: A multilevel analysis of person-context interactions. *Journal of Educational Psychology, 100*, 15–29.

Lau, S., & Roeser, R. W. (2002). Cognitive abilities and motivational processes in high school students' situational engagement and achievement in science. *Educational Assessment, 8*, 139–162.

Liem, A. D., Lau, S., & Nie, Y. (2008). The role of self-efficacy, task value, and achievement goals in predicting learning strategies, task disengagement, peer relationship, and achievement outcome. *Contemporary Educational Psychology, 33*, 486–512.

Liu, W. C., & Wang, C. K. J. (2008). Home environment and classroom climate: An investigation of their relation to students' academic self-concept in a streamed setting. *Current Psychology, 27*(4), 242–256.

Meece, J. L., Anderman, E. M., & Anderman, L. H. (2006). *Annual Review of Psychology, 57*, 487–503.

Meece, J. L., Blumenfeld, P. C., & Hoyle, R. H. (1988). Students' goal orientations and cognitive engagement in classroom activities. *Journal of Educational Psychology, 80*, 514–523.

Midgley, C., Maehr, M. L., Hruda, L. Z., Anderman, E., Anderman, L., Freeman, K. E., et al. (2000). *Manual for the patterns of adaptive learning scales.* Ann Arbor: University of Michigan.

Moller, A. C., & Elliot, A. J. (2006). The 2 x 2 achievement goal framework: An overview of empirical research. In A. Mittel (Ed.), *Focus on educational psychology* (pp. 307–326). Hauppauge, NY: Nova Science Publishers.

Murayama, K., & Elliot, A. J. (2009). The joint influence of personal achievement goals and class-room goal structures on achievement-relevant outcomes. *Journal of Educational Psychology, 101*, 432–447.

Nicholls, J. G. (1989). *The competitive ethos and democratic education.* Cambridge, MA: Harvard University Press.

Nicholls, J. G., Patashnick, M., & Nolen, S. B. (1985). Adolescents' theories of education. *Journal of Educational Psychology, 77*, 683–692.

Pintrich, P. R., Smith, D. A. F., Garcia, T., & Mckeachie, W. J. (1993). Reliability and predictive-validity of the motivated strategies for learning questionnaire. *Educational and Psychological Measurement, 53*(3), 801–813.

Roeser, R. W., Midgley, C., & Urdan, T. C. (1996). Perceptions of the school psychological environment and early adolescents' psychological and behavioral functioning in school: The mediating role of goals and belonging. *Journal of Educational Psychology, 88*, 408–422.

Ryan, R. M., & Deci, E. L. (2000). Self-determination theory and the facilitation of intrinsic motivation, social development, and well-being. *American Psychologist, 55*, 68–78.

Ryan, A. M., Gheen, M. H., & Midgley, C. (1998). Why do some students avoid asking for help? An examination of the interplay among students' academic efficacy, teachers' social–emotional role, and the classroom goal structure. *Journal of Educational Psychology, 90*(3), 528–535.

Schunk, D. H., Pintrich, P. R., & Meece, J. L. (2008). *Motivation in education: Theory, research, and applications* (3rd ed.). Upper Saddle River, NJ: Pearson/Merrill Prentice Hall.

Stankov, L. (2010). Unforgiving Confucian culture: A breeding ground for high academic achievement, test anxiety and self-doubt? *Learning and Individual Differences, 20*(6), 555–563.

Steinberg, L., Lamborn, S. D., Dornbusch, S. M., & Darling, N. (1992). Impact of parenting practices on adolescent achievement: Authoritative parenting, school involvement, and encouragement to succeed. *Child Development, 63*(5), 1266–1281.

Turner, J. C., Midgley, C., Meyer, D. K., Gheen, M., Anderman, E. M., Kang, Y., et al. (2002). The classroom environment and students' reports of avoidance strategies in mathematics: A multi-method study. *Journal of Educational Psychology, 94*(1), 88.

Urdan, T. (2004). Predictors of academic self-handicapping and achievement: Examining achievement goals, classroom goal structures, and culture. *Journal of Educational Psychology, 96*, 251–264.

Wei, J. (2003). An analysis on the influencing multi-factor on mental health of students in middle school. *Journal of Clinical Psychosomatic Diseases, 9*(3), 162–165.

Wellborn, J., & Connell, J. (1987). *Manual for the Rochester assessment package for schools.* Rochester: University of Rochester.

Yeung, A. S., Lau, S., & Nie, Y. (2011). Primary and secondary students' motivation in learning English: Grade and gender differences. *Contemporary Educational Psychology, 36*, 246–256.

Chapter 15
Promoting Mastery-Approach Goals to Support the Success of the *"Teach Less, Learn More"* Educational Initiative

Gregory Arief D. Liem, Wee Kiat Lau, and Elaine Yu Ling Cai

"Teach Less, Learn More"

Singapore has consistently emerged as one of the top performing nations in the international assessments of academic performance (Martin, Mullis, Foy, & Stanco, 2012; Mullis, Martin, Foy, & Arora, 2012; OECD [OECD], 2012). This outstanding feat can be attributed, in part, to the introduction and adaptation of schooling policies and instructional practices that keep the country's educational system relevant and responsive to the time's demands.

"Teach Less, Learn More" (TLLM) is an educational initiative first mentioned by Prime Minister Lee Hsien Loong in 2004 in his inaugural National Day Speech Rally and began its nationwide implementation in 2006. In his speech, Mr. Lee said,

> It [TLLM] would mean that less pressure on the kids, a bit less rote learning, more space for them to explore and discover their talents and also more space for the teachers to think, to reflect, to find ways to bring out the best in their students and to deliver quality results. We've got to teach less to our students so that they will learn more.

Further, as articulated by Mr. Tharman Shanmugaratnam (2005, para. 12), then Minister of Education, "TLLM is a call to educators to teach better, to engage our students and prepare them for life, rather than to teach for tests and examinations." Thus, the policy seeks to ignite the spirit and enjoyment of learning (or intrinsic motivation) in Singapore students beyond studying for educational credentials (or other forms of extrinsic motivation). Further, it also aims to develop youths holistically and nurture the seed of lifelong learning so that they are better prepared to face future life challenges. In other words, the TLLM aims to develop young people who are passionate, engaged, and skilled in both academic and nonacademic arenas.

G.A.D. Liem (✉) • W.K. Lau • E.Y.L. Cai
National Institute of Education, Nanyang Technological University, Singapore, Singapore
e-mail: gregory.liem@nie.edu.sg

© Springer Science+Business Media Singapore 2016
W.C. Liu et al. (eds.), *Building Autonomous Learners*,
DOI 10.1007/978-981-287-630-0_15

Thus far, reviews of the TLLM implementation have shown mixed findings. Schools claimed that the TLLM works. Students have become more reflective and critical, more participative in class, and more intrinsically motivated in pursuing interests beyond their schoolwork (Ng, 2012; Peh, 2007). However, as reported by Hogan and his research team (2013), the 2010 data indicated a different portrayal. A nationally representative sample of 4,000 ninth-grade students from 32 schools claimed that their teachers were inclined to adopt more traditional teaching and direct instructional strategies. These strategies (e.g., drilling, memorization, and emphases on procedural skills) focus more on preparing students for high-stake examinations than developing their understanding and self-regulated learning (e.g., self-monitoring the learning progress, self-set learning goals, self- and peer assessment).

Furthermore, although Singapore students in general perform well relative to their international counterparts, the trend does not generalize to all the students. Recent statistics indicated that only 82.7 % out of 28,221 students in the 2013 cohort scored at least 5 "O"-level passes (Ministry of Education (MOE), 2014), which is a benchmark for Singapore secondary-school students to advance their education to junior colleges or polytechnics. Also, 4.3 % of the students in this cohort failed to complete their secondary education.

As asserted by the current Minister of Education Mr. Heng Sweet Kiat (2014), bringing out the best in every child involves all aspects of the education system: the school, the child's current stage of learning, where the learning initiative should start, and how to create a better environment for children to grow. However, he further expressed, although efforts to create more holistic learning environments for students have begun, this is still limited to a few schools. Thus, there appears to be room in the Singapore education system for a more optimal implementation of its educational policies and instructional practices including the TLLM.

In the last three decades, many research studies have used achievement goal theory as a framework to examine student motivation. The bulk of the studies have shown both the effects of the achievement goals adoption on academic and nonacademic outcomes and the role of teachers and classroom climates in promoting students' achievement goals. Thus, as suggested by Roberts (2012), the popularity of the theory among educational researchers and practitioners is apparently due to the relations of achievement goals to focal educational outcomes and the malleability of achievement goals through the "message" the students receive as emphasized by the teachers in the classrooms (i.e., the classroom goal structure).

In this chapter, we first outline the development of the achievement goal theory and how the different types of achievement goals are measured in the research. We then provide an overview of research findings showing the effects of the different goal adoption on students' behavioral, cognitive, affective, social, well-being, and achievement outcomes. In addition, we will look at how teachers and their classroom practices may foster the adoption of achievement goals in students. Finally, we offer some practical implications of the theory and propose links to key dimensions of the TLLM. For more detailed accounts of the theory and its historical overview, we refer readers to Elliot (2005), Maehr and Zusho (2009), Roberts (2012), and Papaioannou, Zourbanos, Krommidas, and Ampatzoglou (2012).

Achievement Goal Theory

Early Achievement Goal Perspectives

In the late 1970s and early 1980s, early achievement goal theorists (Ames, 1984; Nicholls, 1984, 1989; Dweck, 1986; Maehr, 1989; Maehr & Nicholls, 1980) conceptualized achievement goals as the reasons and purposes that individuals hold in engaging in achievement behaviors, with *task-oriented* and *ego-oriented* goals being the two main achievement goals focused on. Task-oriented goals (also known as *mastery* or *learning* goals in the later development of the theory) refer to the focus on *developing* skills and knowledge, whereas ego-oriented goals (or also called *performance*, *ability*, or *competition* goals) reflect the focus on *demonstrating* competencies.

According to Nicholls (1989), the different types of achievement goal originate from individual differences in the conception of success. When individuals define success in *subjective* terms (e.g., task mastery, personal development), they hold task-oriented goals, whereas when individuals define success in *normative* terms (e.g., becoming wealthy, famous), they pursue ego-oriented goals. As a result, task-oriented goals in the Nicholls scholarly tradition were typically measured by items such as "I feel really successful when I solve a problem by working hard" and ego-oriented goals by items such as "I feel really successful when I beat others" (Duda & Nicholls, 1992). Nicholls (1989) believed that task-oriented goals are adaptive for both individuals and society as they promote social equality and the development of society. Ego-oriented goals, however, are deleterious for individuals – especially those of low ability – and lead to social inequality and the promotion of superiority and inferiority.

Another key feature in Nicholls (1989) perspective of achievement goals lies in the posited synergy between individuals' reasons and aims in motivating their behaviors. This is because "no rational person consistently seeks to achieve something without reason" (Papaioannou et al. 2012, p. 75). The synergy is well reflected in the measurement of goals developed within this tradition such as those in the Patterns of Adaptive Learning Scales (PALS; Midgley et al., 2000) in which the reason and aim underlying achievement behaviors are measured simultaneously ("an important reason why I do my class work is because I like to learn new things" and "the reason I do my class work is so my teacher doesn't think I know less than others" are examples of the mastery and performance-avoidance goal items in the PALS, respectively).

Revised Achievement Goal Model

In the 1990s, Elliot and his colleagues (Elliot, 1999, 2006; Elliot & McGregor, 2001; Elliot & Murayama, 2008; Elliot, Murayama, & Pekrun, 2011) systematically revised the achievement goal perspective in two major ways. First, they separated the two components (reason and aim) of achievement goals and more narrowly conceptualized achievement goals as cognitive representations of competence-related aims that individuals seek to pursue in a given performance setting. Further, the attainment of competence can be defined or evaluated based on either *personal* and *task-referenced* or *normative* and *other-referenced* standards, with the former called mastery goals and the latter performance goals. According to Elliot, any goals – both mastery and performance – can be undergirded by different reasons, for example, to please parents or to gain social approval.

Thus, unlike Nicholls' view of achievement goals that are derived from individuals' broad and society-based conceptions of success, the conceptual scope of achievement goals in Elliot's model is narrowed to the aims of pursuing competence in a specific area of performance (e.g., education, work, sport). The separation of aims from reasons was formalized by Elliot (1999, 2006) in a hierarchical model of motivation. This model hypothesizes the role of achievement goals as a catalyst of achievement-related processes and outcomes and the goals themselves be predicted by contextual or situational factors (e.g., classroom climate, assessment system) and individual differences (e.g., motives, needs) that constitute the reasons underlying the achievement goals adoption. Recent theorizing suggests autonomous and controlled regulations as underlying reasons for achievement goal adoption (Vansteenkiste, Lens, Elliot, Soenens, & Mouratidis, 2014).

The second revision incorporated the classic approach-avoidance dimensions of motivation (Atkinson, 1957; McClelland, 1951) and the bifurcation of these dimensions with mastery and performance goals. This revision resulted in a *2 × 2 achievement goal model* (Elliot & Murayama, 2008) and expanded its preceding *trichotomous model* in which the construct of mastery-avoidance goal was not proposed (Elliot & Church, 1997; see also Papaioannou et al., 2012; Roberts, 2012). Clearly, the consideration of these approach and avoidance dimensions of motivation was absent in the early achievement goal theorizing and research.

Students pursuing *mastery-approach* goals aim to develop academic competence based on their intrapersonal and absolute/task-referenced standards ("my aim is to completely master the material presented in this class" is an example of mastery-approach goal items in the revised Achievement Goal Questionnaire or AGQ-R; Elliot & Murayama, 2008), whereas students pursuing *mastery-avoidance* goals avoid the shortfall of attaining the optimal development and mastery of the task according to their own intrapersonal and absolute/task-referenced standards ("my aim is to avoid learning less than I possibly could"). Students pursuing *performance-approach* goals seek to demonstrate academic competence considered superior by interpersonal or normative standards ("my aim is to perform well relative to other students"), whereas students pursuing *performance-avoidance* goals aim to appear looking less competent relative to others ("my goal is to avoid performing poorly compared to others"). As reviewed below, research evidence has attested to the differential patterns of behavioral, cognitive, affective, social, well-being, and achievement outcomes associated with the adoption of these four achievement goals (for reviews, see Elliot, 2005; Hulleman, Schrager, Bodmann, & Harackiewicz, 2010; Maehr & Zusho, 2009; Papaioannou et al., 2012; Roberts, 2012; Senko, Hulleman, & Harackiewicz, 2011).

Recent Development of Elliot's Achievement Goal Model

Based on the evaluative standards that competence attainment can be defined (task-, self-, or other-referenced) while keeping the approach and avoidance dimensions incorporated, Elliot and his colleagues (2011) recently proposed a 3×2 achievement goal framework. In this model, mastery goals are separated into *task-based* and *self-based* goals. Students pursuing *task-approach* goals aim to do the task correctly, whereas those pursuing *task-avoidance* goals seek to prevent doing the task wrongly. Students motivated by *self-approach* goals focus on attaining a level of competence better than their previous attainment, whereas those driven by *self-avoidance* goals focus on preventing a performance worse than what they did before. Analogous to performance-approach and performance-avoidance goals, *other-approach* and *other-avoidance* goals were also types of achievement goals in the model.

The separation of mastery goals into *task-based* and *self-based* goals was exhibited to be more fruitful in understanding achievement goal effects. Elliot et al. (2011) found that although the combined task-/self-approach (mastery-approach) goals were not a positive predictor of task absorption and learning efficacy, task-approach (but not self-approach) goals were a positive predictor of these two outcomes. This suggests that the pursuit of the development of competence based on the task-related rubrics makes students more engaged and feel more competent at the task at hand, but not when the focus is on becoming more competent than they are before. This is, perhaps, due to the potential moderation of the students' actual levels of performance and their perceptions of competence efficacies in the task.

In sum, the theorization, conceptualization, and operationalization of achievement goals have evolved over the past four decades. The more recent model represents a taxonomy of achievement goals that are more nuanced and more precise in their conceptual scope. This includes the conceptual focus on the aims of attaining competence (rather than the aims and the reasons), the definition of goals according to the evaluative standards of competence attainment (task-based, self-based, and other-based), and the incorporation of the approach and avoidance dimensions characterizing motivated behaviors (the desire to attain success and the desire to avoid failure).

Effects of Achievement Goals

The fundamental tenet of achievement goal theory is that achievement goals provide an interpretative framework for students to appraise and interpret tasks and achievement-related situations, and these appraisals and interpretations shape how they regulate their achievement-related behaviors and, in turn, determine their achievement outcomes (Elliot, 2005; Maehr & Zusho, 2009; Papaioannou et al., 2012; Roberts, 2012). In general, the achievement goal literature has documented evidence for the positive role of mastery-approach goals, the adaptive and less adaptive role of performance-approach goals, and the generally deleterious role of mastery-avoidance and performance-avoidance goals in students' behavioral, cognitive, affective, social, and achievement consequences (Hulleman et al., 2010; Senko et al., 2011). Studies addressing the differential effects of the achievement goal adoption on these outcomes are reviewed below.

Behavioral Outcomes

Achievement goals have motivational implications for students' academic behaviors, including persistence (Miller, Behrens, Greene, & Newman, 1993), perseverance (Cury, Biddle, Sarrazin, & Famose, 1997), class participation (Lau, Liem, & Nie, 2008), and the amount of effort students put into their schoolwork (Sarrazin, Roberts, Cury, Biddle, & Famose, 2002). Elliot, McGregor, and Gable (1999), for example, demonstrated that students who adopted mastery-approach and performance-approach goals were more persistent because they kept revisiting the learning material until they understood it, even when the material was difficult or boring, and these students performed better in examinations than students who held performance-avoidance goals.

However, Chouinard, Karsenti, and Roy (2007) found that when faced with subjects considered difficult such as mathematics, students with mastery-approach goals were found to exert more effort than students with performance-approach goals. This shows that mastery-oriented students are more willing to take up more challenging tasks that provide opportunities for them to develop their skills than performance-oriented students who are more concerned with their grades relative to others.

The effect of the achievement goals adoption on class participation has also received considerable research evidence. Church, Elliot, and Gable (2001) showed that undergraduates with mastery-approach goals were more engaged in lectures than students with performance-approach or performance-avoidance goals because, as the authors argued, those with performance goals tended to be more preoccupied with grades or avoiding looking inapt when participating in class activities.

In a recent Singapore study seeking to examine the mediating role of achievement goals in linking parental behaviors and learning outcomes, Luo, Aye, Hogan, Kaur, and Chan (2013) administered an online survey to 1,667 Singaporean secondary students. Effort regulation ("when the work in math is difficult, I give up") was one of the key outcomes measured in the study. Analyses using structural equation modeling showed that, after controlling for the effects of gender and prior achievement, mastery-approach goals were a positive predictor of effort regulation, whereas mastery-avoidance and performance-avoidance goals were negative predictors of effort regulation. Performance-approach goals, however, were not significantly associated with effort regulation.

In another Singapore study, Luo, Hogan, Yeung, Sheng, and Aye (2013) looked into the attributional beliefs of 1,496 ninth-grade students. The attributional beliefs examined included ability, effort, teachers' help, and tuition classes. Luo and colleagues found that Singapore students rated effort as the highest attribution belief for academic success. The hierarchical regression analysis conducted revealed that mastery-approach and mastery-avoidance goals were positive predictors of effort attribution. On this finding, the authors commented, "Students with high mastery goals are concerned with mastering new knowledge and skills, and [hence] they tend to view ability as incremental with effort and use regulatory strategies in the face of difficulties in their study" (p. 166). Although the positive association between mastery-avoidance goals and effort attribution was somewhat surprising, it was consistent with prior findings showing that avoidance goals are not necessarily inimical and can be equally motivating, in East Asian cultures (Elliot, Chirkov, Kim, & Sheldon, 2001).

Departing from a *normative goal* perspective positing that mastery goals are good and performance goals are bad (Brophy, 2005; Dweck, 1986; Nicholls, 1989), a *multiple-goal* perspective (Harackiewicz & Linnenbrink, 2005; Senko et al., 2011) views that the simultaneous adoption of mastery-approach and performance-approach goals can be beneficial for motivation, engagement, and performance. Studies underpinned by the multiple-goal perspective typically adopt an intrapersonal or person-centered approach by measuring various achievement goals and performing statistical techniques that allow them to examine the effects of multiple-goal pursuit on outcome measures, such as those classifying students according to their motivational profiles using cluster analysis or those assessing the interactive effects of goals using regression analysis.

In a Singapore-based study, for instance, Wang, Biddle, and Elliot (2007) administered a survey to a mixed sample of 647 Singapore secondary-school students (of which 178 were athletes who represented the school in sports competitions) to measure their achievement goals in a physical education context. Their study was based on the 2×2 achievement goal framework. Using a cluster analysis, Wang et al. found that students who were high on all the four achievement goals reported higher rates of effort and participation in physical activity than those who were moderate or low on all the achievement goals. Similarly, in another study looking into Singapore eighth-grade students' motivation in project work, Liu, Wang, Tan, Ee, and Koh (2009) found that students who were high on all four achievement goals and those high on mastery-approach goals and moderate on all the other goals reported higher behavioral regulation skills than those low on all the goals.

These Singapore-based studies provide support to the multiple-goal perspective and also highlight that the avoidance goals are not necessarily costly to behavioral outcomes when they are adopted simultaneously with the approach goals. Indeed, the avoidance goals may provide an additional source of motivation to perform well, at least for some students, such that the foreseen adverse effects resulted from failing to master the required skills or failing to perform as well as others can be avoided or reduced. Future studies, however, are needed to ascertain the extent to which this is the case and if this pattern is only specific to Asian students. Based on the above reviews, it is clear that mastery-approach goals have been found to be consistently associated with behavioral engagement (persistence, participation). Thus, promoting mastery-approach goals in Singapore students is aligned with the TLLM mission of realizing the potential of each student through heightening students' engagement in their learning.

Cognitive Outcomes

Numerous studies have demonstrated the role of achievement goals in the use of cognitive, meta-cognitive, and self-regulated learning strategies such as deep and surface learning and planning and organization (Cury, Elliot, Da Fonseca, & Moller, 2006; Elliot & McGregor, 2001; Lau et al., 2008; Moller & Elliot, 2006). Deep learning has been considered to be a more adaptive form of cognitive engagement that typically leads to a deeper understanding and better academic performance, whereas surface learning characterized by memorization and rote learning is considered to be less adaptive for student learning outcomes (Fredricks, Blumenfeld, & Paris, 2004). In a study of psychology undergraduates, Greene and Miller (1996) found that students with mastery goals reported higher engagement in deep cognitive processing of course contents, while students with performance goals tended to engage in surface cognitive processing. This early study, however, did not include the avoidance dimensions of achievement goals.

In a study of 1,475 ninth-grade Singapore students, Liem, Lau, and Nie (2008) examined the joint role of mastery-approach, performance-approach, and performance-avoidance goals in predicting deep and surface strategies in the context of English learning. Structural equation modeling showed that, beyond the effect of prior English achievement, task values, and self-efficacy, performance-approach goals positively predicted deep learning whereas performance-avoidance goals positively predicted surface learning. Interestingly, mastery-approach goals positively predicted both deep and surface learning. As argued by the authors, the latter finding seemed to be attributed to the fact that many Singapore students are bilingual and, for some students, English is not their first language. Thus, these students may have memorized new vocabularies and grammatical rules to make improvements in their English proficiency. However, Liem and his colleagues called for further studies to ascertain if bilingualism, or the number of languages spoken, moderates the role of achievement goals in the use of cognitive strategies.

Ablard and Lipschultz (1998) conducted a study with 222 seventh-grade high-achieving students who scored 97 % percentile in their cohort. In a series of interviews, these students were asked eight different open-ended questions concerning, for example, how they would prepare for a test, complete their homework, or study at home. They also completed questionnaires on mastery and performance goals (the goals however were not divided into the approach/avoidance dimensions). Ablard and Lipschultz found that mastery-oriented students used self-regulated learning strategies, such as planning, organizing and transforming information, and reviewing lesson materials, especially during challenging tasks that were difficult to comprehend or when doing tasks under distraction. Performance-oriented students, however, adopted self-regulated learning only in conjunction with the intention to master their learning contents, that is, when they saw that the pursuit of performance goals can be facilitated by the pursuit of mastery goals. Although this finding points to the more adaptive effects of mastery goal adoption, it also shows that students simultaneously adopt and pursue both mastery and performance goals and that this multiple-goal adoption facilitates their adaptive learning behaviors.

The adaptive effect of the multiple-goal adoption was also found in Singapore students. In a cluster analytic study with 480 eighth-grade students, Jang and Liu (2012) found five groups of students differing in their 2×2 achievement goal profiles. These clusters consisted of students high on all the four goals (cluster 1), students high on mastery-approach goals and low on mastery-avoidance goals (cluster 2), students low on all the four goals (cluster 3), students high on mastery-avoidance goals and moderate on all the other goals (cluster 4), and students low on both performance-approach and performance-avoidance goals and moderate on mastery-approach and mastery-avoidance goals (cluster 5). In terms of their cognitive strategies, Jang and Liu found that students high on all the goals (cluster 1) reported higher rehearsal, elaboration, organization, critical thinking, and self-regulation skills than all the other groups. Students high on mastery-approach goals and low on mastery-avoidance goals (cluster 2) were found to be similar in their self-regulation to those high on all the goals. For critical thinking, organization, and rehearsal, students low on performance goals (cluster 5) were found to be similar in their endorsement level to those low on all the goals (cluster 3). Thus, while mastery-approach goals were adaptive, performance goals were adaptive only when they were pursued together with mastery goals, providing support to the normative goal perspective (Brophy, 2005; Dweck, 1986; Nicholls, 1989) and also the multiple-goal perspectives (Harackiewicz & Linnenbrink, 2005; Senko et al., 2011).

In sum, achievement goals do play a role in cognitive strategies such that students' pursuit of mastery-approach and performance-approach goals tends to be associated with the use of deep processing in order to better understand the learning content and to score well, while students with performance-avoidance goals tend to use surface learning likely due to the fear of failure and anxiety (Elliot & Church, 1997; Zusho, Pintrich, & Cortina, 2005). However, the research evidence (Jang & Liu, 2012) also suggests that the simultaneous adoption of mastery and performance goals, both their approach and avoidance dimensions, can be adaptive for cognitive strategies. It might be that, for students who study in a competitive educational system, performance and avoidance goals are not necessarily detrimental to their learning. The relationship between mastery-avoidance goals and cognitive processing is still relatively understudied. Future research therefore needs to clarify this relationship. Taken together, these reviews point to the adaptive role of mastery-approach goals in the use of cognitive processing skills (deep, critical, creative thinking) which is one of the key areas highlighted in TLLM. Thus, emphasizing students to pursue mastery-approach goals is consistent with the spirit of the TLLM initiative.

Emotional and Psychological Well-Being Outcomes

Students' emotions and psychological well-being have also been found to be related to various achievement goals that they hold. In the cluster analytic study of Singapore students by Jang and Liu (2012) reported earlier, students high on all the four goals and those high on mastery-approach goals and low on mastery-avoidance goals were significantly higher on enjoyment than all the other students. Further, students high on mastery-approach goals and low on mastery-avoidance goals were lower on anxiety and boredom than the other students, and students high on all the four goals were lower on boredom than those low on all the four goals.

Similarly, in another person-centered approach to studying multiple-goal adoption of Canadian undergraduates, Daniels and colleagues (2008) found four clusters including students high on both mastery and performance goals, students high on mastery goals, students high on performance goals, and students low on both mastery and performance goals (the approach and avoidance dimensions were not distinguished in this study). It was shown that, while students low on both goals had the least adaptive outcomes, students high on performance goals reported more negative cognitive beliefs in the forms of expected achievement and perceived success and greater emotional vulnerability as shown in their lower enjoyment and higher boredom and anxiety than those high on both goals and high on mastery goals. Taken together, these Singapore- and Canada-based findings are consistent with the normative goal theory positing the adaptive role of mastery-approach goals and also with the multiple-goal perspective suggesting that performance goals can be beneficial when they are pursued simultaneously with mastery goals.

In a study by Pekrun, Elliot, and Maier (2006) with Germany and American college students, those with mastery-approach goals experienced positive emotions like joy and hope, students with performance-approach goals experienced pride, whereas students with performance-avoidance goals experienced negative emotions like anxiety and hopelessness. In their subsequent study, Pekrun, Elliot, and Maier (2009) found positive associations between mastery-approach goals and positive academic emotions like hope, enjoyment, and pride but negative associations between mastery-approach goals and negative academic emotions like boredom, anger, hopelessness, and shame. Further, performance-approach goals were positively associated with hope and pride, whereas performance-avoidance goals were positively associated with anger, anxiety, hopelessness, and shame and were negatively associated with hope and pride.

The negative association between performance-avoidance goals and anxiety was also established in various other studies. For instance, McGregor and Elliot (2002) investigated the relationships between achievement goals in relation to university examinations. The findings showed that mastery-approach goals positively predicted students' anticipation of the examination as a challenge, whereas performance-avoidance goals predicted students' anticipation of the examination as a threat and poorer expectations for grades in the examination. Performance-approach goals positively predicted students' anticipation of the examination as a challenge and also their positive expectation for getting good examination grades, but did not predict students' anticipation of the examination as a threat. Further, the study also found that students who adopted mastery and performance-approach goals were calmer and more composed when preparing for the examination, whereas students with performance-avoidance goals were less calm in preparing for the examination.

Altogether, the McGregory and Elliot study suggests that the relations between achievement goals and academic emotions appear to be mediated by students' perceptions of the tasks (e.g., examination, homework). Importantly, studies on the impacts of achievement goals on academic emotions shed light on the links between achievement goals and academic performance because some of the emotions, such as shame, hopelessness, and anxiety, are negatively associated with achievement, whereas some others such as enjoyment, joy, and pride, are positively associated with achievement (Elliot & McGregor, 1999; Pekrun et al. 2009; Valiente, Swanson, & Eisenberg, 2012).

There is also evidence showing the associations between achievement goals and psychological well-being. Students' adoption of mastery-approach goals was associated with more adaptive well-being indicators, such as better emotional and impulse control, than those with performance goals (Kaplan & Maehr, 1999). Further, students high on performance goals were found to report heightened self-blame and adopt maladaptive coping strategies, such as denial and disengagement, in overcoming the sense of failure after receiving poor grades (Neff, Hsieh, & Dejitterat, 2005).

A similar finding was also observed in a study by Ntoumanis, Biddle, and Haddock (1999) who found that student athletes with mastery goals maintained their sense of well-being through problem-centered strategies, while those with performance goals tended to cope with problems using emotion-focused and avoidance mechanisms. Future research is needed to illuminate the psychological mechanism underlying the relationships between achievement goals, academic emotions, coping, and well-being. The reviews above clearly suggest that promoting mastery-approach goals is relevant for optimal psychological well-being and emotional functioning which are elements of students' holistic development targeted by the TLLM policy.

Social Outcomes

The literature has now documented growing evidence for interpersonal effects of the academic achievement goal adoption (for reviews, see Darnon, Dompnier, & Marijn Poortvliet, 2012; Poortvliet & Darnon, 2010). In general, relative to the adoption of performance goals, the adoption of mastery-approach goals is associated with better social adjustment, for example, positive peer relationships (Kaplan & Maehr, 1999; Liem et al. 2008), positive perception of others (Darnon, Muller, Schrager, Pannuzzo, & Butera, 2006), positive attitude toward helping others (Poortvliet & Darnon, 2014), and willingness to cooperate (Levy, Kaplan, & Patrick, 2004).

A recent study by Poortvliet and Giebels (2012) showed that, relative to mastery-approach goals, performance-approach goals were associated more strongly with competitive motives and decisions but more weakly with cooperative motives and decisions. Further, compared to mastery-approach goals, performance-approach goals tended to lead to a reduced willingness to share task-related information with others (Poortvliet, Janssen, Van Yperen, & Van de Vliert, 2007, 2009), adoption of a competitive conflict regulation which focuses on social comparisons of competence and doubting viewpoints of others (Darnon et al., 2006), and engagement in interpersonally harmful behaviors such as sabotaging (Poortvliet, 2013). In contrast, relative to performance-approach goals, mastery-approach goals were more likely to promote willingness to share useful information with others (Poortvliet et al., 2007, 2009), adoption of an epistemic conflict regulation focusing individuals on solving problems and understanding different viewpoints of others (Darnon & Butera, 2007; Darnon et al., 2006), and positive attitudes toward helping others (Poortvliet & Darnon, 2014).

Despite their use of intrapersonal standards of competence, mastery-oriented students are not free of social comparison concerns (Régner, Escribe, & Dupeyrat, 2007). This social comparison orientation, however, was mainly adopted to search for information useful for self-evaluation and self-improvement purposes (Butler, 1992, 1995). Underpinned by the multiple-goal perspective, a study by Darnon, Dompnier, Gilliéron, and Butera (2010) demonstrated that the positive effect of mastery-approach goals on a social comparison orientation was stronger among students with higher levels of performance-approach goals (Study 1) and that mastery-approach goals predicted an interest in social comparison only in a performance-approach situation (Study 2). Further, mastery-approach goal adoption may also lead to engagement in interpersonally harmful behaviors as their relative standing in a group increased (Poortvliet, 2013) which appears to represent a situation where mastery-approach-oriented students may also be competitive when they simultaneously hold performance goals (Darnon et al., 2010). However, as found by Adie, Duda, and Ntoumani (2010), mastery-approach-oriented students were more likely to see competition as a challenge and less likely to see it as a threat, whereas mastery-avoidance and performance-avoidance-oriented students were likely to see competition as a threat.

In a study with Israeli students, Levy et al. (2004) found that, consistent with their focus on skill development, mastery-approach-oriented students were willing to cooperate with peers regardless of social status of the latter as the cooperation was construed as contributing to learning and task mastery. Performance-approach-oriented students, however, were willing to cooperate with peers when their own relative social status could be noticed; hence they were selective in terms of the peers they were willing to cooperate with. Although rather limited evidence has been documented, extant findings pointed to the less adaptive social effects of performance-avoidance goals as reflected in unwillingness to cooperate, derogation of out-group members, and adoption of social avoidance strategies (Levy et al., 2004) as well as poorer qualities of peer relationship (Liem et al., 2008).

In another Israel-based study, Levy-Tossman, Kaplan, and Assor (2007) conducted both variable-centered and person-centered analyses of their data. Their variable-centered analysis showed that the pursuit of mastery-approach goal was associated with mutual sharing of difficulties, trust, and adaptive social problem-solving skills, whereas the adoption of performance-approach and performance-avoidance goals was linked to mistrust, social inconsideration, and tension between friends. Further, their person-centered analysis indicated that students high on mastery-approach goals reported less mistrust among friends than those high on performance goals, suggesting the more adaptive role of mastery-approach goals relative to performance goals in social relationships.

However, a cluster analysis of Singapore students' responses to the 2×2 achievement goal items by Liu et al. (2009) showed that students high on all the four goals and students high on mastery-approach goals and moderate on all the other goals reported higher levels of communication, collaboration, and problem-solving skills than those with moderately high performance-avoidance goals or low on all the goals. While this Singapore-based finding is consistent with the study by Levy-Tossman et al. (2009) showing the positive effect of mastery-approach goals, it also supports the multiple-goal perspective in that performance and avoidance goals are not necessarily detrimental for social outcomes when they are adopted together with mastery-approach goals.

In sum, these reviews show that, relative to other goals, mastery-approach goals are more likely to be associated with adaptive social functioning such as a sense of trust, willingness to collaborate, and attitude toward helping others. Thus, promoting mastery-approach goals in students is relevant to building a learning community which provides a platform for students to work together, learn from each other, and at the same time hone their social skills. This supports the implementation of the TLLM policy seeking to bring out the best in every child in different life areas including the interpersonal domain.

Achievement Outcomes

Research has demonstrated a relatively consistent pattern of the negative predictive effects of mastery-avoidance and performance-avoidance goals on academic achievement (e.g., Elliot & McGregor, 2001; Liem, Martin, Porter, & Colmar, 2012) as well as other psycho-behavioral attributes associated with lower academic achievement such as avoidance of help seeking, test anxiety, disorganization, task disengagement, and surface processing (Elliot & McGregor, 2001; Hulleman et al., 2010; Liem et al., 2008; Moller & Elliot, 2006; but see Madjar, Kaplan, & Weinstock, 2011).

In contrast, the positive relationship between performance-approach goals and achievement has been found to be relatively consistent across studies (Barron & Harackiewicz, 2001; Cury et al., 2006; Elliot & Church, 1997; Harackiewicz, Barron, Pintrich, Elliot, & Thrash, 2002; Linnenbrink-Garcia, Tyson, & Patall,

2008) although this was not always the case (Brophy, 2005; Grant & Dweck, 2003; Hulleman et al., 2010; Midgley, Kaplan, & Middleton, 2001; Pintrich, 2000). This lack of consistency seems to be due to the fact that the adoption of performance-approach goals may lead to both adaptive and less adaptive learning processes such as instrumental and formal help seeking and also avoidance of help seeking and perceptions of help-seeking threats (Moller & Elliot, 2006; see also Senko et al., 2011 for further discussions on this inconsistency).

Unlike performance-approach goals, the association between mastery-approach goals and achievement was reported in a few studies (Cury et al., 2006; Grant & Dweck, 2003) but was nonsignificant in the majority of others (Barron & Harackiewicz, 2001; Elliot & Church, 1997; Liem et al., 2012; Senko et al., 2011). This points to the possibility that although mastery-approach-oriented students are more likely to engage in psycho-behavioral processes leading to higher achievement such as deep processing, persistence, and instrumental help seeking (Moller & Elliot, 2006), they also tend to spend their time and energy on fulfilling their interests in certain content which interests them without paying much attention to grades (Senko & Miles, 2008; see also Dompnier, Darnon, & Butera, 2009).

From a multiple-goal perspective, Daniels et al. (2008) showed that the groups of students high on both mastery and performance goals, high on performance goals, and high on mastery goals obtained similar academic achievement even though, as reported earlier, the performance goal-oriented students tended to be more negative in their expected achievement and perceived success and more emotionally vulnerable. This study, however, did not distinguish the approach and avoidance dimensions of the goals. In the person-centered analysis by Jang and Liu (2012), the finding indicated that students high on all the different achievement goals and those high on mastery-approach goals but low on mastery-avoidance goals were significantly higher in their mathematics performance than those low on all the goals and those high on mastery-avoidance goals. In general, although the pursuit of avoidance goals does not lead to better academic achievement, the reviewed findings appear to lend support to the multiple-goal perspective positing that the pursuit of the approach dimension of performance goals is beneficial for academic achievement and that the pursuit of mastery-approach goals could also be beneficial to academic achievement when students simultaneously adopt performance-approach goals.

Thus, consistent with the positive role of mastery-approach goals in behavioral, cognitive, emotional well-being, and social outcomes, research evidence has also pointed to the benefit of adopting these goals for academic performance – although as noted above, this has not always been the case. While performance-approach goals are often found to be associated with heightened performance, these goals tend to give rise to less adaptive processes (e.g., anxiety, mistrust). Taken together, there is reason to believe that promoting mastery-approach goals is a viable approach that educators may take in facilitating the successful implementation of the TLLM policy. The following section discusses research-based strategies useful in helping students become more mastery-approach oriented.

Reinforcing Mastery-Approach Goals: The TARGET Framework

To pursue its objective of igniting the spirit of learning and developing children holistically, TLLM has spurred the judicious reduction of learning content (the curriculum), the provision of space and time for teachers to be reflective and innovative in their teaching (the pedagogy), and the recognition of different talents beyond academic achievements that students can flourish in (the assessment) (Ministry of Education (MOE) [MOE], 2005). By the same token, achievement goal theory has highlighted the importance of curriculum, pedagogy, and assessment in promoting mastery-approach goals.

Classroom goal structures represent an overarching message pertinent to learning tasks, evaluation criteria, and the overall classroom atmosphere that the teacher conveys and emphasizes in the classroom and the students receive and perceive during their classroom learning (Meece, Anderman, & Anderman, 2006). It constitutes "precursors of students' personal goal orientations which have some influences on motivation and achievements." That is, "... these structures influence student behavior and learning by shaping the type of personal goals students adopt" (Meece et al., 2006, p. 495).

A notable classroom goal-structure study in Singapore was conducted by Lau and Nie (2008) who examined the relationship between classroom goal structures and personal goals. Lau and Nie proposed three hypotheses to test how classroom goal structures and personal goals may affect classroom-level or student-related outcomes such as motivation, engagement, and academic achievement in mathematics. The first hypothesis, the *additive hypothesis*, posited that classroom and personal goals have independent effects on students' motivational outcomes, with classroom goals affecting classroom-level outcomes and personal goals affecting student-level outcomes. The second hypothesis, the *reinforcing hypothesis*, proposed that classroom goals affect the relationships between personal goals and outcomes. The third hypothesis, the *counterbalancing hypothesis*, stated that classroom goals weaken the effects of personal goals on outcomes.

To test these hypotheses, Lau and Nie recruited 3,943 fifth-grade students from 38 primary schools in Singapore. Based on a multilevel analysis, they found cross-level interactions showing that, in classrooms emphasizing social comparisons and competition, students oriented toward performance goals were less likely to engage in their learning, more likely to reduce the amount of effort they put in, and more likely to give up when the work was difficult and boring. Their findings supported the reinforcing hypothesis and suggest that performance classroom goal structures are likely to exacerbate the negative relationships between students' performance-avoidance goals and behavioral engagement in learning mathematics.

In a more recent study on classroom goal structures with Germany high-school students, Schwinger and Stiensmeier-Pelster (2011) not only measured mastery goal structures but also distinguished between performance-approach and performance-avoidance goal structures and examined how students' perceived classroom goal structures were linked to their personal achievement goals. Analyses conducted using hierarchical linear modeling indicated that each type of students' achievement goals (mastery, performance-approach, and performance-avoidance) was best predicted by the corresponding dimension of classroom goal structure. An important note to highlight is that the two interaction effects showed the relationship between students' perceptions of mastery goal structures and their own mastery goals and the relationship between students' perceptions of performance-approach goal structures and their own performance-approach goals were stronger when the students perceived that their classrooms emphasized less performance-avoidance goal structures. This finding suggests that the intended emphasis on knowledge development or competition that the teacher intends to convey in the classroom can be better communicated to students when the classroom does not induce fears of failure and negative judgments.

Classroom goal structures can directly or indirectly be communicated to students not only by teachers and the classroom environment but also by the school policy and practice. When teachers perceive the school environment to be achievement oriented, they tend to use more performance-focused teaching practices, which then lead students to adopt performance goals (Midgley, Anderman, & Hicks, 1995). Similarly, teachers who focus on the mastery of concepts and the development of skills in their teaching practices encourage students to be more mastery oriented (Aunola, Leskinen, & Nurmi, 2006). Further, there is also evidence showing that students had better psychological adjustments and higher positive affects when they perceived that their school environment stressed the adoption of mastery goals than when they perceived that their school environment fostered competition among students (Roeser, Midgley, & Urdan, 1996). Thus, there is a need for educators to create learning environments and activities that reinforce the adoption of mastery goals.

"TARGET"-ing Mastery-Approach Goals

Although our reviews of achievement goal effects have shown the benefits of performance-approach goal on some of the key academic and nonacademic outcomes, the bulk of findings have also indicated the costs of pursuing these goals. Furthermore, consistent with the multiple-goal perspective (Senko et al., 2011), the adoption of performance-approach goals is beneficial on many outcomes only when it is accompanied by the pursuit of mastery-approach goals. Thus, we believe it is important that classroom environments reinforce the adoption of mastery-approach goals rather than performance-approach goals, especially given the fact that the educational system in Singapore, and in many other East Asian countries, is already competitive and, "by default," encourages the pursuit of performance goals (Chong & Liem, 2014).

Achievement goal theory highlights six distinct but interrelated dimensions of the classroom environment that can be modified to better nurture mastery-approach goals. The six dimensions – shortened as "TARGET" – include tasks, authority, recognition, grouping, evaluation, and time (Ames, 1992; Epstein, 1989). The TARGET framework is conceived to identify classroom components that (a) promote mastery-approach goals, (b) allow researchers to examine how the TARGET components interact and influence students' achievement goals, and (c) allow for interventions through the alteration of these components. The practicality of the TARGET framework involves assessing each of the components in the framework. These components can be altered because the TARGET framework represents contextual factors that teachers may adjust and modify to scaffold students' adoption of certain goals.

As articulated earlier, the *"Teach Less, Learn More"* (TLLM) educational initiative aims to nurture the spirit of learning, engage students, build characters, and prepare students to face the twenty-first century challenges, rather than to teach students for examinations (Lee, 2004). In its implementation, the policy calls for teachers to remember why they teach, to reflect on what they teach, and to reconsider how they teach. Thus, the policy cuts across the three key dimensions of education: the curriculum, the pedagogy, and the assessment. The TARGET components and their relevance to the TLLM policy are reviewed below.

Tasks The tasks that students attempt provide them with information to assess their abilities, interests, effort, and satisfaction of their learning process. Students with mastery-approach goals tend to prefer challenging tasks which can bring about the improvement of skills and the acquisition of knowledge (Ames & Archer, 1988). These tasks also provide meaning and values which determine the extent to which students are motivated and engaged in their learning (Blumenfeld, 1992). Thus, when designing tasks/activities for students within the TLLM framework, teachers may ask themselves questions such as, "Is the task meaningful to my students? Is the task optimally challenging to provoke a sense of mastery? Do instructions to the task provide enough support such that my students can succeed in attempting the task? How much scaffolding is needed to help my students attempt the task successfully?" Answers to these questions guide teachers in creating tasks that are personally meaningful and optimally challenging to students so that the students are intrinsically motivated in attempting the task and more likely to adopt deep cognitive processing. Aligned with this principle, teachers can also design tasks that are authentic and related to real-life situations. These tasks are then likely to spark intrinsic interests, curiosity, and, hence, mastery orientations in the students because they can better relate to the tasks.

Authority Teachers are encouraged to reflect upon the extent to which they exercise their authority in class (Anderman & Anderman, 2009). Teacher authority refers, or is related, to the amount of autonomy that teachers share with students in the class (Deci, Schwartz, Sheinman, & Ryan, 1981). Students provided with greater autonomy in learning tend to be more mastery oriented, intrinsically motivated, and better engaged in classroom activities (Greene, Miller, Crowson, Duke, & Akey, 2004; Schwartz, 2006). In providing autonomy in the implementation of the TLLM framework, teachers can get students to choose the "what" and the "how" of learning activities, for example, by having students who are good at a certain subject or topic to lead classroom activities and discussions. That is, the curriculum needs to be student-centered such that students are able to exercise autonomy in their learning experience. In this regard, it is important that teachers allow students to explore alternative ways of learning which the students find more effective or useful in helping them achieve the learning goals. Further, teachers can also provide students opportunities to express themselves so that their ideas and opinions are heard and appreciated (Reeve & Jang, 2006). By implementing these instructional practices, students are expected to develop a sense of ownership of their learning, and, as a result, the students' mastery orientation is inculcated. This is aligned with the TLLM goal in seeking to nurture the spirit of learning.

Recognition Recognition refers to the incentives students receive when they succeed in performing a task. The incentives are typically extrinsic (e.g., gifts, medals, "student-of-the month" awards). Although it is important that teachers recognize students' accomplishments, the frequent administration of external rewards may reduce intrinsic motivation especially when such rewards are no longer present (Lin, McKeachie, & Kim, 2001). Focusing on the level of improvement that students exhibit and highlighting that the improvement is attributable to the effort they have put in are seen as more adaptive ways of reinforcing mastery orientation. In the implementation of the TLLM initiative, it is therefore important that the curriculum does not recognize students' academic and intellectual successes or the "product" of learning alone – as this may cause the students to fixate on performance goals (Anderman & Anderman, 2009) – but more importantly the improvement, effort, and different talents that students may have. In this regard, teachers need to create an assessment system that provides them with opportunities to reward the "process" of learning as well as the students' personal and social accomplishments.

Grouping Grouping refers to the composition of students that make up the class or activity group (Kaplan, Middleton, Urdan, & Midgley, 2002). Students obtain better achievement when the classroom environment stresses on cooperation and teamwork (Cohen, 1994) than on individualistic learning (Johnson, Johnson, & Scott, 1978). Thus, teachers are encouraged to design assignments/activities for small groups that provide opportunities for students to interact while fostering greater motivation for mastery (Meece & Jones, 1996). In raising group cohesion and individual participation, teachers need to remind students of the importance of collective effort (Anderman, Andrzejewski, & Allen, 2011) and design group activities that allow multiple solutions derived from group members (Kaplan & Maehr, 2007). These recommendations can also be factored into the designing of enhanced curricula, the remodeling of instructional practices, and the setting of assessment criteria within the TTLM framework.

Evaluation Evaluation, as defined by Ames (1992), refers to both the teachers' evaluation of students in the class and the way students perceive the meaning of the evaluation. Teachers use various methods, particularly grades, to assess the quality of student learning. In this aspect, the evaluation practice within the TLLM framework is expected to do well in motivating and engaging students when it is focused on the improvement of task mastery and skill development shown by individual students rather than on the comparison among students (Kaplan & Maehr, 2007). Furthermore, assessment should not be limited to one evaluative tool (Anderman & Anderman, 2009). Instead, teachers may consider multiple indicators of assessment, including the amount of effort or the determination of students' improvement in a task. In addition, teachers need to incorporate multiple sources of evaluation, for example, by incorporating peer- and self-assessment (i.e., assessment as learning) into the overall evaluation scheme (Ormrod, 2014; Wiggins, 1989). In doing so, the teachers need to set criteria when assigning tasks, roles, and responsibilities to students. This can be done, for example, by providing students with rubrics on how the evaluation will be done so that students may assess their own performance, monitor their progress, and identify the strengths and areas of improvement for themselves and for their peers.

Time The final component, time, refers to the length of time that teachers provide their students with in gaining the mastery of topics and skills (Anderman et al., 2011). At times, the time given to complete a task may be insufficient. As a result, students are forced to complete the task due to the time constraint (Kaplan & Maehr, 2007). This situation can be remedied by relaxing the time constraint for students to complete their work. However, prolonging deadlines does not enhance students' mastery of the content. Instead, students accomplish more when the teacher sets activities that are to be completed within a reasonable timeframe (Anderman et al., 2011). For example, the time given to students to complete a task can be made flexible within a certain timeframe to allow the students to work at their own pace and not the general pace of the class (Anderman & Anderman, 2009). Importantly, teachers can also design a TLLM curriculum that emphasizes time management or include time management as a pedagogical practice to allow students to master the learning contents without feeling pressured or rushed. Further, teachers may assess whether students complete their tasks on time as an alternative form of assessment.

In sum, teachers seeking to reinforce the adoption of mastery-approach goals in their students are likely to be more effective to do so when they (1) design tasks that are authentic and interesting to the students, (2) provide the students with greater autonomy in making decisions on the "what" and the "how" of their learning, (3) recognize the improvement and effort that the students have put into their work including those in different areas of their school lives (social, cocurricular), (4) promote group work and collaboration with peers, (5) involve the students in the process of monitoring the progress of their own learning, and (6) allow the students to progress at their own pace.

Conclusion

The *Teach Less, Learn More* (TLLM) educational initiative was intended to promote the holistic development of Singaporean youths by igniting the spirit of learning in Singaporean students beyond studying for educational certificates. In this chapter, we have provided an overview of achievement goal theory, reviewed research findings pointing to the effects of goal adoption on key outcomes, and identified the potential implications of the theory to support the implementation of the TLLM framework. Reviews of the literature have indicated the differential effects of the achievement goal adoption on behavioral, cognitive, achievement, social, and well-being outcomes. More specifically, we found relatively more adaptive effects of mastery-approach goals and relatively less adaptive effects of performance-avoidance and mastery-avoidance goals. In the case of performance-approach goals, both positive and negative effects seem to be evident. Further, the simultaneous adoption of multiple goals, particularly mastery-approach and performance-approach goals, appears to be relatively adaptive for cognitive processing and achievement.

Collectively, the research evidence pointed to the fundamental value of promoting mastery goals by modifying the nature of the task, autonomy, recognition, grouping, evaluation, and time (TARGET) dimensions of the curricula and learning environments. That is, effort seeking to promote mastery goals is likely to do well when the process of learning involves more authentic tasks, provides greater autonomy to students, recognizes and centers on the assessment of students' effort and improvement, encourages cooperative learning and teamwork, and allows students to learn in their own pace. The successful implementation of the TLLM initiative is expected to benefit from putting each of the TARGET dimensions into practice.

References

Ablard, K. E., & Lipschultz, R. E. (1998). Self-regulated learning in high-achieving students: Relations to advanced reasoning, achievement goals, and gender. *Journal of Educational Psychology, 90*, 94–101.

Adie, J. W., Duda, J. L., & Ntoumanis, N. (2010). Achievement goals, competition appraisals, and the well- and ill-being of elite youth soccer players over two competitive seasons. *Journal of Sport and Exercise Psychology, 32*, 555–579.

Ames, C. (1984). Achievement attributions and self-instructions under competitive and individualistic goal structures. *Journal of Educational Psychology, 76*, 478–487.

Ames, C. (1992). Classrooms: Goals, structures, and student motivation. *Journal of Educational Psychology, 84*, 261–271.

Ames, C., & Archer, J. (1988). Achievement goals in the classroom: Students' learning strategies and motivation processes. *Journal of Educational Psychology, 80*, 260–267.

Anderman, L. H., & Anderman, E. M. (2009). Oriented towards mastery: Promoting positive motivational goals for students. In R. Gilman, E. S. Heubner, & M. Furlong (Eds.), *Handbook of positive psychology in the schools* (pp. 161–173). Mahwah, NJ: Erlbaum.

Anderman, L. H., Andrzejewski, C. E., & Allen, J. (2011). How do teachers support students' motivation and learning in their classrooms. *Teachers College Record, 113*, 969–1003.

Atkinson, J. W. (1957). Motivational determinants of risk-taking behavior. *Psychological Review, 64*, 359–372.

Aunola, K., Leskinen, E., & Nurmi, J. E. (2006). Developmental dynamics between mathematical performance, task motivation, and teachers' goals during the transition to primary school. *British Journal of Educational Psychology, 76*, 21–40.

Barron, K. E., & Harackiewicz, J. M. (2001). Achievement goals and optimal motivation: Testing multiple goal models. *Journal of Personality and Social Psychology, 80*, 706–722.

Blumenfeld, P. C. (1992). Classroom learning and motivation: Clarifying and expanding goal theory. *Journal of Educational Psychology, 84*, 272–281.

Brophy, J. (2005). Goal theorists should move on from performance goals. *Educational Psychologist, 40*, 167–176.

Butler, D. L. (1995). Promoting strategic learning by postsecondary students with learning disabilities. *Journal of Learning Disabilities, 28*, 170–190.

Butler, R. (1992). What young people want to know when: Effects of mastery and ability goals on interest in different kinds of social comparisons. *Journal of Personality and Social Psychology, 62*, 934–943.

Chong, W. H., & Liem, G. A. D. (2014). Self-related beliefs and their processes: Asian insights. *Educational Psychology: An International Journal of Experimental Educational Psychology, 34*, 529–537.

Chouinard, R., Karsenti, T., & Roy, N. (2007). Relations among competence beliefs, utility value, achievement goals, and effort in mathematics. *British Journal of Educational Psychology, 77*, 501–517.

Church, M. A., Elliot, A. J., & Gable, S. L. (2001). Perceptions of classroom environment, achievement goals, and achievement outcomes. *Journal of Educational Psychology, 93*, 43–54.

Cohen, E. G. (1994). Restructuring the classroom: Conditions for productive small groups. *Review of Educational Research, 64*, 1–35.

Cury, F., Biddle, S., Sarrazin, P., & Famose, J. P. (1997). Achievement goals and perceived ability predict investment in learning a sport task. *British Journal of Educational Psychology, 67*, 293–309.

Cury, F., Elliot, A. J., Da Fonseca, D., & Moller, A. C. (2006). The social-cognitive model of achievement motivation and the 2×2 achievement goal framework. *Journal of Personality and Social Psychology, 90*, 666–679.

Daniels, L. M., Haynes, T. L., Stupnisky, R. H., Perry, R. P., Newall, N. E., & Pekrun, R. (2008). Individual differences in achievement goals: A longitudinal study of cognitive, emotional, and achievement outcomes. *Contemporary Educational Psychology, 33*, 584–608.

Darnon, C., & Butera, F. (2007). Learning or succeeding? Conflict regulation with mastery or performance goals. *Swiss Journal of Psychology, 66*, 145–152.

Darnon, C., Dompnier, B., Gilliéron, O., & Butera, F. (2010). The interplay of mastery and performance goals in social comparison: A multiple-goal perspective. *Journal of Educational Psychology, 102*, 212–222.

Darnon, C., Dompnier, B., & Marijn Poortvliet, P. (2012). Achievement goals in educational contexts: A social psychology perspective. *Social and Personality Psychology Compass, 6*, 760–771.

Darnon, C., Muller, D., Schrager, S. M., Pannuzzo, N., & Butera, F. (2006). Mastery and performance goals predict epistemic and relational conflict regulation. *Journal of Educational Psychology, 98*, 766–776.

Deci, E. L., Schwartz, A. J., Sheinman, L., & Ryan, R. M. (1981). An instrument to assess adults' orientations toward control versus autonomy with children: Reflections on intrinsic motivation and perceived competence. *Journal of Educational Psychology, 73*, 642–650.

Dompnier, B., Darnon, C., & Butera, F. (2009). Faking the desire to learn a clarification of the link between mastery goals and academic achievement. *Psychological Science, 20*, 939–943.

Duda, J. L., & Nicholls, J. G. (1992). Dimensions of achievement motivation in schoolwork and sport. *Journal of Educational Psychology, 84*, 290–299.

Dweck, C. S. (1986). Motivational processes affecting learning. *American Psychologist, 41*, 1040–1048.

Elliot, A. J. (1999). Approach and avoidance motivation and achievement goals. *Educational Psychologist, 34*, 169–189.

Elliot, A. J. (2005). A conceptual history of the achievement goal structure. In A. J. Elliot & C. S. Dweck (Eds.), *Handbook of competence and motivation* (pp. 52–72). New York: Guilford Press.

Elliot, A. J. (2006). The hierarchical model of approach-avoidance motivation. *Motivation and Emotion, 30*, 111–116.

Elliot, A. J., Chirkov, V. I., Kim, Y., & Sheldon, K. M. (2001). A cross-cultural analysis of avoidance (relative to approach) personal goals. *Psychological Science, 12*, 505–510.

Elliot, A. J., & Church, M. A. (1997). A hierarchical model of approach and avoidance achievement motivation. *Journal of Personality and Social Psychology, 72*, 218–232.

Elliot, A. J., & McGregor, H. A. (1999). Test anxiety and the hierarchical model of approach and avoidance achievement motivation. *Journal of Personality and Social Psychology, 76*, 628–644.

Elliot, A. J., & McGregor, H. A. (2001). A 2×2 achievement goal framework. *Journal of Personality and Social Psychology, 80*, 501–519.

Elliot, A. J., McGregor, H. A., & Gable, S. (1999). Achievement goals, study strategies, and exam performance: A mediational analysis. *Journal of Educational Psychology, 91*, 549–563.

Elliot, A. J., & Murayama, K. (2008). On the measurement of achievement goals: Critique, illustration, and application. *Journal of Educational Psychology, 100*, 613–628.

Elliot, A. J., Murayama, K., & Pekrun, R. (2011). A 3×2 achievement goal model. *Journal of Educational Psychology, 103*, 632–648.

Epstein, J. (1989). Family structures and student motivation: A developmental perspective. In C. Ames & R. Ames (Eds.), *Research on motivation in education* (pp. 259–295). New York: Academic.

Fredricks, J. A., Blumenfeld, P. C., & Paris, A. H. (2004). School engagement: Potential of the concept, state of the evidence. *Review of Educational Research, 74*, 59–109.

Grant, H., & Dweck, C. S. (2003). Clarifying achievement goals and their impact. *Journal of Personality and Social Psychology, 85*, 541–553.

Greene, B. A., & Miller, R. B. (1996). Influences on achievement: Goals, perceived ability, and cognitive engagement. *Contemporary Educational Psychology, 21*, 181–192.

Greene, B. A., Miller, R. B., Crowson, H. M., Duke, B. L., & Akey, K. L. (2004). Predicting high school students' cognitive engagement and achievement: Contributions of classroom perceptions and motivation. *Contemporary Educational Psychology, 29*, 462–482.

Harackiewicz, J. M., Barron, K. E., Pintrich, P. R., Elliot, A. J., & Thrash, T. M. (2002). Revision of achievement goal theory: Necessary and illuminating. *Journal of Educational Psychology, 94*, 638–645.

Harackiewicz, J. M., & Linnenbrink, E. A. (2005). Multiple achievement goals and multiple pathways for learning: The agenda and impact of Paul R. Pintrich. *Educational Psychologist, 40*, 75–84.

Heng Sweet Kiat (2014). FY 2014 committee of supply debate: 1st reply by Mr. Heng Swee Keat, Minister for Education: Bringing out the best in every child. Retrieved August 19, 2014, from http://www.moe.gov.sg/media/speeches/2014/03/07/first-reply-by-mr-heng-swee-keat-bringing-out-the-best-in-every-child.php

Hogan, D., Chan, M., Rahim, R., Kwek, D., Maung Aye, K., Loo, S. C., et al. (2013). Assessment and the logic of instructional practice in secondary 3 english and mathematics classrooms in Singapore. *Review of Education, 1*, 57–106.

Hulleman, C. S., Schrager, S. M., Bodmann, S. M., & Harackiewicz, J. M. (2010). A meta-analytic review of achievement goal measures: Different labels for the same constructs or different constructs with similar labels? *Psychological Bulletin, 136*, 422–449.

Jang, L. Y., & Liu, W. C. (2012). 2×2 achievement goals and achievement emotions: A cluster analysis of students' motivation. *European Journal of Psychology of Education, 27*, 59–76.

Johnson, D. W., Johnson, R. T., & Scott, L. (1978). The effects of cooperative and individualized instruction on student attitudes and achievement. *The Journal of Social Psychology, 104*, 207–216.

Kaplan, A., Middleton, M. J., Urdan, T., & Midgley, C. (2002). Achievement goals and goal structures. In C. Midgley (Ed.), *Goals, goal structures, and patterns of adaptive learning* (pp. 21–55). Hillsdale, NJ: Erlbaum.

Kaplan, A., & Maehr, M. L. (1999). Achievement goals and student well-being. *Contemporary Educational Psychology, 24*, 330–358.

Kaplan, A., & Maehr, M. L. (2007). The contributions and prospects of goal orientation theory. *Educational Psychology Review, 19*, 141–184.

Lau, S., Liem, A. D., & Nie, Y. (2008). Task- and self-related pathways to deep learning: The mediating role of achievement goals, classroom attentiveness, and group participation. *British Journal of Educational Psychology, 78*, 639–662.

Lau, S., & Nie, Y. (2008). Interplay between personal goals and classroom goal structures in predicting student outcomes: A multilevel analysis of person-context interactions. *Journal of Educational Psychology, 100*, 15–29.

Lee, H. L. (2004). Our future of opportunity and promise. Address by Prime Minister Lee Hsien Loong on 22 August at the 2004 National Day Rally at the University Cultural Centre, National University of Singapore: Singapore Government Press release.

Levy, I., Kaplan, A., & Patrick, H. (2004). Early adolescents' achievement goals, social status, and attitudes towards cooperation with peers. *Social Psychology of Education, 7*, 127–159.

Levy-Tossman, I., Kaplan, A., & Assor, A. (2007). Academic goal orientations, multiple goal profiles, and friendship intimacy among early adolescents. *Contemporary Educational Psychology, 32*, 231–252.

Liem, A. D., Lau, S., & Nie, Y. (2008). The role of self-efficacy, task value, and achievement goals in predicting learning strategies, task disengagement, peer relationship, and achievement outcome. *Contemporary Educational Psychology, 33*, 486–512.

Liem, G. A. D., Martin, A. J., Porter, A. L., & Colmar, S. (2012). Sociocultural antecedents of academic motivation and achievement: Role of values and achievement motives in achievement goals and academic performance. *Asian Journal of Social Psychology, 15*, 1–13.

Lin, Y. G., McKeachie, W. J., & Kim, Y. C. (2001). College student intrinsic and/or extrinsic motivation and learning. *Learning and Individual Differences, 13*, 251–258.

Linnenbrink-Garcia, L., Tyson, D. F., & Patall, E. A. (2008). When are achievement goal orientations beneficial for academic achievement? A closer look at main effects and moderating factors. *Revue Internationale De Psychologie Sociale, 21*, 19–70.

Liu, W. C., Wang, C. K. J., Tan, O. S., Ee, J., & Koh, C. (2009). Understanding students' motivation in project work: A 2×2 achievement goal approach. *British Journal of Educational Psychology, 79*, 87–106.

Luo, W., Aye, K. M., Hogan, D., Kaur, B., & Chan, M. C. Y. (2013). Parenting behaviors and learning of Singapore students: The mediational role of achievement goals. *Motivation and Emotion, 37*, 274–285.

Luo, W., Hogan, D. J., Yeung, A. S., Sheng, Y. Z., & Aye, K. M. (2013). Attributional beliefs of Singapore students: Relations to self-construal, competence and achievement goals. *Educational Psychology, 34*, 154–170.

Madjar, N., Kaplan, A., & Weinstock, M. (2011). Clarifying mastery-avoidance goals in high school: Distinguishing between intrapersonal and task-based standards of competence. *Contemporary Educational Psychology, 36*, 268–279.

Maehr, M. L. (1989). Thoughts about motivation. In C. Ames & R. Ames (Eds.), *Research on motivation in education: Goals and cognitions* (Vol. 3, pp. 299–315). New York: Academic.

Maehr, M. L., & Nicholls, J. G. (1980). Culture and achievement motivation: A second look. In N. Warren (Ed.), *Studies in cross-cultural psychology* (Vol. 2, pp. 221–267). New York: Academic.

Maehr, M. L., & Zusho, A. (2009). Achievement goal theory. In K. R. Wentzel & A. Wigfield (Eds.), *Handbook of motivation at school* (pp. 77–104). New York: Routledge.

Martin, M. O., Mullis, I. V. S., Foy, P., & Stanco, G. M. (2012). *TIMSS 2011 international results in science*. Chestnut Hill, MA: TIMSS & PIRLS International Study Center, Boston College.

McClelland, D. C. (1951). Measuring motivation in phantasy: The achievement motive. In H. Guetzkow (Ed.), *Groups, leadership and men: Research in human relation* (pp. 191–205). Oxford: Carnegie Press.

McGregor, H. A., & Elliot, A. J. (2002). Achievement goals as predictors of achievement-relevant processes prior to task engagement. *Journal of Educational Psychology, 94*, 381–395.

Meece, J. L., Anderman, E. M., & Anderman, L. H. (2006). Classroom goal structure, student motivation, and academic achievement. *Annual Review of Psychology, 57*, 487–503.

Meece, J. L., & Jones, M. G. (1996). Gender differences in motivation and strategy use in science: Are girls rote learners? *Journal of Research in Science Teaching, 33*, 393–406.

Midgley, C., Anderman, E., & Hicks, L. (1995). Differences between elementary and middle school teachers and students: A goal theory approach. *The Journal of Early Adolescence, 15*, 90–113.

Midgley, C., Kaplan, A., & Middleton, M. (2001). Performance-approach goals: Good for what, for whom, under what circumstances, and at what cost? *Journal of Educational Psychology, 93*, 77–86.

Midgley, C., Maehr, M. L., Hruda, L. Z., Anderman, E., Anderman, L., Freeman, K. E., et al. (2000). *Manual for the patterns of adaptive learning scales (PALS)*. Ann Arbor, MI: University of Michigan. 1001, 48109-1259.

Miller, R. B., Behrens, J. T., Greene, B. A., & Newman, D. (1993). Goals and perceived ability: Impact on student valuing, self-regulation, and persistence. *Contemporary Educational Psychology, 18*, 2–14.

Ministry of Education (MOE). (2005). Transforming learning: Teach less, learn more. *Contact: The Teacher's Digest* (pp. 04–16). Retrieved from http://www.moe.gov.sg/corporate/contact-print/pdf/contact_oct05.pdf

Ministry of Education (MOE). (2014). Results of the 2013 Singapore-Cambridge general certificate of education (Ordinary Level) examination. Retrieved from http://www.moe.gov.sg/media/press/2014/01/results-of-the-2013-singapore-cambridge-general-certificate-of-education-ordinary-level-examination.php

Moller, A. C., & Elliot, A. J. (2006). The 2×2 achievement goal framework: An overview of empirical research. In A. V. Mittel (Ed.), *Focus on educational psychology* (pp. 307–326). Hauppauge, NY: Nova.

Mullis, I. V. S., Martin, M. O., Foy, P., & Arora, A. (2012). *TIMSS 2011 international results in mathematics*. Chestnut Hill, MA: TIMSS & PIRLS International Study Center, Boston College.

Neff, K. D., Hsieh, Y. P., & Dejitterat, K. (2005). Self-compassion, achievement goals, and coping with academic failure. *Self and Identity, 4*, 263–287.

Ng, J. Y. (2012). Teach less, learn more: Have we achieved it? *Today*, p. 4.

Nicholls, J. G. (1984). Achievement motivation: Conceptions of ability, subjective experience, task choice, and performance. *Psychological Review, 91*, 328–346.

Nicholls, J. G. (1989). *The competitive ethos and democratic education*. Cambridge, MA: Harvard University Press.

Ntoumanis, N., Biddle, S. J., & Haddock, G. (1999). The mediating role of coping strategies on the relationship between achievement motivation and affect in sport. *Anxiety, Stress, and Coping, 12*, 299–327.

OECD. (2012). PISA 2012 results in focus: What 15-year-olds know and what they can do with what they know. Retrieved from http://www.oecd.org/pisa/keyfindings/pisa-2012-results-overview.pdf

Ormrod, J. E. (2014). Motivation and affect. In J. E. Ormrod (Ed.), *Essentials of educational psychology: Big ideas to guide effective teaching* (pp. 184–235). Boston, MA: Pearson.

Papaioannou, A. G., Zourbanos, N., Krommidas, C., & Ampatzoglou, G. (2012). The place of achievement goals in the social context of sport: A comparison of Nicholls' and Elliot's models. In G. Roberts & D. Treasure (Eds.), *Advances in motivation in sport and exercise* (3rd ed., pp. 59–90). Champaign, IL: Human Kinetics.

Peh, S. H. (2007, August). Teach less, learn more? It works, schools tell PM. *The Straits Times*, p. 12.

Pekrun, R., Elliot, A. J., & Maier, M. A. (2006). Achievement goals and discrete achievement emotions: A theoretical model and prospective test. *Journal of Educational Psychology, 98*, 583–597.

Pekrun, R., Elliot, A. J., & Maier, M. A. (2009). Achievement goals and achievement emotions: Testing a model of their joint relations with academic performance. *Journal of Educational Psychology, 101*, 115–135.

Pintrich, P. R. (2000). Multiple goals, multiple pathways: The role of goal orientation in learning and achievement. *Journal of Educational Psychology, 92*, 544–555.

Poortvliet, P. M. (2013). Harming others' task-related efforts: The distinct competitive effects of ranking information on performance and mastery goal individuals. *Social Psychology, 44*, 373–379.

Poortvliet, P. M., & Darnon, C. (2010). Toward a more social understanding of achievement goals: The interpersonal effects of mastery and performance goals. *Current Directions in Psychological Science, 19*, 324–328.

Poortvliet, P. M., & Darnon, C. (2014). Understanding positive attitudes toward helping peers: The role of mastery goals and academic self-efficacy. *Self and Identity, 13*, 345–363.

Poortvliet, P. M., & Giebels, E. (2012). Self-improvement and cooperation: How exchange relationships promote mastery-approach driven individuals' job outcomes. *European Journal of Work and Organizational Psychology, 21*, 392–425.

Poortvliet, P. M., Janssen, O., Van Yperen, N. W., & Van de Vliert, E. (2007). Achievement goals and interpersonal behavior: How mastery and performance goals shape information exchange. *Personality and Social Psychology Bulletin, 33*, 1435–1447.

Poortvliet, P. M., Janssen, O., Van Yperen, N. W., & Van de Vliert, E. (2009). Low ranks make the difference: How achievement goals and ranking information affect cooperation intentions. *Journal of Experimental Social Psychology, 45*, 1144–1147.

Reeve, J., & Jang, H. (2006). What teachers say and do to support students' autonomy during a learning activity. *Journal of Educational Psychology, 98*, 209–218.

Régner, I., Escribe, C., & Dupeyrat, C. (2007). Evidence of social comparison in mastery goals in natural academic settings. *Journal of Educational Psychology, 99*, 575–583.

Roberts, G. (2012). Motivation in sport and exercise from an achievement goal theory perspective: After 30 years, where are we? In G. Roberts & D. Treasure (Eds.), *Advances in motivation in sport and exercise* (3rd ed., pp. 5–58). Champaign, IL: Human Kinetics.

Roeser, R. W., Midgley, C., & Urdan, T. C. (1996). Perceptions of the school psychological environment and early adolescents' psychological and behavioral functioning in school: The mediating role of goals and belonging. *Journal of Educational Psychology, 88*, 408–422.

Sarrazin, P., Roberts, G., Cury, F., Biddle, S., & Famose, J. P. (2002). Exerted effort and performance in climbing among boys: The influence of achievement goals, perceived ability, and task difficulty. *Research Quarterly for Exercise and Sport, 73*, 425–436.

Schwartz, S. H. (2006). A theory of cultural value orientations: Explication and applications. *Comparative Sociology, 5*, 137–182.

Schwinger, M., & Stiensmeir-Pelster, J. (2011). Performance-approach and performance-avoidance classroom goals and the adoption of personal achievement goals. *British Journal of Educational Psychology, 81*, 680–699.

Senko, C., Hulleman, C. S., & Harackiewicz, J. M. (2011). Achievement goal theory at the crossroads: Old controversies, current challenges, and new directions. *Educational Psychologist, 46*, 26–47.

Senko, C., & Miles, K. M. (2008). Pursuing their own learning agenda: How mastery-oriented students jeopardize their class performance. *Contemporary Educational Psychology, 33*, 561–583.

Shanmugaratnam, T. (2005). Achieving quality: Bottom up initiative, top down support. Retrieved from http://www.moe.gov.sg/media/speeches/2005/sp20050922.htm

Valiente, C., Swanson, J., & Eisenberg, N. (2012). Linking students' emotions and academic achievement: When and why emotions matter. *Child Development Perspectives, 6,* 129–135.

Vansteenkiste, M., Lens, W., Elliot, A. J., Soenens, B., & Mouratidis, A. (2014). Moving the achievement goal approach one step forward: Toward a systematic examination of the autonomous and controlled reasons underlying achievement goals. *Educational Psychologist, 49,* 153–174.

Wang, J. C. K., Biddle, S. J., & Elliot, A. J. (2007). The 2×2 achievement goal framework in a physical education context. *Psychology of Sport and Exercise, 8,* 147–168.

Wiggins, G. (1989). A true test. *Phi Delta Kappan, 70,* 703–713.

Zusho, A., Pintrich, P. R., & Cortina, K. S. (2005). Motives, goals, and adaptive patterns of performance in Asian-American and Anglo-American students. *Learning and Individual Differences, 15,* 141–158.